# The Clinical EFT Handbook:
## A Definitive Resource
## for Practitioners, Scholars,
## Clinicians, and Researchers

## VOLUME 2

Edited by
Dawson Church and Stephanie Marohn

Energy Psychology Press
3340 Fulton Rd., #442, Fulton, CA 95439
www.EFTUniverse.com

Library of Congress Cataloging-in-Publication Data

The clinical EFT handbook / edited by Dawson Church and Stephanie Marohn. — First edition.
    pages cm
    multiple volumes
ISBN 978-1-60415-212-8
1. Emotional Freedom Techniques. 2. Emotion-focused therapy. I. Church, Dawson,
1956- editor of compilation. II. Marohn, Stephanie, editor of compilation.
RC489.F62C55 2013
616.89'142—dc23
                                2013038885

Cover design by Victoria Valentine
Editing by Dawson Church and Stephanie Marohn
Typeset by Medlar Publishing Solutions Pvt Ltd, INDIA
Printed in USA by Bang Printing
First Edition

10 9 8 7 6 5 4 3 2 1

Chapter 47, "EFT for the Beginning of Life: Supporting Wholeness, Human Potential, and
Optimal Relationships," is included by permission of the author, Wendy Anne McCarty,
PhD, RN, and Wondrous Beginnings Publishing, copyright 2013.

Chapter 53, "Group Energies and Sports: Some Preliminary Speculation and Research,"
by Eric Leskowitz, is adapted, with permission, from an article that originally appeared in
*Spirit of Change* magazine, Spring 2009.

# Important Disclaimer

# Contents

# Integrative Medical Settings

# Chapter 39
# Strategies for an Integrative Medicine Practice
*David Lake*

### Abstract
This chapter is a general overview, purely from my personal experience, of utilizing meridian stimulation ("tapping") in medical practice. As one of the relatively few medical practitioners doing this, I report on my own 14 years of intensive experimentation, workshop teaching, and supervision in this new field of energy psychology. It has changed my life personally and professionally because of its compelling results. I am not being comprehensive in this chapter but wish to inspire others to try it out, and investigate further. I find tapping to be a valuable resource in physical and emotional healing. As an alternative treatment from the world of natural medicine, it can find a place as a powerful relaxation technique, a self-soothing and stress-management technique, a unique and ideal treatment partner for anxiety, fear, and trauma, and a useful tool for helping to process negative emotions. As well, it can have beneficial results for any condition by helping the mind-body function optimally, in the best balance. It is a partner for most general therapy modalities. It is ideal as self-help in any situation. And it is simple, safe, and easy to learn and do. Tapping provides the best example, in my life as a doctor, of a technique that brings the best of natural and orthodox medicine together—where they belong.

**Keywords:** continuous tapping, integrative medicine, natural medicine, CBT, PTSD, anxiety, phobia, depression

**David Lake**, a medical practitioner and psychotherapist in private practice since 1977, has extensive experience in helping people overcome the effects of posttraumatic stress. Dr. Lake also has considerable expertise in assisting couples and individuals with relationship problems. He is the author of four books on energy psychology. Send correspondence to David Lake, PO Box 738, Newport, NSW, Australia 2106, or dlake@optusnet.com.au. www.eftdownunder.com.

# Introduction for Doctors

I write this as a doctor who practiced as a general family physician for 25 years and gradually moved afterward to full-time psychotherapy and energy psychology. This shift happened because of my interest in treating the ever-present anxiety I saw in ordinary people with illness. It is fair to say that I had little to offer anxious patients early on, other than reassurance. I explored the world of innovative psychological treatments purely from the criterion of practical effectiveness; I am only ever interested, then and now, in what actually works in the real world. I have thus had severe disappointments in my investigations of standard psychological approaches, as well as many traditional talking therapies. Other modern techniques were effective, although no one technique can do everything. But the moment I was introduced to EFT remains in my mind as a watershed in my career. EFT is both highly effective and easy to learn and use.

In this chapter I refer descriptively to EFT and the other methods based on meridian points as "tapping" because of the fact that touching and tapping such points is the most popular way to stimulate that energy system. It is not the only way, of course, and there are many other esoteric ways to use the body's energy. There are some five original meridian techniques and, now, many derivative ones, but "tapping" covers it all for me.

I now think of my therapeutic effectiveness as falling into two periods of my professional life: before learning tapping, and afterward. I wish I had known about this method when I worked in the emergency room. Equally, I now wish I could get the attention of my conservative colleagues in order to introduce them to a whole new world of positive outcomes, far closer to the world I dreamed about inhabiting when I entered medicine. And on a personal note, I lost my lifelong phobia of public speaking in 1998 after one tapping treatment (when so many other treatments had failed miserably), and tapping has been a godsend for the small and big upsets and setbacks of all my family members. The technique itself is simple and straightforward—and quick.

For example, within a few years of learning EFT I was able to organize for certain family members the following single-session tapping-based outcomes:

- Being able to tolerate and have a blood test without trauma
- Passing a driving test involving reverse-parking with confidence
- Recovering completely from the trauma of a near-drowning experience
- Overcoming a cockroach phobia
- Emotional healing and recovery after being blown up in a major terrorist attack

The basic assumptions of tapping are a true mixture of Eastern and Western medicine: that there is an energy system (no matter how you conceptualize it), and that somehow the more severe aspects of traumatization and anxiety are eminently treatable as a body-based approach (not a psychological intervention, since the problem is not in the mind). The feeling reactions might then diminish dramatically, while the thoughts remain unchanged. But where, then, is the problem? If in time it becomes "just a thought," then it can go back into the world of thoughts, and have no power over the person. Psychologist and tapping authority Steve Wells (see Chapter 55) likes to emphasize that it is only our emotionally charged thoughts that have such power. This particularly applies to fears and negative thinking.

My own theory is that tapping disrupts the body's ability to express toxic levels of negative emotion since it seems to help the body eliminate the "stuck" or excessive reactive feelings. This is particularly and dramatically obvious when treating trauma.

I certainly was not taught this at university! This is a new paradigm, and would be psychologically ridiculous but for the growing evidence base of its effectiveness. Its results are not due to suggestion or distraction, and I know this from several decades of using both. It also sometimes has direct effects on physical disease processes that I cannot explain (and I have used it with sufferers of multiple sclerosis and immune deficiencies, for example). In many conditions, it helps the body function at the highest level possible, and it is a boon for healing, rehabilitating, and convalescing generally. Best of all, it is safe, simple, gentle in effect, and a natural facilitator of the body's innate processes. The only adverse effect I have seen rarely in treating thousands of patients is the sudden release in some of intense emotion; unlike a true abreaction, it passes very quickly and I don't consider it a direct result of tapping itself. My experience is that the worst thing that can happen when using tapping is nothing.

I have found this result, for example, when trying over six sessions to gain an improvement in drug-reaction symptoms to interferon (necessary treatment for hepatitis-B exposure). Likewise, I have not found any effect on the basic disease process of schizophrenia (although tapping can, with daily practice, significantly ameliorate the associated anxiety). Tapping does not rewrite the results book when treating personality disorders, obsessive-compulsive disorders, anorexia, autism spectrum disorders, or severe depression. Generally, however, the tapping process initiates strong positive change in the inner world of the person using it for whatever reason.

Thanks to my extensive experience using tapping with thousands of people, I no longer think of psychological problems as being "all in the mind." I no longer think that the standard medical textbooks accurately describe what is possible to achieve in all cases of physical illness. I keep an open mind at all times now, without knowing nearly as much as I thought I did when I graduated from medical school. When talking to a patient, I never use the words "there is nothing we can do" or "you just have to learn to live with it." There is definitely a new way to offer more to patients in distress. The real question for any patient must be something along the lines of: "How would you like to get into the best balance your body can achieve?" For me as the treating doctor, the question is always: "If I can help more by relieving suffering for this patient, what is the most practical and efficient way?" I will do whatever works.

The main reason that people around the world are using energy psychology methods is because of the compelling results—particularly with anxiety, fear, and trauma symptoms. When I consider how much of any consultation involves such symptoms, I start thinking about helping techniques. The meridian-based therapies are usually specific and focused ones, and that is good. Yet the indirect, nonspecific approach of "just tapping" can bring tremendous changes for the better to an aroused autonomic nervous system: Tapping is innately relaxing.

I find the results from tapping are essentially the same as other useful modern methods, specifically NLP (neuro-linguistic programming); hypnotherapy, and EMDR (Eye Movement Desensitizing and Reprocessing), to name three. After using each modality over many years, I find

that tapping is the simplest, easiest, and safest to use as self-help.

I have a reputation as a "natural" doctor because I use a natural method. I actually spend a lot of my time encouraging patients to use the best of both orthodox and natural medicine. There is a lot of fear in the community about illness and risk and authoritarian treatment, and it often seems to ordinary people like an either-or decision. Doctors are often not holistic thinkers about patients, and natural practitioners are not careful enough with their words when implying what remedies can do for clients. Both make mistakes accordingly. It is hard for the person seeking help to understand what the practitioner's words really mean. Words like "treat," "manage," "heal," "help," and "change" can be maddeningly vague, in a clinical sense, when used unthinkingly. When you avoid the flowery language that some overenthusiastic proponents use, and use instead sensible and honest descriptions of tapping's relaxing effects, patients can get on with using a practical tool without false hope or magical thinking.

In describing the potential of tapping approaches, I think it is very important for the doctor to have a personal experience of what tapping can do; then the doctor is congruent in the consultation. In my opinion, the ideal therapeutic situation for the treating doctor is to introduce an added self-help method to patients that will help them recover and heal as quickly as possible, both psychologically and physically. This is a true mutual contract, with the added satisfaction for both of real progress. The simple forms of tapping qualify here as empowering for the patient. Clear descriptions and clear thinking are required from the doctor for this ethical contract. I think of tapping as helping the mind and body function together at the best level by, over time, facilitating healing, soothing anxieties and fears, and helping release emotions connected to hurt and loss.

Finally, I am presenting an overview as a treating psychotherapist. My descriptions and comments here are not meant as dogmatic. They reflect my own anecdotal and empirical experience with tapping since 1998. I am skeptical in a healthy way and hope to remain so. But I am very glad that being in a conservative profession has not made me miss out on the discovery of tapping and its subsequent enormous benefits for me and for my patients.

## Methodology

Tapping cannot be "removed" from most energy therapy approaches, as it is their foundation. This may seem obvious, but some of the clever accoutrements of energy methodology detract from this simple fact. In my experience, however, using tapping alone opens up a new world of physiological benefits.

Most EFT is used in a remedial sense, and used directly, as a specifically focused and problem-solving approach based on desensitizing core issues of a problem. This is extremely effective. But there is another level of tapping results, which is attained from more indirect and nonspecific efforts. This approach is about the quantity of tapping, and the effects of that on the autonomic nervous system over time. This is energy toning and it can be done automatically without thought, like a fitness program. It is "just using tapping" as a beneficial process for the body and as a resilience building program (emotional fitness). It does not require being clever or psychologically minded or even aware! The sequence of use of tapping points is not important; meridian point stimulation itself is.

The simplest way to do enough tapping is to do it "continually." Here the finger points are most useful, and the thumb taps on each of the finger points up and down the fingers without stopping. Ideally, you link this practice to your habitual life, such as tapping while you watch TV, talk on the telephone, or wait at a red light. In this way you can tap in short bursts, for up to an hour a day (total) with little effort. This is the key to applying tapping to some complex physical issues, and to integrating tapping into other psychological therapies.

One of the enduring problems with EFT seems to be that people often have unrealistic expectations when applying the techniques. Often they attempt self-help alone for very complex problems requiring assessment and team effort. Sometimes they are discouraged by having to do a lot of sessions when that was always the path to take.

I think EFT excites magical thinking, leading to the outcome dream of the "one-minute wonder." In addition, it is easy to get discouraged if you think you have to know what words to say for every issue (as a Setup Statement).

In the simplified approach covered in this chapter, there are few words or statements when working more directly with issues; you merely add the tapping to the problem as you become aware of its manifestations. Accept the thoughts, feelings, and negativities—and add tapping. If you experience a block of some kind, treat that as the "next problem." And you can add tapping to most medical problems and most psychological therapies.

## The Issue of Natural Versus Orthodox Medicine

May I offer a little perspective after years of observing the inherent differences in the two branches of medicine from both sides of the fence? Essentially, there is a clash of values between the two branches. I think of tapping as the ultimate holistic treatment and perfect ancillary treatment for all problems. For some conditions, such as phobic anxiety, panic disorder, PTSD, and convalescence, it is itself the treatment of choice (in my opinion).

It is downright dangerous, however, to think of alternative treatments as curative, or highly effective, if they are not. It is likewise reprehensible to ignore the body and its natural resilience mechanisms in treating complex conditions (or any condition). Getting better requires help on all levels. It is only rigid black-and-white thinking (the mind's dealing in opposites) and ideology that prevents the branches of medicine from working harmoniously together. Sometimes the orthodox treatment is the main one, sometimes the natural treatment will do the most good in promoting recovery; sometimes it is the combination.

Doctors seem to be troubled by the casual approach to objective proof that natural medicine may include, even if the remedy works. Natural practitioners seem to be in an internal political struggle with conservatives and drug companies and see themselves as the voice of freedom for natural health. Both camps have a good point but occupy a polarized position. I say, start finding ways to work together, as common sense says you should; this is not an either-or matter!

The negative effect of rapid technological change and authoritarian corporate medicine has made using orthodox medicine far less humanistic than it was. It is less appealing in many ways than natural medicine. Primitive fears are easily triggered by ignorance and superstition. Fear gives rise to mistrust. Doctors, medications, and illness itself can trigger these negative feelings. There is always the wonderfully attractive possibility of getting better or staying well all your life without medications.

A short visit to the Third World will make it obvious that in the West we might have the luxury of wanting to live a completely natural life—without medications—in a society where few die of infection before their first birthday, and illnesses have actual cures as well as folk remedies. But the fears surrounding modern drug treatments are mostly irrational. Antibiotics and antidepressants have their place. Nobody really wants to go back to the early part of last century when polio, tuberculosis, and infections raged, and cancer was always fatal. They just want to find a better balance of treatments, something more holistic, including the best of modern science.

## Practical Applications

I am making some statements here based on my empirical experience with utilizing tapping in many medical situations. As I am a doctor, people assume that I have somehow treated every possible condition with tapping and, then, more than one case. They think I can expound on the intricacies of how effective it will be generally and specifically: "Does it work on…?" Because I find it such a safe modality, I do "try it on everything," as long as I know what I am treating (diagnosis) and follow up the result. Common-sense observation will give you some objectivity.

This is how I discovered that tapping alone is of little use generally in treating severe depression. Very few alternative practitioners are willing to believe this, possibly because the results in treating anxiety-based conditions are so much better and possibly because the default treatment is then medication (antidepressants). Among my patients are a large and growing number of grateful naturopaths, homeopaths, chiropractors, and counselors whose chronic depression finally lifted after using medication as the main treatment.

Equally, I have treated, with tapping, a large number of medical colleagues, and their family members, for diverse emotional problems. This is unremarkable except for the fact that few of these colleagues have then sent me any of their own patients to treat! They know that the tapping works, but for them, as conservative doctors, to

recommend it more widely is a "bridge too far" at present.

Finally, teaching patients how to tap will bring ancillary results in their personal lives if they use it. It is routine to observe how having a trauma or phobia treated somehow allows that patient to start making significant positive changes in his or her habitual thinking, relationships, and goals, even if these are not addressed. For example, I once treated a mother for trigeminal neuralgia attacks and taught her the continual tapping. Her reclusive and nervous adult daughter accompanied her (as her carer) in these sessions, but I said little to the daughter apart from showing her the technique too. The mother informed me that several months later the daughter had moved away from home, lost 30 pounds, found a job, and started going out and dating—and said that the tapping had "saved her life"! All she had done was practice continual tapping.

## In General

Doctors spend an inordinate amount of time preaching the benefits of good diet, exercise, relaxation and stress management, and common sense. The only thing missing in my opinion is tapping! Such a skill belongs in the teaching toolbox of every practitioner interested in real change.

Tapping is something that it is possible to "do" yourself, as self-help. It gives a multilevel benefit, including automatic relaxation, while helping you avoid a kind of helplessness (depending on the condition). It is a pattern interruption to the "trance" of being the patient with a particular condition (e.g., cancer). I consider it the ultimate stress-management self-help technique, which aids in processing negative or dysfunctional emotion while also building resilience.

You can add tapping to the processes of engaging with the medical system, dealing with the uncertainties of being ill, and recovering your health. It has a harmonizing and balancing effect on your body's reactive nervous system. Tapping is a wonderful help when you are undergoing invasive tests (e.g., blood tests and biopsies), having procedures or investigations (e.g., CT or MRI scans), and also getting the results. And let's mention our esteemed dental practitioner colleagues in this treatment context since their efforts are often accompanied by anxiety and fear in the patient!

I advise adding tapping to most ordinary medical presentations because the condition represents an imbalance and the symptoms might benefit. Sometimes tapping can have what seems to be a direct effect on disease states (e.g., oncoming viral illness, acute allergic states).

Please note the very important caveat regarding chest and head pain, infections, and dental and eye conditions: These always deserve a diagnosis. Beware the treatment of symptoms alone—especially pain—without diagnosis. For example, a workshopper in a demonstration treated only with tapping for loin pain was admitted to hospital the next day for acute kidney infection. In another case, a "headache" treated with tapping in a workshop setting without diagnostic acumen produced poor results and there followed an immediate deterioration, requiring urgent admission to the hospital, with a bleeding cerebral aneurysm.

Being able to relieve symptoms does not mean being able to cure the underlying condition. In one case, I helped a patient with a terminal brain tumor avoid being hospitalized so frequently due to exacerbations of headache, when her wish was to die at home. Additionally, I have seen serious exacerbation of lumbar disc disease and of "frozen shoulder" pathology after tapping relieved most of the pain symptoms, and the patient strained the area soon afterward.

Using tapping to keep calm and to desensitize immediate traumatic responses is a new way to manage accidents, emergencies, and other urgent conditions. It is also an excellent way for the treating doctor to remain as capable as possible under duress. I wish I had known about tapping when I was a doctor in the emergency room years ago. I have spent many hours treating my residual PTSD symptoms with tapping as a result of that exposure to trauma. If you can treat such trauma as it occurs, you stand a very good chance of having little further distress. For example, at an EFT workshop at which I presented, two participants were involved after lunch in a head-on collision with an oncoming truck. Because they had learned the continual tapping beforehand, they were actually tapping as the accident occurred! They continued as the emergency services got them out of their car and to the emergency room. There they were treated and returned to the venue quite physically stiff and sore (and still tapping). Significantly, they experienced no symptoms of emotional trauma at all after that incident. The couple gave tribute to the continual tapping I had mentioned in my trauma presentation as a practical guide for them when under duress.

Every doctor and nurse knows of patients who have had miraculous recoveries. Some patients tend to heal better and more quickly. This is the invisible and mysterious world of the healing process. In days gone by, we used to pay far more attention to the healing environment. Today it can be an endurance test merely to be in a hospital ward. The new discipline of psychoneuroimmunology comes to mind here as it seems to encompass the process whereby you can learn to function at the highest physiological level possible in any situation. This is a fancy way of saying that doctors have to consider the role of the mind and nervous system when they wish to aid in the healing process. The old belief that the body will heal automatically, by itself, is not sufficient.

In the case of dealing with serious illness, doctors are often asked whether alternative treatments will help. I deal with such enquiries regularly. It is an opportunity for the physician to impart hope and a positive attitude; words are powerful, and need to be used well. Here is a typical answer from an e-mail exchange regarding cerebellar ataxia and the use of tapping:

*Thank you for your enquiry. If I read about EFT, I too would certainly be asking this question, if the partner I loved had a serious illness. You wrote: "Could you tell me if your treatment will work?" My answer is that the new method you have read about will not cure cerebellar ataxia, unfortunately. Please read on.*

*What I have learned after some years of using such methods is that they can have surprising effects on serious diseases. Sometimes they can help the body to stabilise and work as best as it is capable of doing, in the best balance, so to speak. As well, it is certain that they help very much with the anxieties and worries of having such a dreadful condition (this is not a minor problem). Then they can also offer the other partner or family members something valuable, when it comes to handling the stress of the many difficulties involved.*

*When the doctor says, "There is no treatment" and that it "will get worse," this may be correct in a strict sense. But there is treatment that can aid and assist and help your wife be more comfortable. And sometimes the progression of the disease is not as expected and is a lot slower. I have seen positive effects myself in cases of multiple sclerosis and brain tumour and pain cases that were beneficial for the sufferer (all "incurable conditions"). I think it is unfair to say to someone that nothing can be done if that is the meaning they take from the statement. You might be thinking this.*

*Every doctor has seen cases of an incurable condition that behave a lot better than expected. I think the aim here is to be hopeful that using tapping can have some effect on the whole situation that is positive. Here is my Golden Rule: "With every serious illness there is always a group of people that do well." Surely the aim here is to find out what this means for your wife. If she develops more peace of mind at least, using tapping, I would think this worthwhile. The aim here is quality of life.*

*I know that many people surprise doctors with the strength of their responses to treatment. I also know that medical statistics apply to groups, not individuals. My own wife has trained extensively in oncology as a physician so she has seen the positive variation and unpredictability of the human condition.*

*Your treating physicians will unpack the figures for you, of course, but when you consider "length of life," it is hard to work out where you fit in. Without preempting your own discussions, I would like to mention that a combination of prayer and treatment healed several people I know in a seemingly impossible medical situation. If it is possible at all for some, then that door remains open in theory for others.*

*There are many things that you both need to do to stay well and to stay positive.*

I have found that I could help manage exotic medical conditions better by adding the possibility of symptom change—even if small: e.g., multiple sclerosis, schizophrenia, prostatic hypertrophy, ventricular palpitations. In treating the many issues involved in paraplegia and quadriplegia, it seems that the energy system remains unaffected, and can be influenced by tapping treatment. Tapping can help "facilitate" remission or recovery.

Any condition prone to exacerbations and remissions is worth using tapping on. That fluctuation in the level of symptoms shows that the system is not fixed, that there can be good days and bad days.

I consider it to be the best self-help method available for all rehabilitation and convalescence. I have found it to be particularly useful in the management of injuries (postoperative and posttraumatic) and stroke. Any procedure or operation, or hospital experience, is a strain on the body on one level. For example, recovering from the chemical effects of a general anaesthetic takes a day or two at least; having sutures inside the body (whether by ordinary or keyhole surgery) requires much longer for complete healing than people expect. Patients are expected to adapt to the hospital routine as an in-patient when, paradoxically, this routine is designed mainly for the convenience of staff, and patients yearn to be home—where they can finally get better!

The results from any bodywork or physiotherapy can be improved by teaching the recipient how to tap. The meridian stimulation also works well at the end of a physical session to "seal" the result. If a patient is requiring acupuncture regularly, then some of that treatment effect is available to them via self-help if they know continual tapping.

Obviously, in the world of somatic medicine, it does so much for repairing the so-called mind-body balance and functioning. Any condition which may be caused or aggravated by "stress" (e.g., skin disease, gut reactivity, immune conditions, migraine) can benefit from sufficient tapping. Then there is the "second problem" (the emotional reaction) after a patient has the "first problem" (the diagnosis). This reaction can become emotionally larger than the noxious effect of the original problem (e.g., experiencing chronic pain, joint problems, urinary problems, cancer). The reaction most often takes the form of self-blame and criticism. Ideally, the patient taps when experiencing such negative reactions.

The transitions of life are often accompanied by fear of the unknown and fear of change. Tapping facilitates the healthy emotional processing that leads to a more balanced perspective. While it won't resolve an authentic and appropriate negative emotion (I have found it's impossible to "tap it away" in a misguided effort to remain unaffected by such feelings), so often in these situations there is a toxic or excessive overlay of negative emotion. Here, a processing technique is ideal. You deal with the situation more easily and can usually do it more quickly.

Everyone seems to have heard of the placebo effect, but what about the nocebo effect? This is also part of medicine. Having a personal tapping antidote available to treat the noxious effects of fear of the negative is empowering. Equally, I think that our own negative thoughts and beliefs are our biggest block to just being who we are. These blocks prevent the full expression of innate cheerfulness and happiness.

## Specific Conditions

Each condition I mention briefly here is worthy of a chapter of its own. Tapping can be introduced for all of the following conditions with useful results. Often there is the initial problem followed by the patient's reaction to having the problem. Tapping can help alleviate the intensity of both issues.

## Anxiety, Fear, and Trauma-Based Conditions

In treating these we are dealing with a huge patient population and conditions that are overrepresented in clinics and surgeries. The global current prevalence of anxiety disorders adjusted for methodological differences is 7.3% (4.8–10.9%) and ranges from 5.3% (3.5–8.1%) in African cultures to 10.4% (7.0–15.5%) in Euro/Anglo cultures (Baxter, Scott, Vos, & Whiteford, 2013).

The usual medical approach to anxiety disorders is based on cognitive behavioral therapy (CBT), medication, and counseling. I suggest that adding tapping as a strategic technique has the potential to facilitate resolution of the acute and chronic manifestations, and to act as a maintenance program like no other. Because it is both a relaxing and an emotional processing technique, it has great potential.

**Phobic anxiety.** This is the condition for which tapping truly shines. A simple phobia in an otherwise well person can usually be treated rapidly with tapping, sometimes within minutes. A thorough, specific treatment is best, of course, and some cases can take several sessions. Paradoxically, tapping has no effect on the actual phobic thoughts. They persist. But when the previous associated emotional reaction is gone (as a result of comprehensive tapping treatment), then

there is no nervous system link remaining (which is commonly the cause of the negative feeling). Thus there is no "problem" without such feeling, as a thought alone gives no such reaction. Then the thoughts fade and move away. And, most intriguing of all, I have seen some phobias vanish without specific treatment after enough indirect tapping work. Occasionally, the treatment of one phobia will extinguish the symptoms of another. Presumably, the mechanism of expression of the anxiety is disrupted.

**Panic disorder.** Much of conventional advice to those prone to anxiety attacks involves their learning relaxation, meditation, thought control, and right living habits. I have found that the multilevel benefits of tapping make daily tapping practice indispensable, and extremely effective as a preventive measure. As a result of treating this disorder with tapping alone (where suitable, as in the majority of cases without underlying depression or thyroid problems), I have discovered that combining common-sense precautions and daily tapping practice, as stress management and to build up resilience, can prevent attacks and render the underlying tendency quiescent. Typically, that self-help program in the acute phase of the problem lasts some 4 weeks, and the maintenance part is indefinite (some "automatic" tapping each day, which is the practice of tapping continually without having to think: just tapping).

**Posttraumatic stress disorder (PTSD).** Based on my professional experience and results, I consider that using tapping thoughtfully and comprehensively for treating PTSD is the "gold standard" of treatment. I have used it for hundreds of sufferers of major assaults, war traumas, traffic accidents, and holdups. Used in this context it provides the most gratifying professional results, as far as I am concerned. It is also true that those who suffer the most are predisposed by virtue of their makeup and prior life experiences, and those other life traumas also respond to more extensive treatment and therapy. One day I hope meridian-based therapies will be accepted and used for sufferers everywhere; unfortunately, the evidence base for wider medical acceptance is, as yet, insufficient. After so many successful outcomes, notably including that of treating the trauma of my eldest daughter, I am not waiting for that day for formal approval to continue this work.

Treating minor variations of PTSD (not conforming to the strict definition), which can be quite debilitating for the patient, is also very rewarding. Among the common traumatic situations I have used it for are:

- For the new mother, after a difficult birth experience.
- After minor car accidents (ideally used as soon as possible).
- Losing a job.
- Divorce and readjustment.
- Parent's reaction to the severe illness/disability of a child.
- Court appearances, especially being cross-examined.
- Examination fears and "freezing" in examinations.
- Being bullied in any way.
- Helping carers (especially those caring for people with dementia) avoid burnout.

## Relationship Problems

Some comics say that relationship and trauma are the same thing. Certainly, using tapping as "first aid" for the hurt and upset of dealing with the dark side of your partner's behavior is a good beginning if you wish to avoid having primitive reactions that fail miserably to resolve problems. Ultimately, you have to deal with your own reactions as best you possibly can (think tolerance and patience). Any couple getting professional help will benefit from knowing and using tapping in sessions and at home. If you want to stop struggling with your partner about whose values are going to prevail in the relationship, and eventually reach the point of devotional acceptance in a long-term relationship, tapping is indispensable, in my opinion. It can help you be happy rather than "right."

## Cravings and Addictions

Tapping is very good at helping postpone the reaction to the craving impulse, that is, it helps postpone acting on the impulse. Treating the underlying anxiety and driving emotions of addiction is a multilevel process, however, and typically requires a team of helpers for a successful outcome. Some professionals maintain that three things are needed for the effective treatment of addiction: group work (typically a 12-step program; individual help, ideally some therapy and support; and a spiritual purpose and reason for

living. Tapping is a specific tool that can be used in therapy, group work, or as self-help.

## Grief and Loss

The mixed emotions and waves of feeling that accompany grief and loss make this a situation in which it is often difficult to identify the emotional problem you want help with. Sometimes it just hurts, and sometimes it feels like you will die yourself, from a broken heart. As a process you can become stuck in "pathological grief" if all the old personal and family issues replay in a dark way for too long. Tapping is a godsend for helping retain the right kind of control. What I mean is that it seems to help the release of emotion (often with tears) and the processing of hurt and shock. It helps integrate the new understanding we receive after the death of someone close. I found when both my parents died that the grieving process was nothing like what I had expected. It was much "better" and not as "bad" as I expected. Of course, I was tapping continually.

## Working with Children

The fears and upsets of little children respond very quickly to tapping, often in a matter of seconds, but you need to have a context for them to understand it (as a game) and some ritual in which they experience it as a good and soothing routine (ideally, some tapping for them at night just before sleep). They don't have the belief systems of adults and can let things go easily if the parent is also relaxed. There is little need for words as the problem reaction is manifesting and ready for processing. Mostly, you don't need statements with children; just mention the issue and tell them that you love them. It's best to tap on your own upset feelings about your child's problems before trying anything with the child. If the parent holds a very young child while tapping on him or herself, the child can often benefit from such tapping indirectly.

## Pain Management

Pain is pain, and suffering is the emotional reaction to having the pain, filtered through the belief system and values of the patient. Chronic pain is a new disease state apparently, with its own autonomic conditions. When a sufferer can use tapping in a way to affect autonomic processes for the better (this is easy to demonstrate over time), then it's possible to relieve suffering as well as potentially having some direct effect on the pain. It is particularly useful to have tapping available as self-help. This is empowering for the sufferer. For one thing, it naturally facilitates the relaxation so necessary for dealing with the pain more effectively. I have found it to be the essential ancillary tool in pain treatment.

## Palliative Care

In a situation of palliative care, orthodox medications won't cure but are used to treat symptoms of pain and distress. Natural medications can help balance the body during this difficult time. Every medical symptom might appear, but the patient is likely to have to deal with pain, lethargy, body dysfunction, and sometimes despair (on the road toward acceptance). This is also the world of self-help in a situation in which the patient gradually loses autonomy. It is interesting to note that having a cancer prognosis can in itself be life-threatening. Some patients might find the actual terminal diagnosis to be overwhelming and feel completely helpless. Professor Gerald W. Milton (1973), writing about terminal melanoma, says that some patients can fail to adjust and actually hasten their own death like this (as if they are the victims of witchcraft).

I think that tapping is essential for support staff too, since they are confronted daily with some serious philosophical and spiritual issues and are vulnerable to burnout, like all of us in the helping professions.

## The Question of Depression

Depression is an important, common, and potentially dangerous condition. I consider it to be one of the main reasons for misery and suffering in relationships and families. It can be a complex, multilevel matter. I have seen far too many tragic outcomes with the incorrect treatment for depression and thus I have ethical concerns about the proper treatment approach to the more severe forms of depression (particularly recurrent, long-lasting, or familial forms). Postpartum depression, severe mood disorders, and suicidal thinking must have effective treatments. Despite occasional anecdotal reports, I don't find that EFT or any tapping technique offers this effectiveness consistently.

There is still a belief that depression is the fault of the sufferer and that depressed individuals should cure themselves by thinking more positively. The whole issue of using antidepressants thus attracts judgment in a way that using medication for diabetes never does (although diabetes is often the end result of obesity and overindulgence, according to some researchers). Natural treatments are not thought of as having side effects or causing problems because they are natural. There is very little scientific evidence—or even practical, experiential, empirical evidence—that natural treatments help a significant number of depressed people who have more than mild depression. Tapping is a good tool to use for mild depression but is not sufficient in itself to resolve moderate to severe depression. Any natural practitioner who can prove me wrong and show me results that consistently disprove this will earn the gratitude of millions of sufferers.

Treatment needs to address the domain of depressive thinking and negative beliefs too, but this can't happen unless the depression first lifts. Typically, the depression has been there for some time. Proper diagnosis and assessment is vital here. There are promising results from early trials of fish oil supplements and transcranial magnetic stimulation, as well as certain kinds of acupuncture, but many sufferers need urgent help. For most, this means antidepressant medication as the main modality. It is the only consistent way I know to lift the severe form of depression for most people. Here is where orthodox and natural medicine could work together—but rarely do.

## Adding Tapping to Any Therapy

Continual tapping during a therapeutic session can enhance the benefits of any modality. I regard tapping as the "great integrator"; it transforms any modality into one in which tapping can facilitate the essential emotional shift. Thus thinking techniques can offer emotional shift and potential change in therapy that is more profound. This is an integration of the worlds of thinking and feeling. The worlds of psychotherapy, counseling, coaching, supervision, and debriefing are transformed by the addition of tapping. Tapping is foremost an emotional processing technique and occurs in the body. Thus it is ideal to add to a cognitive process that helps bring focus to the issues.

With permission or agreement from the therapist, the patient can tap continually before, during, and after the session. If preferred, the patient can rub the points instead of tapping, or touch the points and breathe. After training in the technique, even imagining the tapping works for most people.

The concept of continual tapping during a therapeutic session means you don't have to find an EFT practitioner. People seeking help may assume that only an EFT practitioner can apply the benefits of tapping. In reality, many therapeutic approaches can be ideal if you add tapping. Much of the modern plethora of energy therapies consists merely of adding the concept of tapping onto a framework of strategies and mix of ideas from other therapy modalities, such as NLP concepts, Inner Child work, CBT ideas, and straight positive suggestion from hypnotherapy.

In this way, too, a good match between therapist and patient may be easier to find because the available practitioners and disciplines are more numerous. Many excellent therapists who do not utilize tapping are now available to the patient who knows how to tap during the session. Tapping is merely a technique, and I think it works best within the context of a therapeutic relationship. Being your own therapist is a lonely business! We all need to be heard and understood, to be validated. This is the path to acceptance and healing.

## Cognitive Behavioral Therapy

If, as part of the new energy psychology paradigm, our emotionalized thoughts can be treated with tapping, and those noxious effects lessened dramatically, then the concept of thoughts influencing behaviors may actually work. One of the frustrations of using CBT strategies is that the negative emotion persists, even if the patient learns how to walk through the world and mentally perform the difficult things. You can tell somebody not to think a negative thought, but the mind is far more sneaky than mere willpower can control. I tell my patients to add tapping to the problem: Whenever they find themselves thinking a toxic thought, tap. This not only helps lessen the emotionalized part of the thought, but it also prevents the patient from feeling like a failure (for "allowing" the negative thought in the first place). Now there is the feeling of success for that patient, followed by more compliance with the treatment framework and better results. A traditional program of desensitization for phobic anxiety, for example, will not be necessary if the driving emotion is no longer present (because of specific

and direct treatment with tapping), regardless of whether the thoughts have changed or not!

## Hypnotherapy, Eye Movement Desensitization and Reprocessing (EMDR), Transactional Analysis, Gestalt Therapy

I have had extensive training in these modalities. Tapping can be used to assist in facilitating the processing of excess negative emotion during a session, to "finish" a session, and to promote ongoing relaxation training afterward. I find it a useful addition and not necessarily a replacement approach.

## 12-Step Programs and Group Therapy

When a group is tapping, the shared universal emotions flow more freely. When one member is talking, others will resonate emotionally. The great therapist Frank Farrelly says, "What's most personal is most universal." This is particularly apt and useful in the mass treatment of trauma. A survivor goes through their experience while all can make emotional progress together as long as the whole group is tapping. It is a shared experience. This processing function of tapping adds major benefit to mere debriefing, as talking by itself is both cumbersome and slow as an emotional processing technique.

## Psychoanalytically Oriented Psychotherapy

I taught tapping to six patients who were in this traditional treatment over several years, in keeping with the long-term time frame of this type of therapy. Usually, the progress is notoriously slow, but both the patients and the therapists were pleasantly surprised by the benefit overall (without changing the analytic frame). Since real change depends on emotional shifting in a life-affirming direction, tapping promotes quicker progress. I regard it as the missing link in the many "talking therapies" that are relatively inefficient despite the training and skill of the therapist.

## Conclusion

I have a dream. I hope that one day all the people in the helping professions make their treating decisions based on results, not on ideology. I believe in evidence-based medicine. I also see many good examples of alternative treatments that work without such evidence. Sometimes the "evidence" in orthodox medicine is paltry or sparse. There is also a vast array of orthodox medical thinking that owes nothing to evidence but exists due to tradition. Still, on both sides of the medical fence people respect results.

In energy psychology, there is a core of marvelous efficacy. The field is not taken as seriously as it should be because it is new (with relatively little research), as is the paradigm (guaranteed to upset peers). Practitioners who indulge in magical thinking and over-promise undermine the field. More common-sense input from trained medical people is one answer here. Over some 14 years I have applied as much of the new paradigm as I can, in many medical conditions, both mental-emotional and physical. For me it has been the most rewarding time of my professional life. It has made a huge difference in the life of my family. If my dream comes to pass, professionals everywhere will be able to integrate the techniques into their field. Anyone will be able to learn the simple refinements of tapping, and have it "on hand" when necessary.

I consider tapping an essential, life-affirming skill and I look forward to the day when the majority of my medical colleagues regard it this way as well.

## References

Baxter, A. J., Scott, K. M., Vos, T., & Whiteford, H. A. (2013, May). Global prevalence of anxiety disorders: A systematic review and meta-regression. *Psychological Medicine, 43*(5): 897–910. doi:10.1017/S003329171200147X

Milton, G. W. (1973, June 23). Self-willed death or the bone-pointing syndrome. *Lancet, 301*(7817), 1435–1436. doi:10.1016/S0140-6736(73)91754-6)

# Chapter 40
# Building Ethical Mindfulness to Maximize Your Practice of EFT

*Dorothea Hover-Kramer*

## Abstract

This chapter explores the ways that ethical mindfulness can enhance EFT practice by focusing on four distinct areas for increased awareness: (1) the current context of energy therapies as a whole within the larger picture of leading national health care disciplines; (2) the exceptional aspects of a new energy therapy, such as EFT, that require practitioner awareness beyond the usual considerations needed for cognitive therapies; (3) criteria for selection of clients most appropriate for EFT interventions such as client willingness, responsiveness, and ability to give feedback; and (4) the best risk management practices to avoid pitfalls in one's practice while enhancing safeguards and rapport.

**Keywords:** ethical mindfulness, client selection criteria, cautions for using EFT, risk management, energy medicine ethics

**Dorothea Hover-Kramer, EdD, RN, DCEP**, a pioneer in the field of energy medicine, died on January 15, 2013, a month after writing this chapter. Cofounder and past president of the Association for Comprehensive Energy Psychology (ACEP), she was also a founding elder of the Healing Touch movement, and served on the leadership council of the American Holistic Nurses Association. She authored nine textbooks about energy therapies, including the award-winning ethics book *Creating Healing Relationships: Professional Standards for Energy Therapy Practitioners*.

Since EFT (Emotional Freedom Techniques) was first introduced some 15 years ago, practitioner acceptance for addressing a large range of client issues with EFT has made it one of the most widely known of the energy therapies. EFT's easy accessibility and effects of rapid change for clients, however, often disguise the depth and breadth of possible outcomes—a shortcoming this volume seeks to correct. In addition, as explored in this chapter, ethical mindfulness can greatly enhance EFT's effectiveness and maximize client learning.

My personal experience comes from more than 20 years of teaching energy modalities, in both Healing Touch and energy psychology certification programs, to people who are not licensed in a specific mental health discipline. Based on my learning from students, I offer the following perspectives to enhance practitioner mindfulness in utilizing the innately powerful tools of EFT:

- The public context of a new, innovative complementary modality such as EFT.
- The exceptional aspects of energy modalities of which practitioners must be aware.
- Criteria for selecting the clients most appropriate for EFT interventions.
- Best risk management practices.

We'll explore each of these themes to allow you as a practitioner to bring these ideas into your own way of offering EFT's person-centered, caring approaches to your clients. One might say that many of the considerations are simply good common sense; in fact, you may already have thought about many of these ideas. Nevertheless, reality proves that common sense is, after all, not so common unless acknowledged and reinforced. The price of a client relationship gone in the wrong direction is much too high, both for the individuals concerned, and also for the future of EFT practice as a whole.

## I. The Public Context of the Innovative, Complementary Modality of EFT

Although many practitioners of EFT have met with public recognition, it is important to remember that this practice is only one of the approximately 50 approaches that fall under the broad category called "energy psychology" (EP). New protocols and methods are continually being developed by creative psychotherapists to address various forms of emotional distress with energetic means. Energy psychologies are a subset of a much larger popular and growing discipline named "energy medicine" (EM) which includes more than 250 training programs (Thomas, 2010, p. 6). Both EP and EM are sought out by the American public because complex client issues such as chronic pain, persistent stress reaction patterns, and the challenges of aging are not adequately addressed within the framework of current Western medical approaches.

Of course, conventional medical care is required for most people who seek out the large number of "complementary/alternative modalities" as identified and accepted by the National Institutes of Health (NIH). As new methods are being researched, they begin to be recognized as "probably efficacious" by the large organizations of conventional medical and psychiatric practitioners, the purveyors of so-called "mainstream medicine." Energy medicine, also dubbed "frontier medicine," is the last item on NIH's long list of innovative modalities, such as herbal medicine, vitamin therapy, massage, and homeopathic practice, among others, that are currently being researched for future acceptance. It's valuable to recall that acupuncture, despite its 5,000-year history of providing pain relief, was only approved by the American Medical Association in the last decade for a specific number of applications. In November 2012, after a 12-year battle led by the Association for Comprehensive Energy Psychology (ACEP), the American Psychological Association (APA) approved energy psychology courses as acceptable material for psychologists' continuing education credits. APA still considers all energy therapies to be "experimental, and probably efficacious" despite the large, growing body of EP research (ACEP, 2012).

The bottom line is that energy medicine, energy psychology, and EFT specifically are still a long way from being a standard part of the nation's health care picture. The required cautions for practitioners are therefore to use the work wisely, with carefully selected clients (more discussion in Section III), and always to ensure client informed consent.

Clients always have the right to choose whether to receive EFT or not, regardless of the practitioner's wish for good outcomes. They are not at fault if the results practitioners wish for them are not achieved. Other methods may actually be more effective for individual client issues. Networking, referral-making, and expanding practitioner resources are essential elements of all professional EFT practice.

Another aspect of client informed consent is for practitioners to educate clients about EFT clearly before beginning their work. This includes stating the possible benefits and risks of the innovative, experimental EFT treatment they will receive. Benefits are by now well known, but several of the benefits also have inherent client risks. For example, the rapid change induced by EFT can affect the client's family or occupational systems. If, for example, a low-key family member recalls her inner strengths and becomes effectively assertive, the whole family system will be affected, with reverberations to all family members.

Another benefit/risk now well documented is that clients' memories change. While this appears an adaptive change for the better in most cases, it could limit testimony in legal settings. The client and his or her environment must steadily be considered as client/practitioner agreements are made within a mutually set therapeutic contract.

## II. Exceptional Aspects of EFT Requiring Practitioner Awareness

Unlike most cognitive, conversational therapies, EFT communicates on an energetic level. Far more than words is involved in the interaction between client and practitioner energy fields. The very presence of the practitioner can evoke hope and new possibilities if the caregiver is "walking his talk"— a living example of self-care and balanced mental, emotional, and spiritual energy. Every communication is sensed by both participants within the sacred, caring contract to reach the whole person. It is an art to communicate this degree of presence to others, and caregivers, especially in energy modalities, are mandated to engage in regular, daily self-care. (For further discussion of self-care, see Hover-Kramer, 2011, pp. 63–110.)

Another safeguard is to know your scope of practice. Specifically, what are your skills, background, and strengths as well as the areas in which you have limited or no expertise? Keeping a growing self-inventory allows insights to come from each client session. (For further discussion of scope of practice considerations, see Hover-Kramer, 2011, pp. 93–96, 139, 142–147.)

In addition to creating the setting for multi-dimensional healing to take place, practitioners are charged with recognizing their own perceptual limitations so they do not pass them on to their clients. Practitioner attachment to a specific outcome with the use of only one method such as EFT may be one of the most prominent of such projections. There are also, however, the clients' tendencies of wanting to please their helpers by agreeing too readily, not choosing what they need carefully, or becoming overly dependent. There is a real power differential, whether acknowledged or hidden, and all practitioners need to take it into account in obtaining informed consent and building the trusted healing relationship.

Because of the rapid and deeper rapport that occurs in energy therapies, clients may have increased and unrealistic emotional attachments to their practitioners. Client expectations may well exceed anything that can be offered. This is why mutual agreements around treatment goals are so vital at the outset. In addition, I encourage taking the last 10 minutes of every session to ask clients to tell you what they learned, how their view of themselves is changing, and to discuss what was helpful and what was not.

In addition to rapid rapport and the opportunity for full dimensional healing, another unusual feature of energy therapies is the possible presence of varying degrees of trance. The repetition of phrases combined with stimulation of acupoints readily brings clients to deeper awareness of themselves, which may include nonordinary states of consciousness. On a continuum, these may range from mild trance or reverie, to reliving a traumatic event, stepping into a childhood memory, or recalling a period of human history, or moving to a sense of transcending the present, experiencing a sense of spiritual Oneness. Since all these possibilities are healthy signs of human functioning, practitioners must be prepared to normalize these experiences. Validating and honoring clients' unusual responses helps clients accept and integrate whatever material surfaces from the rich treasures of their unconscious minds. The intention of the psyche in opening doors to new awareness is always positive, toward growth and increased wisdom.

Another exceptional feature of energy therapies is that archetypal patterns are often much more active and conscious than in talk therapies. Archetypes are elemental individual and relationship patterns that have been repeated throughout human history. One of the most readily understood is the Parent/Child archetype. As the therapeutic relationship develops, the Child archetype may become activated in a needy client; the helper may respond by temporarily comforting or parenting the client. If the Parent archetype becomes activated more extensively by giving advice or direction, however, the client can slip into dependency on the practitioner in ways that hamper positive outcomes in areas such as personal decision-making, individuating, or becoming more assertive. Other possible archetypes that can be seen in many therapeutic relationships are the Master/Slave or Helper/Victim patterns. Some caregivers may also think they are evoking the Healer archetype when they are actually living from Servant or Martyr archetypal patterns.

Practitioner mindfulness is thus essential in handling rapid rapport, the closeness of biofield interactions, the likelihood of nonordinary states of consciousness, and the possibility of falling into archetypal patterns—all of which can occur in energetic interventions. These cautions exist for EFT practitioners *in addition* to the usual safeguards and practitioner guidelines emphasized in the standard ethics courses for licensed mental health practitioners. (For a summary of standard ethical guidelines in licensed mental health practices, see Hover-Kramer, 2011, pp. 124–125.)

## III. Criteria for Selecting Clients Who Can Most Benefit from EFT

Careful assessments of clients before beginning EFT work with them is essential in avoiding possible later dilemmas. Some clients seek out energy therapies to avoid receiving conventional medical care; others have simply heard about EFT and want to try it for themselves; and some who have experienced many treatment failures in other settings may seek you out as their "last hope." Whatever the motivation, it's helpful to know what brings clients your way before contracting to work together or developing a treatment plan.

Remember that you are not the only resource or "last hope" for anyone; there are plenty of referral or consultation resources available via the Internet to connect practitioners and specialists in all time zones. Some clients may benefit from having a good medical evaluation first because early symptoms of many illnesses such as cancer or diabetes can show up as depression, nightmares, or negative thinking patterns. Others may benefit from learning self-care practices to manage their emotional distress long before you introduce tapping or another EFT intervention.

The kinds of clients who can make the best progress with a good, basic knowledge of EFT and your self-insights as a practitioner are those who are: interested in the work, have well-defined issues such as a recent trauma or anxiety, willing to make mutual agreements to work with you, and willing to participate in their personal growth through homework and giving feedback.

These parameters then remind us of the personality patterns that may hamper reaching positive outcomes: lack of interest in EFT or personal development, suspiciousness, feeling scattered, becoming easily confused or distracted, having poor recall, holding unrealistic expectations, being unwilling to engage in treatment planning or following suggestions, and having severe physical issues or allergies or enmeshed, complex problems. Although some of these individuals may be helped by some of what EFT can offer, they may actually do much better, more rapidly with more intensive in-depth psychological or medical work that fits your personal scope of practice or inclinations.

Matching client needs to the best possible treatment is an essential skill for EFT practitioners, as many do not have long-term study in mental health or social sciences. Of course, given our world of natural and political disasters, human suffering continues to be extensive. There are many, many relatively healthy people who can benefit greatly from the accessibility and effectiveness of EFT without needing more in-depth, long-term interventions. Mindful, ethical EFT practitioners know their strengths and limitations in selecting the clients that can most benefit from what they have to offer.

## IV. Best Risk-Management Practices

To summarize and embellish on the previous considerations, here are some of the most effective and elegant ways to maximize building healing relationships with your clients:

- Make sure every bit of publicity, including websites and e-mail signatures, about you is accurate. This includes your credentials, educational background, interests, years of practice, and strengths.

- Make realistic and proven statements about the method you're using. Avoid making unfounded claims about EFT. Although many positive outcomes have been noted, neither EFT nor any other energy-oriented method can totally cure illness, prevent disease, or answer every problem.
- Keep backup materials of EFT theory and research so you can readily answer client or public questions. Enhance your library and knowledge base regularly.
- Carefully document initial informed consent about using EFT with clients and thereafter "check in" regularly with clients with every intervention you offer. Ask for permissions respecting client wishes; keep confidentiality except in cases where the client's or another person's life is at high risk.
- Ensure that all clients have recent and adequate medical evaluation and care as needed.
- Develop a wide and experienced referral network. Make clients aware that you may consider referral to more expert practitioners or leaders from other disciplines as needed.
- Utilize consultation on a regular basis. No one person can anticipate the challenges you may encounter, but always know you are not alone.
- Be proactive in noting signs of reduced or missing client rapport and ask frequently for feedback.
- Know your scope of practice, your personal strengths and weaknesses, and also what kinds of practice are legally permitted in your community.
- Set goals together with your clients and hold them to the boundaries that you establish regarding visits, telephone calls, emails, fees, and so on.
- Hold the stance of "facilitating being led" by your clients. They know the truth about who they are; it is not your place to guess or assume you know what they need.
- Avoid dual or complex relationships such as seeing several members of one family unless there are clear, up-front agreements to do so.

Though no one can guarantee success in all endeavors because clients can come from widely divergent experiences, these considerations will go a long way toward helping you maximize your effectiveness and minimize unhappy experiences. EFT practice allows you to share your intention of goodwill with skill and inner wisdom in a world of need. Mindful, ethical practice is the heart of EFT in action!

# References

Association for Comprehensive Energy Psychology (ACEP). (2012). APA approves ACEP to provide CE credits for psychologists. Retrieved from http://energypsych.org/displaycommon.cfm?an=1&subarticlenbr=329

Hover-Kramer, D. (2011). *Creating healing relationships: Professional standards for energy therapy practitioners*. Santa Rosa, CA: Energy Psychology Press.

Thomas, L. (2010). *The encyclopedia of energy medicine*. Minneapolis, MN: Fairview Press.

# Chapter 41
# Client Safety

*Phil Mollon*

## Abstract

In general, EFT is gentle and safe. Nevertheless, a variety of hazards remain. It is important that practitioners remain within their scope of practice. Mental health conditions involve complexities of thought, emotion, and behavior that need to be addressed for optimum effect. Some clients react adversely to EFT. Those with a fear of relaxation, personality disorder, severe childhood trauma, autistic spectrum traits, or serious mental illness all require particular care and knowledge. The end of the session should be a point of risk assessment. Care should be taken to provide scientifically sound explanations of EFT. Attention to professional boundaries is crucial. Practitioner self-care is also important.

**Keywords:** risk, boundaries, scope of practice, PTSD, personality disorders, adverse reactions, intuition, recovered memory, dissociation, self-care

**Phil Mollon, PhD**, is a British psychotherapist, psychoanalyst, and clinical psychologist. He has worked in the National Health Service for over 35 years and has taught energy psychology widely in the UK. He is the author of 10 books, including *Psychoanalytic Energy Psychotherapy.* Send correspondence to Phil Mollon, Mental Health Unit, Lister Hospital, Stevenage, Herts. SG1 4AB UK, or phil_mollon@yahoo.co.uk.

In general, EFT and other modalities of energy psychology are remarkably gentle and safe. They tend not to involve vivid or prolonged reliving of trauma. Distressing emotions that emerge during a session tend to pass quickly as tapping continues. The techniques of EFT are designed to approach distress in a graduated and tolerable way, titrating exposure to otherwise unbearable trauma that may have previously overwhelmed the client's coping capacities. Unlike sessions of more conventional psychotherapy, the client is usually not left with lingering distress when he or she leaves, since EFT facilitates both the emergence of relevant psychodynamic material and the clearing of its emotional charge. Despite these positive characteristics of EFT, a variety of potential hazards do remain. These may involve the possibility of harm to both client and practitioner.

There are broadly three categories of hazard:

- Unexpected or untoward reactions to EFT.
- Failure to provide the client with optimum assistance, thereby potentially depriving him or her of the most appropriate help.
- Various forms of boundary violations in the therapeutic relationship.

## Scope of Practice

Many of the dangers concern the practitioner's "scope of practice." This has to do with the practitioner's area of legitimate expertise, in which he or she has received specialist professional knowledge and training. In most parts of the world, it would not be considered appropriate or legal for a practitioner to diagnose or treat medical disorders (including mental health conditions) unless he or she is trained and licensed to do so. Practitioners of EFT who have not received specific clinical training may believe they know the nature of conditions such as PTSD, depression, or anxiety disorders, but their understanding may be more limited than they realize. The danger is that the client's condition is more serious and more complex than the practitioner initially appreciates. For example, there are likely to be considerable differences between the following forms of PTSD: (1) persisting anxiety after a traffic accident in which the person suffered minor physical injuries; (2) intense fear and nightmares, along with episodes of violence, and drug and alcohol misuse, associated with combat trauma; and (3) severe malformations of personality, with pervasive distrust and intense sexual anxieties, associated with extensive childhood sexual abuse.

If an EFT practitioner has not also been trained in (or studied) clinical psychology or psychotherapy, he or she may not appreciate the details of the processes known to take place in the mind, brain, and behavior of people with mental health conditions. A good book on cognitive therapy could be helpful (e.g., Clark & Beck, 2010) since such texts often set out clearly what is known scientifically of the relevant mental processes. For example, it is known that in anxiety disorders, there are contributory processes at: (1) an *automatic* lower brain level (amygdala-based classically conditioned fear responses); (2) a higher cortical level of dysfunctional cognitive strategies involving a bias toward perception of threat and filtering out information incongruent with danger; and (3) a metacognitive level of perceiving anxiety itself as dangerous, thus generating a *fear of fear*. EFT is likely to be more effective if it addresses these different levels, using relevant sentences and phrases.

## Adverse Reactions

A common feature of people with generalized anxiety disorders, and also those who have suffered severe trauma, is the belief that "It is not safe to feel safe." Such people operate on the principle that, in order to be safe, they have to be on their guard—hypervigilant—all the time. For them, being anxious is, paradoxically, the way to be safe. By contrast, they may react with high levels of anxiety if undergoing a procedure that tends to have a calming effect. As a result, such a person may react to EFT by becoming more anxious, or may experience the procedure once but then subsequently refusing to engage in it again, perhaps dismissively saying, "It doesn't work." The belief that it is not safe to feel safe is not usually conscious. Therefore such clients cannot usually spontaneously give the true reason for their negative reaction to EFT, although once this belief has been voiced—as in "Do you think you might feel it is not safe to relax and feel safe?"—they may readily agree.

Clients with a pronounced need for control may have a related form of negative reaction to EFT. Such people may be highly disconcerted by the often rapid and marked effect of EFT, even though this is of a positive and benign nature. As a result, they may react with secondary anxiety and hostility, or even a somewhat paranoid suspicion that some kind of trick is being played on them. EFT and other forms of energy psychology are particularly prone to elicit this response in some people because the changes brought about, in terms of reduction of stress and clearing of negative emotions, are difficult for the brain and mind to track and make sense of. The change is not processed through the mind but occurs at a deeper level. Thus the conscious mind is in the position of a computer searching for a missing file or program that has been deleted; the icon has been clicked, but the emotional program does not open. Whereas most clients are simply pleased that a previous distressing response has been removed, some react with a kind of outrage that their system has been tampered with in ways they do not understand. For such people, talk of mysterious energies, meridians, and so forth simply adds to the confusion and suspicion.

The effect of EFT and other methods can create a state of "cognitive dissonance" in some clients. A change has taken place, but it does not make sense to them. Those who are strongly invested in a "left-brain" rational stance (McGilchrist, 2010), which they may believe to be "scientific," may find this particularly challenging. Roger Callahan (2001) referred to what he called the "Apex Problem," whereby some clients distort their perception of reality in order to reduce their perplexity over the therapeutic effect. This may range from declaring that they feel relaxed and peaceful because the therapist's office is so calming to denying they had a problem in the first place.

Some years ago, I treated a woman's work-related trauma effectively with a single session of EFT, addressing also its childhood roots, and she returned to work, having been on sick leave for some weeks with quite severe anxiety. She was sent a routine feedback questionnaire; on this she indicated that she was no longer suffering any anxiety, but she rated the therapy as "not helpful at all." I made a friendly phone call to enquire further. She said she was feeling absolutely fine, that people said she looked better than ever, and that she felt a fraud, since there must have been nothing wrong with her since she was now so well. I responded by saying it was wonderful that she was feeling so much better, but I was puzzled by her rating the therapy as not helpful. She said, "Well, I thought I needed to be seen for longer—people told me I would need counseling for months—and that I would need to talk about all my nightmares and anxieties, and I couldn't see what good that tapping stuff would have done." I asked if she still experienced any nightmares or anxieties. She replied, "Oh, no, they have all stopped." I then explained to her that she was not a fraud, she had been suffering significant work-related stress and this is what we had addressed, but we had used a technique that was effective but not what she had expected—and now she was better and back at work. I further explained that people are often confused by the nature of the technique since it appears to work at a deeper level that the conscious part of the brain cannot track, so that often people have the kind of perplexed and dismissive reaction she had described. She was immensely relieved by this explanation, which allowed her not to have to invalidate either her previous state of stress or the therapy she received.

## Personality Disorders

Unexpected responses to EFT can also be shown by clients who have personality disorders (O'Donohue, Fowler, & Lilienfeld, 2007). These are distortions of mental and relational life that pervade the personality, and are thus not limited to the presenting problem. Such conditions will commonly be missed by practitioners unless they have undertaken specific training or study in this area. Clients would rarely state explicitly that they have a personality disorder, usually because they do not know, and the presenting problem (such as anxiety, depression) would often appear similar to those presented by people who do not have such a disorder. Clues to the presence of a personality disorder include:

- A history of failed therapies.
- The client presents an increasing number and range of problems.
- Although the client appears to benefit from each application of EFT, he or she does not overall make progress toward recovery and moving on.
- It becomes apparent that the client has entrenched attitudes of "entitlement," of believing he or she is superior to other people in general, or is deserving of special privileges.

- The client appears relentlessly angry and blaming toward others who are perceived as the source of the problem, and seems reluctant to allow any modification of this stance.

Although the concept of personality disorder is, like many other psychiatric diagnoses, a matter of some controversy, there is broad agreement that the following constellations do occur:

- Histrionic Personality Disorder—where the person is continually seeking drama and attention.
- Borderline Personality Disorder (also known as Emotionally Unstable Personality Disorder)—where the person has difficulty managing the strong negative emotions that he or she is prone to, and experiences recurrent difficulties in relationships. A well-known book on this condition has the very apt title *I Hate You—Don't Leave me* (Kreisman & Strauss, 1991). Despite the term "borderline," this is not a mild personality disorder. People with BPD may self-harm.
- Dependent Personality Disorder—where the person seems fearful of making independent decisions and forms particularly dependent relationships.
- Narcissistic Personality Disorder—where the person displays characteristics of entitlement, grandiosity, and limited empathy for others.
- Paranoid Personality Disorder—where the person tends to maintain an unwarranted stance of suspicion toward others, and to perceive conspiracies or malevolence without evidence to support these perceptions.

These personality constellations cannot be diagnosed by EFT practitioners unless they have received specific training and are licensed to do so. The dangers are: (1) the client does not benefit from the work because the underlying personality disorder is missed; and (2) the practitioner finds that he or she has a confusing, or even alarming, client who does not get better. If the practitioner suspects the client may have a personality disorder, and the client is not improving as a result of the EFT work, it would be sensible to suggest a referral to an experienced clinical psychologist, psychotherapist, or psychiatrist. On the other hand,

if the practitioner is familiar with these conditions, then EFT or other energy psychology modalities can be extremely helpful. Understanding personality disorders requires a good knowledge of early developmental processes.

## Childhood Abuse Trauma

Another group of clients for whom any form of psychological therapy is hazardous is those who have experienced extensive childhood abuse trauma. Such people can be greatly helped with EFT and related approaches, but their mental equilibrium is such that even the gentle and benign work of energy psychology can potentially be destabilizing. These clients, for whom childhood trauma and their reactions to this are woven deeply into their personality, can be destabilized by any change to their system, even if this is positive. As one layer of trauma is addressed and its emotional charge cleared with EFT, the next layer may step into the vacated space, with the result that the person is overwhelmed with further trauma-related thoughts, images, and emotions.

Working with extensive childhood trauma can be more hazardous than work with PTSD rooted in adult trauma. EFT and related methods may be safer modalities for severe trauma than more standard methods (including EMDR) since it does not necessarily involve a detailed reliving of the trauma. Nevertheless, it is not without hazard. Consultation with colleagues is strongly advised when working with clients extensively abused in childhood. Severe and repeated childhood trauma may give rise to dissociative reactions, whereby the person may shift unpredictably from one state of mind to another, sometimes experiencing amnesic boundaries between these states, such that the person in one state of mind does not remember what he or she has done in another state of mind. These conditions are rare but extremely hazardous and risky to work with (Mollon, 1996; van der Hart, Nijenhuis, & Steele, 2006).

On occasion a practitioner may encounter a client, with a background of severe and repeated trauma, whose energy system is pervasively and persistently "reversed," that is, organized against recovery (Callahan, 2001; Diamond, 1988; Mollon, 2008). In rare cases, this can take a form analogous to a *black hole vortex*. Though such clients may consciously desire to resolve their difficulties, their system is organized to maintain the disturbance. When the practitioner's energy system, and therapeutic efforts, comes into contact with the client's reversed system, there can be a kind of energetic storm, resulting in worsening disturbance. This can have a darkly deleterious effect on both participants. For some clients, "less is more"—teaching a little EFT for self-soothing may be more helpful than attempting to resolve fundamental issues and traumas.

## Other Mental Health Vulnerabilities

There are yet other clients who have serious mental illness vulnerabilities, which may not be immediately apparent. These vulnerabilities may include severe depression, bipolar disorder, and schizophrenia. Addressing areas of intense emotional pain or trauma can trigger these illness states. In potentially suicidal patients, EFT may alleviate anxiety and energize them sufficiently that they put the suicidal intention into action. This relates to the well-recognized danger that as a severely depressed person begins to feel slightly better, the risk of suicide may temporarily increase. Enquiries about psychiatric history should be routine for the EFT practitioner.

A group of clients who may not respond very much, if at all, to EFT, comprises those with autistic spectrum traits, including Asperger's (Atwood, 2008). For these people, emotional and energetic processing often seems slow. Their thoughts and mental attitudes are very rigid. They may report no effect with EFT or they may actually find it unpleasant, although some others may indeed benefit.

Some clients with obsessive-compulsive disorder (OCD) may report positive effects with EFT but may then incorporate it into their rituals, sometimes doing EFT for hours or using it as an obsessional "magical" means of warding off "bad" thoughts and feelings. Others may develop a stance of believing they cannot undertake any anxiety-evoking task without extensive preparation with EFT, which then becomes an unhelpful form of avoidant or "safety" behavior.

In general, it is inadvisable for EFT practitioners to take on clients of a kind that they have not already worked with using other approaches. It is important to make clear to clients the limits of the practitioner's expertise, and to suggest other appropriate specialists when these may be required. Providing EFT support for emotional relief while the client is under the care of a conventional medical or other licensed professional can often work well if all parties agree. However, discouraging a client from taking prescribed medication would usually be regarded as highly irresponsible and can indeed be very dangerous. For example, stopping antidepressant medication abruptly can result in highly unstable mental states, including severe suicidal depression. Ceasing antipsychotic medication would potentially result in an eruption of psychotic illness.

Sometimes clients seek help with EFT for physical illness. It is certainly the case that emotional stress can play a part in physical illness, and EFT, or other energy psychology modalities, can help alleviate this. EFT can reduce emotional stress, including that associated with the distress of the illness itself and the medical treatment for it, and may even contribute to alleviating the illness itself. Such work with the emotional aspects of an illness is often of great benefit. It should be clear, however, that the EFT practitioner does not diagnose or treat physical illness, unless trained and licensed to do so. Moreover, care should be taken not to collude with a client's efforts to deny (as an unconscious defence against painful reality) a need for conventional medical intervention. Any clinical symptom, other than the most commonplace and ordinary, should be investigated by a medical doctor.

## The End of the Session

The end of an EFT session should be a routine point of risk assessment. A crucial question for the practitioner to consider is: "What state of mind is the client in?" It is not unusual for clients to be in a slightly altered state of consciousness, somewhat like a trance or dream state, and sometimes slight euphoria. They may be relatively oblivious to normal dangers. If clients are driving, it can be important to warn them to be sure of feeling alert and in a fit state to drive before setting off. It can also happen that clients feel more anxious as a result of some new train of thought that has arisen during the session, perhaps one that they do not spontaneously voice. Clients do often conceal thoughts and feelings that they feel are shameful. Some may be practiced at pleasing others and may give the practitioner a plausible but misleading impression of positive effects of the EFT, when, in fact, they are feeling something quite different. Even when the positive effect is genuine, it can still be important to warn the client that other negative emotional states may subsequently come to the fore.

EFT contains various procedures for minimizing distress and the danger of the client feeling overwhelmed. Despite these valuable strategies, it sometimes happens that high levels of negative emotion do emerge. At such times, it can be helpful to keep the client tapping but without using any further emotionally arousing words. Another effective step is gently to remind the client, while tapping, that the traumatic event is "not happening now" and that what is being recollected is "just a memory."

## Scientifically Valid Explanations

Another aspect of client safety is attention to the truth and validity of the information given. Although some practitioners, including this author, may find the concept of subtle energy meridians meaningful, and the hypothesis that these play a part in the experience of negative emotions may seem plausible, there is relatively little sound evidence for such notions. We do know that EFT and related methods work, and that they are effective for a variety of conditions (Feinstein, 2012). However, we do not know *how* they work, and a variety of hypotheses are possible (Feinstein, 2010). To assert that, for example, "the cause of all negative emotions is a disruption in the body's energy system" is not at present a scientifically defendable position, although there is considerable and varied evidence for the subtle energy system per se (Swanson, 2009; Tiller, 2007). It is truthful and realistic to tell the client that tapping on acupoints has been found to alleviate emotional distress, and that practitioners have found ways of enhancing this effect with the judicious use of forms of words that target crucial experiences, thoughts, and emotions, and to add that we are still exploring why this might be the case. If clients are given a fanciful explanation that is not congruent with other areas of scientific knowledge, then they may be placed at a disadvantage when appraising other forms of medical or paramedical treatment.

## Professional Boundaries

Many risks to both client and practitioner arise from violations of appropriate professional boundaries. Just as the management of the boundary of the human body, and that of each cell within it, are crucial to biological survival, so the maintenance of psychological boundaries in relationships have profound consequences for the health of the mind and the personality. It is a matter of being mindful of what belongs where. Physical toxins and viral and parasitic organisms are best kept out of the physical body. Similarly, the practitioner's personal life, needs, and vulnerabilities are best excluded from the therapeutic relationship. The client's session should contain only what the client brings, and the practitioner's professional response to this. Contact beyond this should be minimized.

Overt sexual interactions between practitioner and client are obviously completely inappropriate, but there are many lesser violations of boundaries that are unhelpful and, unfortunately, common. Telling the client unnecessary details about the practitioner's personal preoccupations, beliefs, lifestyle, and so forth contaminates the therapeutic space and is a misuse of the professional relationship. It interferes with a clear perception of what the client is bringing to that space. Moreover, some clients, with a dependent stance or an uncertain sense of identity, may seek the approval of the therapist by identifying with his or her personal views and attitudes. Ultimately, this does not foster the individual's autonomy and authentic development. When clients seek help with emotional problems, the more childlike and needy aspects of the personality are engaged—parts that may seek "magical" solutions, suspending the more critical faculties of the adult personality. Energy psychology methods can play into such desires by means of their often-startling effects and mysterious mode of action. There is nothing wrong with a little magic, but the vulnerability of the client to uncritical idealization of a charismatic therapist must be protected. It is part of the practitioner's duty of care toward the client.

## Intuition and Other Nonobjective Information

Further boundary considerations arise from the practitioner's potential use of "information" from intuition or other nonphysical and essentially private sources. Work with the subtle energy system seems to increase the availability of intuitive data. The problem with material derived in this way is that it is mostly not open to explicit scrutiny or objective evaluation. In some instances, particularly if presented in an appropriately tentative way, intuitive data can be helpful, but such data can also be experienced as violating. For example, one client became quite troubled by a misguided practitioner suggesting she had been a temple prostitute in a previous life. The client was particularly disturbed by this suggestion since it conflicted with her current religious beliefs. Not only did this idea arise essentially from the practitioner's subjective perceptions, it was a hypothesis that could not be tested or disproved. It also contained a metaphysical belief—the notion of past lives. Some would argue that all such metaphysical and intuitive notions are without logical or scientific meaning because they are beyond any realm that is open to evidence of the senses (i.e., evidence that can ultimately be translated into data that can be seen, heard, or felt; Ayer, 1960). Others regard such notions as potentially open to appraisal by thoughtful enquiry and evidence of some kind, even if this is not based on purely sensory data. Human perception is easily distorted or fooled, resulting in all kinds of illusions (Chabris & Simons, 2011), even though intuition can sometimes be a source of good information (Myers, 2004).

These concerns also relate to the complex issues of "recovered memory" and "false memory" (Conway, 1997; Loftus, 1996). Recollections of childhood are prone to error, and false narratives of abuse can give rise to immense anguish within families (Atkins, 2007; Maran, 2010). The practitioner should treat such accounts with care and caution, bearing the painful reality that, without evidence, the objective truth can be difficult to ascertain. Neither hypnosis (Yapko, 2009) nor energy psychology contains methods that can objectively validate or disprove hypotheses regarding childhood events (Mollon, 2002).

## Practitioner Self-care

Maintaining client safety also depends on the practitioner attending to self-care. In general, prolonged work as a psychotherapist may be somewhat toxic, as the practitioner is exposed for lengthy periods to negative energetic and emotional states. Fortunately, work with EFT tends to be less energetically and emotionally draining than more traditional forms of therapy, since the distress and disturbance is continually discharged from the practitioner's system as well as that of the client. In most styles of EFT, the practitioner taps at the same time as the client. This also helps the attunement between them. However, this attunement itself can have the negative effect, in some instances, of the practitioner taking on a mirror impression of the client's disturbance. Additional energetic tools can be helpful, many of which are described in Eden's book on energy medicine (2008).

Further reading on ethics and professional standards is recommended (e.g., Feinstein, 2012; Hover-Kramer, 2011).

## Client Safety Quick Checklist

- Remain within your *scope of practice* and *scope of knowledge*.
- Be alert to adverse reactions to EFT, which can occur in those with a pronounced need for control or a belief that it is not safe to relax, and the "Apex Problem."
- Be alert to potential personality disorders.
- Enquire about psychiatric history.
- It is advisable not to use EFT with types of client you have not worked with previously using other methods.
- Do not discourage conventional medical care. Never advise a client to discontinue medication (unless you are a medical practitioner).
- Avoid explanations of EFT not grounded in science. Consider an explanation along the lines of: "Tapping on acupoints calms the body and brain. We use language to target particular memories and other areas of distress."
- Maintain professional boundaries. Avoid unnecessary personal disclosure.
- Take care in using nonphysical sources of data. These can be misleading.
- Be cautious regarding the veracity of memories of early childhood.
- Attend to self-care.

## References

Atkins, A. (2007). *Fractured families: The untold anguish of the falsely accused.* Bradford on Avon, UK: British False Memory Society.

Atwood, T. (2008). *The complete guide to Asperger's syndrome.* London, UK: Jessica Kingsley.

Ayer, A. J. (1960). *Language, truth, and logic.* London, UK: Victor Gollancz.

Callahan, R. J. (2001). *Tapping the healer within*. New York, NY: Contemporary Books.

Chabris, C. & Simons, D. (2011). *The invisible gorilla: And other ways our intuition deceives us*. New York, NY: Harper Collins.

Clark, D. A. & Beck, A. T. (2010). *Cognitive therapy of anxiety disorders: Science and practice*. New York, NY: Guilford Press.

Conway, M. (Ed.). (1997). *Recovered memories and false memories*. New York, NY: Oxford University Press.

Diamond, J. (1988). *Life-energy analysis: A way to cantillation*. South Salem, NY: Enhancement Books.

Eden, D. (2008). *Energy medicine: How to use your body's energies for optimum health and vitality* (2nd ed.). New York: Tarcher/Penguin.

Feinstein, D. (2010). Rapid treatment of PTSD. Why psychological exposure with acupoint tapping may be effective. *Psychotherapy Theory, Research, Practice, Training, 47*(3), 385–402.

Feinstein, D. (2011). *Ethics handbook for energy healing practitioners: A guide for the professional practice of energy medicine and energy psychology*. Fulton, CA: Energy Psychology Press.

Feinstein, D. (2012). Acupoint stimulation in treating psychological disorders: Evidence of efficacy. *Review of General Psychology, 16*, 364–380. doi:10.1037/a0028602

Hover-Kramer, D. (2012). *Creating healthy relationships: Professional standards for energy therapy practitioners*. Santa Rosa, CA: Energy Psychology Press.

Kreisman, J. J. & Straus, H. (1991). *I hate you—don't leave me: Understanding the borderline personality*. New York, NY: Avon.

Loftus, E. M. (1996). *The myth of repressed memory: False memories and allegations of sexual abuse*. New York, NY: St. Martins Griffin.

Maran, M. (2010). *My lie: A true story of false memory*. San Francisco, CA: Jossey-Bass.

McGilchrist, I. (2010). *The master and his emissary: The divided brain and the making of the Western world*. New York, NY: Yale University Press.

Mollon, P. (1996). *Multiple selves, multiple voices: Working with trauma, violation, and dissociation*. New York, NY: Wiley.

Mollon, P. (2002). *Remembering trauma: A psychotherapist's guide to memory and illusion* (2nd ed.). London, UK: Whurr.

Mollon, P. (2008). *Psychoanalytic energy psychotherapy: Inspired by Thought Field Therapy, EFT, TAT, and Seemorg Matrix*. London, UK: Karnac Books.

Myers, D. G. (2004). *Intuition: Its powers and perils*. New York, NY: Yale University Press.

O'Donohue, W. T., Fowler, K. A., & Lilienfeld, S. O. (2007). *Personality disorders: Towards the DSM-V*. New York, NY: Sage.

Swanson, C. V. (2009). *Life force: The scientific basis*. Tucson, AZ: Poseidia Press.

Tiller, W. A. (2007). *Psychoenergetic science: A second Copernican-scale revolution*. Walnut Creek, CA: Pavior.

Van der Hart, O., Nijenhuis, E., & Steele, K. (2006). *The haunted self: Structural dissociation and the treatment of chronic traumatization*. New York, NY: W. W. Norton.

Yapko, M. (2009). *Suggestions of abuse: True and false memories of childhood sexual trauma*. New York, NY: Simon & Schuster.

Chapter 42
# Integrating EFT with Chiropractic Care: Addressing the Emotional Aspects of Pain
*Craig Weiner*

## Abstract
There is minimal material in the scientific literature regarding the integration of Emotional Freedom Techniques (EFT) with other health care disciplines. This chapter explores the author's view on how EFT can be utilized complementary to, and integrated into, the chiropractic field, which is the third largest doctoral-level health care profession in the United States. While individual state laws dictate a chiropractor's scope of practice, an understanding of how a neuromusculoskeletal-based paradigm can work in health care in conjunction with an energy medicine paradigm is a worthy investigation. A core philosophical tenet of chiropractic is the importance of removing interference (subluxation) in order for the nervous system to operate fully and enable the innate healing capacity of the body to flourish and heal the body. One hypothesis of how EFT works is that it resolves disruptions in the body's energy system, which have resulted from negative emotions and which correspond to various symptoms and imbalances in a person's physical, mental, and emotional states. The combination of collaborative insight and the complementary practice of these two professions holds great potential for healing, especially of chronic physical conditions. Scientific research continues to demonstrate that chronic conditions, most notably chronic back pain, have, to a large degree, emotional components that are unlikely to be resolved by physical interventions alone. This chapter serves to open the door to further communication and collaboration between these two fields, as well as potentially opening the discourse between EFT practitioners and other more established health care professions. Such collaboration has the potential to reduce patients' physical symptoms, improve resolution of acute and chronic conditions, and prevent possibly injurious interventions such as intense pharmaceutical regimens and surgical procedures. Another potential result of collaboration is a significant savings on the health care dollars currently spent in the United States and abroad on nonresolving chronic pain conditions.

**Keywords:** chiropractic, EFT, integrative medicine, CAM, complementary and alternative medicine, pain

**Craig Weiner, DC**, director of the Chiropractic Zone, has practiced integrative wellness care for over 25 years, incorporating massage therapy/bodywork, EFT, and other techniques with chiropractic. A magna cum laude graduate from Life Chiropractic College West, he was honored as the 2003 LCCW alumnus of the year. Send correspondence to Craig Weiner, The Chiropractic Zone, PO Box 1258, Freeland WA 98249, or drcraig@chirozone.net.

*A* caveat: This chapter is not a consensus view in the chiropractic profession. It is a personal perspective, supported by study, research, and clinical experience, and should be read as such.

As a chiropractor in private practice for over 21 years, I've seen the profession grow in numbers and acceptance. Chiropractic is now licensed by all 50 states in the United States and in over 70 other countries, with over 60,000 licensed U.S. chiropractors in the United States and 90,000 more worldwide. Scientific research coupled with a high rate of patient satisfaction has helped chiropractic become the largest, most regulated, and best recognized of the complementary and alternative medicine (CAM) professions in the United States. It is the third largest doctoral-level health care profession, after medicine and dentistry.

During the past five years, I have witnessed the EFT profession go through meteoric growth from its initial development by Gary Craig. Its development has been accompanied by challenges natural for any emerging profession. Though EFT practitioners are not granted licensure status on a state or federal level, the acceptance of EFT as a valid treatment intervention for a variety of conditions continues to grow.

At the end of 2012, the American Psychological Association granted continuing education credit status for EFT to be taught to psychologists on behalf of the Association for Comprehensive Energy Psychology (ACEP), which is a significant step toward acceptance of EFT as a valid treatment option in the mental health world. EFT appears to be the largest and fastest growing of all the energy psychology techniques, of which there are many.

It is an exciting time to be working at the cutting edge of incorporating and integrating EFT into a chiropractic practice. I am honored to have the privilege of offering my perspective on integrating these two modalities, as I am unaware of any other literature reporting such collaboration. I hope that this serves as a starting point from which further literature and case studies can be generated, as there is currently not only a paucity of research regarding EFT as an effective modality for pain reduction, but also there is no peer-reviewed literature comparing EFT and chiropractic as interventions or a combination approach using both methods.

Five years ago, upon my introduction to EFT, I was initially skeptical at hearing "It works, try it on everything." The key to understanding the idea "try

it on everything" is knowledge of the role that stress and its associated neurohormonal effects play in a plethora of physical conditions. Stress hormones, especially the glucocorticoid cortisol, when elevated over prolonged periods, can have serious and devastating effects on nearly all systems of the body, including the cardiovascular, musculoskeletal, digestive, neurocortical system and more. As current theories postulate, if EFT is able to reduce cortisol and stress levels in a consistent way, and possibly alter neurocognitive function, then "try it on everything" is not an unreasonable suggestion, given EFT's documented minimal risk of side effects. My personal experience has clinically validated the effectiveness of EFT for a wide variety of physical musculoskeletal pain conditions (including neck and back pain, headaches, migraines), stressful emotional states, phobias, panic attacks, and more. I feel fortunate to have witnessed and facilitated many life-changing results in others due to the efficacy of EFT in my clinical population.

My original chiropractic training was inadequate regarding the emotional causality of pain, primarily because this factor was not well understood 25 years ago. It has always been clear to me, however, that emotions play a significant role in the health status of my patients. When they were going through divorce, loss of a loved one, times of financial distress, or other stressful episodes, they were much more likely to have episodes of "a crick in the neck" or "the back going out" without any real causal event. They would come into my office reporting that they had "slept wrong" or just bent over to tie their shoes and could not get back up. Over time it became obvious that the single factor that most often preceded the onset of non-traumatic pain was a challenging life circumstance that had caused the patient to become stressed, overwhelmed, angry, depressed, or another significant negative emotion. By the time they walked or limped into my office, they would be inflamed, in pain, subluxated (i.e., misaligned), and in spasm. They would often ask me why they were in pain, and I would have to answer honestly that I didn't truly know. I wasn't living in their body and could not know all the factors they were dealing with, especially when they offered me no physical explanation for why their pain began.

In my training as a chiropractor, I had been thoroughly conditioned to find and treat the physical cause of patients' problems. One popular meme in chiropractic school was "Find it, fix it, and leave it alone." The chiropractic approach to a patient in pain is that there is nearly always a physical correlate of signs and symptoms that needs to be formulated into a diagnosis based on their subjective symptoms (what the patient feels) and objective signs (what is observed by the doctor). So I observed patients' posture and gait and measured their range of motion and, without necessarily documenting it, always got an intuitive feeling or hunch as to how the patient was generally doing the moment I saw their body and looked into their eyes. But becoming a skillful chiropractor meant accurately using tools such as visual observation, physical examination, and X-rays; acquiring the skills necessary to document findings and treatment provided for insurance company reimbursements; and abiding by legal documentation requirements. This was all for the purpose of determining why the patient was not in optimal health and then providing effective treatment to help restore balance to the patient's nervous system.

Treatment styles vary widely within chiropractic, as they do in the world of energy psychology. There are hundreds of techniques practiced throughout the profession, from manual techniques to instrument-adjusting methods to more energy-based approaches. In fact, one technique known as applied kinesiology (AK) was created by a chiropractor, George Goodheart, DC, and was a forerunner to the development of EFT.

The core tenet of chiropractic philosophy has always been that there is an art, science, and philosophy to chiropractic and that the body has the ability to heal itself when the interference to the nervous system is removed. This ability to self-heal is a universal and individual innate intelligence in the body that, if not obstructed, ensures that health is the default status. The founder of chiropractic, Daniel David Palmer, was known as a "magnetic healer" and performed energetic laying-on of hands in the late 1800s. With regard to a larger approach to healing, he wrote, "The dualistic system—spirit and body—united by intellectual life—the soul—is the basis of this science of biology…I have answered the time-worn question—what is life?" (Palmer, 1966, pp. 17–19).

I offer this historical perspective so that it may be understood that the heart of chiropractic and EFT offer multiple similarities. Both professions were begun by outside-the-box thinking, charismatic, paradigm-shifting founders. Chiropractic and EFT were initially shunned and ridiculed by the more popular and populous mainstream professional associations that may have been threatened by their effectiveness. Nevertheless both grew in popularity through word of mouth via individuals who found the techniques to be effective where more traditional forms of treatment had failed.

The fundamental principle or "discovery statement" of EFT, as articulated by its founder, Gary Craig, is: "The cause of all negative emotions is a disruption in the body's energy system." Current neuroscientific research, including the Polyvagal Theory of Stephen Porges, PhD, (2011) and the concept of "trauma capsules" developed by Robert Scaer, MD, (2005) offer revelatory explanations of the mechanisms by which physical and emotional traumas may lead to neurophysiological mechanisms that result in suffering that goes on long beyond the original traumatic emotional events. Similarly, chiropractic was founded on the notion that when nerve interference is removed by removing the spinal subluxation (misalignment or "disruption"), the body has a significantly enhanced chance of healing itself.

## Integrating EFT into Chiropractic Practice

In terms of clinical application of EFT in combination with chiropractic, I speak from my personal experience as a practicing chiropractor in the state of Washington in the United States. Chiropractic scope-of-practice regulations vary by country and by state. While the heart of chiropractic, the spinal adjustment, is always permitted, chiropractic and state licensing boards determine the breadth of practice parameters to include or not include various therapeutic modalities, including physiotherapy devices, nutritional advice, physical rehabilitation approaches, and even the use of meridian-based techniques such as acupuncture and EFT. As a chiropractor reading this chapter, you are obliged to find, read, interpret, and follow the regulations and practice laws of your state or pertinent governing licensing body. The current law governing chiropractic in the state of Washington (Revised Code of Washington) relevant to EFT reads as follows:

> **RCW 18.25.005(3)** The commission finds that the following treatment modalities, by whatever name known, are not within the definition of "chiropractic" as specified. In subsection 2…

(f) The use of meridian therapy, whether known as "acupressure" or the same type of therapy under any other names, unless complementary or preparatory to a chiropractic spinal adjustment.

My interpretation of this is that, as a chiropractor, I can only employ meridian-based techniques such as EFT in conjunction with or in preparation for a chiropractic adjustment, so that is what I do. My hope is that this regulation will be expanded, but for now my license mandates compliance. When patients come to me with complaints varying from whiplash, neck pain, back pain, and sciatica to tension headaches and migraines, I evaluate what I think is the source of their pain and *dis*-ease. Over the years I have learned to ask questions that are not only relevant to making a chiropractic diagnosis, but also most relevant to EFT and potential underlying issues. I have made these inquiries a standard part of my new patient consultation.

Examples of such inquiries might be: What was happening in your life just before the pain started? What significant stressors or stressful events happened in the 6 to 12 months prior to your pain's onset? Did you change jobs, move homes, lose a loved one, go through any stress at home or work? I also always keep an eye out for psychological reversal/secondary gains issues—the unconscious benefits the condition might be providing, including things like disability payments, time off from work, increased attention at home, or avoidance of stressful situations at work.

Besides knowing how intense and frequent their pain is and what activities aggravate or ameliorate the pain, I also ask questions about how their symptoms are affecting their lives beyond their physical pain, such as: What enjoyable activities can you no longer perform? How has your injury or pain affected your relationships, your ability to exercise, and your ability to do the activities that bring you pleasure? Before learning EFT, I had inquired with the purpose of determining my patients' physical limitations, but now my questions are honed to reveal deeper aspects, what underlies their pain, much of which I would have ignored previously.

Listening carefully to how people describe their pain is also critically important in being able to pick up clues as to what may be going on for a patient. People reveal much in their choice of words when describing their condition. When I hear descriptions like "It feels like I was just stabbed in the back" or "It's like I am carrying the weight of the world on my shoulders" or "It seems as if this pain will never get off my back." All of these descriptions beg the question of who or what might be at cause for the underlying issue revealed in the language. The way in which patients describe or reference their pain with regard to potential emotional contributions is an area of great interest to me.

## A Deeper Questioning

Observing a patient's body posture, affect, communication style, and other cues may lead a clinician to suspect that emotional stress may be underlying or affecting the physical symptoms for which a patient is seeking assistance. Inquiring whether the complaint is a recurrent one and, if it is, exploring the first experience related to this condition will often prove valuable for permanent resolution. Obtaining insight into the relevant emotional sequelae of the pain—for example, resentment toward their boss for making them work a double shift, resentment held toward their back, anxiety over how they will pay their mortgage if they have to miss any more work, or fear that their condition will not get better and might require surgery—can provide important clues to help a clinician work with client and resolve the emotional/energetic component of the client's condition.

Research on EFT supports the idea that its application can reduce sympathetic nervous system tone and increase parasympathetic tone. It is my experience that even a few minutes of EFT can cause a significant relaxation response. A paper published by Larry Burk, MD, describes the use of single-session EFT for three post motor vehicle accident victims and describes possible mechanisms for the reduction of symptoms in acute and chronic posttraumatic cases (Burk, 2010, pp. 65–71). Tapping appears to allow patients to be in a more relaxed physical state in preparation for their adjustment. Tapping is especially helpful if there is anxiety or apprehensiveness that treatment will exacerbate their painful condition. Tapping also offers them a self-help tool that they can employ at home to decrease symptoms, which also reduces their sense of helplessness and is empowering to them. Providing an integrated, collaborative approach to working with an individual's pain is, I believe, the most effective way to help people resolve symptoms and perhaps even find meaning and purpose in those symptoms.

## A Broader View of Pain Symptoms

Pain can be classified in several different ways. It can be described by where the pain originates, as in nociceptive pain (due to tissue damage), neurogenic pain (due to nerve damage), or psychogenic pain (pain that begins as nociceptive or neurogenic pain, which is then prolonged or increased by psychological or emotional factors such as stress, anxiety, or depression. Another way to categorize pain is acute versus chronic pain. Acute pain is usually a sensory type of pain that comes on quickly and is elicited when, for example, whiplash injures or strains tissues and damages the pain receptors in the cervical spine, with resultant inflammation, pain, and muscle spasm. This type of pain usually resolves within a short period of time (depending on the severity and care provided, though dysfunction can last for much longer). Chronic pain is longer lasting and over time this type of pain can alter the brain in such a way that it continues to cause a person pain, even though evidence of the injury may no longer be seen in the injured tissues

According to Sean Mackey, MD, chief of the Division of Pain Management at the Stanford School of Medicine, "The standard model of pain still taught in every medical school is that you treat the pain by fixing the underlying pathology. But the reality of pain is much more complicated. We're now beginning to recognize that you can't talk about chronic pain without talking about its psychological aspects. It's a condition in which signals from the body are literally distorted by the brain" (Lehrer, 2009).

Research by A. Vania Apkarian, PhD, a neuroscience professor at Northwestern University, found that chronic back pain even appears to cause loss of gray matter in the brain. He estimates that each year of chronic severe lower back pain can cause a reduction of up to a cubic centimeter of gray matter. His research also uncovered that chronic pain-activated brain regions typically associated with negative emotions point to a relationship between chronic pain and emotions. Apkarian says, "It's as if people with chronic pain have internalized the pain. It's become part of who

they are. That's why you can't just treat the body" (Apkarian et al., 2004).

## Clinical Applications

When patients come to my clinic, they see me first through the lens of seeking pain relief via chiropractic treatment. They may or may not know that I also employ EFT in my practice, so it is my responsibility both morally and legally to evaluate and treat them with that in mind. At the first visit, my intake consultation includes a history of their complaints, personal and family medical history, a systems review, and a physical chiropractic exam relevant to their concerns. How I broach the subject of exploring relevant stressful emotional factors that may be related to their pain involves a combination of intuition, 25 years of experience, and a willingness to look beyond the patient's perception of or insistence on the cause of their complaint being solely physical. If on the first visit I sense openness to the subject, I may simply talk about how stress can cause increased muscle tension via increased sympathetic nervous system tone, which in turn causes the body to become tighter and more vulnerable to injury from movements that would normally not cause strain. I then explain how feeling annoyed or angry at your body for hurting or getting injured can cause even greater tension and may result in repressed negative emotions, which then can aggravate a condition. Such an explanation is usually well received and understood. Though I generally provide only chiropractic treatment on the initial visit, along with home recommendations of ice/heat and stretching exercises, I may send the patient home with an EFT book, DVD, or website links to introduce the technique. (Only once have I had a patient return saying that they were not at all interested in doing EFT.) If, when I ask what they thought about the material and they are interested in trying EFT, I usually take 10 minutes to review with them the shortcut points and do a round or so with them, focusing on their physical symptoms first. Based on how the round went, I determine whether they might be open to going a little deeper with the associated emotions. On that visit, my intention is simply for them to see that they can have some effect on and control over their pain, not to open up a large emotional issue that I cannot complete, given that another patient is waiting in the lobby. If that initial experience is a positive one,

I then offer them the opportunity for a lengthier session in which I can allot sufficient time for a combination of chiropractic and EFT.

Some might question how EFT can be effectively employed in a busy chiropractic office, where patient appointment times typically last from five to 15 minutes. I believe that there are models yet to be explored for the application of EFT in busy health care clinics. As one example, the chiropractic assistant or other staff person can explain EFT to patients and teach them the tapping points before the actual EFT session with the doctor. The chiropractor can create a handout or short video for the patient to watch prior to EFT application. In the field of dentistry, where apprehension or anxiety about treatment also exist, Graham Temple, DDS, employed EFT to reduce this dental anxiety, offering patients four minutes of explanation and six minutes of tapping (Temple, 2011, pp. 53–56). This example confirmed for me that there are many ways in which EFT can be utilized, even in busy medical, dental, or chiropractic offices. Research has shown statistically significant results in phobia reduction, for example, with EFT sessions of less than five minutes (Waite and Holder, 2003, pp. 65–71). This issue could become relevant for a patient who has significant fears about the application of adjustment techniques; for example, a patient may be fearful of a particular movement of the neck or the sound of a joint "popping" (cavitation) when it is adjusted.

Certain professions, specifically certain mental health professions, mandate whether the clinician can touch a client. This is not a concern for chiropractic practitioners, as kinesthetic contact is standard care in the profession. A chiropractor may, however, want to eliminate tapping on the liver acupoint, which lies below the breast tissue; this point need not be used, according to current Clinical EFT protocols.

## Conclusion

Chiropractic offers individuals a drugless method for restoring homeostasis to the body via the adjustment or correction of dysfunctioning joints in the spinal column and its corollary neurological effects on the rest of the body. EFT effectively reduces the harmful effects of stress-inducing negative emotions and affects the body's energy system in such a way as also to restore homeostasis. The integration of these two techniques holds tremendous promise as an emerging holistic body-mind approach to improved health and peace of mind.

*A note of gratitude and acknowledgment for editing assistance and feedback goes out to Mark Brady, PhD.*

## References

American Chiropractic Association. Origins and history of chiropractic. Retrieved November 13, 2012, from http://www.acatoday.org/pdf/Chiro_History.pdf

Apkarian, A. V., Sosa, Y., Sonty, S., Levy, R. M., Harden, R. N., Parrish, T. B., & Gitelman, D. R. (2004, November 17). Chronic back pain is associated with decreased prefrontal and thalamic gray matter density [Abstract]. *Journal of Neuroscience, 24,* 10410–10415. doi:10.1523/JNEUROSCI.2541-04.2004

Association for Comprehensive Energy Psychology (ACEP). (2012, November 19). APA approves ACEP to provide CE credits for psychologists. Retrieved from http://acepblog.org/2012/11/19/apa-approves-acep-to-provide-ce-credits-for-psychologists

Burk, Larry. (2010) Single session EFT (Emotional Freedom Techniques) for stress-related symptoms after motor vehicle accidents. *Energy Psychology, 2*(1), 65–71.

Chapman-Smith, D. (2000). Facts on chiropractic. *Chiropractic Report.* Retrieved November 13, 2012, from http://chiropracticreport.com/portal/index.php?option=com_content&task=view&id=18&Itemid=33

Lehrer, J. (2009, January 9). Back pain. Posted on the Frontal Cortex Science Blogs. http://scienceblogs.com/cortex/2009/01/09/back-pain

Palmer, D. D. (1966 [1910]). *The chiropractor's adjuster* (original title: *The text-book of the science, art and philosophy of chiropractic*). Portland, OR: Portland Printing House.

Porges, Stephen W. (2011). *The Polyvagal Theory: Neurophysiological foundations of emotions, attachment, communication, and self-regulation.* New York, NY: W. W. Norton.

Revised Code of Washington. Retrieved from http://apps.leg.wa.gov/RCW/default.aspx?cite=18.25.005; last updated December 27, 2012.

Scaer, R. C. (2005). *The trauma spectrum: Hidden wounds and human resiliency.* New York, NY: W.W. Norton.

Temple, G. P. & Mollon, P. (2011). Reducing anxiety in dental patients using Emotional Freedom Techniques (EFT): A pilot study. *Energy Psychology, 3*(2), 53–56.

Waite, L.W. & Holder, M.D. (2003). Assessment of the Emotional Freedom Technique: An alternative treatment for fear. *Scientific Review of Mental Health Practice, 2*(1), 20–26.

World Federation of Chiropractic. Facts on chiropractic. Retrieved on November 13, 2012, from http://www.wfc.org/website/index.php?option=com_content&view=article&id=122&Itemid=138&lang=en

# Special Populations

# Chapter 43
# Searching for New Myths
*Stanley Krippner*

## Abstract

A "myth" can be defined as an imaginative statement or story about an important human issue. A myth has consequences for behavior, the way a person, a family, or a group makes decisions and manages life. The advent of the new century provides an opportunity for old, dysfunctional myths to be replaced by new myths that work on behalf of human welfare and happiness. Paramount in this multicultural, divisive world are myths that emphasize community and sustainability. Community myths enable disparate peoples and groups to work in tandem for mutually beneficial goals. Sustainability myths assist individuals, families, and cultures in conserving resources that do not inflict injury upon the planet and its life forms. The word "myth" has advantages over terms such as "world view" and "belief system" because it can be associated with archetypal symbols and metaphors from classical myths and from contemporary dreams, visions, and inspirational speeches and texts.

**Keywords:** personal mythologies, personal myths, functional myths, dysfunctional myths, belief systems, archetypes

**Stanley Krippner, PhD**, professor of psychology at Saybrook Graduate School in San Francisco, is a fellow in three divisions of the American Psychological Association (APA), coauthor of *Extraordinary Dreams* and *Haunted by Combat: Understanding PTSD in War Veterans*, and coeditor of *Varieties of Anomalous Experience: Examining the Scientific Evidence*. Send correspondence to Stanley Krippner, Saybrook University, 747 Front Street, San Francisco, CA 94111, or skrippner@saybrook.edu.

At the end of the 20th century, a number of writers heralded the 21st century as one of untold possibilities and new guiding myths. These became known as "Millennium Myths" and portrayed a New Golden Age, the New Jerusalem, the Peaceable Kingdom, or the City of the Sun. In some of these mythic narratives, it was told that Heaven will come down to Earth, or at least that we would experience a kind of earthly Paradise. Other narratives foretold the arrival of the Messiah, the return of Quetzalcoatl, the appearance of Maitreya, or the emerging of the Goddess.

Joseph Campbell cautioned that one cannot predict the next mythology any more than one can predict the night's dreams. He was very clear, however, that if humanity was to survive, its dysfunctional myths must be transformed. Instead of looking at myth from a metaphysical and esoteric perspective, I prefer to define it within the context of common sense. A myth, then, can be seen as an imaginative story about an important, existential human issue that has behavioral consequences. Some myths, such as those held by most religions, are considered to be "sacred"; but the myths that guide our daily behavior are simply examples of "self-talk," even though they often have dimensions of which we are dimly aware.

As you can see, my definition contains words that are psychological in nature rather than esoteric. It encompasses personal myths, which give guidance for daily living, as well as cultural myths that involve gods and goddesses, spirits and demons, and various creation stories. The first part of this definition sees myths as imaginative narratives. Thus, a myth could be one sentence long or it could comprise an entire saga such as *Tristan and Isolde* or the *Odyssey*. These narratives are usually expressed in words, but sometimes they include pictures, architecture, sculpture, dance, or song.

Second, myths concern themselves with important, existential human issues. They are not about trivial matters, but about life and death, birth and rebirth, starvation and bounty, love and war. Myths confront us with the here and now: What do we do when we are in the middle of a crisis? What do we do if we want to make changes in our lives? What do we do when a moral choice is demanded of us? Whether we know it or not, we fall back upon personal, cultural, or religious myths to direct our behavior.

Third, myths have behavioral consequences. They are not just fanciful tales of fantasy, they impact the way we make decisions and live our lives. They play an important role in determining who we will marry, what work we will choose, the way in which we will raise our children, and how we will relate to God, the Tao, the Ground of Being, or whatever we believe to be greater than ourselves. For Carl Jung and other writers who saw the relevance of myths to contemporary times, mythology was of critical importance because it contained profound psychological insights essential to the art of "soul making."

Campbell and Jung both wrote about such critical concepts as the survival of humanity and the fate of the Earth. Yet when individuals think in these terms it can be overwhelming. "Global warming, social crises, and paradigm shifts are happening right now," we think. And then we ask, "What can I do in the face of such tremendous obstacles and such widespread dysfunction?" It is at this point that people need to feel empowered, to know that positive change is possible, and that their vitality—or inner energetic capacity—is the key to mythic change, on both the personal and the cultural levels.

Such cultural myths as the *Iliad* and the *Aeneid*, the Shiva and Shakti stories, and the Australian aborigines' Dreamtime, posed the same questions. These issues also are addressed by religious myths and are proclaimed in churches, temples, and mosques, often giving the worshippers contradictory messages. World leaders, when they make crucial decisions about war and peace, neglect the world of mythology at their peril.

In addition to personal, religious, and cultural myths, there are distinct family mythologies. Some families, for example, expect their children to marry within the same religion, and there is often a crisis if they don't. They reflect one's family mythology, one's cultural mythology, one's religious mythology—or the lack of it. Personal mythologies are derived from our biology, our cultural environment, our interpersonal relationships, and our transpersonal experiences. They are the microcosm of the macrocosm.

Why do I use the term "mythology" as opposed to "world view" or "belief system"? Beliefs are very intellectual; mythology is not only intellectual, it is attitudinal and emotional. Mythology combines the unconscious as well as one's conscious inclinations, and it involves symbols (such as mandalas and crucifixes) and metaphors (such as "running with the wind") in addition to straightforward language.

We can ask if a myth is "functional" or "dysfunctional." Does the myth support a person's life and well-being or does it lead to fanaticism, depression, or constant anxiety? A basic guideline could be that functional myths are those that enhance our vitality, while dysfunctional myths are those that hamper our vitality.

Functional myths will differ from person to person, yet even the most functional mythic structures continually evolve if they are to further a person's optimal adjustment and development. The symbols and metaphors that are inherent in our myths have the power to transcend polarities and unite opposites, fostering a transition from psychic conflict to the achievement of greater unity. Sometimes a superficial mythic structure is revealed by one's "persona," a term Jung adopted from the Greek word for "mask," which is basically a role that is enacted to adapt to the requirements of specific life situations. This persona can reflect deeper layers of the psyche or it can disguise what people actually feel, think, and believe. In other words, it may be a mask for the deep-set personal myths of the person wearing it.

Personal conflicts in one's inner life and external circumstances are natural markers of times of transition. A myth is a narrative, yet beneath the words and images there are feelings, there are convictions, and there are attitudes that we don't often put into words. A personal myth is more than intellectual; it has an emotional component to it. And in working to transform our personal myths, it is essential that we create new myths that pack an emotional punch. Many resolutions for the New Year are never carried out because they are simply words that lack the emotion, the intention, and the vitality to bring about a long-term behavioral change.

Year after year, Marie resolved to improve her habit of procrastinating, but by the end of January she had lapsed into her previous dysfunctional behavior patterns, telling herself, "It really doesn't matter if I put off an assignment or am late for an appointment; everyone else does it." A friend suggested that she add an exercise routine to her agenda. Marie discovered that half an hour of vigorous exercise five times each week provided her with a source of vitality she had ignored. For the first time, she was able to finish job assignments on time, appear punctually for appointments, and turn around the personal myths that she had used as an excuse for procrastination. Other people have enhanced their vitality through changing their diet, by setting aside some time each day for meditation or contemplation, or simply by getting an extra hour of sleep each night.

Personal myths that have been with us since childhood are very difficult to change. Something that is learned early in life is hard to unlearn later in life. We don't just stop what we are doing; we must learn to behave differently. Yet this is not how we commonly go about trying to make change. Instead, people who have the urge to keep doing something over and over again—like a compulsive sex or drug addict, for example—tell themselves, "When I have enough will power I will just stop." But the behavior does not stop because the verbal resolution does not reflect the deepest layers of the addict's psyche.

Embodying a new myth is one of the best ways to make a change. Our bodies usually tell us whether we are ready to make a beneficial change. Our bodies provide clues that inform us in our dreams, in our periods of meditation and contemplation, and in our bodily symptoms, or lack of them. Can we relax easily? Are we beset with aches and pains? If a medical examination can reveal no reason for bodily discomfort, we might look into our personal myths to see if there are some that are dysfunctional and not working on our behalf. Do we spend too much time with people who give us "a pain in the neck"? Do we have "gut feelings" that we ignore when making decisions? Physical vitality usually accompanies emotional vitality, intellectual vitality, social vitality, and spiritual vitality.

I learned a great deal from Albert Ellis, the founder of Rational-Emotive Behavior Therapy. Early in his career Ellis realized that what he was then calling Rational Therapy was not descriptive enough. He changed the name because he understood that it was necessary to bring emotions and behavior into the process. His books and those of Joseph Campbell are just a couple of examples of the many resources that provide access to wisdom on how to change our dysfunctional myths.

We in the "First World" have more options and choices than are available in developing countries. Even so, many people still suffer from depression and apathy. More often than not, this suffering is a part of a collection of dysfunctional personal myths, an insight that the Buddha grasped centuries ago. These men and women have imagined the way their world "should be." When the world does not measure up to their expectations, they suffer. Remember that I defined "myths" as "imaginary" narratives. If we have imagined the world in an unrealistic way, we can learn to imagine the world in a realistic way. And when we improve our mythology on the personal level, we will have an opportunity to change our interactions with people on the social and cultural level.

Jackie Robinson grew up in poverty, but wanted more than anything to play major league baseball. However, the cultural myths of the time told him that black athletes couldn't be baseball players. The best they could hope for was to get a decent job and play baseball on weekends, or perhaps participate in one of the so-called "Negro leagues" that consisted only of black athletes. Robinson started out by playing baseball in one of the "Negro leagues," where he was noticed by talent scouts such as Branch Rickey, a team manager for the Brooklyn Dodgers. Rickey courageously signed him up and that action changed the face (and the color) of baseball. Neither Robinson nor Rickey accepted the current mythologies. Together they made a paradigm shift—not in the world-at-large but certainly in the world of sports.

Jackie Robinson walked his talk, fighting for civil rights the rest of his life, even after he retired from baseball. When he and Rickey changed the mythology of the baseball community, that began to change the cultural myths about racial relations. In time, people began to see that if Jackie Robinson could excel in baseball, and if Duke Ellington could excel in music, and if Harry Belafonte could excel in movies, the cultural myths of the era were dysfunctional. Eventually, African American candidates for the presidency of the United States emerged in both the Democratic and Republican parties.

I am not an advocate of the one-person theory of history, nor do I hold that there is a simple cause-and-effect relationship between events. However, one person or a small group of people can initiate a change; if the times are ready for it the change very well might occur, especially if there are social supports in place to reinforce and to build upon the new cultural myths that have come into play.

But in order to accelerate this process, it would help each of us to know just what we want to do, and to establish a belief system that supports what we want and not what we don't want. One way to discover the belief system that underlies our current personal myths is by finding out the underlying intention that is running our mythology. Here are some myths that reveal various intentions: "I want peak vitality because I want to win every basketball game this season for my team." "I want peak vitality because I want to be a better sexual athlete in bed." "I want peak vitality because I want to live a long and healthy life." "I want peak vitality because my body is the temple of God." "I want peak vitality so that I can do all of my tasks and not be fatigued at the end of the day." "I want peak vitality so that I can be a role model for my children." "I want peak vitality so that I can maintain my mental and spiritual health."

We incorporate belief systems from many sources. Four sources of personal myths are: our biology, our culture, our interpersonal relationships, and our transpersonal experiences. Any of these, alone or in combination, can produce a personal myth. So, peak vitality will differ according to the person and also from gender to gender. Often, peak vitality relates to bodily health, as it is necessary to be in optimal condition if our intention focuses on athletics, on longevity, on sexual prowess, on spiritual development, or any number of other goals.

When I talk about physical vitality I take a very holistic approach, since physical vitality overlaps with emotional vitality, intellectual vitality, even spiritual vitality and social vitality. Vitality is all part of one piece as far as I am concerned. But its components can interact. Instead of complimenting one another they can conflict and interrupt one another if they are not synchronized and headed in the same direction.

When we discuss functional myths and dysfunctional myths, we need to relate them to brain functioning. Our awareness of myths comes in the form of a narrative, and language originates in the brain. But beneath those words, there are feelings, there are images, and there are attitudes that we don't put into words. They are grounded in the brain as well, but in different areas than words and language. So we use the total brain when we form and act out our personal myths. When there is a mythic conflict, there is also a neurological conflict because our neural networks are at odds with each other. This saps our physical vitality, and produces the "mixed messages" that we give ourselves and that we give others.

A person might make the statement, "I have the intention of being personally fit and vital until I am well into my 80s and my 90s." That intention sounds positive, but how deep does that intention go? It might come from the prefrontal cortex, but what is happening in the amygdala and other parts of the limbic system that are associated with emotion? A person may see a Twinkie and go for it because the pleasure centers of the brain are taking over. This part of the brain simply is at odds with the more rational parts of the brain's cortex that knows better.

Then there is the person whose stated personal myth is, "I know that to get through high school and college I have to be focused on my academic work and coordinate my social life accordingly." Once again, an invitation to a party stimulates those pleasure centers and the noble, high-minded intention is tested. Personal awareness and self-monitoring can help us regulate our behavior in ways that keep us focused on our goals, not distracted from them.

Something that is learned is very difficult to unlearn. Old myths die hard. In order to unlearn a dysfunctional personal myth, one does not simply stop in one's tracks and say, "I will better next time." One learns to do something differently by changing behavior, by diligently practicing the new behavior, and by surrounding oneself with people who will support the new behavior. It is not enough to say "When I have enough will power I will just stop." I have heard people apply this personal myth to smoking (and other addictions), to overeating, to gambling, and to procrastinating. The problem is that their will power never quite materializes. They have neglected feelings, emotions, intentions, and the practice that is needed to change a personal myth and to eradicate a harmful habit.

Your body is an excellent guide to finding your bliss. Do you feel good about what you are doing? Do you sense accomplishment when your task is finished? If you have been eating properly, exercising well, and getting enough rest and sleep, you can trust your body to help you make crucial decisions. But if your body is filled with aches and pains that a physician cannot explain, something is disconnected. Re-examine your personal mythology, your work situation, and your love life. Are they working together or are they at odds?

Physical vitality is the bottom line to connecting your bodily feelings with your personal mythology. If your life is synchronized, you will feel vital and energetic. Some exercise programs are designed to coordinate mind and body, feelings and intellect, your inner life and outer life. Yoga is one path, and the martial arts are another; for some people, aerobics is the key and for others, a daily run or swim produces results.

In his classic book called The *Nature of Things,* the Roman philosopher Lucretius discussed free will and how difficult it is to exercise it. He used the term "swerve," and gave several recipes to help people bring "swerve" into their lives. This is exactly what David Feinstein and I have been doing in our workshops and books about personal mythology. We have advised our workshop members and our readers to empower themselves, to take charge of those aspects of their lives where change is possible, and to direct their personal vitality in ways that will anchor those changes. We believe that personal vitality is not just a catch phrase. It is the product of an optimistic, life-affirming, compassionate personal mythology. It starts with the individual, spreads to that person's associates, and can even affect society at large. When enough people transform their personal mythology, there will be changes in family mythologies, cultural mythologies, and even religious mythologies.

The need for a new unifying mythic vision amidst the disorienting cacophony of competing myths presses on. Abraham Lincoln's Civil War–era plea is now more appropriate than ever. In a famous speech he observed that "the dogmas of the past are inadequate to the stormy present. As our case is new, so we must think anew and act anew." This is not inconsistent with the mythology of the North American Iroquois Indians who ask in what way the decisions we make today will affect the seventh generation that follows us.

As a result of studying Native American and other indigenous people's mythologies, some contemporary anthropologists and psychologists have proposed a number of strategies for implementing new functional mythologies:

1. "Learned Optimism" counters the tendency to believe that when something terrible happens to one's group or nation it will be permanent and pervasive.
2. "Subordinate Goals" are mutually beneficial outcomes that transcend the separate interests of conflicting groups.

3. "Synergy" leads to beneficial outcomes that transcend the separate interests of the group and the individual.
4. "Emotional Education" supplements reasoning and critical thinking with the development of children's ability to defer gratification, control their anger, cultivate insight about their own feelings, and develop empathy for others.
5. "Spiritual Enrichment" can clarify an individual's values and ethics, as well as those held by groups.

In conclusion, Joseph Campbell understood the importance of myth for our time, and he popularized this understanding through his books, his lectures, and his television series. Other scholars have reached the same conclusion even though they might use different terms than "mythology." But time is running out. We need to translate theory into action. A living mythology is more than belief, more than attitude, more than emotion. If dysfunctional myths and paradigms are going to shift, the new narrative needs to lead to new behaviors. Vitality is a canvas and we need different paints on our palette in order to create a beautiful picture. Every day, we are painting a self-portrait as well as a representation of our environment. It is naïve to claim that we "create" our reality. But it is accurate to state that we "construct" our reality. To cite Epictetus, a Greek philosopher, our life is determined not so much by what happens to us, but by our interpretation of what happens to us. Thus, our self-portrait is composed, in great part, of our personal myths. We need to select those self-statements, beliefs, attitudes, and behaviors that will keep us physically, intellectually, emotionally, socially, and spiritually vital. Indeed, we must think anew and act anew.

# Chapter 44
# Long-Term Weight Loss
*Peta Stapleton*

## Abstract

There is little doubt as to the adverse physical effects of being overweight or obese. Obesity increases cardiovascular disease risk factors, type 2 diabetes, and overall mortality. Current approaches to addressing this epidemic have included combined dietary and physical activity approaches and, of late, behavioral strategies to influence the weight loss process such as motivation strategies. However, it appears the more time that elapses between the end of a diet and the follow-up period, the more weight is regained. Although studies have examined factors that contribute to longer-term weight maintenance, they still continue to highlight aspects relating to individual willpower and self-control (e.g., low-energy, low-fat and high carbohydrate diets; high intensity and frequent physical exercise; and self-weighing). It may be that comprehensive psychological treatment in conjunction with physical and dietary approaches is necessary, essential, and the key to successful weight loss and maintenance, particularly for those individuals who find the self-control behaviors difficult to sustain. Psychological research that combines cognitive strategies with somatic procedures adapted from acupuncture and related systems for altering the cognitive, behavioral, and neurochemical foundations of psychological problems has been showing promise in the weight loss field. Research examining meridian-based procedures (e.g., Emotional Freedom Techniques, EFT), often referred to as "psychological acupuncture," for food cravings found that significant improvements occurred in weight, body mass index, food cravings, subjects' perceived power of food, craving restraint, and psychological coping from pre to 12-months after a 4-week treatment. When compared to traditional approaches (e.g., cognitive behavioral therapy, CBT), pilot studies have indicated EFT is more significant in explaining differences over time between food craving measures than is CBT treatment. This chapter highlights the common psychological concerns that are present in many overweight and obese individuals and offers a structured, practical approach to using EFT to resolve them. Future research directions are discussed and case studies are offered to demonstrate its clinical application.

**Keywords:** overweight, obese, weight loss, food craving, cravings, craving restraint

**Peta Stapleton, PhD, MAPS, MCCP, MHCP,** is a registered clinical and health psychologist and assistant professor at Bond University in Australia. With 16 years in academia, she recently led the world's first randomized clinical trial investigating EFT in the treatment of food cravings in overweight and obese adults. Send correspondence to Peta Stapleton, Faculty of Humanities and Social Sciences, University Drive, Bond University, Robina, Gold Coast 4229, Queensland Australia, or pstaplet@bond.edu.au.

## Overview

Obesity is now being treated as a chronic disease estimated to account for between 0.7% and 2.8% of a country's total health care expenditures (Withrow & Alter, 2010). While the prevalence rates for overweight and obese people differ worldwide, there is general agreement that the Middle East, Central and Eastern Europe, and North America have higher prevalence rates (James, Leach, Kalamara, & Shayeghi, 2012). Across countries, women typically present with a greater body mass index (BMI) distribution and with higher obesity rates than do men (James et al., 2012).

Obesity is a leading cause of death and disease and being an overweight or obese adult results in physical issues such as cardiovascular disease; type 2 diabetes; some cancers; musculoskeletal, skin, and respiratory problems; and psychosocial problems including eating disorders and depression (NHMRC, 2012). It is also commonly associated with poverty (James et al., 2012). As a multifaceted and complicated health disorder now drawing worldwide attention due to its consequences, the costs of being obese extend into areas previously reserved for protracted and enduring health conditions and now include employment absenteeism, disability, workers' compensation costs, and premature mortality (Trogdon, Finkelstein, Hylands, Dellea, & Kamal-Bahl, 2008).

Unfortunately the prevalence of obesity in children and adolescents is also increasing. The number of overweight children and adolescents in the United States has doubled in the last three decades, and similar rates are occurring worldwide (Deckelbaum & Williams, 2001). Comorbid conditions and complications that have always previously been associated with adulthood are now presenting in children: type 2 diabetes (Kaufman, 2011), hypertension (Sorof & Daniels, 2002), lipid abnormalities (Morrison, Sprecher, Barton, Waclawiw, & Daniels, 1999), and pulmonary problems including obstructive sleep apnea and exacerbation of asthma (Mallory, Fiser, & Jackson, 1989). Psychological outcomes of being overweight in childhood include depression, self-esteem, social adjustment, body size dissatisfaction, and weight-related teasing and exclusion by parents and peers (Young-Hyman et al., 2012). Gender and ethnicity is important in the experience of being overweight and in weight-related distress, but increasing weight has been associated with emotional and weight-related distress in children regardless of these (Young-Hyman et al., 2012). Finally, there is evidence that higher levels of BMI during childhood can predict being overweight later in life, and this is independent of parental obesity status (Li, Goran, Kaur, Nollen, & Ahluwalia, 2012).

## Defining Obesity

The internationally accepted standardized classification of overweight and obese is based on the BMI, which allows a comparable analysis of prevalence rates worldwide (World Health Organization, 2000) and is a weight-to-height ratio, calculated by dividing one's weight in kilograms by the square of one's height in meters. While the consensus is that the full normal range is a BMI between 18.5 and 24.9 kg/m$^2$ (for both sexes and for all ages over 18.0 years), in children, the International Obesity Task-Force age-, sex-, and BMI-specific cutoff points are increasingly being used (Wang & Wang, 2000). Obesity is defined as a BMI above 30 kg/m$^2$, while overweight is defined as a BMI above 25 kg/m$^2$. Morbid obesity occurs at a BMI above 40 kg/m$^2$ (World Health Organization, 2000).

An additional measure of obesity that is related to BMI is waist circumference. A high waist circumference is associated with an increased risk for type 2 diabetes, dyslipidemia, hypertension, and cardiovascular disease in patients with a BMI in a range between 25 and 34.9 kg/m$^2$ (Chan, Rimm, Colditz, Stampfer, & Willett, 1994). Furthermore, waist circumference provides an independent prediction of risk over and above that of BMI, and can be used to indicate increased abdominal fat even when BMI changes. A high-risk waist circumference for men is that which is greater than 102 centimeters (or 40 inches), and for women greater than 88 centimeters (or 35 inches). It is important to note that waist circumference cutpoints lose their incremental predictive power in patients with a BMI of 35 kg/m$^2$ because these patients exceed the cutpoints noted ("Clinical guidelines," 1998).

## Etiology of Obesity

Obesity has typically been purported to result from a range of causes including metabolic factors (Bray & DeLany, 2012), excessive consumption of obesogenic foods (Wilding, 2012), genetics

(Lyon & Hirschhorn, 2005), and environmental contributions such as increased use of transport (e.g., cars) resulting in more sedentary behavior, and decreased cost of energy-dense food making it more easily accessible to lower socioeconomic groups (Wilding, 2012). While the likely explanation may well be a combination of these complex and often interacting processes, what is interesting is that health care providers in a range of specialty areas endorse stereotypical assumptions about obese patients and attribute obesity to blameworthy causes (Puhl & Heuer, 2012).

It is well known that obese individuals are highly stigmatized because of their weight and face various forms of prejudice and discrimination (Sechrist et al., 2005; Teachman et al., 2005), but more recently it has been noted that physicians view obesity as largely a behavioral problem caused by physical inactivity and overeating (Foster et al., 2012). Nurses, too, consistently express biased attitudes toward obese patients, reflecting common weight-based stereotypes that obese patients are lazy, lacking in self-control, and noncompliant (Lee & Calamaro, 2012); and medical students exhibit the same attitudes as their experienced colleagues (Magliocca, Jabero, Alto, & Magliocca, 2005). Fitness/health professionals (Hare, Price, Flynn, & King, 2000), registered dietitians, and those still studying express similar negative weight bias to obese adults (Harvey, Summerbell, Kirk, & Hill, 2002; Puhl, Wharton, & Heuer, 2009). Interestingly, the increasing worldwide prevalence of obesity has not mitigated or reduced negative societal attitudes toward obese people.

## Benefits of Long-Term Weight Loss

Given the complexity of physical health related conditions, psychosocial consequences, and co-occurring psychological concerns, it has become an international priority to target the obesity epidemic and devise strategies to instigate weight loss and improve quality of life. A 5 to 10% decrease in body weight for obese adults is associated with significant improvements in blood pressure, serum lipid levels, glucose tolerance (Goldstein, 1992), and a reduction in diabetes (Colditz, Willett, Rotnitzky, & Manson, 1995) and hypertension (Huang et al., 1998; Kirk et al., 2005). Current approaches to addressing this epidemic have included combined dietary and physical activity

approaches (Fujioka, 2012; Wing & Hill, 2001) and, of late, behavioral or motivation strategies to influence the weight loss process (Bandura, 1986; Prochaska, DiClemente, & Norcross, 1992; Prochaska, Norcross, Fowler, Follick, & Abrams, 1992).

Weight loss and weight maintenance are complex issues. Research suggests dieting regularly results in weight loss in the short term (Perri & Fuller, 1995), but meta-analysis indicates that the more time that elapses between the end of a diet and the follow-up period, the more weight is regained (Mann et al., 2007). Short-term studies of weight loss do not often indicate the benefits on health related outcomes, and also do not address what occurs when weight is regained (Mann et al., 2007). Indeed weight cycling has been associated with decreased perceptions of health and well-being (Foster, Sarwer, & Wadden, 2012), excess body weight, and abdominal fat accumulation (Cereda et al., 2011). Weight instability has been related to lower health satisfaction and self-esteem, higher body dissatisfaction, dieting, and binge eating for both men and women (Serdar et al., 2011). Unfortunately, it is clear that dieting alone does not lead to sustained weight loss and individuals who diet are more likely to gain back more weight than they lost (Mann et al., 2007).

## Successful Long-Term Weight Loss

The area of *successful* weight maintenance is new and under-researched. Similar to many therapeutic models, treatment characteristics such as continued therapist contact have been shown to increase the likelihood of weight maintenance (Perri, Nezu, Patti, & McCann, 1989). More recently, the National Weight Control Registry (Hill, Wyatt, Phelan, & Wing, 2005; Wing & Hill, 2001), which is the largest observational study examining weight loss maintainers of more than a year, has identified four factors used by those who are successful. These include: consuming a low-energy, low-fat, and high-carbohydrate diet (Shick et al., 1998); regularly eating breakfast (Wyatt et al., 2002); engaging in high levels of physical activity (Wing & Hill, 2001); and self-weighing at least once per week (Klem, Wing, McGuire, Seagle, & Hill, 1997). Indeed decreasing self-weighing has been independently associated with weight gain (Butryn, Phelan, Hill, & Wing, 2007). Additionally, the overall conclusion in the recent Raynor,

Jeffery, Phelan, Hill, and Wing (2012) review of the weight registry participants to date has also highlighted that to be successful at weight loss maintenance over time, individuals must have *limited variety in food groups,* and consume a low-energy diet as well as dedicate to a consistent exercise regimen (McGuire, Wing, Klem, & Hill, 1999). In sum, the theme present in the weight maintenance literature appears to be that of behavioral control, self-control and willpower in maintaining restricted food choices, and engaging in frequent and strenuous physical activity.

Though it appears then the addition of these behavioral strategies result in longer weight loss maintenance over time, it seems there may be a missing link in the weight loss/obesity field: that of recognizing the complex psychological factors involved, and therefore the need for comprehensive psychological treatment in conjunction with physical and dietary approaches. A recent study investigated the psychological, cultural, and social contributions to overeating in obese people (Grant, Buckroyd, & Rother, 2008). The authors found that eating for comfort for the morbidly obese is rooted in using food to manage experiences of emotional pain and difficult family and social relationships. Participants reported that what had been missing from all treatment programs they had tried was the *opportunity to work on the psychological issues concurrently with weight loss* (Grant et al., 2008).

## Psychological Interventions for Weight Loss

The addition of psychological techniques indicates that people who are overweight or obese benefit from psychological interventions to enhance weight reduction (Shaw, O'Rourke, Del Mar, & Kenardy, 2005). A Cochrane review (Shaw et al., 2005) highlighted that cognitive behavior therapy (CBT) and behavior therapy (BT) significantly improved the success of weight loss for overweight and obese people. Cognitive therapy alone was not found to be effective as a weight loss treatment. The evidence available for other strategies, such as relaxation therapy and hypnotherapy, also indicated that these might be beneficial in improving weight loss (Shaw et al., 2005).

Energy psychology (EP) strategies are emerging as techniques that can change emotional, behavioural, and cognitive concerns by combining physical interventions that target the body's electrical or energy fields, often with a cognitive element (Feinstein, 2008). Addressing symptoms in this way is in its infancy in modern, evidenced-based approaches, but has existed for thousands of years in Eastern philosophies (Meyers, 2007).

Emotional Freedom Techniques (Craig, 2011) is one such EP strategy and is a type of exposure therapy that includes a somatic and cognitive component for altering the cognitive, behavioral, and neurochemical foundations of psychological problems. Similar to acupuncture, EFT is believed to use the body's meridian or energy system to counter negative or distressing sensations. Whereas acupuncture uses fine needles to stimulate the end points of the meridian system, EFT uses a tapping technique (with two or several fingers). It is widely understood that the parts of the brain involved in hyperarousal include the amygdala, and recent studies of the use of EFT have indicated a decrease in amygdala and hippocampus activity (Dhond, Kettner, & Napadow, 2007). It would then appear that the mechanism at work here has an impact on physiological systems in the body that regulate stress, and EFT treatment can influence the strength of emotional intensity and associated neural frequencies (Diepold Jr. & Goldstein, 2009; Feinstein, 2010).

There is now evidence that emerging techniques such as EFT can have an immediate and lasting effect on food cravings. Food cravings frequently lead to consumption of the craved food (Hill & Heaton-Brown, 1994), are positively correlated with BMI (Delahanty, Meigs, Hayden, Williamson, & Nathan, 2002; Franken & Muris, 2005) and obese adults report preferences for high fat foods (Drewnowski, Kurth, Holden-Wiltse, & Saari, 1992). Therefore addressing these cravings in treatment is paramount.

A randomized clinical trial that offered a 4-week EFT treatment program to 96 overweight and obese participants with severe food cravings, and then assessed their progress 6 and 12 months after treatment ended (Stapleton, Sheldon, Porter, & Whitty, 2011) found BMI, degree of food craving, individual's perceived power of food, restraint capabilities, and psychological symptoms significantly improved. Weight loss over the 12 months was significant from the start of treatment (mean difference, $-5.05$ kilograms or 11.1 pounds, $p < .05$) and the decrease in BMI was also significant (mean difference, $-2.28$, $p < .05$; (Stapleton, Sheldon, & Porter, 2012b).

In the same study, a small pilot of EFT (N = 40) versus cognitive behavioral therapy (CBT, N = 7) versus a psycho-education intervention (N = 7) versus a waitlist (N = 40) was conducted to assess the effectiveness of EFT against a gold standard psychological treatment (CBT). The results indicated through paired sample t-tests that the CBT group resulted in a significant reduction in total food craving pre to post a 4-week treatment and a significant reduction in total food craving and increase in an individual's power over food. An increase in restraint ability pre to post also occurred for the psycho-education group. The EFT results indicated significant reductions on all measures pre to post, except restraint ability. However, increased restraint was significant at the 6- and 12-month point, indicating a time lag.

One-way ANOVAs (analysis of variance tests), however, showed significant differences *between groups* for total food craving, power over food, and restraint ability. Post hoc analyses showed CBT to contribute to explaining one of these differences (total food craving; waitlist versus CBT, p = 0.022); the psycho-education group did not reach significance in explaining any differences. The waitlist versus EFT was significant in explaining differences between groups for food craving, power over food, and restraint ability—consistent with the Stapleton, Sheldon, Porter, and Whitty (2011, 2012) publications. Current research is examining the effects of CBT versus EFT in a larger clinical trial (for a full review of session topics and case study vignettes from the trial, see Stapleton, Sheldon, and Porter, 2012a, 2012b).

## Common Themes in Weight Issues

Common emotions individuals may have that trigger food cravings and food consumption were explored in Stapleton, Sheldon, Porter, and Whitty (2012b; 2011) and included: deprivation, abandonment, loss/grief/sadness, loneliness/emptiness, anxiety/stress, guilt, fear, anger, shame, and feeling inadequate/not good enough. Issues in the "present" included: specific foods craved, problem times of the day and current feelings about weight, size or shape, as well as potential "future" issues (e.g., "Imagine yourself in the future at an event or at a usual trigger time. Imagine yourself not eating your food craving food. How do you feel?"). The other significant issue that arose was centered on wastage

and disposing of craved foods. The most common emotional issues raised were feelings of loss and guilt from food wastage. Often participants highlighted messages from their childhood (e.g., "I feel guilty if I throw food away, because there are other people who are hungry"). Similarly, a feeling of guilt often resulted from an idea of being disloyal to a faithful friend (the food), and not seeking comfort in the food left participants with a sense of loss, emptiness, and unhappiness. Questions that assist in eliciting underlying emotional issues related to overweight, obese, or food cravings include:

1. How do you feel in your stomach when you eat a food that you crave?
2. How do you feel in your stomach when you eat a food you don't crave?
3. Seeing and smelling the food you crave, what do you feel?
4. Imagine yourself throwing this food away; how do you feel?
5. What's your first memory of eating the food you crave?
6. As a child, were you given food to comfort you?
7. What's your best memory that involves food?
8. What's your worst memory that involves food?

## Application of EFT for Weight Issues

The application of EFT for weight issues is far reaching and often complex. EFT can reduce immediate food cravings; EFT can target and eliminate the negative or distorted body images; EFT can neutralize issues from the past that have led to overeating; and EFT can be used to target future situations that might trigger a relapse (Look, 2001). Everyday stress is often what causes an individual to try to treat his or her anxiety with food. It is well known that EFT can help people manage this stress. EFT can confront and "loosen" the unconscious and conscious irrational beliefs individuals have about food, weight, and hereditary factors that may contribute to them being overweight. EFT can target and eliminate the negative or distorted body images that individuals hold about themselves, and can enhance a person's positive successful image of self. EFT can be used to target future situations that might trigger a relapse, and can assist individuals in eliminating limiting beliefs about reaching their ideal weight and shape goals (Look, 2001). Feedback from the food craving trial (Stapleton et al., 2012b; Stapleton et al., 2011) highlighted many of the issues raised thus far: One 70-year-old male wrote: "I found the programme extremely enlightening and it has helped me with some deep-seated emotional issues that I have carried since childhood (some 70 years)."

Interestingly, weight issues are often believed to be just that (devoid of any emotional content), as highlighted by a participant who chose not to engage in the food craving trial:

> *Having perused your food craving questionnaire, I have decided that my eating problems are not so much craving-related, but quantity-related! By that I mean both portion sizes, and "doubling up" with either a second helping of the main course, or following a main with dessert, or fruit, etc. Added to that is the ever common "grazing" between meals!*
>
> *Compounding that, is the fact that I have had Ross River virus for 15 years, meaning I experience pain and discomfort in my joints, particularly my feet, knees, and wrists (typical RRV symptoms). This limits the amount of exercise I do, even though I do physical work three days a week in my job. Thank you for the opportunity for me to give thought to my eating problems, and hopefully, I can head in a different direction to achieve the results that I "crave"!— 64-year-old male*

The often desperate pleas from would-be participants in the food craving trial flag a complex and deeply emotional weight journey, intertwined with life experiences and theories about weight issues:

> *My craving has been sugar for the past 4 years. I've put it down to hormones? My GP said, "Just say no"! I'll be 53 in 11 days and weigh 95 kg, 168 cm. Due to an accident, I have been unable to do a lot of exercise the last 2 years; yes, I'm using this and hormones as my excuse! Wrong. I hope tapping those areas taught in the right way would help me shed the 20 kilos I have put on the past 4 years. Please can I be in your study?—53-year-old female*
>
> *I saw with interest the results of your recent diet trial on Channel 9 this evening. I go to the gym 4 to 5 times a week, do weights,*
> *pump class, boxing, and kick boarding. I eat healthily and only drink occasionally. BUT and the big "but" is my sweet tooth—lollies, chocolate. My BMI is approx 28 and I am 7 to 8 kilos over my ideal weight. I am fit but fat.—Female*
>
> *Finally I have read your chapter. I am not too overweight as I am about 170 cm and weigh about 69 kg, but I have constantly been up and down in my weight all my life. I diet and then go back to eating. I absolutely love and live for food! I absolutely binge eat and lollies, chocolate, etc. I cannot stop once I start. I get very depressed when I have to give them up. Could I please come to your trial, as I would like to help you but also do something about this situation that I have battled all my life.—Female*
>
> *I am interested in taking part in the trial. My BMI is 44. I have been overweight most of my life and on two occasions, I have managed to lose 60 kilos and then put it back on both times. I am constantly craving food (especially sweets) and I hope your program can help me. Apart from my weight, I am in great health. I hope to hear from you soon.—Female*

## Practical Application of EFT for Food Cravings

The original Stapleton, Sheldon, Porter, and Whitty (2011) study is now available as a self-guided program available at www.foodcraving.com.au (Sheldon, Stapleton, & Porter, 2010). It originally offered 8 hours of therapist instructed session over a 4-week period and covered the topics of psycho-education about EFT, the nature of food cravings and how they can be addressed with EFT, feelings and food and how to treat with EFT, and relapse prevention (using EFT for stress and relaxation, and future goal setting). Participant feedback from this original clinical trial indicated a strong desire for more sessions and instruction, despite 12-month results indicating significant statistical change on all measures used (Stapleton et al., 2012a). Practical components of this original program are discussed in Stapleton, Sheldon, and Porter (2012b), but as a result of the feedback current research is examining the effectiveness of EFT against CBT across eight weekly sessions (16 hours). The topic areas being explored include: psycho-education about EFT and how it works, the nature of food cravings and how they are cognitively formed, feelings and food, cognitive restructuring with EFT, stress and relaxation training, goal setting with EFT, good nutrition, and relapse prevention.

## Example Setup Statements for Weight Issues—Stage 1 EFT

The remainder of this chapter is dedicated to practical Setup Statements and Reminder Phrases, which resulted from the clinical trials and may be used with clients as per the Basic Recipe. Please note that though EFT has been reported to be of clinical use with other eating disorders (e.g., anorexia nervosa), the focus here is on its application to weight issues relating to being overweight and obese. It could also be applied, however, to eating disorders such as bulimia nervosa and binge eating disorder.

**Theme or Issue.** A food (usually junk) is regularly/frequently craved by the subject with a history of rarely or never resisting its consumption once the craving arises.

**Examples of Setup Statements.** *Even though I love sugary foods (or insert own food craving here), I completely accept myself. Even though I crave something sweet (or whatever it is after meals), I completely accept myself.*

**Reminder/Shortened Phrase.** *This craving, my craving; Love sugar; I crave this food; I love this food, desperate to eat this yummy _____.*

**Common Negative Belief or Thought.** Afraid to let go of this problem; don't believe in myself.

**Examples of Setup Statements.** *Even though I'm **afraid to let go of this problem**, I deeply and completely accept myself; Even though I **don't believe** I can reach my goal, I deeply and completely accept myself anyway.*

**Reminder/Shortened Phrase.** Afraid to let go; Afraid to change; *Don't believe in myself; Can't reach my goal.*

## Feeling: Deprivation

**Examples of Setup Statements.** *Even though I feel deeply deprived, I deeply and completely accept myself anyway. Even though I can't eat like others, I deeply and completely accept this about myself. Even though when I restrict my intake, I feel deprived, I truly and sincerely accept myself.*

**Reminder/Shortened Phrase.** *Feel deeply deprived; Can't eat like others; Feel deprived; Feel restricted.*

## Feeling: Anxiety

**Examples of Setup Statements.** *Even though I can't stop feeling anxious/can't control my anxiety, I completely love and accept myself. Even though I am afraid and I won't know what to say and will make a fool of myself, I choose to accept myself anyway. Even though I'm afraid that I will lose control at _____, I completely love and accept myself anyway. Even though I know I tend to eat to relieve my feelings of anxiety or stress, I deeply and completely accept myself.*

**Reminder/Shortened Phrase.** *Feeling anxious; Can't stop being anxious; Can't control my anxiety; I'm afraid I might make a fool of myself; I might lose control; I'm afraid; This fear; This anxiety; Eat to relieve anxiety; Eat to relieve stress; Stressed.*

## Feeling: Loneliness

**Examples of Setup Statements.** *Even though I feel this deep loneliness, I completely love and accept myself. Even though I feel lonely and completely empty inside, I love and accept myself. Even though I use food as my reliable friend because I feel so lonely, I completely love and accept myself anyway. Even though food keeps me company and stops me being aware that I am alone and afraid, I completely love and accept myself.*

**Reminder/Shortened Phrase.** *I feel alone; Lonely and empty; Empty inside; Completely alone; Food has been my friend; Food keeps me company; Food stops my fear; I'm afraid to be alone; Food stops me being lonely; Food is reliable; This loneliness; Loneliness.*

## Situation: Exercise and Motivation Issues

**Examples of Setup Statements.** *Even though I loathe exercising, I deeply love and accept myself. Even though I feel fatigued and too tired to exercise, I choose to know that my energy levels will improve as I get fitter and I choose to be fit and healthy anyway. Even though exercise feels like punishment, I choose to know that it will help me and I completely love and accept myself anyway. Even though I have no motivation to exercise, I completely love and accept myself. Even though I'd rather eat than jog, I completely love and accept myself. Even though exercise frightens me because I expect to get hurt* or sore, I choose to know that it will help me and I completely love and accept myself anyway. Even though I don't want to get too sweaty/hate getting sweaty, I completely love and accept myself. Even though I'm afraid I'll look too muscly and big, I choose to know that it's in my imagination and I completely love and accept myself anyway. Even though I feel people think I look silly exercising, I choose to know that it's in my imagination and I completely love and accept myself anyway.

**Reminder/Shortened Phrase.** *Loathe exercise; Hate exercise; Feel too tired; Feel fatigued; Choose to be fitter; Choose to know I'll improve; It's too hard; Feels like punishment; No motivation; No energy; I feel too tired; Rather eat; Hate jogging; Don't want to; Exercise frightens me; It's scary; It might hurt; Hate getting sweaty; It feels yucky; Too sweaty; Exercise makes you big; Too muscly; Too big.*

## Situation: Given Food as Comfort as a Child—Family Issues

**Examples of Setup Statements.** *Even though my mother let me eat more biscuits/lollies/chocolate/junk food whenever I cried, I choose to love and accept myself. Even though my grandmother always overfed me to keep me quiet when I visited her, I choose to completely love and accept myself anyway. Even though my mother gave me ice cream to distract me from feeling sad and disappointed when my friends wouldn't let me play, I deeply and completely accept myself. Even though my dad started to buy me chips to make me feel better when I was disappointed about losing the football match, I deeply and completely accept myself. Even though I was fed to make me feel better when I was sick with _____, I deeply and completely accept myself.*

**Reminder/Shortened Phrase.** *(Whatever food) when I cried; Chocolate (whatever food) made me feel better; Grandma and food; Overfed to keep quiet; Eat and be quiet; Ice cream (whatever food) to avoid disappointment; Eat to avoid the feeling; Ice cream (whatever food) for comfort; Chips (whatever food) to handle disappointment; Chips (whatever food) for comfort; Chips (whatever food) and my dad; Food to feel better; Fed to combat sickness.*

## Situation: Don't Like Drinking Water

**Examples of Setup Statements.** *Even though I dislike the taste of water, I deeply and completely*

accept myself. Even though I don't like drinks that have no smell, I deeply and completely accept myself. Even though I'd prefer to drink (say the name of what you'd prefer to drink) than drink water, I deeply and completely accept myself. Even though I'm worried that drinking more water will mean going to the toilet too often, I deeply and completely accept myself. Even though drinking water is a nuisance to me, I deeply and completely accept myself. Even though drinking water doesn't excite me, I deeply and completely accept myself.

**Reminder/Shortened Phrase.** *Dislike the taste; Smells horrible; Hate the feeling in my stomach; I'd rather drink something else.*

## Feeling: Using Food to Change Mood

**Examples of Setup Statements.** *Even though I used food as entertainment and to stop myself feeling bored, I completely love and accept myself anyway. Even though I used food as security, I choose to accept myself anyway. Even though I overate to distract myself from _____, I completely love and accept myself anyway. Even though I overate to avoid _____, I completely love and accept myself anyway.*

**Reminder/Shortened Phrase.** *Food for entertainment; Food to stop boredom; Food for security; Food makes me safe; Food for distraction; Didn't want to feel anything; Food blocked the pain; Overate to avoid; This avoidance.*

## Situation: Benefits to Staying Overweight

**Examples of Setup Statements.** *Even though staying heavy/overweight/fat reduces the pressure on me so that people won't expect more, I deeply and completely accept myself. Even though staying overweight makes me feel invisible and safer, I choose to love and accept myself anyway.*

**Reminder/Shortened Phrase.** *Staying heavy; Less pressure; It's easier; Feel safer.*

## Situation: Negatives or Costs to Reaching a Natural (Ideal) Body Shape

**Examples of Setup Statements.** *Even though I need the distraction of overeating and hating myself, I choose to let this go and be slim anyway and completely love and accept myself.*

*Even though I'm afraid of disappointing myself/ my partner if I regain the weight/fat, I choose to accept myself anyway. Even though I'll have no excuses anymore to not _____, I completely love and accept myself anyway.*

**Reminder/Shortened Phrase.** *Need the distraction; Need to hate myself; Afraid I'll regain it; Afraid I'll find it again; Afraid I'll yoyo; Afraid I'll be back where I started; I'll be disappointed; _____ will be disappointed in me; No more excuses; I can't hide behind excuses anymore.*

## Situation: Other Negative Consequences to Reaching Goal Weight or Body Shape

**Examples of Setup Statements.** *Even though I can't afford new clothes, I choose to be slim anyway and completely love and accept myself. Even though I don't want to feel the pressure of keeping my new shape, I choose to be slim anyway and completely love and accept myself. Even though I won't be able to hide behind the extra fat anymore, I choose to completely love and accept myself anyway. Even though I resent having to maintain and be responsible for my control, I completely love and accept myself anyway.*

**Reminder/Shortened Phrase.** *Can't afford new clothes; Cost money; The pressure; It's too stressful; I'll feel trapped; Can't hide away anymore; I'll be noticed; No excuses; Scary; Resentment; Responsibility; No excuses.*

## Situation: A Lack of Belief in Achieving Weight Goals

Here is a formula for discovering any lack of belief in being successful:

1. Say out loud the body shape goal and fully associate (be in it) as if it has already been achieved. Feel it, smell it, notice what's happening around.
2. Now listen carefully to that negative inner voice, listen to any tail-enders or "yes buts"
3. If there is any "yes but," then rate the belief in the affirmation from 0 to 10 with 10 being absolute belief. If it is a low number, then the next step would be to tap with the statement *"Even though I don't believe I will succeed because of _____, I choose to let that go now and love and accept myself anyway."*

4. There may be numerous negative self-statements in relation to this affirmation or goal. Tapping on each negative feeling or statement until it no longer feels true, then rerating the belief in the Setup Statement will highlight any other discrepancies.

## Application of Positive EFT Phrases for Weight Issues—Stage 2 EFT

The use of positive affirmations during the EFT process has largely been pioneered by Patricia Carrington (2001) and is useful in a second-stage approach. While Stage 1 focuses on food issues, underlying emotional issues, and related aspects, Stage 2 focuses on empowerment and installing positive reminder phrases.

For example, if the problem is "fear of change," have the client rate the intensity of this issue on the subjective units of distress (SUD) scale. Wolpe (1969) introduced this self-assessment measure wherein the intensity of distress or disturbance being experienced by an individual is self-reported on a scale of 0 to 10, where 0 represents no disturbance, and 10 represents the worst distress or disturbance the individual can imagine experiencing. After ascertaining a client's SUD rating, construct the appropriate Setup Statement, such as "Even though I'm afraid of the changes I know are coming, I completely accept myself," and then tap with a Reminder Phrase such as "afraid of change." If other aspects (feelings or thoughts) arise while tapping, such as "resent having to change," construct a Setup Statement for resentment and tap with a Reminder Phrase. Once the SUD rating has decreased for the feeling and associated aspects have reduced to a 1 or 0, then follow with tapping on the same points with positive Reminder Phrases. These may include: I do want to change; They can handle it; I could be safe embracing this change; I love realizing my potential; I deserve _____; I appreciate all the abundance I have already; I appreciate who I am; I feel free to release this conflict once and for all.

In addition to positive phrases, individuals can include a choice or an "I Choose" statement such as *"Even though a part of me is afraid to change, I deeply and completely accept all of me and I **choose** to succeed anyway."* The Choices Method (Carrington, 2001) can assist individuals in consolidating and making permanent the beneficial changes brought about by EFT and help the changes generalize to many aspects of their lives.

Examples of positive or "I Choose" Setup Statements include:

*Even though I don't enjoy drinking water, I deeply and completely accept myself and I choose to give my body all the precious water it needs.*

*Even though I don't feel thirsty until I have a headache, I deeply and completely accept myself and I choose to drink water often/10 times a day even when I'm not thirsty.*

*Even though I don't like the idea of drinking tap water, I deeply and completely accept myself and I choose to find a way to give my body the best quality water I can.*

*Even though I have all these feelings about food, my eating behaviors, and my body, I completely accept myself and choose to be slim, in control, happy, and healthy.*

*Even though I have these issues in my past that are affecting my behavior about food and how I feel about myself now, I choose to let them go and be slim, in control, happy, and healthy.*

*Even though I have some doubts about my success, I choose to believe in myself, be in control, slim, happy, and healthy.*

## Working with Aspects in Food and Weight Issues

In EFT, aspects describe the different layers or facets of an identified problem, or coexisting feelings or thoughts about the same problem. For example, if someone suffers from a phobia related to air travel, separate aspects might be fear of crashing, dread of confined spaces, in-flight nausea with a fear of vomiting, and panic about descent and landing. Generally, for EFT to be effective, it is expected to differentiate between, and then address, all the different aspects of the presenting problem. Sometimes a client may report that the treatment "didn't work," whereas, in fact, upon closer questioning, the recurring distress is found to be due to the emergence of a new aspect. In relation to food and weight issues, particular issues or events that seem resistant to resolving could indicate the presence of other aspects that are yet to be remedied. Common examples include memories related to food (positive or negative) as a child; first experiences with food soothing a distressed feeling; and family patterns and beliefs around weight, food, and social acceptance. One EFT technique that is useful in identifying and addressing aspects is the Movie Technique. This uses the client's visualization of the event or situation as if watching a film on a movie screen (i.e., the client imagines sitting in the audience watching the event) and stopping the movie whenever an aspect arises in the form of a significant emotion, sensation, negative thought, or memory. EFT is applied to each aspect as it arises until the "movie" seems to come to a natural conclusion; that is, there seems to no more of the story to be told. The Movie Technique assists the client and practitioner in evaluating whether all the aspects have been discovered and treated.

## Client Feedback and Length of Treatment

While an outstanding advantage of using EFT is its brevity and precision in achieving change very quickly, the standout difference between the original 4-week and 8-week food craving program (Stapleton et al., 2012a) was the changes the more elderly participants received later in the program. It was often not until session seven or eight that "light bulb" moments occurred or emotional release was achieved. This may well be vital to remember when working with individuals who have had many years of ingrained behavior patterns, and require more time to learn and accept the power of techniques such as EFT.

## Conclusion

EFT is essentially a technique of awareness and insight without judgment. It can be a private and safe discovery process that highlights the personal truths about one's own discomforts or about the changes an individual wants to achieve in life. EFT can be used on many issues related to weight—emotional or physical, specific or general, past present or future—and its application to the worldwide phenomenon of obesity and long-term weight loss and subsequent longevity in life is profound.

*Acknowledgments: Terri Sheldon and Brett Porter for their combined superhuman efforts in being part of the clinical trial research, and reviewers of this chapter. They know how special they are to me. The Association of Comprehensive Energy Psychology for making seed funding available to pioneer clinical research in the area of food cravings and EFT.*

# References

Bandura, A. (1986). The explanatory and predictive scope of self-efficacy theory. *Journal of Social and Clinical Psychology, 4*(3), 359–373.

Bray, G. A. & DeLany, J. (2012). Opinions of obesity experts on the causes and treatment of obesity: A new survey. *Obesity Research, 3*(S4), 419S–423S.

Butryn, M. L., Phelan, S., Hill, J. O., & Wing, R. R. (2007). Consistent self-monitoring of weight: A key component of successful weight loss maintenance. *Obesity, 15*(12), 3091–3096.

Carrington, P. (2001). The power of using affirmations with energy therapy. In W. Lammers and B. Kircher (Eds.), *The energy odyssey: New directions in energy psychology* (pp. 179–188). Eastbourne, UK: DragonRising.

Cereda, E., Malavazos, A. E., Caccialanza, R., Rondanelli, M., Fatati, G., & Barichella, M. (2011). Weight cycling is associated with body weight excess and abdominal fat accumulation: A cross-sectional study. *Clinical Nutrition, 30*(6), 718–723.

Chan, J. M., Rimm, E. B., Colditz, G. A., Stampfer, M. J., & Willett, W. C. (1994). Obesity, fat distribution, and weight gain as risk factors for clinical diabetes in men. *Diabetes Care, 17*(9), 961–969.

Clinical guidelines on the identification, evaluation, and treatment of overweight and obesity in adults—The evidence report. (1998). *Obes Res, 6*(Suppl 2), 51S–209S.

Colditz, G. A., Willett, W. C., Rotnitzky, A., & Manson, J. A. E. (1995). Weight gain as a risk factor for clinical diabetes mellitus in women. *Annals of Internal Medicine, 122*(7), 481.

Craig, G. (2011). *The EFT manual.* Fulton, CA: Energy Psychology Press.

Deckelbaum, R. J. & Williams, C. L. (2001). Childhood obesity: The health issue. *Obesity Research, 9*(S11), 239S–243S. doi:10.1038/oby.2001.125

Delahanty, L. M., Meigs, J. B., Hayden, D., Williamson, D. A., & Nathan, D. M. (2002). Psychological and behavioral correlates of baseline BMI in the diabetes prevention program (DPP). *Diabetes Care, 25*(11), 1992–1998.

Dhond, R. P., Kettner, N., & Napadow, V. (2007). Neuroimaging acupuncture effects in the human brain. *Journal of Alternative and Complementary Medicine, 13*(6), 603–616.

Diepold Jr., J. H. & Goldstein, D. M. (2009). Thought Field Therapy and qEEG changes in the treatment of trauma: A case study. *Traumatology, 15*(1), 85–93.

Drewnowski, A., Kurth, C., Holden-Wiltse, J., & Saari, J. (1992). Food preferences in human obesity: Carbohydrates versus fats. *Appetite, 18*(3), 207–221.

Feinstein, D. (2008). Energy psychology: A review of the preliminary evidence. *Psychotherapy: Theory, Research, Practice, Training, 45*(2), 199.

Feinstein, D. (2010). Rapid treatment of PTSD: Why psychological exposure with acupoint tapping may be effective. *Psychotherapy: Theory, Research, Practice, Training, 47*(3), 385.

Foster, G. D., Sarwer, D. B., & Wadden, T. A. (2012). Psychological effects of weight cycling in obese persons: A review and research agenda. *Obesity Research, 5*(5), 474–488.

Foster, G. D., Wadden, T. A., Makris, A. P., Davidson, D., Sanderson, R. S., Allison, D. B., & Kessler, A. (2012). Primary care physicians' attitudes about obesity and its treatment. *Obesity Research, 11*(10), 1168–1177.

Franken, I. H. A. & Muris, P. (2005). Individual differences in reward sensitivity are related to food craving and relative body weight in healthy women. *Appetite, 45*(2), 198–201.

Fujioka, K. (2012). Management of obesity as a chronic disease: Nonpharmacologic, pharmacologic, and surgical options. *Obesity Research, 10*(S2), 116S–123S.

Goldstein, D. J. (1992). Beneficial health effects of modest weight loss. *International Journal of Obesity and Related Metabolic Disorders: Journal of the International Association for the Study of Obesity, 16*(6), 397.

Grant, P. G., Buckroyd, J., & Rother, S. (2008). Food for the soul: Social and emotional origins of comfort eating in the morbidly obese. In J. Buckroyd & S. Rother (Eds.), *Psychological responses to eating disorders and obesity: Recent and innovative work* (pp. 1121–1137). Hoboken, NJ: John Wiley & Sons.

Hare, S. W., Price, J. H., Flynn, M. G., & King, K. A. (2000). Attitudes and perceptions of fitness professionals regarding obesity. *Journal of Community Health, 25*(1), 5–21.

Harvey, E., Summerbell, C., Kirk, S., & Hill, A. (2002). Dietitians' views of overweight and obese people and reported management practices. *Journal of Human Nutrition and Dietetics, 15*(5), 331–347.

Hill, A. J., & Heaton-Brown, L. (1994). The experience of food craving: A prospective investigation in healthy women. *Journal of Psychosomatic Research, 38*(8), 801–814.

Hill, J. O., Wyatt, H., Phelan, S., & Wing, R. (2005). The National Weight Control Registry: Is it useful in helping deal with our obesity epidemic? *Journal of Nutrition Education and Behavior, 37*(4), 206–210.

Huang, Z., Willett, W. C., Manson, J., Rosner, B., Stampfer, M. J., Speizer, F. E., & Colditz, G. A. (1998). Body weight, weight change, and risk for hypertension in women. *Annals of Internal Medicine, 128*(2), 81.

James, P. T., Leach, R., Kalamara, E., & Shayeghi, M. (2012). The worldwide obesity epidemic. *Obesity Research, 9*(S4), 228S–233S.

Kaufman, F. R. (2011). Type 2 diabetes mellitus in children and youth: A new epidemic. *Journal of Pediatric Endocrinology and Metabolism, 15*(Supplement), 737–744.

Kirk, S., Zeller, M., Claytor, R., Santangelo, M., Khoury, P. R., & Daniels, S. R. (2005). The relationship of health outcomes to improvement in BMI in children and adolescents. *Obesity Research, 13*(5), 876–882. doi:10.1038/oby.2005.101

Klem, M. L., Wing, R. R., McGuire, M. T., Seagle, H. M., & Hill, J. O. (1997). A descriptive study of individuals successful at long-term maintenance of substantial weight loss. *The American Journal of Clinical Nutrition, 66*(2), 239–246.

Lee, S. H. & Calamaro, C. (2012). Nursing bias and the obese patient: The role of the clinical nurse leader in improving care of the obese patient. *Bariatric Nursing and Surgical Patient Care, 7*(3), 127–131.

Li, C., Goran, M. I., Kaur, H., Nollen, N., & Ahluwalia, J. S. (2012). Developmental trajectories of overweight during childhood: Role of early life factors. *Obesity, 15*(3), 760–771.

Look, C. (2001). *How to lose weight with energy therapy: A training manual.* New York, NY: Author.

Lyon, H. N. & Hirschhorn, J. N. (2005). Genetics of common forms of obesity: A brief overview. *American Journal of Clinical Nutrition, 82*(1), 215S–217S.

Magliocca, K. R., Jabero, M. F., Alto, D. L., & Magliocca, J. F. (2005). Knowledge, beliefs, and attitudes of dental and dental hygiene students toward obesity. *Journal of Dental Education, 69*(12), 1332–1339.

Mallory, G. B., Fiser, D. H., & Jackson, R. (1989). Sleep-associated breathing disorders in morbidly obese children and adolescents. *Journal of Pediatrics, 115*(6), 892–897.

Mann, T., Tomiyama, A. J., Westling, E., Lew, A. M., Samuels, B., & Chatman, J. (2007). Medicare's search for effective obesity treatments: Diets are not the answer. *American Psychologist, 62*(3), 220.

McGuire, M. T., Wing, R. R., Klem, M. L., & Hill, J. O. (1999). Behavioral strategies of individuals who have maintained long-term weight losses. *Obesity Research, 7*(4), 334–341.

Meyers, L. (2007). Serenity now: East meets West as psychologists embrace ancient traditions to enhance modern practice. *Monitor on Psychology, 38*(11), 32–34.

Morrison, J. A., Sprecher, D. L., Barton, B. A., Waclawiw, M. A., & Daniels, S. R. (1999). Overweight, fat patterning, and cardiovascular disease risk factors in black and white girls: The National Heart, Lung, and Blood Institute Growth and Health Study. *Journal of Pediatrics, 135*(4), 458–464.

NHMRC (National Health and Medical Research Council). (2012). *Clinical practice guidelines for the management of overweight and obesity in adults, children and adolescents.* Canberra, Australia: Department of Health and Ageing. Retrieved from http://consultations.nhmrc.gov.au/public_consultations/obesity-guidelines

Perri, M. & Fuller, P. (1995). Success and failure in the treatment of obesity: Where do we go from here? *Medicine, Exercise, Nutrition, and Health, 4,* 255–272.

Perri, M. G., Nezu, A. M., Patti, E. T., & McCann, K. L. (1989). Effect of length of treatment on weight loss. *Journal of Consulting and Clinical Psychology, 57*(3), 450.

Prochaska, J. O., DiClemente, C. C., & Norcross, J. C. (1992). In search of how people change: Applications to addictive behaviors. *American Psychologist, 47*(9), 1102.

Prochaska, J. O., Norcross, J. C., Fowler, J. L., Follick, M. J., & Abrams, D. B. (1992). Attendance and outcome in a work site weight control program: Processes and stages of change as process and predictor variables. *Addictive Behaviors, 17*(1), 35–45.

Puhl, R., Wharton, C., & Heuer, C. (2009). Weight bias among dietetics students: Implications for treatment practices. *Journal of the American Dietetic Association, 109*(3), 438–444.

Puhl, R. M. & Heuer, C. A. (2012). The stigma of obesity: A review and update. *Obesity, 17*(5), 941–964.

Raynor, H. A., Jeffery, R. W., Phelan, S., Hill, J. O., & Wing, R. R. (2012). Amount of food group variety consumed in the diet and long-term weight loss maintenance. *Obesity Research, 13*(5), 883–890.

Sechrist, G. B., Stangor, C., Brownell, K., Puhl, R., Schwartz, M., & Rudd, L. (2005). Social consensus and the origins of stigma. In K. Brownell (Ed.), *Weight bias: Nature, consequences, and remedies* (pp. 97–108). New York, NY: Guilford Press.

Serdar, K. L., Mazzeo, S. E., Mitchell, K. S., Aggen, S. H., Kendler, K. S., & Bulik, C. M. (2011). Correlates of weight instability across the lifespan in a population-based sample. *International Journal of Eating Disorders, 44*(6), 506–514.

Shaw, K., O'Rourke, P., Del Mar, C., & Kenardy, J. (2005). Psychological interventions for overweight or obesity. *Cochrane Database of Systematic Reviews,* Issue 2, Art. no. CD003818. doi:10.1002/14651858.CD003818.pub2

Sheldon, T., Stapleton, P., & Porter, B. (2010). *The food craving and tapping program* (pp. 1–201). Queensland, Australia: Slim Minds Proprietary.

Shick, S. M. Wing, R. R., Klem, M. L., McGuire, M. T., Hill, J. O., & Seagle, H. (1998). Persons successful at long-term weight loss and maintenance continue to consume a low-energy, low-fat diet. *Journal of the American Dietetic Association, 98*(4), 408.

Sorof, J. & Daniels, S. (2002). Obesity hypertension in children a problem of epidemic proportions. *Hypertension, 40*(4), 441–447.

Stapleton, P., Sheldon, T., & Porter, B. (2012a). Clinical benefits of Emotional Freedom Techniques on food cravings at 12-months follow-up: A randomised controlled trial. *Energy Psychology: Theory, Research, & Treatment, 4*(1), 1–11.

Stapleton, P., Sheldon, T., & Porter, B. (2012b). Practical application of Emotional Freedom Techniques for food cravings. *International Journal of Healing and Caring, 12*(3), 1–9.

Stapleton, P., Sheldon, T., Porter, B., & Whitty, J. (2011). A randomised clinical trial of a meridian-based intervention for food cravings with six-month follow-up. *Behaviour Change, 28*(1), 1.

Teachman, B. A., Mallett, R. K., Brownell, K., Puhl, R., Schwartz, M., & Rudd, L. (2005). Measurement of bias. In K. Brownell (Ed.), *Weight bias: Nature, consequences, and remedies* (pp. 121–133). New York, NY: Guilford Press.

Trogdon, J. G., Finkelstein, E. A., Hylands, T., Dellea, P. S., & Kamal-Bahl, S. J. (2008). Indirect costs of obesity: A review of the current literature. *Obesity Reviews, 9*(5), 489–500. doi:10.1111/j.1467-789X.2008.00472.x

Wang, Y., & Wang, J. Q. (2000). Standard definition of child overweight and obesity worldwide: Authors' standard compares well with WHO standard. *British Medical Journal, 321*(7269), 1158.

Wilding, J. (2012). Are the causes of obesity primarily environmental? Yes. *British Medical Journal, 345.* doi:10.1136/bmj.e5843

Wing, R. R. & Hill, J. O. (2001). Successful weight loss maintenance. *Annual Review of Nutrition, 21*(1), 323–341.

Withrow, D. & Alter, D. (2010). The economic burden of obesity worldwide: A systematic review of the direct costs of obesity. *Obesity Reviews, 12*(2), 131–141.

Wolpe, J. (1969). *The practice of behaviour therapy.* New York, NY: Pergamon.

World Health Organization. (2000). Obesity: Preventing and managing the global epidemic. Report of a WHO consultation. *World Health Organization Technical Report Series, 894,* i–xii, 1–253.

Wyatt, H. R., Grunwald, G. K., Mosca, C. L., Klem, M. L., Wing, R. R., & Hill, J. O. (2002). Long-term weight loss and breakfast in subjects in the National Weight Control Registry. *Obesity, 10*(2), 78–82.

Young-Hyman, D., Tanofsky-Kraff, M., Yanovski, S. Z., Keil, M., Cohen, M. L., Peyrot, M., & Yanovski, J. A. (2012). Psychological status and weight-related distress in overweight or at-risk-for-overweight children. *Obesity, 14*(12), 2249–2258.

Chapter 45
# EFT for Procrastination: Six Steps to Success
*Gloria Arenson*

**Abstract**

Millions of people are procrastinators. The habit of putting things off is a signal from the unconscious mind that the individual is avoiding facing something. Unless procrastinators uncover the root cause of the problem, they will continue to suffer unpleasant negative consequences. Despite the many books and articles written about overcoming this behavior, why is it that the majority of procrastinators still procrastinate? Chronic procrastination is not a sign of laziness, poor organization, or lack of willpower. Procrastination is a compulsion. This chapter details the application of EFT to Arenson's Six Steps to Success. This process enables procrastinators to understand and successfully overcome this frustrating problem.

**Keywords:** procrastination, EFT, compulsion, belief, cognition

**Gloria Arenson, MFT, DCEP**, past president of ACEP, specializes in EFT for compulsive behaviors and is author of *Five Simple Steps to Emotional Healing, How to Stop Playing the Weighting Game, Born to Spend, Desserts Is Stressed Spelled Backwards, EFT for Procrastination,* and *Grownup Love: Getting It and Keeping It.* Send correspondence to Gloria Arenson, 1429 Las Positas Place, Santa Barbara, CA 93105, or glotao@cox.net.

Procrastinators are people who either put things off or don't finish what they start. They come in all sizes and shapes, young and old, all colors, denominations, from all walks of life and many cultures. We tend to think that it is just a weakness or a bad habit and make jokes about it. But procrastinators are not stupid, weak, or bad. Procrastination is also not a disease and it cannot be cured with any medication. Many millions of people are procrastinators.

The habit of putting things off is a signal from the unconscious mind, a reminder that the individual is avoiding facing something. Unless procrastinators uncover the root cause of the problem, they will continue to suffer the negative consequences. Friendships can erode when a procrastinator consistently comes late to social events, doesn't return calls in a timely manner, and seems to let friends down. Procrastination at work may lead to loss of a job when the person doesn't complete projects on time, is late for appointments or meetings, and is a poor team member. People who don't pay bills on time incur punitive late fees. The painful consequence for one college student who didn't hand an important paper in on time was to pay a great deal of money to repeat the semester.

Hundreds of books and articles have been published that advise procrastinators how to control their time better, use "willpower," and find ways to reorganize their life in order to overcome this widespread problem. Despite all this information, why is it that the majority of procrastinators still procrastinate? Chronic procrastination is not a sign of laziness, poor organization, or lack of willpower. Procrastination is a compulsion.

My definition of compulsion is: *If you cannot control when you start or when you stop a substance or behavior, you have a compulsion.* In other words, procrastinators can't stop stopping themselves! Scientific research maintains that compulsion is a state in which self-induced changes in neurotransmission result in problem behaviors (Ruden, 2000). That means that your behavior affects your brain, which then affects your behavior. This happens over and over and turns into what looks like a bad habit.

Procrastination as a compulsion is a dysfunctional way of going through life that many people cannot control. It is a compulsion to *not do*. Putting things off may also be a solution to other problems. Once I recognized that dynamic, I decided to apply the same approach with procrastinators

that I use with other compulsive clients. The unstoppable urge to overeat compulsively, spend compulsively, or engage in other activities without being able to control them is usually triggered by a kind of stress that results from feeling powerless and angry because of a situation or relationship that you can't change. I call this "Super Stress."

All compulsive people, including procrastinators, are looking for a way out of the discomfort of Super Stress. Addicts use pleasure to medicate their pain; procrastinators use avoidance. Avoidance takes many forms. Procrastinators may also turn to overeating, spending, drinking, and so on as a distraction to keep them away from the project they are reluctant to approach. It is also easy to get lost in a book, hobby, TV show, the Internet, DVDs, CDs, podcasts, or phone calls rather than buckle down to the job. Some of my clients have even escaped into sleep!

## Six Steps to Success

After working with procrastinators for over 30 years, I have created a simple six-step guide that will help any procrastinator stop holding him or herself back from beginning or completing goals. Here are the steps. I will explain each one in greater detail in the following pages and also add instructions in using EFT to heal and release the negative experiences and beliefs that keep procrastinators slaves to this self-defeating habit.

1. Set a goal. Name the task, job, or project you want to finish. Check that it is specific, reasonable, attainable, and that this the right time to attempt it.
2. List excuses. Say or write down all the excuses you can think of that you are tempted to use to stop yourself from starting, going on with, or completing this endeavor. Next, cross them out since they are merely a smoke screen that keeps you from taking action.
3. Look for the hidden fear. Use the Worst-Case Scenario method. Quiz yourself and keep pushing to discover what your fear thoughts are.
4. Look for the Negative False Belief. Some common fear thoughts are: "Failure is unacceptable," "People will dislike me if I don't do it right," "Success is dangerous," "I'm afraid of what the future holds," and

"I shouldn't have to do what you want me to do."

5. Ask yourself: What happened to me that made me decide that this Negative False Belief was the truth?
6. What self-fulfilling prophecies have I been living out as a result?

## Negative False Beliefs Lead to Avoidance

When I teach classes about using EFT to overcome procrastination, I write this sentence on the board: *Procrastination is your way of avoiding your fantasy of reality*. What I hope my students will come to realize is that this negative behavior is a symbol that something isn't going well in their life. Putting things off or not finishing is the behavior that many adopt to avoid uncomfortable feelings of pain, guilt, shame, anxiety, or fear.

There are five common Negative False Beliefs that plague procrastinators; however, not all procrastinators dread all five. Each procrastinator's fear results from an unconscious belief that is untrue. These are the main Negative False Beliefs that create the fears that keep most procrastinators from moving forward:

- Failure is unacceptable. I must excel and be perfect.
- People will dislike, ridicule, exclude, or harm me if I don't do it right.
- Success is dangerous. People will harm me if I am better than they are.
- I'm afraid of what the future holds.
- I don't have to do what you (parent, teacher, authority) want me to do!

## The Worst-Case Scenario

Playing the Worst-Case Scenario Game is a quick way to find out which of the Negative False Beliefs are causing you to procrastinate over and over again. Begin by thinking of something specific you are putting off beginning or completing.

Ask yourself, "What is the *worst thing* that will happen if I clean out my garage, pay my taxes, go for my mammogram, send Christmas cards in time for the holiday, sign up for school, wash my car, etc?" Write or say aloud the first thing that comes to mind. Don't judge yourself on your answer.

Ask again, "If that happens, then what am I *afraid* will happen next?" Make sure you use the word "afraid" because that is what this is all about. Keep this up until you have run out of the easy answers like "I'll be happy" or "I'll be healthy." Eventually, you'll hit pay dirt. The answer that springs to mind may have nothing to do with the project you are dawdling over. That is the point. Once you find out which Negative False Belief is to blame, use EFT to reassess it and install a new and reasonable alternative. Here is an example.

Kathy's husband was nagging her to clean out the garage because he couldn't park his car in it. She kept putting it off until they had a big fight. Here is what she discovered.

Q: What am I *afraid* will happen if I clean up the garage?
A: The garage will look nice and my husband will be able to park his car and stop nagging me.
Q: Then what am I *afraid* will happen when the garage is clean?
A: Nothing. I will feel good and be able to put things away and get organized.
Q: Then what am I *afraid* will happen when I put things away?
A: I will have to give away the toys my daughter has outgrown.
Q: Then what am I afraid will happen when I give the toys away?
A: It means that she is growing up and will soon graduate from school and leave home.
Q: Then what am I afraid will happen?
A: I will feel so sad when she is gone. I don't want to feel that loneliness.

## EFT Speeds Results

Once Kathy realized that what she was avoiding was not the garage mess but the fear of what it would be like when her daughter grew up and moved on with her life, she used EFT to deal with the sadness. She tapped about her fantasy of how lonely she would be and how she was scared about the future and continued tapping until she felt acceptance and love instead. She realized that, no matter where her daughter might be in the future, they could still have a close and loving relationship.

Doris was flabbergasted when she discovered that her messy desk was really a metaphor for an unhappy life and a fear of a terrible future. Doris was so fed up with her cluttered desk that she finally sought my help. No matter how many times she promised herself that she would organize her work space, she put lots of other things first. "It's not a big desk. I should be able to finish the job in a few hours," she explained. I proceeded to play the Worst-Case Scenario Game with Doris in order to find her underlying Negative False Belief.

Q: What is the worst thing that will happen if you clean up your desk?
A: I'll feel better.
Q: Then what are you afraid will happen?
A: It will look better.
Q: And then what?
A: I'll have time to clean out the bookcase.

I pushed and pushed, asking her to imagine the very worst after each of her comebacks, until the light dawned. "If I clean up my desk I'll have to clean up my life, and I'll have to divorce my husband," she explained. No wonder she wasn't able to get her desk in order. Since her Negative False Belief had to do with fear of the future, she was putting off exploring an issue that was too upsetting for her conscious mind to contemplate.

One of the reasons I don't discuss time management techniques or how to organize personal belongings with my clients is for exactly this reason. Doris's problem was not her desk. It was her marriage. Using the Worst-Case Scenario approach helped Doris free herself to organize her desk after she used EFT to address her feelings about her marriage. Here are some of the Setup Statements she used:

- *Even though a part of me is unwilling to look at the state of my marriage, I am exploring that now.*
- *Even though, I am not happy with my marriage and am avoiding looking into that by distracting myself with my messy desk, I am doing the best I can.*
- *Even though I know there are problems in my marriage, I am willing to tap about them now.*

A client named Rita was frustrated over her closet. Rita said, "My closet is a mess. I should organize it. I have too many clothes that I'm not even wearing anymore. There's no more room for anything new, and I keep putting off cleaning it out. I am so disgusted with myself for being lazy."

When procrastinators tell me that they are lazy, I know immediately that the Negative False Belief has to do with the authority figures in their early lives. Lazy is what the grownups call you when you don't do what *they* want you to do! Rita was not aware of this, but she discovered that the part of her that wasn't organizing the closet was a much younger Rita whose mother was the cause.

In this case I suggested that she use EFT, saying: *"Even though I am resisting organizing my closet, although I really want to complete it, I am exploring that now."*

Here is what she learned after each round of tapping:

- I am resisting.
- I feel annoyed with my husband because he always searches through the bag with the things I am going to give away.
- Feeling annoyed toward him, very annoyed!
- Why is he prying?
- I feel violated when he does this.

She continued to tap five more rounds, focusing on the feeling of being violated. Here is what she discovered:

- There was no privacy in my family when I was growing up.
- My mother read my diary when I was 10 and made fun of me.
- I was embarrassed that she read my private thoughts.
- How dare she!

Rita kept tapping about that memory of when her mother and then later her husband invaded her boundaries until all her anger and embarrassment were neutralized. This took only a few minutes. Next, I asked her to test the effectiveness of EFT by remembering what happened and trying to feel angry and upset. She rated her emotions as 0, neutral. The following weekend she cleaned out her closet without any problem.

Beverly figured out that her fear of being a success in business stemmed from the False Belief "Success is dangerous." She was procrastinating about finding an office for her new business. When she pondered the worst-case scenario if she opened her own office, she immediately said, "If I am too successful, no man will want to marry me and take care of me."

As she tapped, she told me that each time she went office hunting and imagined her name on the door, she heard her mother's voice inside her head, whispering, "If you are too independent, what man will want to marry you and take care of you?" Her mother's generation was mostly homemakers who thought their mission in life was to look good and make a lovely home for their husbands. What if her mother was right? Would she jeopardize her chances if she competed successfully with men? After a few more rounds of EFT, she knew without a doubt that she could be as successful as she wanted to be and still be lovable. She soon found the perfect office.

When Zack tried the Worst-Case Scenario Game about not handing in a report on time at work, he discovered that he was afraid that his boss might not think it was good enough. He asked himself, "What am I afraid will happen if it isn't good enough?" The answer was "My coworkers will laugh at me because it isn't perfect and I might not get promoted." At that moment Zack realized that he operated under the Negative False Belief that there were only two options: perfect and failure. Therefore the report had to be perfect or he couldn't risk handing it in.

The perfectionistic procrastinator must avoid the negative outcome he imagines if he fails. This belief usually leads to the creation of standards that are impossible to live up to such as: "I must be perfect or I will be rejected," "If I make a mistake, I will be humiliated," "If I can't do something really well, there is little point in doing it," or "If I make a mistake, I am worthless."

Zack used EFT, saying: "Even though I am holding back because I am afraid I will fail, I am now releasing all the times and all the ways I have harmed myself because I believed that failure was unacceptable." With each round of tapping, his anxiety decreased. As the fear of failure disappeared, he came up with a solution. He decided to ask a trusted friend to look over his work in the future and give him feedback when he doubted himself.

## Origins of Negative False Beliefs

Once procrastinators learn how to recognize the Negative False Beliefs that are encouraging them to avoid completion of tasks and goals, the next step is to find out the source of those beliefs. It is important to understand how the brain works in order to get to the heart of procrastination. Just pinpointing the thought that is creating the fear will not lead to permanent change.

Recent studies have shown that feelings come before thoughts. Dr. Daniel J. Siegel, well-known neuroscientist and author, claims that emotions exist at a stage prior to language. These emotions drive the brain toward deciding on an appropriate reaction to a particular situation. Only then do the thoughts start. Therefore, in order to transform negative thoughts, it is necessary to go back to the time of the initial emotional reaction—the time when that damaging belief emerged (Siegel, 1999).

The part of the brain involved in these emotional reactions is called the limbic system, which maintains and guides the emotions and behaviors necessary for self-preservation and survival of the species. Procrastinators need to know two vital facts about this part of the brain:

- There are no words in the limbic system; there are only emotions.
- There is no time in the limbic system; the past and the present exist simultaneously.

Within the limbic system are two structures: the hippocampus and the amygdala. The hippocampus is the repository of our memories from the time we were about 2 years old onward. The amygdala, the region of the brain responsible for processing emotional memories, is like a smoke alarm. It works around the clock sensing danger in the environment. If there is danger, the amygdala signals the rest of the brain, which creates a survival reaction. When the danger seems extremely threatening, it signals an alert that sends the body into an immediate survival reaction of fight, flight, or freeze. There is no time to think! The thinking part of the brain goes offline.

When the danger has passed, the thinking part of the brain comes back online and tries to make sense of what happened. Therefore we rationalize, after the fact, to explain it to ourselves. After a frightening episode some people decide, "I'm not good enough," while others resolve, "I survived. I am a lucky person." Some think, "I am a failure" or "I don't deserve love." These decisions, often made in childhood, are stored in the brain, stay with us, and mold our adult behavior. They often lead to putting things off, not even beginning them, or failing to complete them.

## The Power of the Past

Lily was barely making ends meet financially but procrastinated about looking for a higher paying job.

She was working at a very boring, low-paying job despite her education and ability yet kept finding excuses for not going back to school to hone her skills so she could find something better. When Lily used EFT to explore her procrastination, she was surprised to find that she was still living out a decision she made as a child that *if she didn't do things right, people would embarrass or criticize her.*

Apparently, she had been traumatized in kindergarten when her teacher called her stupid and embarrassed her in front of the entire class. When that happened, Lily froze. She couldn't say anything because she was so mortified. As a result, she decided that the teacher was right and she was stupid. She vowed that she would never let that happen again. She had to stay away from groups and from critical authority figures.

Lily felt safe in her present job even if it was a dead end because she told herself that if she got a new job she might have a mean boss who would tell her she was incompetent and embarrass her in front of coworkers. Each time she planned to go job hunting, she turned into that helpless 5-year-old and found excuses to stay put.

When Joel was a child, his physically abusive mother often warned him, "People won't like you if you stand out!" Although Joel was an expert in computers and wanted to share with others, he kept putting it off. Finally, he decided to face his fear and volunteered to give a class at the community center. He reported that when he stood up in front of the small group, his voice suddenly gave out. "I could feel my mother's hands around my throat, choking me," he said. "I remembered her words."

Joel's body reexperienced his mother's cruelty as though it were happening again. As a result of her threats, Joel's childhood decision was that "Success is dangerous." He learned to avoid putting himself in any situation where he might stand out. When Joel tapped on that specific memory, it led him to remember many other times he was the victim of his mother's angry outbursts.

Using EFT to heal other memories of her physical and emotional abuse of him, Joel felt sad about how she caused him to avoid calling attention to himself in other areas of his life. He tapped about his sadness in not being assertive with his wife and his coworkers. He also tapped about his anger with himself for not being more ambitious since he was very good at his job but rarely called attention to his potential. EFT helped released his

negative emotional blocks and he realized that he was still living his life as dictated by a ghost, and he finally freed himself of her curses.

## Two Kinds of Memory

There are two kinds of memories stored in the brain and body: explicit and implicit. Explicit memories are autobiographical. You can remember yourself being there. They are like movies in your head or pictures in a photo album. We all can remember both happy and unhappy events we participated in like birthday parties, going to the circus, or falling off our bike. Lily's procrastination about moving forward in her career resulted from a terrible event she remembered clearly.

Our unconscious mind makes most of our everyday decisions, and that information is stored as what is termed implicit or body memories. It is astounding to realize how much of what we do is determined by mysterious memories and the emotional forces associated with those memories.

Implicit memories are recollections of what the body experiences during trauma. They are hardwired in the brain. These memories are acquired in a flash and stored for our lifetime unless we recognize and clear them. When the amygdala signals that we are in danger, these unconscious memories are unleashed instantly as a survival mechanism in the face of perceived danger. Then we reexperience the scary past, and it is as though it were happening again in the present.

That is what happened to Joel. Standing in front of a group made him nervous. His throat tightened, and that sensation triggered the body memory. He not only felt his mother's hands around his throat, he also remembered her words. In some cases implicit memories go back to birth and can influence our present behavior even if we are totally unaware of them. Body memories are often to blame at times when we can't account for our actions by thinking back to something that happened to us, no matter how hard we try. Each time a procrastinator like Joel is triggered, he unwittingly turns into the child he was when his mother abused him. That causes the adult Joel to stop himself from taking positive action.

## Self-fulfilling Prophecies

So far I have described people who were chronically procrastinating in their personal, school, or work life and explained how, after they identified the Negative False Belief that triggered their troublesome behavior, they were able to uncover the original unpleasant or threatening experience from which it arose, an experience that occurred earlier in their life. As noted previously, after such a scary event, the brain tries to make sense of the experience and creates a rationalization that is interpreted as fact.

Although we may believe that we are free to control our lives and steer them in any direction we want, the direction we follow is determined by the decisions we have made as our lives have unfolded. With each experience, whether positive or negative, the brain has stored opinions about who we are and the meaning of our life. As a result, our choices are dependent on these thoughts. These are called self-fulfilling prophecies. Self-fulfilling prophecies are core decisions that are like the software that runs a computer.

Certain negative decisions about ourselves may become the foundation on which we build our lives and lead to the choices we make and the actions we take. These are some of the most common self-fulfilling prophecies procrastinators live by:

- I am not good enough.
- I am unlovable.
- I am unacceptable.
- I am incompetent.
- I don't belong.
- I am powerless.
- I am unimportant.
- I am to blame.
- I don't deserve (love, health, success, etc.).
- I am a victim.
- I am stupid.

We also decide what kind of world we were born into: frightening, beautiful, challenging, welcoming, or hard and dangerous. Many procrastinators tell themselves, "Life is hard," "There is no justice in the world," "Life is dangerous," or even "God is punishing me." These beliefs turn into their life scripts. All of us become the authors of a play and then star in it. Whether we create a drama, comedy, or tragedy is influenced by our False Negative Beliefs combined with our self-fulfilling prophecies. Most procrastinators don't remember making those decisions about themselves and the world until they use EFT to heal and release their negative emotions and beliefs.

Many self-fulfilling prophecies bring misery and pain because procrastinators unwittingly keep reliving them. Here are examples of self-fulfilling prophecies that lead to lives that resemble soap operas. For example, if a person believes, "My life is about never being good enough, therefore, I am supposed to be abused, treated like a victim, blamed, or a loser," he or she will unconsciously make this come true.

Nick was the son of an unwed teenaged mother who later married a man who resented Nick. Therefore his childhood was filled with loneliness, criticism, and lack of nurturing. Nick's procrastination led to an inability to follow through on his plans and lost him jobs and friends. He used EFT to defuse his painful childhood memories of physical and emotional abuse, challenge his beliefs about not being good enough, and look at his procrastinating behaviors using statements such as:

- *Even though my mother made what was fun into hard work, I love and accept myself.*
- *Even though my stepfather's harsh rules and disapproval stopped me from having fun when I was growing up, I am letting go of my anger now.*
- *Even though I didn't feel safe with my stepfather's rage, I survived and I am safe now.*
- *Even though I have many unhappy and unpleasant memories of being unloved and unwanted, I am willing to release the pain now.*

Frequently, people who believe that they are worthless will continue to punish themselves the way that others treated them earlier. They may harm themselves by putting off going to the dentist, getting into debt, having to declare bankruptcy, or being attracted to unloving relationships. Those who live by the idea that "There is no justice in the world" or "Everything is my fault" may allow physical or emotional abuse from family members or lovers, or on the job.

I have also come across procrastinators who started out in life with experiences that taught them that "Life is dangerous." Some of these depressed people become losers because they are unconsciously telling themselves that they are better off not being here at all or that life sucks so why even bother. Therefore they set themselves up for mistreatment through their inability to complete goals.

## Three Sources of Self-fulfilling Prophecies

Self-fulfilling prophecies are created in three ways. The first way is that they evolve from individuals trying to rationalize negative life events that they endured, as was the case with Nick and Lily. The second way is through strict commandments taught by authority figures (parents, teachers, or clergy) in childhood that become embedded as rules that must be obeyed. Their words, sometimes harsh or critical, felt as though they were handed down from God. They must be followed without question, or else! That was what Joel had to deal with whenever he heard his mother's voice in his head.

The third way that self-fulfilling prophecies are created is through the body's response to emotional happenings. Psychologist Wendy Anne McCarty, researcher and author in the innovative field of prenatal and perinatal psychology (see Chapter 47), maintains, "Our earliest experiences can hold the key to recognizing and healing our current limiting and debilitating life patterns" (McCarty, 2012).

When I interviewed Dr. McCarty, I asked her how a person's pre-birth or birth experience could possibly lead to procrastination. She commented that the birth experience might lead to a person developing difficulty getting started on a project or become someone who begins but doesn't finish. She informed me that studies show that, when the environment of the womb is negative, the fetus doesn't "move toward life" but moves away. She also indicated that some procrastinators report feeling numb as they think about fulfilling an assignment or project. Some who were born caesarian section and didn't get to complete the journey into life through the birth canal may become procrastinators who likewise get started but stop partway and don't finish the job.

health problems, a therapist who specializes in energy psychology can help the person heal the difficult memories and release the self-fulfilling prophecies.

Memories of awful happenings are hard to extinguish. EFT can actually disconnect the fear loop that was put in place a long time ago. According to Ronald Ruden, MD, PhD, clinician and scientist, EFT raises the serotonin level in the brain (Ruden, 2000). Serotonin is a brain chemical that plays an important role in mood regulation, allowing a person to feel calm. In addition to raising serotonin, EFT also helps raise the levels of two other brain substances, glutamate and GABA, which are also involved in de-linking the fear loop.

Dr. Ruden suggests picturing the amygdala like a beach filled with holes; each hole represents a painful emotion, event, or memory. When we focus on that unpleasant memory or emotion and stimulate EFT energy points, that hole in the beach fills with glutamate. Then when a serotonin wave flows in, the chemical GABA is released, allowing that particular glutamate-filled hole to interact with the serotonin and solidify. The hole is now gone. The negative reaction can no longer take place. Although a person may still remember what happened, he will no longer feel any intense emotion. It will be as if he is looking at a photo in an album, just another memory. If, like Joel, your body remembered the original memory, it will stop reacting to the old trigger.

That is why attempting to change negative thoughts through talk therapy alone will not necessarily help someone stop procrastinating once and for all. In order to transform negative thoughts, procrastinators need to go back to the time of the initial emotional reaction—the time when they first created the Negative False Belief or self-fulfilling prophecy—and use EFT to eliminate the familiar negative urge to procrastinate.

## Retrain the Brain with EFT

When procrastinators learn how to erase their negative self-fulfilling prophecies, they can create and live with new positive beliefs and rewrite a script free of procrastination. Sometimes it is necessary to investigate the level beyond awareness, the place that holds the person's history and memories, especially those that were stressful and unpleasant. If a procrastinator suffers from problems with depression or other serious mental

## Blocking Beliefs

If a procrastinator follows the Six Steps to Success without seeing improvement, it may indicate that there is an impediment in the form of a negative blocking belief. Here is a list of some of the most common ones:

- I don't deserve to get over this problem.
- God is punishing me.
- It's impossible to get over this problem.

- If I get over this problem, I won't be safe.
- I'm not sure I want to get over this problem.
- If I get over this problem, I will lose my identity.
- If I get over this problem, it will be bad for someone else.
- I don't have the strength or willpower to get over this problem.
- If I get over my problem, it means that someone who should be punished will get away with it.

Barry, a man approaching 50, made very little money, couldn't afford his own apartment, and had to rent a room in someone's home. He kept putting off looking for a job that paid more. His excuse for not job hunting was that he didn't have enough energy after working the long hours he had to work to make ends meet. He had put himself into a double bind, and it seemed impossible to get free. Even after using EFT in an attempt to eliminate his Negative False Beliefs and self-fulfilling prophecies, nothing changed. What he didn't know was that unconsciously he *wasn't sure that he wanted to get over his problem* with procrastination. He had a hidden belief that, if he took power over his life and was more successful, he would *lose his identity* as a victim.

Barry's early years were filled with horrible abuse. He was still furious at being injured by both his parents and wanted his dad to make restitution, but his father was cold and distant. Barry tapped as he explored his situation and frustration about procrastinating. He discovered that in addition to a blocking belief there was also another irrational belief that was holding him back: *Money is love.*

He said, "If I am powerless enough, my dad will have to take care of me and give me money to make my life easier to make up for the awful things he did to me when I was small. If he gives me money, it means he loves me." In order to get love, Barry had to remain a financially destitute victim who needed rescuing. Meanwhile, his father couldn't care less that he was miserable. The only one really suffering was Barry.

More tapping enabled Barry to realize that the past was past. Although he had felt powerless as a child and needed a grownup to take care of him, he was now an adult and had skills to survive. He decided he wanted to stop living the way he had been, and took action to improve his life. A while later he was able to move into his own place in a beautiful neighborhood.

Another person with an unconscious blocking belief was Hannah, who desperately wanted to lose weight but kept putting off starting a diet because she was immobilized by the belief that, if she succeeded, she wouldn't be safe. Hannah was angry with herself for not taking action. She was filled with self-hatred because of how she looked and her lack of willpower. When she explored what she was afraid would happen if she dieted, she discovered that, if she went on a diet, she would lose weight and look thin. When she thought of how she would appear, she imagined looking into her mirror and seeing someone who was skeletal, just like her Jewish relatives who had died in concentration camps during World War II had looked. The thought came to her that if she got too thin and another holocaust occurred, she would not live through it. In this case, it wasn't Hannah's experiences that were affecting her; it was the trauma of her close relatives and her cultural history.

Hannah used EFT, focusing on:

- *Even though my relatives died in the Holocaust, it's over. I am okay today and releasing this terror.*
- *Even though I am scared of getting so thin that I might die like my family, I am tapping on that now.*
- *Even though I am worried about getting too thin, I can control how much weight I choose to lose and do it safely and healthfully.*

EFT helped her put this fear into perspective so she was able to understand that just for today she was safe and she could be a healthy weight.

## Moving Forward

Procrastination is a self-sabotaging set of behaviors. All behavior is communication. Procrastinators are people who keep themselves from moving forward because of fears about what will happen if they do. These fantasies are so frightening that the procrastinator is willing to endure the negative consequence of not doing rather than face the fear. Yet, in almost all cases, the fear is a product of Negative False Beliefs that arose from that person's life experiences. Procrastinators lock themselves in a prison of compulsive putting-off behaviors due to their self-fulfilling prophecies. They are unaware, however, that the prison door has no lock.

The Six Steps to Success is a guide for self-awareness and self-efficacy that, when combined with EFT, will enable procrastinators to heal traumatic memories, transform untrue beliefs, create positive expectations, and eliminate the negative avoidance behaviors.

# References

Linden, D. J. (2011). *The compass of pleasure: How our brains make fatty foods, orgasm, exercise, marijuana, generosity, vodka, learning, and gambling feel so good.* New York, NY: Viking.

McCarty, W. A. (2012). *Welcoming consciousness: Supporting babies' wholeness from the beginning of life—An integrated model of early development.* Santa Barbara, CA: Wondrous Beginnings Publishing. (Originally published as eBook in 2004 under same title.)

Ruden, R. A. (2000). *The craving brain: A bold new approach to breaking free from drug addiction, overeating, alcoholism, gambling* (2nd ed.). New York, NY: Harper Perennial.

Scaer, R. C. (2007). *The body bears the burden: Trauma, dissociation, and disease* (2nd ed.). New York, NY: Haworth Medical Press.

Siegel, D. J. (1999). *The developing mind: How relationships and the brain interact to shape who we are.* New York, NY: Guilford Press.

# Chapter 46
# EFT for Veterans
*Marilyn McWilliams*

## Abstract

"This EFT technique is the best hope that I have *ever* seen of helping all of our veterans," states former VA psychiatrist and psychotherapist Rick Staggenborg (2013). With veteran suicide rates at an all-time high and President Obama having issued an executive order calling for the development of better prevention, diagnosis, and treatment of posttraumatic stress disorder (PTSD), there is a greater urgency for efficacious intervention. EFT is a drug-free technique that pairs attention to discomfort with self-applied tapping to resolve problems ranging from physical pain to PTSD symptoms. It is fast, flexible, and economical. The logistics of delivery are uncommonly simple. EFT is effective when delivered via Skype. Many studies confirm that it is astonishingly effective. After six EFT sessions, in the first randomized, controlled clinical trial applying EFT to veteran PTSD, 86% of the veterans no longer tested positive for PTSD and gains were maintained on follow-up. The Veterans Stress Project is continuing this research, including a replication of the first trial. It also makes EFT available to veterans at no cost. The statistics represent real veterans who returned home incapable of living normal lives. After EFT, their theme is "Thank you. I have my life back. How can we make EFT available to other veterans?" Anyone can learn enough EFT to improve his or her quality of life. Expertly delivered, EFT is extraordinarily effective in resolving even complex PTSD. The Veterans Administration may be the logical delivery system. Veterans, doctors, therapists and politicians are asking the VA to use EFT, but bureaucratic change is slow. Our veterans can't wait. Fortunately, we can help by using and sharing EFT in our own way. I found my place by providing EFT directly to veterans and participating in the clinical trials. You can play an even more important role by helping EFT go viral. This work allows us to acknowledge the problem while staying focused on the vision and personally engaged in the solution. The first critical step is introducing EFT to veterans, their families, and their communities. The next step is incorporating EFT into the family culture. This may be one of the most effective means of serving our veterans and ourselves. EFT carries the promise of unimagined gifts of freedom and peace.

**Keywords:** veteran, posttraumatic stress disorder, PTSD, PTS, stress, combat trauma, war trauma, Veterans Stress Project

> *The war is just a training mission compared to the real battle. The personal combat starts when vets come home. Without EFT you go in unarmed.*
> —Ken Self, MSG, USMC (Ret.), 4-tour Iraq and Afghanistan veteran

**Marilyn McWilliams** is a certified EFT practitioner, specializing in trauma resolution, and a research coach, providing EFT and collecting data for clinical trials. She serves on the advisory board of the nonprofit National Institute for Integrative Healthcare, which runs the Veterans Stress Project and the Foundation for Epigenetic Medicine. Send correspondence to Marilyn McWilliams, 1905 NE 16th Avenue, Suite 4, Portland, OR 97212, or Marilyn@EFTCatalyst.com. www.EFTCatalyst.com.

## Veteran PTSD: The Individual and Social Costs Are Immeasurable

It is impossible to calculate the number of veterans suffering from military trauma. Fewer than 40% of U.S. veterans are enrolled in the VA health care system. The VA estimates that nearly 31% of Vietnam veterans suffer from posttraumatic stress disorder (PTSD; NIH, 2009). Much of the VA's increase in overall mental health patient load is made up of newly diagnosed Vietnam and other earlier era veterans. (Rosenheck & Fontana, 2007). According to the Pentagon approximately 40% of soldiers and 50% of national guardsmen returning from the Middle East report mental health problems (Dept. of Defense, 2007). Given these and other estimates, one can conservatively project that millions of U.S. veterans suffer from PTSD. In 2010, the VA provided PTSD treatment to morethan 400,000 of our 22.5 million veterans (Congressional Budget Office, 2012).

It is well established that we lose more soldiers to suicide than to combat. In *Nam Vet,* Chuck Dean (1990) makes a compelling argument that suicide-related losses among Vietnam-era veterans outweigh combat losses by nearly 3 to 1. A CBS News investigation of 2005 data found that veterans were more than twice as likely to commit suicide as non-veterans; among veterans aged 20 through 24, those who have served during the war on terror had the highest suicide rate among all veterans, estimated between 2 and 4 times higher than civilians the same age (Keteyian, 2009). The VA estimates that 22 U.S. veterans kill themselves every day, butthis number is extrapolated from extremely limited data (Dept. of Veterans Affairs, 2012, p. 15). These estimates are likely to be low, as reliable numbers are not available for suicides disguised as "accidents." This crisis led President Obama to sign an Executive Order in August 2012 mandating interagency focus on the development of better prevention, diagnosis, and treatment of PTSD, traumatic brain injury (TBI), and related injuries.

## PTSD: The Inability to Function Normally after Trauma

The American Psychiatric Association first included a definition of PTSD in its *Diagnostic and Statistical Manual of Mental Disorders* in 1980 (3rd edition, *DSM-III*). In *DSM-IV-TR,* published in 2000, the definition requires that a certain mix of symptoms must follow a traumatic event, last at least a month, and keep the individual from functioning normally. *DSM-V,* scheduled to replace *DSM-IV* in 2013, will add a few symptoms and adjust the symptom grouping. The updated definition includes not only directly experiencing an event, but also knowledge or threat of an event ("New Diagnostic Criteria," 2013).

## Diagnosis and Measurement: The PTSD Checklist–Military

The PTSD Checklist–Military (PCL-M) was developed within the VA and includes the symptoms included in *DSM-IV.* It is one of the most widely used assessments for screening, diagnosis, and monitoring symptom change. Some veteran centers use the same assessment without reference to military experience, which is called the PTSD Checklist–Civilian (PCL-C). Scores over 49 generally indicate PTSD. As a practitioner, completing the PCL-M assessment for yourself (see Table 1), ignoring reference to military experience, provides a useful familiarity for discussion of symptom change and will increase your appreciation for the challenges faced by veterans who navigate each day with a PCL-M score of 50, 60, 70, or 80.

PTSD occurs when a person's expectations are violated by a strong threat for which the person has no effective strategy or coping mechanism. Resources are reallocated, leaving the brain unable to appropriately file memories. Unprocessed information remains an unfinished memory, resulting in nightmares and intrusive thoughts and/or physical pain until that information is processed and filed as a normal memory. Unfinished or traumatic memories seem to jump to mind by themselves and trigger involuntary emotional or physical responses such as anxiety or flashbacks, which are the physical reexperiencing of the event. Normal memories are accessed voluntarily and do not trigger involuntary responses. EFT "re-resources" the system that facilitates the completion of the memory-filing process. In short, in EFT, the brain gets a "do over," this time with the benefit of the resources it didn't have the first time around. After receiving EFT, veterans report that they simply have the memories instead of the memories having them.

Psychologist James R. Lane provides a medical explanation of what happens during acupoint stimulation:"Recent research indicates that manual stimulation of acupressure points produces opioids,

**Table 1.** *PTSD Checklist–Military (PCL-M)*

Below is a list of problems and complaints that veterans sometimes have in response to stressful military experiences. Use the following scoring to indicate how much the patient has been bothered by that problem in the past month.
1 = Not at all; 2 = A little bit; 3 = Moderately; 4 = Quite a bit; 5 = Extremely

| | | | | | |
|---|---|---|---|---|---|
| 1. Repeated, disturbing memories, thoughts, or images of a stressful military experience? | 1 | 2 | 3 | 4 | 5 |
| 2. Repeated, disturbing dreams of a stressful military experience? | 1 | 2 | 3 | 4 | 5 |
| 3. Suddenly acting or feeling as if a stressful military experience were happening again (as if you were reliving it)? | 1 | 2 | 3 | 4 | 5 |
| 4. Feeling very upset when something reminded you of a stressful military experience? | 1 | 2 | 3 | 4 | 5 |
| 5. Having physical reactions (e.g., heart pounding, trouble breathing, sweating) when something reminded you of a stressful military experience? | 1 | 2 | 3 | 4 | 5 |
| 6. Avoiding thinking about or talking about a stressful military experience or avoiding having feelings related to it? | 1 | 2 | 3 | 4 | 5 |
| 7. Avoiding activities or situation because they reminded you of a stressful military experience? | 1 | 2 | 3 | 4 | 5 |
| 8. Trouble remembering important parts of a stressful military experience? | 1 | 2 | 3 | 4 | 5 |
| 9. Loss of interest in activities that you used to enjoy? | 1 | 2 | 3 | 4 | 5 |
| 10. Feeling distant or cut off from other people? | 1 | 2 | 3 | 4 | 5 |
| 11. Feeling emotionally numb or being unable to have loving feelings toward those close to you? | 1 | 2 | 3 | 4 | 5 |
| 12. Feeling as if your future will somehow be cut short? | 1 | 2 | 3 | 4 | 5 |
| 13. Trouble falling or staying asleep? | 1 | 2 | 3 | 4 | 5 |
| 14. Feeling irritable or having angry outbursts? | 1 | 2 | 3 | 4 | 5 |
| 15. Having difficulty concentrating? | 1 | 2 | 3 | 4 | 5 |
| 16. Being "super-alert" or watchful or on guard? | 1 | 2 | 3 | 4 | 5 |
| 17. Feeling jumpy or easily startled? | 1 | 2 | 3 | 4 | 5 |

Subtotals by column:

Total Score:

serotonin, and gamma-amino butyric acid (GABA) and regulates cortisol. These neurochemical changes reduce pain, slow the heart rate, decrease anxiety, shut off the fight/flight/freeze response, regulate the autonomic nervous system, and create a sense of calm. This relaxation response reciprocally inhibits anxiety and creates a rapid desensitization to traumatic stimuli" (Lane, 2009).

## Traditional VA Treatments: Talk Therapy, Prolonged Exposure, and Drugs

The VA uses a limited number of approved treatment methods. One is "talk therapy," which includes cognitive behavior therapy (CBT) and longer-term psychotherapy and counseling. Another method is prolonged exposure, which, as its name indicates, involves extended focus on a specific traumatic event. Although veterans who stay the course report relief, prolonged exposure is highly unpopular with veterans. It is also *counterindicated* for those who have been acutely traumatized. The list of counter-indications includes many symptoms associated with PTSD (Bryant & Harvey, 2000): extreme anxiety, panic attacks, anger, severe depression, suicide risk, substance abuse, marked dissociation, as well as complex comorbidity (i.e., multiple disorders and unresolved prior traumas).

Selective serotonin reuptake inhibitors (SSRIs) such as Prozac, Zoloft, and Paxil are prescribed widely for depression and anxiety. Benzodiazepines such as Xanax, Ativan, Klonopin, and Valiumare prescribed for anxiety and can be highly addictive. A veteran participating in our research told me that his VA doctor had begun weaning him off of the benzodiazepine he had been prescribed for over a dozen years in light of a recent study indicating that benzodiazepines significantly increase the risk of dementia. The 15-year study published in the *British Medical Journal* indicates that use of benzodiazepines is associated with an approximately 50% increase in the risk of dementia (Billiotti de Gage, 2012). VA counselors tell me that current generation veterans resist (and/or resent) prescription drugs both because of immediate side effects such as sexual dysfunction and emotional numbness and because of the prospect of life-long symptom management.

Some VA facilities also make available what are considered complementary methods of stress reduction such as meditation, yoga, breathing, and Eye Movement Desensitization and Reprocessing (EMDR).

## EFT Is an Effective Treatment for PTSD

### Anecdotal Evidence

Do EFT and related meridian activation modalities "work" to resolve PTSD? In Kosovo, South Africa, Rwanda, and the Congo, teams providing relief to 337 disaster relief victims recorded a total of 1,016 traumas, of which 1,013 (99.97%) were resolved (Feinstein, 2008). Abused adolescents with PTSD symptoms no longer tested positive for PTSD a single session of EFT while the control group (which did not receive treatment) showed no improvement (Church, Piña, Reategui, & Brooks, 2012).

In 1994, the founder of EFT, Gary Craig, used EFT with veterans at the Los Angeles VA. In the video of the sessions, *Six Days at the VA,* viewers see veterans transform before their eyes. In 2008, nine veterans and two families received EFT in a 5-day intensive in San Franciscoas documented in *Operation: Emotional Freedom—The Answer.* In this open trial, Gary Craig and EFT practitioners delivered EFT. Dawson Church, PhD, collected data on the mental and emotional condition of the participants before, during, and after the retreat, using well-recognized measurement tools including

the PCL-M. The group's average opening PCL-M scores of 65 dropped precipitously then settled and stayed at 33 on 1-year follow-up (Church, 2010b).

Dr. Stephen Nagy, MD, a psychiatrist specializing in PTSD who observed the 2008 study, provided this context for the magnitude of the improvement show in the PCL-M scores: "A 5- or 10-point change in a PCL-M score is regarded as a significant improvement... When asked whether results like those I witnessed in San Francisco would be considered a success if they were produced by conventional treatment, I would have to say that if conventional treatment produced these same results, it would be considered to be miraculous, unexpected, and amazing" (Nagy, 2009).

## Randomized, Controlled Clinical Trials

Division 12 of the American Psychological Association set standards for declaring a practice to be "evidence based."Multiple, randomized, controlled clinical trials are required and must demonstrate that the treatment is more effective than the control group or wait list. These studies are conducted with enough subjects to show a statistical significance of 95%, stated as ($p < .05$), meaning there is only one possibility in 20 that the results are due to chance.

Randomized, controlled trials are being conducted by the nonprofit National Institute for Integrative Healthcare both through its research arm, the Foundation of Epigenetic Medicine, and through the Veterans Stress Project. The first randomized, controlled clinical trial applying EFT to veteran PTSD involved 59 veterans and was published in February 2013 in the *Journal of Nervous and Mental Disease* (Church et al., 2013) Individually, 86% of veterans who received EFT no longer tested positive for PTSD and stayed PTSD free on 3- and 6-month follow-up. Statistically, there is a 99.99% certainty ($p < .0001$) that these results are not random. In addition, the size of the effect was dramatic; with EFT, the veterans' mean PCL-M scores dropped *31 points,* falling from 66 to 35. Even a reduction of 5–10 points indicates reliable change (Weathers, Litz, Herman, Huska, & Keane,1993).

A common measure of effect size is *d,* which is the difference in the two groups' means divided by the average of their standard deviations (as when comparing the mean of the control group and the intervention group). This means that if we see a *d* of 1, we know that the two groups' means differ by one standard deviation; a *d* of .5 tells us that the two groups' means differ by half a standard deviation; and so on. A *d* of .02 is considered a "small" effect size because if two groups' means don't differ by 0.2 standard deviations or more, the difference is trivial, even if it is statistically significant; 0.5 represents a "medium" effect size and 0.8 a "large" effect size. How much larger than "large" is the effect size in this first published EFT study? The *d* for the PCL-M scores is *2.019!*

Certainly, multiple studies are required to prove EFT can reliably produce such impressive and long-lasting resolutions. As of this writing, the Church et al. study is in the process of being replicated. Surprisingly, the largest challenge to completing the studies has been locating veteran volunteers to receive confidential EFT sessions and provide anonymous feedback. You can directly facilitate this ground breaking research by letting veterans know about the opportunity to be a study participant. The Veterans Stress Project plans to continue to offer free EFT to veterans and to gather trial data.

In July 2010, Dr. Church and clinical psychologist David Feinstein, PhD, testified before Congress about the efficacy of EFT on PTSD. Dan Lungren (then U.S. Congressman and former California attorney general) arranged a second congressional hearing in September 2010. As a result, multiple members of Congress signed a letter to the secretary of the VA, Eric Shinseki, saying:"It is vital that our returning troops have access to effective PTSD treatments if they are affected by this debilitating condition. Research has shown EFT to reduce PTSD symptoms effectively. Previous studies have also found that it can be self-applied, quickly learned and is free of side effects. Its military implications cannot be underestimated."

VA counselors tell me that the VA responds to written letters from veterans' physicians outside the VA. Veterans are encouraged to put their own requests in writing.

## Case Examples from Veterans

### Ken Self: "I was Given a Tool and I Used it"

Ken served four tours in Iraq and Afghanistan. In our first session, we tapped on his most traumatic memory of shooting a child who'd been strapped in explosives. He had not told this story since getting out of the military and his chest was tight at the very thought of talking about it. We tapped the tightness

down to 0 on the subjective units of distress (SUD) scale (i.e., intensity rating). We interrupted the telling of his story frequently to tap on the components of the memory. Afterward, he calmly said, "I was in charge. It was my responsibility and I did what I had to do to protect the lives of my men."

A few days later Ken said he felt "fabulous."For over 10 years, he hadn't been able to sleep well, even after drinking a fifth of alcohol a night to get to sleep. He had nightmares, and would wake to the smell of gunpowder and burning oil. Shortly after he started tapping, he said, "Something happened and I forgot to drink." He also reports that he now "sleeps like a baby" for 7+ hours.

Ken resolved his second most traumatic memory entirely on his own. Since resolving "the kid" memory and being able to sleep without alcohol, he'd been tapping for himself. He said he could now willingly (i.e., painlessly) think about the death of one of his closest friends who had been blown apart when their transport took a direct hit. Ken said he'd tapped on every aspect he could think of, including "the smell of the camel crap."After resolving this memory, he reported calmly, "We were in the wrong place at the wrong time."

Ken's SUD level remained at 0 throughout his detailed retelling of the story. He said he was surprised that his good feelings had returned. "For over 10 years every part of that day was off limits because it was a chain of thoughts and once you started you couldn't stop and it never ended well."He said that EFT had given him his friend back because he had regained the good memories of their times together. After three hours of EFT coaching, and some very effective personal tapping, his PCL-M assessment showed him to be free of PTSD symptoms, including insomnia.

Ken calls this experience with EFT "his Personal Stand Down" through which he was finally able to stop fighting the dreams and memories. He now practices EFT as a life skill and taps down his daily stressors. Ken says, "There's no limit to how often a soldier will risk his life to bring another injured soldier back in from the battlefield. If they have PTSD, they're still out there, and we need to bring them in."

### David's Story in His Own Words

"My life was in shambles. I was in the middle of a disastrous divorce. My wife blamed the Army. My job was sitting in limbo. My youngest son was born and I was not allowed to be present. My diagnosis of PTSD only made things more difficult. I had angry outbursts, migraines, nightmares, flashbacks, and bouts of depression regularly. My mind and my body began suffering from the effects of the VA medicines (i.e., lack of sexual libido, weak and dizzy in the morning hours, and vertigo every time I blinked my eyes). I had no emotions or compassion anymore. I was falling apart with no hope of gaining control again. Thoughts of suicide entered my mind daily. All I had were my combat memories. I felt alone.

"I believe the mind is a very powerful tool; however, I was not prepared for what was defined to me as a therapy. Repeating words, tapping…how could this help me? Skeptical is an understatement to what was going through my mind. It was this or the end of a rope…I chose life (a big step for me). I began to explore the thought of attempting this EFT psychobabble therapy. What did I have to lose? Besides, it was free, and I was rock-bottom broke at the time anyway. Together, Marilyn and I began to take the first steps to save my life.

"I was in Texas. Marilyn was in Oregon. We scheduled our first 'face-to-face' appointment via Skype. I ignored Marilyn on how the process works, what would be asked of me, and how I may feel during this process. All I thought about was reliving horrible memories repeatedly.

"I broke my neck in Iraq and had suffered from excruciating migraines, sometimes as many as three a day, ever since. On a scale from 1 to 10, with 10 being the most horrible pain imaginable, I had a 10-size migraine for our first session. Marilyn's first priority was to prove to a skeptic that the EFT works on everything…even migraines. "Whatever, let's get this over with so I can swallow a bottle of Excedrin Migraine and go to sleep!"

"Within 10 minutes, I was a believer! For the first time in 5 and a half years, I was migraine-free! Amazing! Her Vulcan mind meld and voodoo witchcraft worked on me, and I wanted more. We began to work on one of my top five worst experiences. Marilyn let me tell my story at my pace. We stopped and tapped every time I began to feel an emotional or physical response to my story.

"I fell asleep that night easily and stayed asleep for more than 2 hours, which was unheard of for me at the time. I felt a difference the next morning in my memory of the story I'd told. Funny thing, it was just a memory now, not a living nightmare.

"Marilyn and I continued for five more sessions. She taught me how to proceed with my EFT outside of our sessions. I took advantage of it, and I no longer considered it homework. These emotions were just memories now. I remember how I used to feel when I recalled these events, but I do not feel them anymore.

"The day arrived when we tapped on my worst memory. This was the memory that put me over the top. This event changed my life forever; it caused me to retreat into myself, it cost me my personality, my marriage, my job, and worse, my children. I was dreading this day, but we did it. We removed my emotional response to the memory that had haunted me for over 6 years. That was the first time I ever spoke about what happened that horrible day in Iraq. Marilyn, again, allowed me to take charge. We did it!

"Now I can sleep at night without the aid of sleeping pills. I have only had two migraines of low intensity in the past 11 months. I am no longer on antidepressants; I am engaged to a very beautiful young woman; my ex-wife allows my boys extended stays with me; I have a great job; I have friends; and the best of all, I have my life back! For the first time since my combat days ended, I can share my stories with my loved ones without the fear of my own emotional responses. I now have the ability to face my past and my memories with confidence and security that I will be safe and comfortable.

"Because of the Veteran Stress Project, I am not a victim of PTSD anymore. I am no longer an insomniac. The proof is in the numbers."

[Note: Figure 1 shows David's scores on two commonly used assessments. On the VA's PCL-M, scores of over 49 typically indicate PTSD. On the Insomnia Severity Index (ISI), David had the highest score possible, indicating "severe clinical insomnia."On recently received follow-up, scores fell further on both assessments.]

"I continue to use EFT as a means to defuse stressful memories and other activities that may cause me discomfort or an emotional response. I share my experience with EFT with other veterans. I have spoken of the Veteran Stress Project in my VA PTSD group sessions and to the VA counselors as a means to end the pain and suffering of veterans everywhere. I wish to 'pay it forward.'

"I find it amazing that the Veteran's Stress Project intends to continue to offer sessions at no cost, especially considering the project counselors are volunteering their personal time. The more

| | Before Session 1 | After Session 3 | After Session 6 | % of improvement within range of possible scores |
|---|---|---|---|---|
| PCL-M (possible scores: 17 to 85) | 80 | 62 | 28 | 83% |
| ISI (possible scores: 0 to 28) | 28 | 28 | 2 | 93% |

*Figure 1.* David's assessment scores.

veterans who sign up for the project, the more evidence will be available to encourage the VA to incorporate EFT tapping as a holistic healing process for the masses.

"Thank you, Veteran Stress Project. Thank you, EFT. Moreover, most notably to me, thank you, Marilyn, you saved my life! When asked how I feel, my only response is, 'I'm free!'"
—David S-B, Afghanistan and Iraq War Veteran, Army, December 2012

David and Ken are two of the real-life people behind the statistics. Keep them in mind as you read the following sections describing the characteristics of EFT and the approaches I have personally found valuable in working with veteran trauma.

## EFT's Characteristics

*The results were dramatic, swift, and lasting.*
—Vietnam veteran

## EFT Maximizes Veteran Comfort, Control, and Acceptance

In contrast to talk therapy and prolonged exposure, EFT involves only brief, imagined exposure to discomforts or memories of traumatic events. Veterans appreciate that they maintain personal control of the exposure level when using EFT. Exposure is often confined to one narrowly defined aspect of an event, such as a sound or a specific visual component of a memory. The very process itself, with its resource-building neurochemistry, minimizes the likelihood of discomfort. Experienced practitioners can often guide a veteran through his or her most traumatic event without the veteran ever being "triggered." Should discomfort occur, EFT has the distinct advantage of being able to quickly and painlessly bring the veteran back out of distress. Veterans themselves become proficient in self-care as they are coached to stop, pull back, freeze-frame, or otherwise disengage at the first

indication, or even preemptively at the very anticipation of physical or emotional intensity.

Consequently, veterans typically exhibit no aversion to further sessions. On the contrary, it is fascinating when Vietnam-era veterans, who have employed a primary strategy of avoiding trauma triggers for over four decades, instead enthusiastically engage in a "Search and Resolve" mission. In one veteran's words: "In talk therapy, they want you to tell all the details of the story over and over no matter how bad it feels, but with EFT you're just never even allowed to get uncomfortable."

I had the privilege of attending a training in which EFT/Matrix instructor Alina Frank provided EFT to Korean War veteran Carl Anderson. Matrix Reimprinting is an advanced EFT technique, but Alina intentionally used almost very basic EFT to demonstrate the effectiveness of even EFT's most basic, easy-to-learn technique. (A video of the full session is available at www.stressproject.org.) Seven months later, Carl provided this follow-up: "I served with the Army in Korea in 1951 and for 60 years have had a very painful/emotional memory that has plagued me all these years. So I told 'my story' to Alina and went through the process of tapping it down. After 1 hour I could mentally revisit that Korean experience and it was as though I was watching an old newsreel of a 20-year-old GI's (me) experience. ... and there was absolutely no emotional charge to it. I have been free of it ever since!!13 years of group therapy or 1 hour of EFT/Matrix: take your pick. I'm sold on EFT!!"

Veterans appreciate tools that work and are willing to train to become competent and self-reliant. Many will experiment and improvise. One veteran reported that by using EFT while sharing his stories, he and his girlfriend were successfully resolving one traumatic war memory after another. His girlfriend understood that he would leave to apply EFT at his first sign of physical or emotional discomfort and would return later to continue the story. This is a practical example of incorporating EFT into family culture: Communication is encouraged and family members are expected to take personal responsibility to "resource up" when they either anticipate or are faced with challenges.

## EFT Is Extraordinarily Economical

An army physician at Madigan Army Medical Center cautioned colleagues that a PTSD diagnosis could cost the army up to $1.5 million over the lifetime of a soldier (Dao, 2012). (Note: the concept of needing to provide PTSD treatment "over the lifetime of the soldier" is outside of the model of most EFT practitioners.) Without knowing the average cost of "treating" a PTSD veteran with current methods for life, we can reliably conclude that the average cost of current, long-term therapy multiplied by millions of suffering veterans results in an astronomical cost that cannot be practically integrated into any budget.

EFT can be delivered for a fraction of the cost of traditional treatment methods. The fact that EFT can be effectively delivered via Skype provides unprecedented economic advantage. Tele-video delivery virtually eliminates the logistical challenges of serving rural veterans as well the many urban veterans whose PTSD symptoms are themselves barriers to treatment. Many veterans report that visiting VA facilities often triggers their PTSD. One trial shows that even when six EFT sessions were delivered to veterans without the benefit of video (i.e., strictly over the telephone) two-thirds of the veterans had PCL-M scores reduced to below the minimum threshold for PTSD diagnosis (Hartung & Stein, 2012). An analysis of trial results indicates that trained EFT coaches and licensed mental health practitioners are equally effective in reducing PTSD diagnostic criteria in veterans (Stein& Brooks, 2011).

If EFT were delivered within the constraints and culture of the VA, it might be appropriate to increase the number of sessions. However, even if a standard of 10 to 12 sessions were established, the cost to deliver a full sequence would still be relatively small, and would have an end point. Prolonged exposure therapy often involves a 10- to 12-week sequence dedicated to reducing the intensity of a *single* traumatic event. Using EFT, veterans are often able to fully resolve even their most traumatizing events in one or two sessions. EFT requires no investment in equipment. Since results are typically permanent, ongoing costs are drastically minimized.

Regarding a group of 300,000 returning Middle East veterans with PTSD, Dr. Church made the argument to Congress:"Just 1,000 full-time clinicians can provide six one-hour-long sessions of EFT (the minimum number we've found it takes) to every one of those 300,000 veterans in only a single year. Such a treatment plan would also cost only one-third of the $584 million Congress has already spent on PTSD research in the last 3 years. It is thus an achievable and affordable goal, and one which would restore the possibility of normal lives to hundreds of thousands of sufferers who, right now, have no prospect of such a bright future"(Church, n.d.-a).

Dr. Church notes, "During the last 10 years, the Veterans Administration (VA) and the Department of Defense (DOD) spent $791 million on a drug called risperidone. Initially touted as a treatment for PTSD, a clinical trial published in the *Journal of the American Medical Association* eventually showed that it was no more effective than a placebo-an inert comparison pill [Krystal et al., 2011].

"The price of drugs can be compared with the cost of treatment with EFT. An estimated 500,000 Iraq and Afghanistan veterans suffer from PTSD. The cost of six sessions with an EFT practitioner for every one of them comes to $300 million. For less than half of what the military spent on an ineffective drug treatment, it could have purchased this effective and safe behavioral treatment for every veteran with PTSD. If the results were as good as those in the studies, nearly nine out of ten of those veterans would be PTSD-free today"(Church, n.d.-b).

Dr. Church also lays out a detailed argument that modalities such as EFT can save the overall U.S. economy $65 billion per year (Church, 2010a). In light of the government's economic challenges, a rational observer might conclude that at some point the sheer economic efficiency of EFT will come into play.

## Other Advantages of EFT: Flexibility and Simplicity

- *Prolonged exposure therapy is structured to deal with a single traumatic event.* EFT can be applied to an event, or a particular aspect of an event such as a single sight, sound, or physical sensation. It can be applied to an attitude, an idea, an image, a word—to any of the full range of emotions and virtually every form in which distress might appear. A Vietnam veteran I'll call "Len" managed his life for over 40 years before landing in the VA psych ward. Suddenly, Len had an uncontrollable obsession to know the details of an event that had occurred over four decades earlier, but there was no way for him to know for sure what happened. Using EFT, we resolved the trauma surrounding both possible versions of the story. Afterward, Len stated, "It doesn't matter. I can live with either one."Veterans may initially identify a "Top 40 playlist" of traumatic events, which make up most of their nightmares, flashbacks, and intrusive thoughts. After resolving their first half-dozen events, they are frequently hard pressed to identify a remaining specific event to which they have an involuntary response.

- *EFT does more than just "take away" pain; it opens the door to additional healing and growth.* Veterans and EFT practitioners alike are delighted by what regularly surfaces after well-executed EFT. A Vietnam veteran I'll call "Bill" resolved his horror and rage at a newsman who shot a child in the head in reaction to the child's having stolen his wristwatch. The correspondent had been in Vietnam less than 2 days. Bill was the father of a young child. It took all Bill's self-control to keep from doing violence to the war correspondent. The sight of the mother rocking her son's body in her arms and the sound of her anguished voice had haunted Bill in the form of painful involuntary responses for over four decades. At our next session I asked Bill to tell the story again, which he did without any involuntary responses. At the end he looked at me with surprise and genuine compassion, saying, "I'd never thought before about how the correspondent must have felt."

- *EFT often eliminates insomnia and restores healthy sleep patterns.* Many veterans have told me:"I don't want to sleep. Sleep is the enemy."One Vietnam era veteran woke every night in "violent hand-to-hand combat" until we devoted one of our six sessions to tapping on the

aspects of his most violent nightmare. The nightmares stopped immediately. In many cases restful sleep is restored even without tapping directly on the content of any specific nightmare.

- *Clinical EFT can be used to enhance the effectiveness of many other modalities and therapies.* Body workers are beginning to use EFT to relax clients. Many therapists report that EFT has "super-charged" their effectiveness in areas such as counseling, hypnotherapy, timeline work, neuro-linguistic programming, EMDR, and many other modalities. Extremely effective advanced EFT techniques are evolving, such as Matrix Reimprinting (see Chapter 59), which elegantly incorporates elements of guided imagery, timeline, and resource generation into an EFT framework. The physical aspects of Clinical EFT are already based on 5,000-year-old meridian activation practices, which we know "work."Ideally, Clinical EFT's codification of the physical processes will assist students at all levels by ensuring that the all-important neurochemical benefits are always present, even as we welcome the growing richness of advanced EFT applications based on imaginal and linguistic variations.

- *The very structure of EFT renders suicide highly unlikely.* Suicide is not chosen; it happens when pain exceeds the resources for coping with that pain. You can survive suicidal feelings if you: (1) reduce your pain, or (2) increase your coping resources. EFT reduces pain and increases resources at the same time. The mere physical act of tapping the EFT points triggers the body's production of natural opioids and endorphins (Lane, 2009).

## The Realities of Hands-on EFT with Veterans

### Chronic Pain Amplifies PTSD Symptoms; EFT Reduces Pain

Physical pain is not one of the symptoms of PTSD listed in the DSM. Veterans with PTSD, however, frequently not only report chronic pain, but also report chronic pain that is not well managed by pain-killers. There is scientific evidence that chronic pain keeps portions of the brain's frontal cortex associated with emotion in a perpetual state of agitation, leading to depression, anxiety, sleep disturbances, and decision-making abnormalities (Baliki, Geha, Apkarian, & Chialvo, 2008). It follows that resolving chronic pain can significantly reduce the number and intensity of PTSD symptoms. Multiple studies show that EFT reduces pain by an average 68%. Taken together, these studies (Church& Brooks, 2010; Karatzias et al., 2011; Brattberg, 2008) have a statistical certainty of 99.9% (p < .001).

A VA counselor tells me that pain-killers are extremely easy to get from the VA, but when pain-killers aren't effective for the pain, the veterans often land in this counselor's Substance Abuse Treatment Program. The counselor referred to me a Vietnam veteran I'll call "Joe."Joe had suffered for a few years from chronic, debilitating shoulder pain, which on a 0-to-10 scale, was usually at 8 or 9, despite high levels of prescription pain-killers. The doctors said nothing else could be done. In our first EFT session, the intensity of the pain was reduced from 8.5 to 1. At the next session, Joe reported, "It's not a problem anymore, but if it starts to hurt, I just tap. I never let it get above 2.5."Later, he mentioned that he no longer takes any pain medication. Joe brought a friend for an EFT session and the friend's pain was also relieved. The friend said, "I knew there was something to this because Joe hasn't been able to take his motorcycle out for a couple of years, and now we're out riding again."Pain relief often does not require any detective work or language about emotions. Many pains will diminish or vanish in response to tapping along with attention-focusing language as simple as *"Even though I have this pain. This pain. This pain. This pain and everything it stands for."*

## Unraveling Complex PTSD

PTSD is considered complex if it involves the combined trauma from multiple events. Complex PTSD is typical in the veteran population. Many veterans describe their entire deployment as one continuous traumatic event. Research regularly confirms that unresolved childhood trauma, adversity, and stressors result in increased risk for PTSD following a traumatic event in adulthood (Emery, Emery, Shama, Quiana, & Jassani, 1991; Koenen, Moffitt, Poulton, Martin, & Caspi, 2007; Lapp, 2005; APS, 2012).

Thus in working with veterans with PTSD, it is often necessary to apply EFT to non-combat military incidents and incidents that predate military service. Reactions to multiple events may both trigger one another and intensify one another. Entangled involuntary reactions may appear to be a bio-neuro-emotional Gordian knot. However, systematic application of EFT to the parts of the puzzle that present themselves to "view" leads to a comfortable and natural unraveling of even highly complex trauma. The facilitation of a trained EFT practitioner, combined with the fact that the body generalizes its learning, can bring resolution to a trauma with surprising speed.

## The Body Can't Defend and Repair Itself at the Same Time

The body needs to both protect and maintain itself. When the sympathetic nervous system is active, the body is optimized for defense but is unable to carry out processes for growth and repair. When the parasympathetic nervous system is active, the body is optimized for digestion, rest, and repair but is not configured to deal with stress or danger. Under chronic stress, the system gets stuck in the sympathetic mode and cell maintenance is neglected. The sympathetic state is characterized by low levels of the hormone DHEA (dehydroepiandrosterone) and high levels of the body's main stress hormone, cortisol. Low levels of DHEA are found among those with cancer, cardiovascular disease, Alzheimer's, diabetes, depression, hypothyroidism, and adrenal fatigue (McEvoy, 2011). In contrast, the parasympathetic state is characterized by high levels of DHEA, which is associated with "anti-aging," and with low levels of cortisol. Cortisol levels have been shown to drop an average of 24% following an hour of EFT. Cortisol reductions mirror reductions in psychological distress (Church, Yount, & Brooks, 2012). At a neurochemical level, EFT lets the body know that the danger is over and it is time to switch from sympathetic or defense mode to the parasympathetic or repair mode.

## The Magic of the EFT Setup Statement

The Setup Statement, which introduces each round of EFT, pairs the recipient's attention to a discomfort (such as a physical pain or a traumatic memory) with a positive statement, such as one of self-acceptance: for example, "Even though

I have/feel this burning back pain (discomfort), "I deeply and completely accept myself (self-acceptance or other positive statement)." By referring to the discomfort as *"this* [problem]" the Setup Statement elegantly differentiates the person from the problem. The combination of the statement and the tapping typically allows a peaceful though sometimes paradoxical and comical coexistence of the person and the negative experience while it opens the door to comfortable change.

## Veteran Themes: All Are Tappable

Individual veterans often demonstrate the PTSD symptom of "isolation," in which they assume they are the only ones who have certain feelings. In practice, themes reliably emerge throughout the veteran population.

- Distrust and feeling misunderstood are tappable. Although EFT coaches should certainly learn what they can of military culture, I believe coaches make a mistake if they try to "fake it" by memorizing military abbreviations. A nearly universal belief among war veterans is that only someone who was there could possibly understand. The easiest way to be trusted is to actually be trustworthy. Those who are not trustworthy will quickly fail the veteran's "sniff test." Sample Setup Statements: *Even though I've been through more than anyone can ever know, I choose to be surprisingly okay with that. Even though I have this isolation, I accept myself with or without it. Even though I can't trust anyone, I'm open to the possibility of something working out for me.*
- Inconsistency and self-judgment about inconsistency are tappable. *Even though I have this self-judgment, I accept myself, or at least like the idea of accepting myself. Even though this doesn't make any logical sense, I'm still here.*
- Hypervigilance, grief, anger, injustice, outrage, overwhelm, guilt, shame, betrayal, abandonment, anxiety, and emotional numbness are all tappable. *Even though I can't even imagine ever not having this grief, I accept myself with or without it. Even though I have been on "high alert" for years, I allow myself to consider the possibility that I've been safer since I came*

*home than I was over there. Even though I have this overwhelming shame, my heart is still beating. Even though I have this numbness, I'm open to the possibility of being pleasantly surprised.*

It is a common but stereotypic assumption that veteran PTSD always involves direct combat situations. Veterans just as often ask for help resolving trauma around being in defensive situations in which they could do nothing but wait for either death or the all-clear signal, whichever came first. Since EFT reduces cortisol levels by moving the nervous system into a parasympathetic state, tapping directly on the aspects of those experiences allows the body to finally experience the long-awaited "all-clear signal."

## EFT for Veterans: Useful Tools and Practices

### Robert Scaer's Elements of Trauma

Trauma specialist and neurologist Robert Scaer (2007) identifies four factors involved in trauma. In my experience, veterans feel understood when the elements are acknowledged and visible during sessions. I often have them in big print on a single page, as follows:

### Elements of Trauma

1. An interruption or violation of our expectations
2. A perceived threat to identity or physical survival
3. A feeling of isolation
4. A feeling of powerlessness to cope with the situation; having no strategy.

In session, veterans frequently refer directly to the key elements as doorways to communicating their experience. They say things like, "I couldn't believe it was happening" or "That's it. I knew I was dead." They may reach over and touch item 4 on the page saying, "Exactly; there just wasn't anything I could do about it."

## The Emotional Scale: a Context for Feeling

An emotional scale is an invaluable tool to help veterans find words for their experience. Many lists are available. I use the one that follows. By applying EFT to the worst feeling about some particular issue or incident (i.e., starting at the bottom of the list), it is surprisingly easy to work upward. SUD ratings can still be used on each emotion. Many veterans appreciate the insight that anger feels better and feels more "alive" than any of the dozen emotions listed below it. After tapping on discouragement, one veteran said, "Good news! I can see disappointment from here." Indeed, the higher, better feeling emotions only become visible or accessible after EFT has been applied to the lower, worse feeling ones.

## The Emotional Scale

Joy/Appreciation/Empowered/Freedom/Love
Passion
Enthusiasm/Eagerness/Happiness
Positive Expectation/Belief
Optimism
Hopefulness
Contentment
Boredom
Pessimism
Frustration/Irritation/Impatience
Overwhelment
Disappointment
Doubt
Worry
Blame
Discouragement
Anger
Revenge
Hatred/Rage
Jealousy
Insecurity/Guilt/Unworthiness
Fear/Grief/Depression/Despair/Powerlessness

*(Hicks & Hicks, 2004, p. 297)*

## Helpful Practices and Shortcuts

- A simple *hand signal* can indicate the veteran's level of intensity. This can be as simple as having one's hand position range from "low" to "high" and allows the practitioner to ask about intensity without interrupting the veteran.(Young children often indicate comfort with their hands close together and discomfort by holding them far apart.)

- Setting a *low intensity ceiling* and frequently verifying the veteran's comfort often allows tapping through even the most intense events with little or no triggering. I may let the veteran know that the story can only be told if the veteran's intensity does not exceed a level of 3 or 4(on a 0-to-10 scale.) As, in many veterans' previous experience, that would be impossible, veterans will often say, "Well, then, I'm not going to be able to tell you the story."Then, with the benefit of preemptive tapping, the veteran goes on to comfortably do what the veteran thought was impossible.

- Encourage veterans to learn by doing. I encourage veterans to use their own words. This allows the veteran to provide critical information. The coach can make adjustments immediately or incorporate the veteran's words into the next Setup Statement. Veteran participation provides the direct experience that allows the veteran to more easily begin tapping at home.

## Visions for the Future

### Veterans Helping Veterans

*These days MIA stands for Missing In America.*
—Vietnam veteran

Veteran Ken Self said in his story that veterans with PTSD are injured soldiers who need to be brought back to safety. At long last, EFT gives veterans the opportunity to bring their buddies in from the battlefield of involuntary stress responses. Veterans are ideally positioned to provide peer-to-peer EFT support. To the extent that veterans with excessive stress trust anyone, they trust other veterans.

Imagine a self-appointed army of veterans reaching out to one another as only veterans can. Imagine veterans gathering to support themselves and one another in free, drop-in EFT groups coordinated by veterans who have already benefited from EFT. Alcoholics Anonymous and all of the "Anonymous" programs have shown it is possible to make free peer-to-peer support widely available.

By tapping along with videos, resources such as Battle Tap (www.BattleTap.org), or in veteran-based group settings, veterans can receive the benefit of EFT participation without having to talking about their specific issues, or sometimes without talking at all. Veterans frequently mention that EFT needs to be taught in Basic Training so soldiers can apply EFT in the field, promptly after a traumatic event.

## Helping Military Families with EFT

Imagine military family EFT support groups. Studies show that wives of men with PTSD also exhibit symptoms of traumatization (Ben Arzi, Solomon, & Dekel, 2000) and that veteran spouses have a disproportionately high incidence of psychiatric disorders (Manguno-Mire et al., 2007). Facilitators are recommended for EFT support groups for military family members. Imagine EFT being taught in kindergarten, used in the home, and considered a basic life skill.

## Innovation Through Strategic Partnerships

With such compelling research results, the Veterans Stress Project hopes to inspire additional research. Its resources and experience are available to support larger, better funded organizations to undertake larger-scale studies. Until EFT is recognized by the VA, the nonprofit Veterans Stress Project is also seeking strategic partners with whom to explore the logistics of contracting to deliver EFT to the government privately. California Congressman Mike Thompson, cochair of the bipartisan Military Veterans Caucus, introduced legislation supporting innovative treatments for veterans and active duty soldiers suffering from TBI and PTSD. This legislation would ensure access to private treatments while reserving payment only for treatments that work (Editor, 2012). This "pay only for performance" model is compatible with EFT's high success rate. Imagine a collaborative effort of strategic partners resolving veteran PTSD and using the profits to fund further research and education.

## How You Can Help

*Do what you can, with what you have, where you are.*

— Theodore Roosevelt

If this issue touches your heart as it does mine, or if PTSD touches the lives of those for whom you care, you can be part of the solution. Whether you are a parent, neighbor, teacher, or coworker, you can let veterans and family members know where free EFT support is available. Then ask the VA to provide EFT. The VA responds best to written requests from veterans, their health professionals, and their political representatives. You can download the Veterans Stress Project brochure (www.stressproject.org), forward it to friends, and print it for distribution to local Vet Centers, American Legion and VWF posts, student veterans associations, and thousands of other organizations dedicated to serving veterans. Anyone can learn enough basic EFT to improve the quality of his or her daily life and, in so doing, be better able to make a contribution to the lives of others. Anyone can spread awareness of EFT through social media. Anyone can bring EFT to the attention of his or her local and national politicians and ask for their support. (Please forward the contact information of interested parties to the Veterans Stress Project so these representatives will have the opportunity to add their names to future letters to the VA.) Anyone can let veterans and families of veterans know they can help themselves and others by asking for EFT from the VA and by having their physicians or other professionals make written requests to the VA that it use EFT. Anyone can help make EFT a household word. Links to locate veteran related facilities nearest you are listed in the resources section at the end of this chapter.

## Practitioner Volunteer Networks

EFT and other energy psychology practitioners can join a nationwide network of volunteers providing support to veterans and family members by listing themselves on the Veterans Stress Project website. EFT practitioners who are also licensed mental health professionals can volunteer through many nonprofit organizations modeled along the lines of Give An Hour (GAH; www.giveanhour.org), which has a network of nearly 6,500 mental health professionals who provide pro-bono support to veterans.

## EFT Training for VA Counselors

Dawson Church, PhD, supports VA counselors interested in EFT in a refreshingly practical way. Through EFT Universe (eftuniverse.com), he offers VA counselors Level 1 and Level 2 EFT training at no cost on a space-available basis. Other counselors who directly serve veterans may also apply for this sponsorship.

# Conclusion

*There is nothing more powerful than an idea whose time has come.*

—Victor Hugo

In the decades I spent studying, delivering, or teaching in the areas of counseling, personal growth, NLP, and hypnotherapy, I was always searching forever-better means of alleviating human suffering. I wantedan effective, accessible, economical "silver bullet" with no negative side effects, which would enable and encourage people to engage directly in their own healing and growth. I found it in EFT. When I realized I could play a significant role in making EFT available to the VA and mainstream medicine by participating in the Veterans Stress Project's ground breaking clinical trials, I knew I had found my place.

What could be better than saving lives and setting individual veterans free?

What could be better than sharing with all veteran supporters that this drug-free self-help technique comfortably resolves PTSD and its host of physical, mental, and emotional challenges?

What could be better than building a sound, scientific bridge from energy medicine to mainstream medicine? The credibility delivered by the Veteran Stress Project's research is critical to allowing the VA to take advantage of the fact that that America does have a solution to PTSD right now.

EFT is not only a solution to PTSD. It is a life skill. EFT's Personal Peace Procedure allows individuals to systematically eliminate barriers to experiencing personal well- being. Peace is not possible when an individual is trapped in fear or locked in defense mode. Peace is not sustainable when humans are in physical, emotional, or mental pain. EFT makes it possible to resolve or manage pain and stress. EFT frees humans from being "stuck in stress" and from feeling continually under attack. This is true of individuals and of families. It is true of communities and of nations. EFT provides the resources that make lasting peace possible.

In the words of Thich Nhat Hanh, "Veterans are the light at the top of the candle, illuminating the way for the whole nation. If veterans can achieve awareness, transformation, understanding, and peace, they can share with the rest of society the realities of war. And they can teach us how to make peace with ourselves and each other, so we never have to use violence to resolve conflicts again"(Willis, 2003, p. 124).

## EFT Resources for Veteran PTSD
### Books and DVDs

*EFT for PTSD,* by Gary Craig (Fulton, CA: Energy Psychology Press). This book draws from the 2008 open trial and includes guidelines and instructions on applying EFT with veterans.

*An Introduction to Releasing War Trauma with EFT4Vets,* by Ingrid Dintner. Download this free eBook at www.EFT4Vets.com.

*Operation: Emotional Freedom—The Answer* video by Eric Huurre documents the 2008 open trial in which Gary Craig, a team of EFT Masters, Dawson Church, and others met to helpnine veterans and two family members and measure the results.www.operation-emotionalfreedom.com/dvd.php

*PTSD and Trauma: Treating Posttraumatic Stress,*12 DVD set by EFT practitioner Carol Look, documenting work with a married couple who participated in the 2008 open trial. www. attractingabundance.com/eft/dvd-ptsd-trauma

*Six Days at the VA* video documents Gary Craig's work with veterans at the Los Angeles VA in 1994. Original purchasers of the DVD were granted a license to make 100 copies of the DVD to be given away but not sold. Contact Marilyn McWilliams at Marilyn@EFTCatalyst.com to request a copy (subject to license limits).

*The Tapping Solution* by Nick and Jessica Ortner and Nick Polizzi is a DVD documentary on a four-day tapping retreat that includes a Vietnam veteran who suffered from severe PTSD and his turnaround due to EFT. www.thetappingsolution.com

Veterans Stress Project videos demonstrate veterans working with EFT, veteran testimonials, and related research. Download a brochure offering free EFT to veterans. www.stressproject.org

### Battle Tap

Battle Tap (www.battletap.org) is an interactive website to assist veterans in applying EFT to their own symptoms. Dr. Olli Toukolehto is a veteran who himself struggled with PTSD before finding relief with EFT. He and his father, Tim Toukolehto, made a phenomenal contribution by developing this unique resource, which customizes EFT sequences in response to the user's input. Although the expertise of a skilled EFT practitioner is recommended to maintain a safe, comfortable environment when working through the details of intense traumatic memories, substantial and measurable progress can be made by veterans using the Battle Tap resource in the privacy of their own homes. Users can set up anonymous accounts to track their own progress relative both to the reduction of intensity ratings of specific events or feelings and to the scores on a large number of self-assessments available on the site. I routinely ask veterans to supplement their personal practice of EFT by taking advantage of Battle Tap's electronic coach, available 24 hours a day, including those hours when many vets have trouble sleeping.

# References

Association for Psychological Science (APS). (2012, November 19). Embattled childhoods may be the real trauma for soldiers with PTSD [Press release]. Retrieved from http://www.psychologicalscience.org/index.php/news/releases/embattled-childhoods-may-be-the-real-trauma-for-soldiers-with-ptsd.html

Baliki, M. N., Geha, P. Y., Apkarian, A. V., & Chialvo, D. R. (2008, February 6). Beyond feeling: Chronic pain hurts the brain, disrupting the default-mode network dynamics. *Journal of Neuroscience, 28*(6), 1398–1403.

Ben Arzi, N., Solomon, Z., & Dekel, R. (2000). Secondary traumatization among wives of PTSD and post-concussion casualties: Distress, caregiver burden and psychological separation. *Brain Injury, 14,* 725–736.

Billiotti de Gage, S., Bégaud, E., Bazin, F., Verdoux, H., Dartigues, J. F., Pérès, K. Kurth, T., & Pariente, A. (2012, September 27). Benzodiazepine use and risk of dementia: Prospective population based study. *British Medical Journal, 345.* doi:10.1136/bmj.e6231

Brattberg, G. (2008). Self-administered EFT (Emotional Freedom Techniques) in individuals with fibromyalgia: A randomized trial. *Integrative Medicine: A Clinician's Journal, 7*(4), 30–35.

Bryant, R. A. & Harvey, A. G. (2000). *Acute stress disorder: A handbook of theory, assessment, and treatment.* Washington, DC: American Psychological Assocation.

Church, D. (n.d.-a). EFT hearings in Congress [Press release]. Retrieved from http://www.eftuniverse.com/press-release/eft-hearings-in-congress

Church, D. (n.d.-b). For cost of one drug, military might have cured 86% of veterans with PTSD [Press release]. Retrieved from http://www.eftuniverse.com/press-release/cost-of-ptsd-eft-risperidone

Church, D. (2010a). The economic cost savings of energy psychology treatment (Editorial). *Energy Psychology: Theory Research, and Treatment, 2*(1), 9–12. doi:10.9769. EPJ.2010.2.1.DC

Church, D. (2010b). The treatment of combat trauma in veterans using EFT (Emotional Freedom Techniques): A pilot protocol. *Traumatology, 16*(1), 55–65. http://dx.doi.org/10.1177/1534765609347549

Church, D. & Brooks, A. J. (2010). The effect of a brief EFT (Emotional Freedom Techniques) self-intervention on anxiety, depression, pain and cravings in healthcare workers. *Integrative Medicine: A Clinician's Journal, 9*(4), 40–44.

Church, D., Hawk, C., Brooks, A., Toukolehto, O., Wren, M., Dinter, I., & Stein, P. (2013). Psychological trauma symptom improvement in veterans using EFT (Emotional Freedom Techniques): A randomized controlled trial. *Journal of Nervous and Mental Disease, 201,* 153–160.

Church, D., Piña, O., Reategui, C., & Brooks, A. (2012). Single session reduction of the intensity of traumatic memories in abused adolescents after EFT: A randomized controlled pilot study. *Traumatology, 18*(3), 73–79. doi:10.1177/1534765611426788

Church, D., Yount, G., & Brooks, A. J. (2012). The effect of Emotional Freedom Techniques (EFT) on stress biochemistry: A randomized controlled trial. *Journal of Nervous and Mental Disease, 200,* 891–896.

Congressional Budget Office. (2012, February 9). The Veterans Health Administration's treatment of PTSD and traumatic brain injury among recent combat veterans. Retrieved from http://www.cbo.gov/sites/default/files/cbofiles/attachments/02-09-PTSD.pdf

Dao, J. (2012, February 2). Branding a soldier with "personality disorder." *New York Times.* Retrieved from http://www.nytimes.com/2012/02/25/us/a-military-diagnosis-personality-disorder-is-challenged.html?_r=3&sq=ptsd&st=cse&scp=3&pagewanted=all&

Dean, C. (1990). *Nam vet: Making peace with your past.* Portland, OR: Multnomah Press.

Department of Defense. (2007, June). *An achievable vision: Report of the Department of Defense Task Force on Mental Health* (Executive summary, p. 2). Retrieved from http://www.health.mil/dhb/mhtf/mhtf-report-final.pdf

Department of Veterans Affairs. (2012). *Suicide data report, 2012.* Retrieved from http://www.va.gov/opa/docs/Suicide-Data-Report-2012-final.pdf

Editor of the *Lake County News.* (2012, May 19). House passes Thompson's bipartisan amendment to improve TBI, PTSD treatment for troops, vets. *Lake County News.* Retrieved from http://www.lakeconews.com/index.php?option=com_content&view=article&id=25085:house-passes-thompsons-bipartisan-amendment-to-improve-tbi-ptsd-treatments-for-troops-vets&catid=41:veterans&Itemid=285

Emery, V. O., Emery, P. E., Shama, D. K., Quiana, N. A., & Jassani, A. K. (1991, July). Predisposing variables in PTSD patients. *Journal of Traumatic Stress 4*(3), 325–343.

Feinstein, D. (2008). Energy psychology in disaster relief. *Traumatology, 14*(1), 124–137.

Harrell, M., C. & Berglass, N. (2011, October 31). *Losing the battle: The challenge of military suicide.* Washington, DC: Center for a New American Security. Retrieved from http://www.cnas.org/losingthebattle

Hartung, J. & Stein, P. (2012). Telephone delivery of EFT (Emotional Freedom Techniques) remediates PTSD symptoms in veterans: A randomized controlled trial. *Energy Psychology: Theory, Research, & Treatment, 4*(1), 33–42.

Hicks, E. & Hicks, J. (2004). *Ask and it is given.* Carlsbad, CA: Hay House.

Karatzias, T., Power, K., Brown, K., McGoldrick, T., Begum, M., Young, J., ... Adams, S. (2011). A controlled comparison of the effectiveness and efficiency of two psychological therapies for posttraumatic stress disorder: Eye Movement Desensitization and Reprocessing vs. Emotional Freedom Techniques. *Journal of Nervous and Mental Disease, 199*(6), 372–378. doi:10.1097/NMD.0b013e31821cd262

Keteyian, A. (2009, February 11). Suicide epidemic among veterans. CBSNews. Retrieved from http://www.cbsnews.com/2100-500690_162-3496471.html

Koenen, K. C, Moffitt, T. E., Poulton, R., Martin, J., & Caspi, A. (2007). Early childhood factors associated with the development of post-traumatic stress disorder: Results from a longitudinal birth cohort. *Psychological Medicine, 37*(2), 181–192.

Krystal, J. H., Rosenheck, R. A., Cramer, J. A., Vessicchio, J. C., Jones, K. M., Vertrees, J. E., ... Stock, C.(2011, August 3). Adjunctive risperidone treatment for antidepressant-resistant symptoms of chronic military service–related PTSD: A randomized trial. *JAMA, 306*(5), 493–502.

Lane, J. (2009). The neurochemistry of counterconditioning: Acupressure desensitization in psychotherapy. *Energy Psychology: Theory Research and Treatment 2009, 1*(1), 31–44.

Lapp, K. G, Bosworth, H. B., Strauss, J. L., Stechuchak, K. M., Horner, R. D., Calhoun, P. S., . . . Butterfield, M. I. (2005). Lifetime sexual and physical victimization among male veterans with combat-related post-traumatic stress disorder. *Military Medicine, 170*(9), 787–790.

Manguno-Mire, G., Sautter, F., Lyons, J., Myers, L., Perry, D., Sherman, M., Glynn, S., & Sullivan, G. (2007, February). Psychological distress and burden among female partners of combat veterans with PTSD. *Journal of Nervous and Mental Disease, 195*(2), 144–151.

McEvoy, M. (2011, March 6). Cortisol & DHEA: The major hormone balance. *Metabolic Healing.* Retrieved from http://metabolichealing.com/key-integrated-functions-of-your-body/hormone-and-endocrine/cortisol-and-dhea-the-major-hormone-balance

Nagy, S. S. (2009). Observing veterans with PTSD being treated with EFT. In G. Craig, *EFT for PTSD* (pp. 36–47). Fulton, CA: Energy Psychology Press.

New diagnostic criteria for PTSD to be released: DSM-5. (2013). Retrieved from National Center for PTSD, http://www.ptsd.va.gov/professional/pages/dsm-IV-tr-ptsd.asp

NIH (National Institutes of Health). (2009, Winter). PTSD: A growing epidemic. *NIH Medline Plus, 4*(1), 10–14. Retrieved from http://www.nlm.nih.gov/medlineplus/magazine/issues/winter09/articles/winter09pg10-14.html

Rosenheck, R. A. & Fontana, A. F. (2007, November–December). Recent trends in VA treatment of post-traumatic stress disorder and other mental disorders. *Health Affairs, 26*(6), 1720–1727.

Scaer, R.C. (2007). *The body bears the burden: Trauma, dissociation, and disease* (2nd ed.). New York, NY: Haworth Medical Press.

Staggenborg, R. (2013, February 15). Healing the wounded warrior with Marilyn McWilliams [Radio interview]. Retrieved from http://www.blogtalkradio.com/sfpiradio/2013/02/15/healing-the-wounded-warrior-with-marilyn-mcwilliams or http://stressproject.org/Recordings/mm_blogtalkshow_4415027.mp3

Stein, P. & Brooks, A. J. (2011). Efficacy of EFT (Emotional Freedom Techniques) provided by coaches vs. licensed therapists in veterans with PTSD. *Energy Psychology: Theory, Research, & Treatment, 3*(1), 11–17.

U.S. Census Bureau. (2012). Table 521. Veterans living by period of service, age, and sex: 2010. Retrieved from http://www.census.gov/compendia/statab/2012/tables/12s0521.pdf

U.S. Department of Veterans Affairs: National Center for Veterans Analysis and Statistics. (2011, September 30). Veteran population statistics at a glance. Retrieved from http://www.va.gov/vetdata/docs/quickfacts/Homepage-slideshow.pdf

Weathers, F., Litz, B., Herman, D., Huska, J., & Keane, T. (1993, October). The PTSD Checklist (PCL): Reliability, validity, and diagnostic utility. Paper presented at the Annual Convention of the International Society for Traumatic Stress Studies, San Antonio, TX. Retrieved summary from http://www.ptsd.va.gov/professional/pages/assessments/ptsd-checklist.asp

Willis, J. S. (Ed.). (2003). *A lifetime of peace: Essential writings by and about Thich Nhat Hanh.* New York, NY: Marlowe.

Chapter 47

# EFT for the Beginning of Life: Supporting Wholeness, Human Potential, and Optimal Relationships

*Wendy Anne McCarty*

## Abstract

As we move from a biology-based Newtonian paradigm into a consciousness-based paradigm in which our perspectives expand to hold the multidimensional nature of reality, human nature, communication, and healing, our views of what wholeness, coherence, and right relationship mean also evolve. Nowhere are the implications of this paradigm shift more profound than in our evolving understanding of babies and our earliest developmental period. Emotional Freedom Techniques (EFT) practice with families at the beginning of their baby's life is explored within the context of the broader consciousness-based landscape of the Integrated Model of early development and the corresponding therapeutic Integrated Approach, which incorporate prenatal and perinatal psychology clinical findings, heart intelligence research, and consciousness studies. Priority is given to meeting the needs of the multidimensional baby to support human potential and optimal relationships. A transcript of a session with a pregnant mother and baby illustrate an Integrated Approach using EFT in which the baby is included.

**Keywords:** Emotional Freedom Techniques, EFT, pregnancy, birth, infant, consciousness, heart intelligence, prenatal and perinatal psychology, energy psychology

**Wendy Anne McCarty, PhD, RN**, is a holistic educator/consultant for professionals and families specializing in prenatal and perinatal psychology, consciousness, and energy healing. She is the author of *Welcoming Consciousness: Supporting Babies' Wholeness from the Beginning of Life— An Integrated Model of Early Development*. Send correspondence to Wendy Anne McCarty, 315 Meigs Road A306, Santa Barbara, CA 93109, or drwmccarty@gmail.com.

An enlightened culture would attend to the developmental needs of its newborn and unborn with exquisite care and consciousness (Eden, 2012).

> *Imagine a World ...* where every baby is welcomed, loved, nurtured, and seen for the amazing, conscious, and aware being they are from the beginning of life. As these babies grow, so does their capacity to love, to empathize with others, to be in relationship and to live in joy. As our first generation matures, we would see the ripple effect grow to encompass greater learning capacity, emotional intelligence and creativity, the emergence of new leaders, and healthier families and communities. Our potential is unlimited. (McCarty & Glenn, 2008, p. 134)

Helping families as they welcome, conceive, carry, birth, and care for their babies is an honor. It is a sacred time of bringing in new life and is filled with immense power and potential to set in motion lifelong patterns not only for the baby, but also for each member of the family and the family as a synergistic whole.

## Our Core Nature

We live in an exciting time. Our understandings of who babies are, what they are capable of, what they need, and what is happening during their time in the womb, birth, and newborn period are in the midst of quantum change. The 20th century Newtonian worldview that considered our core nature to be biological is expanding into a 21st century multidimensional, consciousness-based paradigm. Our consciousness-based holistic, integrated, and integral lens guides us in new possibilities for health and healing and in what it means to be human.

As Schlitz and Amorok (2005) suggest, "Consciousness shifts our healing efforts and results from a change that expands the range and scope of what is possible, to a change that actually transforms the entire landscape" (p. 4). Nowhere is that more true than for babies and families at the beginning of life.

## My Evolving Worldview, Theory, and Practice

For the past 40 years, I have had the privilege of supporting families as they carry, birth, and raise their babies and children. My journey has taken me into the heart of this quantum change of worldview regarding our core nature and human potential. I began as a western-trained obstetrical nurse, childbirth educator, and parent-infant specialist and then practiced as a Marriage and Family Therapist (MFT) for 10 years. I thought I understood a lot about babies, but in 1988 that was turned upside down when I attended an Association for Prenatal and Perinatal Psychology and Health (APPPAH) conference. There I entered the world of prenatal and perinatal psychology (PPN) and discovered a very different multidimensional lens being used to more fully understand babies.

Prenatal and perinatal psychology (PPN) has been studying our earliest human development *from the baby's point of view* for over 30 years. The PPN field coalesced in the 1980s when APPPAH was formed. Therapists came together to share their discoveries of clients' current issues found to be anchored in their experiences in the womb, during birth, and in the newborn period. Their stories portrayed babies as having greater awareness and capacities than traditionally held to be possible. Over the years, PPN-oriented therapies were developed to identify and treat not only adults with early-origin issues, but also to work directly with babies and children to assess and heal early trauma, unmet needs, and attachment issues, based on the PPN understandings of babies' capacities and needs.

During the APPPAH conference, Dr. William Emerson's presentation, *Psychotherapy with Infants,* included a video of his session with a 3-month-old in which he and the baby addressed the baby's difficult birth. As I watched, my normal ways of perceiving babies were suspended and I found myself sensing the meaningfulness of the baby's verbal and nonverbal communication and dialogue with Dr. Emerson. I experienced the baby's depth of presence and what appeared to be the baby's appreciation for Dr. Emerson's "being with him" in that difficult place and understanding him in the moment. That moment changed me, and it changed what I considered to be the "whole" baby.

I perceived a grander SELF being expressed by that baby than I had previously thought possible. The repercussions of this realization were enormous. Why had I never perceived this deeper level of conscious being in babies before? Could it be that my Newtonian mindset had limited my perceptions? I wanted to find out.

As I trained and worked with a PPN orientation, I experienced endless expanding perceptions of the very essence of who we are and how to communicate and care for babies to help set in motion greater human potential and optimal relationships. Since 1990, I've specialized in prenatal and perinatal psychology working with families and their babies and children who have experienced early trauma, unmet needs, and life-diminishing imprints during the earliest stages of life.

I began by opening my MFT practice to young children and for several years saw toddlers through grade school age children who had experienced some trauma or difficulty during their birth or prenatal experience. (For clinical stories of young children from those years of practice, see McCarty, 2012.) Later, I cofounded BEBA (Building and Enhancing Bonding and Attachment), a nonprofit clinic, to treat babies and their families. Throughout those years, my intention was to let go of my preconceived notions and to be receptive to what babies were showing me. I was stunned, awed, touched, challenged, and surprised by the depth of consciousness that babies expressed. (For clinical stories of work with babies at BEBA, see McCarty, 2002.)

Thus my journey as a practitioner dramatically evolved from biology-based to consciousness-based therapeutic practice. Not only was I using a multidimensional lens to relate to and treat babies and children, but I incorporated more energetic and nonlocal aspects of relating to babies and healing as well. I was grateful to have the opportunity to study biodynamic craniosacral therapy, Somatic Experiencing, and other energy psychology/medicine modalities. I was involved in consciousness studies and my own spiritual practice.

I specifically searched for energy psychology (EP) techniques that would be effective and gentle to use during pregnancy. I wanted EP tools that I could both use in sessions with families and teach parents to use at home for their children and themselves. Emotional Freedom Techniques (EFT) met those criteria and has been an integral part of my work with families and my PPN-EP trainings and practice for many years.

In 1999 I coauthored and was the founding chair of the first PPN graduate degree program, and for 12 years I taught therapists-in-training how to work with young families during pregnancy, birth, and after the baby is born, including EP and specifically EFT.

When teaching, I felt the tension of the paradigm "divide" between Newtonian biology-based views and the PPN multidimensional view of babies. Although PPN had many clinical findings and effective therapies to address early trauma, we needed to articulate new early development models that were consciousness-based, held the integrity of PPN clinical findings, and could guide our practice. Through an academic grant, I reviewed findings from a wide range of related fields and developed the new consciousness-based Integrated Model published in *Welcoming Consciousness: Supporting Babies' Wholeness from the Beginning of Life—An Integrated Model of Early Development* (2004, 2012), which includes over 30 pages of reference and bibliography. (For other writings about the Integrated Model, see McCarty, 2004, 2005, 2006a, 2006b.)

Thus what I share with you in this chapter are selected key concepts, principles, and approaches that I have garnered as an academic, researcher, theorist, educator, and practitioner utilizing what I call the Integrated Approach to working with families. My theoretical Integrated Model and its guiding principles inform my practice with families. Many of the basic EFT steps and techniques you have learned as general EFT practice can be applied during pregnancy, birth, and baby's first years. Yet I believe situating our EFT practices within the broader landscape of consciousness-based understandings of the beginning of life, clinical findings from prenatal and perinatal psychology, and the integrated lens of early development can transform our work and offer families a more conscious way of being with their baby and themselves.

## An Integrated Approach

Although families often come wanting help with a specific issue or difficulty, what fundamental principles and overarching goals guide our work during this momentous moment in their lives?

## Healing: Wholeness, Coherence, and Right Relationship

I would suggest that supporting *wholeness, coherence,* and *right relationships* be pillars of our healing intentions, as they as are within the holistic nursing community. From *Holistic Nursing: A Handbook for Practice:*

> When the theoretical physicist David Bohm was asked, "How can anything become more

whole if everything is already part of the indivisible wholeness of the implicit order of the universe?" he responded with one word. "Coherence." ... Increasing the wholeness of a system is about establishing a pattern of relationships among its elements that is more and more coherent. ...

Healing, if it is a process of being or becoming whole, must be an emerging pattern of relationships among the elements of the whole person that leads to greater integrity, connection, and cohesion of the whole system. This pattern of relationships can be called right relationship. Thus, healing is the emergence of right relationship at or between or among any and all levels of the human experience. It is a process rather than a state. (Quinn, 2013, p. 109)

These core dynamic, living processes—wholeness, right relationship, and coherence—are all involved in supporting healing and human potential. They can be applied to an individual, such as the baby, or to the "whole" mother-baby relationship, or to the "whole" family. Supporting greater wholeness, coherence, and right relationship guides my work with families. I ask myself where these are diminished or impaired. How is our work together serving to bring them into a higher level of functioning?

As we move from a biology-based Newtonian paradigm into a consciousness-based paradigm in which our perspectives expand to hold the multidimensional nature of reality, human nature, communication, and healing, our views of what wholeness, coherence, and right relationship mean also evolve. Nowhere are the implications of this paradigm shift more profound than in our expanding understanding of babies and our earliest human developmental period.

## The Integrated Model of Early Development: The Integrated Self

In the 20th century, the Newtonian worldview and the corresponding understandings of babies were based on a biological view of human development. Our core nature was seen as biological. Brain development was considered the foundation for a baby's capacity to perceive, communicate meaningfully, and learn. Consciousness was seen to develop from their biological development. Our core sense of self was thought to develop over the first 18 months of life. In recent decades, great strides have been made in understanding the importance of early experience and secure parent-infant relationships for optimal brain development, yet these findings are all still held within the Newtonian biological paradigm. Most of us grew up with these views, were educated and also trained with these understandings.

Yet PPN findings bring us full circle to the nearly universal ancient wisdom (prior to the modern era) that suggests that our human self is the manifested expression of our more encompassing and primary nonphysical, spiritual being. Prenatal and perinatal psychology findings demonstrate that our transcendental awareness, our sense of ourselves as a person (sense of self), and many of our multidimensional abilities are present *as we come into human life and throughout our lives.*

**Core principles from the integrated model.** Here is a succinct list of core principles of the Integrated Model of early development, originally published in *Shift: At the Frontiers of Consciousness,* the journal of the Institute of Noetic Sciences (McCarty, 2005, pp. 19–20):

1. We are sentient beings—conscious and aware from the beginning of life. We have a sense of self as we enter physical form that is present prior to, during, and after our human life.
2. From conception on, we have dual perspectives of awareness: a transcendent perspective and a human perspective. Our earliest experiences involve an intricately woven relationship between these two distinct perspectives. Together they form the Integrated Self.
3. From the moment of conception we perceive, function, communicate, and learn on nonlocal consciousness, energetic, and physical levels.
4. We have an ability to transmit and receive communication during the prenatal and perinatal period and participate in a reciprocal relational process.
5. During our gestation, birth, and early infant stages, we learn intensely and are exquisitely sensitive to our environment and relationships. Through our transcendent perspective, we have omni-awareness of our parents and others' thoughts, feelings,

and intentions that arise from their conscious and subconscious mind. Through our human self, our experience is intricately related to our mother's experience, the health of our womb, and the physical and emotional journey at birth. During this period we form a foundational holographic blueprint from our experience.

6. This blueprint becomes the adaptive unconscious core infrastructure from which we grow and experience life at every level of our being—physical, emotional, mental, relational, and spiritual.

7. Our early experiences become part of our implicit memory reflected in our subconscious and in our autonomic functioning. These affect us below the level of our conscious awareness and directly shape our very perceptions and conceptions of reality.

8. We already are making intentional choices and forming adaptive strategies in the womb and at birth that establish potentially lifelong patterns.

9. Young babies show us established life patterns already developed from their experiences in utero, birth, and the early postnatal period (McCarty, 2002). The majority of babies born in the United States show signs of stress or traumatic imprinting (Emerson, 1998).

10. Many of the needs we have considered essential for healthy development during infancy and childhood are needs we have from the beginning of life: to be loved, wanted, welcomed, safe, nourished, seen, heard, included, and communicated with as the sentient beings we are. From the beginning of life, stress and trauma inhibit or interfere with the natural relationship between the baby's Transcendent Self and human self.

11. As many indigenous cultures have done for centuries, communicating with babies and relating to them as conscious beings during the preconception, prenatal, birth, and infancy period on is one of the most powerful ways to support babies and can mitigate the impact of potentially traumatizing events.

(For an in-depth discussion of each of these principles and clinical stories that illustrate them, see McCarty, 2012.)

**The integrated self.** For me, these findings and principles mark a celebration of remembering more of who we are, our spiritual heritage, and our early development that shaped our core human self. These findings also guide our welcoming and caring for babies in ways that support wholeness, consciously include their primary Transcendental Self, and seek to provide a continuity in the transition to becoming human.

My premise is that prior to human life we have a Transcendent Self that has a sentient, aware sense of "I AM." With our human conception, our human self and our Transcendent Self form a holonomic, holographic, self-organizing, dynamic self-system that I refer to as the *Integrated Self*. In other words, our Integrated Self represents the ever-evolving relationship between our physical human perspective and our nonphysical transcendental perspective.

Thus, when I speak of supporting wholeness in babies, I am focused upon the baby's primary relationship with his or her SELF. When there is greater coherence and alignment (right relationship) between the Transcendent Self and human self, there is greater wholeness, higher levels of complexity, self-organization, well-being, and a fuller expression of the SELF in human experience. During the Newtonian era this relationship was undermined and disrupted, resulting in a cascading diminution of our wholeness when babies are viewed solely through a biological lens.

How can we help families welcome and care for the whole multidimensional baby in ways that promote a coherent, right relationship with the Transcendental Self? I would suggest, therein lies the promise of a quantum change in human potential and expanded avenues for positive, self-actualizing life patterns.

We begin with building the inner alignment of our own Integrated Self and helping parents to nurture their own alignment as a way of family living. We learn not only to align our SELVES more fully, but also to access and utilize our capacities more consciously at multiple levels of being—physical, energetic, and nonlocal—as a fuller embodiment of our multidimensional Integrated Self.

## A Therapeutic Integrated Approach

Building upon the foundation of the consciousness-based landscape of healing and wholeness and my understandings of early development as expressed in the Integrated Model, I want to introduce some of the key concepts and principles that I value in my therapeutic Integrated Approach. I discuss these with families and help families benefit from them in their daily life. I have previously discussed coherence and holographic relational fields in McCarty (2006a, 2012). I build upon them here.

## Coherence

Coherence is increasingly being used as a way to describe the state of health and well-being. In energy psychology we speak in terms of coherent energy flow and disruptions in energy. In the infant literature, babies who are thriving are often described by such terms as coherent, organized, regulated, connected, securely attached, and oriented toward growth. Babies who are functioning in more protected survival ways are described as disorganized, disregulated, disconnected, incoherent, or insecurely attached.

For the holonomic, holographic Integrated Self, building coherence is helping the person's whole being at every level—physical, emotional, mental, and spiritual—come into the most coherent alignment (right relationship). The whole organizes the parts, and when we align our physical human self with our nonlocal primary consciousness, we optimize our human potential and positive relationships with others and our world. When we are in coherent states, our connection between our human self and nonphysical self is clearer, and when our primary nonphysical Self is more available and present, our human self becomes more coherent.

Coherence can be viewed intrapersonally, interpersonally, and globally to include environmental factors. When I relate to babies, children, or adults, I envision their multidimensional wholeness, and my healing intention is to help create more coherent connections within their multidimensional being. I model and help parents do this with their baby, and as a way of being within themselves.

## Holographic Relational Fields of Experience

When we come into relationship, we share information at every level of our being (physical, emotional, mental, and spiritual) and reality (local,

energetic, and nonlocal). These can be shared consciously or at unconscious levels. We share information from past and present experiences and from future events. We can influence and be influenced by one another in this shared holographic field of experience (McCraty, 2003; Radin, 2006).

## Heart Fields and Heart Coherence

In my work with families, I share findings with them from the Institute of HeartMath. The institute's extensive research suggests that our heart's electromagnetic rhythmic field acts as a global synchronizing carrier wave for our whole body; that when our heart field is more coherent, our brain and our whole system becomes more coherent; and that our emotional states are correlated with the patterns of heart coherence. When we experience expansive emotions of love, well-being, gratitude, and joy, we are more coherent. When we are in constricted emotional states, such as frustration or anger, we lose coherence (McCraty, Trevor, & Tomasino, 2005). I teach parents to use EFT to help shift their constricted emotional states to more coherent positive states.

When considered interpersonally, Heartmath research suggests that we share information from our heart's electromagnetic field with others in proximity. The more coherent we are, the more we can synchronize with others, becoming more empathic and sensitive to them and helping them synchronize with us. The research suggests that the more the social (relational) field is coherent, the more influence it has in helping its members be coherent (McCraty, 2003; McCraty, Trevor, & Tomasino, 2005). For more information, visit www.heartmath.org.

One of my primary goals is to empower mothers to be able to improve their emotional state with EFT. Mothers readily understand the connection between their emotional state and coherency. A mother can sense how her own coherent heart acts as a carrier wave of coherence for her baby, supporting optimal prenatal development. Mothers understand that when they are in a heart-open, positive, coherent state, they also help stabilize their babies' emotional states, regulation, and brain development, and promote optimal coherence for growth. When mothers are more coherent, babies feel more secure and the relationship is enhanced. When mothers understand how vital their emotional states are, it can sometimes inspire guilt or fear of the responsibility this implies. EFT can help overcome any guilt or fear, and empower mothers to be able to care for themselves and their baby in this way.

Fathers appreciate the importance of their own coherence and their vital role in helping their partner and baby create and sustain heart coherence and positive emotional states. EFT empowers fathers to be able to shift their state of being more readily.

## The Holographic Therapeutic Field

When we work with an individual or family, we enter and form a *therapeutic holographic field* of interaction. As we bring our intentions and attention into focus, while we discuss and address events and issues, we are *coming into phase* with that particular aspect of their experience. Some call this a *thought field*. I prefer the term *holographic field,* because the field is more than thoughts. This therapeutic holographic field is ever-evolving and has memories, sensations, somatic patterns, emotions, thoughts, images, patterns of being, energetic qualities, and relational patterns held at conscious and unconscious, and local and nonlocal levels.

This is how I conceptualize what is happening in our EFT sessions. The client is coming into phase with a specific holographic field of experience of the issue we are addressing and I am participating in that experience. As practitioners, when we are in phase with our clients' experiences, we feel empathic and are intuitively in sync, often finding words and expressions of that field that we bring into the tapping focus and language with our clients. Together we are in an intuitive, creative dance with the material that is arising. During the EFT session, as we explore and work with that field of experience, the holographic field changes and reorganizes, and new thoughts, feelings, sensations, and meanings emerge. Magic happens, the field of experience evolves into something new, and the whole holonomic, holographic Integrated Self changes.

This is also true when I work and relate to babies. I intend to come into phase with their holographic field of experience, and as I build my skills to do that, I become more in tune with their behaviors and communications at all levels.

## An Integrated Approach with Families

Whether working with families while their baby is in the womb or has grown into an adult, these selected principles are essential to my therapeutic lens and interventions.

## The Holographic Family Field

This specific application of relational fields is a core conceptualization and focus in my work with families. It is worth a much fuller discussion than is possible here, but let me introduce its essentials.

The Newtonian model simplified and narrowed our understanding of what "information" babies meaningfully or consciously interact with. With our new lens of babies as holographic, multidimensional beings, we see babies read and respond meaningfully to a greater range of information in the multidimensional holographic fields that surround them.

For example, in sessions with families, I attend to how babies and children respond to what their parents and I are discussing, such as stories of what happened during the child's time in the womb and during birth and bonding. Whether they are very young babies or older children, they appear to resonate with and respond to the material meaningfully. The young ones often talk about or display somatic behaviors that portray their earlier experiences, respond with feelings that arise as we discuss that circumstance, or interact with us in a way that is a meaningful dialogue about the subject.

During those sessions, we are all, including the babies, coming into phase with the holographic field of experience of that moment in their lives back then. The sessions then focus on helping the babies or children with their unresolved trauma and constricted patterns through a conscious, direct interaction with them about what they are showing us. We slow down, acknowledge the babies/children's responses, and process the event or circumstances together with them. Sometimes they are the ones leading us into a specific focus, and we come into phase with their field of experience and start to explore the territory together from there. (This therapeutic process is illustrated in clinical stories in McCarty, 2002, 2012.)

*In my practice over the years, from what babies and children have shown us, I have come to appreciate that babies grow, live, learn, adapt,* and communicate within the interconnected holographic field of their family and personal environment from prior to conception forward. That is a big and very significant statement. The family field contains ancestral material, historical experiences from the past—this or other lifetimes—unprocessed or unresolved issues of the parents or other family members, as well as information of current experience and responses to it. The family field also resonates with/within the fields of the extended family and significant others, community, culture, other planes of reality and the unified whole. Sometimes in sessions babies and young children would show us or talk about things that happened to their parents during their parents' infancy, some unresolved material their parents had from earlier life experiences, or other sources of information and material. After we addressed them, the babies and children didn't seem to resonate with or hold on to them anymore.

The clinical literature of prenatal and perinatal psychology is filled with stories of babies' capacities to accurately remember complex events and relational dynamics, parents' intentions and actions, and their parents' emotional states while they, the babies, were in the womb or during their birth and newborn period. Thus, in a session when we begin talking about an earlier time, or the baby/child is triggered into a pattern set in motion from back then, understanding the notion of the shared family field is very helpful in successfully supporting a therapeutic shift.

Thus I have come to appreciate that babies are exquisitely sensitive and responsive to relational fields from the very beginning of life. We develop and learn to be "human" by being within our mother's and family's holographic field of human experience. Mothers and babies have 9 months in which they are uniquely connected physically but also sharing conscious and unconscious holographic fields of information between them. This unique rapport continues after birth. Knowing babies are more aware and functioning at these levels can add to the possibility of greater communication and bonding by attending to subtle cues, somatic sensations, thoughts and feelings, energetic intuitive knowing, and mind-to-mind rapport with the baby that arise while we seek to come into phase with them and the relational field between us. Thus, expanding our conscious ways of interacting with the family holographic field of experience is an opportunity to meet the whole baby and

help the baby function from his or her Integrated Self from the beginning of life.

Sometimes we may do this by understanding a particular constriction babies are expressing. Babies often resonate with unresolved trauma, grief, or unspoken family secrets and express them in some manner until we identify and shift them. For example, if there is some unspoken conflict and tension between parents, the baby resonates with that conflict and may be more disregulated or fussy. Working with the parents' conflict first, utilizing EFT, can shift the whole family's field and the baby often naturally becomes more balanced. Thus, when parents come for help for their baby, I assess and keep my awareness attuned to issues the parents, grandparents, or others have with which the baby could be resonating and identifying as well. I often work with the adults' contributions first and then see if the baby needs further help.

## Deepening Our Relationship with the *Integrated Self* Baby

As described previously, one of the distinct characteristics of PPN-oriented therapeutic work with babies, children, and families is that we work directly with babies and young children. We include them in the family's therapeutic process, rather than the adults talking *about* them without acknowledging or including them. This is true for babies in the womb and after birth if they are present during the session.

The inclusion of babies in the session *is* the therapeutic process that transforms babies' experiences and how families relate. Even though there remains great mystery in babies' inner worlds, we know enough to understand that babies want to be communicated with, included, and have the capacity to relate as conscious beings prior to conception and forward.

This is still a newer perspective for parents, and many want help knowing how to communicate with their baby and read their baby's cues. Parents may have heard about talking to babies in the womb or that babies can experience trauma at birth, but their information is often sketchy. What I have found is that the more comfortable I am with this new lens of babies and with modeling how to bring the baby into our EFT process, parents quickly experience the real interchange with the baby and begin including the baby more in their daily lives and in their own EFT practice. Deepening parent-baby communication and bonding from the very beginning is one of the primary components of building human potential and optimal relationships.

Much of my focus with families is modeling and mentoring them in how to relate to their baby as a full being, how to come "into phase" with their baby prior to conception forward, and how to nurture that sense of welcome and security for their multidimensional baby.

To summarize, in the work with families, a mainstay of my approach is to suggest to parents that (1) babies resonate, connect, and respond to the family field, and changes in the field, from the very beginning of life in the womb; (2) we can, with our intention and attention, come into phase and check in with the baby's field of experience as we would our own; (3) we can work with the baby's field of experience with EFT to promote healing and well-being; and (4) we can do that with babies in the womb, and we can do it nonlocally after birth when babies are not with us physically. (A description of an EFT session illustrating this in detail came be found in McCarty, 2006a.)

## Authentic Truths—The Heart of Healing

I believe when we reach an authentic truth, when we address something genuinely that has remained unresolved or unspoken, and when we come to acknowledge and compassionately hold the experience of that truth, our Transcendent Self and human self come into a beautiful alignment and we become more whole. This is the heart of healing.

In EFT sessions, we see moments of transformation unfold as clients acknowledge what is genuinely true for them with love and acceptance as they tap. Feeling the relief and resolution possible with EFT, clients learn not to be afraid or stand in judgment of their authentic process, but rather become more at ease to discover, acknowledge and allow healing to unfold.

The most treasured gift I have received from babies and children is watching the spontaneous transformations they experience when we are authentically honest with them about what is going on in the moment or about what transpired in the past. Babies align, parents align, and healing of their relationships unfolds. This is especially true when we recognize and acknowledge something from the babies' earlier experiences during conception, pregnancy, birth, and the newborn period that may have left them with unresolved trauma, unmet needs, or inner conflicts. The circumstance may have just happened, or it may have happened decades ago. But when these earlier circumstances are spoken of with loving care with the intention of helping the babies understand more of their early story and giving them a chance to express their feelings and responses and have them honored and heard, and when parents express their own feelings and regrets or remorse, the heart of healing is touched and the multidimensional self of both align. When parents experience their child's healing in this way, it changes how they interact with the child from then onward.

As adults and parents, we want to protect babies from pain, hurt, or difficulties. In the past, we have thought that babies didn't remember early experiences and we assumed that those things really wouldn't affect them. Often parents are hesitant to talk about when things weren't ideal. They are especially hesitant to talk to their children about their own feelings or problems. But now that we understand that babies' early experiences are recorded and held within them, and we understand that babies are resonating with what is going on in the relational fields and family fields, especially what is left unspoken and unresolved, it changes our fundamental approach. I believe this way of being with babies and this therapeutic process is *the* most important change to help babies thrive and align with their whole self.

I address this process and phenomenon every time I teach or write. If you read my work, you will find many stories that illustrate this. But, because this is so critical, I want to include a story here that I shared in an ISSEEEM *Bridges* article:

One of the most remarkable phenomena was the spontaneous change that would occur when parents decided to talk to their children about what really happened during their birth or prenatal period. Time and time again current challenges dissolved and parent-child relationships improved with these conversations. One mother wrote after she "took my advice" to talk to her 4-year-old son about his difficult birth. She had always told him a "positive version" on his birthday, and now told him the more "real" story that included the complications, pain, disappointments, and his coming out screaming with deep indentations in his forehead and bruising. "That must of hurt your head and you cried so loud for a very long time ... and I couldn't come to hold you. I'm so sorry. That must have been really hard for you."

He didn't say much, but later, at home she said to herself, "Something's different. What is it?" Then she realized that her son's lifelong pattern of talking very loudly had gone away. She shared that as a baby he cried very loudly and when he talked, he always shouted. It was such a problem they got his hearing checked. No matter how much they worked with him, he consistently shouted. In that moment, she realized he was no longer shouting, nor did he return to that pattern after their talk about his birth. The remarkable healing power of acknowledging what really happened and showing empathy for the baby's experience I have witnessed hundreds of times over the years. (McCarty, 2011, p. 13)

When we do EFT, we are doing these steps for ourselves while we tap. We recognize something, and then we acknowledge and honor our own experience of it with loving care. In the Integrated Approach, we are essentially building upon the notion of helping babies to know and heal with their authentic truth, their authentic life story. Now we can add EFT into that process and tap for the baby.

## Honor and Heal Our Own Prenatal and Perinatal Experiences

Most adults were conceived, carried, birthed, and raised in the traditional Newtonian mindset and practices. Much of what we have seen in PPN-oriented therapies are the unfortunate effects of our not recognizing the primary consciousness of the baby and not understanding the full impact of what the baby experiences during this time. When I reviewed the PPN literature and thought about what babies had taught me, underlying all the other issues was the need to be recognized, communicated with, included, and considered as a conscious being—a person. I like to say we are *sentient beings–sensitive human beings* as we begin human life. Whether I am working with a family that is trying to conceive or one with an infant, I consider and relate to the baby as a whole multidimensional being. I want babies to feel they are valued, that they matter, and to encourage communication and a conscious relationship with them from the very beginning.

So whether I'm working with babies or adults revisiting their prenatal and perinatal experiences, I envision them as the Integrated Self and support their alignment and access to their holographic wholeness during their early experiences. Profound healing often comes when we connect their current life difficulties and their prenatal and perinatal experiences in which they were not related to nor considered as a conscious being and had unrecognized trauma, unmet needs, or limiting life-imprints.

Working with the pre- and perinatal issues of clients at any age often triggers practitioners' early unconscious, unresolved material. This is especially true when working with families during this developmental period. I highly recommend when you work with families having babies, that you honor your own experience by working with your own pre- and perinatal experiences and patterns using EFT. If you are a parent who has been pregnant and/or had your own children, reflecting upon and working with whatever unresolved trauma, depression, loss, regrets, and disappointments you and your children may have from pregnancy, birth, and the postnatal period can offer wonderful healing and can improve your ability to be clear and present with families and babies. My motto is that *it is never too early or too late* to work with prenatal and perinatal issues to create transformational shifts.

## Pacing, Stillness, Orienting, Differentiating, and Integration

We know from working with trauma that maintaining the right pacing during the session is important. From craniosacral therapy principles we know that when we come into inner stillness, we are aligned with our deepest, most restorative rhythms, and our system is the most coherent, and best able to let go of constrictive patterns and spontaneously reorganize in greater alignment. As practitioners we value our skill to be heart-coherent, still within ourselves, and attuned to slower rhythms in order to help clients access their own stillness.

When working with pregnant mothers and babies in the womb or postnatally, it is essential to be aware of pacing. Babies process more slowly. A priority in the session is to help babies stay oriented and regulated in the moment and able to integrate their process and experience. Slowing down, pausing, and reading those cues are important skills. Also, when parents are working with their own earliest experiences, it can be more challenging for them to stay present and oriented. They can become disoriented and charged more easily. Attending to slowing down the pace, pausing, and helping them orient in connection with themselves and to you can be an important part of their successfully resolving those early life issues and integrating their healing experience.

Another therapeutic tool to help orient is differentiation, which is especially helpful in working with families and babies. There are two aspects of differentiation: differentiating between people, and differentiating between past and present. The traditional Newtonian view of babies in the womb is that their experience is one of being merged with their mother and their environment, and they have no capacity to have a sense of self or have their own experience. In the Integrated Model, we see that babies do experience merging with their mother's experience and their environment, but they also have a sense of personhood, a sense of themselves as a separate entity with their own experience and perspective.

Oftentimes when we are working with parents and babies, we are helping to "orient" them to what is going on with something that they are experiencing in which there may be a lack of clarity as to "who is who and what is what." Here is an example from a BEBA clinic session that illustrates differentiation and several of the principles we have been discussing.

A mother and her 9-month-old baby have come in for their last BEBA session. The family is moving out of town. The session begins with the baby being very fussy. We bring our attention to helping the baby by slowing things down, acknowledging with him that we are aware of his fuzziness, and yet nothing seems to help. I remember our principle of family field and wonder if he is resonating with something the mother is holding, and I ask the mother, "How are you feeling about moving and not having our support any longer?" She looks down, and silent tears roll down her cheeks. "I'm sad and scared," she whispers. At the very moment she begins authentically acknowledging her inner truth, the baby rolls over, looks at her, smiles, and relaxes. I say to the baby, "Yeah, Mom's feeling sad and scared about moving and not seeing us again. You may have been feeling those hard feelings she was feeling. Those are Mom's feelings. And she's talking with us about them now and I see you are feeling better. Yeah." ... And the whole tension pattern in the room releases. That is differentiating between people.

Differentiating the past from the present is also an essential part of helping babies or individuals at any age address very early material. We understand that babies imprint and develop belief patterns from their earliest experiences. They are held at the unconscious level and often, as we grow, we are like the fish in the water—we don't understand why we are this way, we just are. When we acknowledge what was true in the past, it is also helpful to acknowledge how things are different now. Both help orient us in relationship to the pattern rather than being in the pattern.

To bring together several of the principles we just covered and illustrate differentiating past from present, I want to share one of my favorite father stories that was originally published in the ISSSEEM publication *Bridges*. The father, who was from Mexico, approached me at a workshop and said he wanted to talk with me:

> Luis said, "Do you remember years ago telling us a story of your therapy work with babies? You told us of a father who was just realizing that his baby really was conscious even while still inside his wife's womb. The father had not wanted this baby when he heard his wife was pregnant. He had not truly welcomed this baby at birth.
>
> "You told us that during the therapy, you suggested that the father talk directly to his baby now in his arms. Looking him straight in the eyes, the father tells him gently what really happened. 'I did not want you then,' he says, 'because I wasn't ready for a baby then. There's nothing wrong with you. I love you now.' You recounted that when the father saw the sadness in his baby's eyes, he felt the sorrow and spoke deep words of truth. 'I'm so sorry. I didn't know you felt this. I didn't know you were conscious of this. I am sorry. I love you so much now. You are a beautiful boy,' the father spoke softly."

Luis said, "When I got on the plane that night, I started thinking and feeling honestly how this story applied to what happened with my fourth child. We had had three children and they had grown up enough so that we could go skiing and take vacations. My wife got pregnant and I was silently angry and distant during the whole pregnancy. I was never close to this child and our relationship had always been 'tense.' I had no patience with her and of course, we were far from being caring and tender with each other. At that moment on the plane, I decided I wanted to talk to her about this.

"One morning a few days later, I went into her bedroom and quietly sat on her bed. 'I want to talk to you about when you arrived in your mother's tummy.' Paula, now 5 years old, listened. 'When you arrived, I wasn't happy about your coming. I sometimes resented you being here. I did not always treat you well, even until now. I've made a mistake. I am very sorry. Now I realized you felt my anger and resentment in some way. I'm sorry and I now realize what a magnificent being you are. I'm so grateful you choose this family and choose me to be your father. I love you from the bottom of my heart. I am so sorry I did not honor you in the way you needed from the beginning.'"

Luis' eyes filled with soft tears as he continued, "She didn't say much at the time. Wendy, this conversation happened 7 years ago. After that conversation, she changed; the tension between us that had been there from the beginning was replaced with a wonderful relationship. Today she is 12, and my love and caring for my daughter flows with ease and joy. I realized it all had an enormous impact in my relationship with Paula, but it also had much to do with my understanding that each one of my children is a complete human being and needed to be addressed as such from the first day they came." (McCarty, 2003, pp. 2–3).

## An Integrated EFT Approach with Families

Ideally, parents come prior to their baby's conception to work with their own material as a way of "clearing the channel" for their baby and preparing to be parents. If these issues aren't addressed prior to conception, then I suggest assessing and working with them as soon as possible during the pregnancy. When doing EFT during pregnancy, include the baby in the process. Although there are myriad possible issues important to the well-being of the mother-baby and the father during this early period, I highlight four here that I believe are critical to address. My emphasis is on working with mothers, but these issues are for fathers as well.

First, I recommend parents have the opportunity to work with their own prenatal, birth, infant experiences, imprints, unresolved trauma, and unmet needs from that period. How a woman carries, connects, and births is greatly influenced by her own experience during this developmental period. How a father can show up and be involved and supportive of mother and baby is influenced by his early beginnings.

Second, I highly recommend taking great care to work with previous losses—failed fertility procedures, miscarriages, abortions, stillbirths, losses of babies after birth, failed adoptions, or other significant losses a mother has previously had. In my experience, the effects of these losses can leave a great weight upon the mother's psyche, often for years without help to process them, and can greatly diminish her well-being and connection with her babies in pregnancies that follow. Babies are also greatly affected by this legacy of unresolved loss. Thus I give the highest priority to helping mothers address these issues.

Third, I recommend you assess and work with previous pregnancies, births, and postnatal experiences of the mother and baby. Unfortunately, too many mothers are left with unresolved trauma, regrets, disappointments, and fears from what happened previously when having a child. These carry over and can permeate the whole pregnancy with the next baby's arrival.

And fourth, when things have not been ideal earlier in the current pregnancy, then I highly recommend helping mother and baby process that now, not waiting until later. This includes any circumstance in which there is regret when realizing the impact it could be having on the baby, for example, when a pregnancy is unwanted or caused conflict between partners, or the mother realizes how her unresolved loss has kept her from connecting with her baby. I suggest a dialogue such as Luis had with his daughter, even while the baby is in the womb, and doing EFT as part of that process.

We want mothers to feel unencumbered by their pasts so they can be happy, well, and enjoy becoming a mother and connecting with their baby. We want babies to experience being fully welcomed, loved, and connected, and to have that sense of well-being too. Helping mothers and fathers with these issues during pregnancy can help support those goals greatly and significantly influence the type of birth and bonding experience they have.

In a moment I want to share an EFT session I had with a pregnant mother so that you can see how I weave the Integrated Model lens and Integrated Approach together in a live session. But first, I want to say just a few things about working with families after the baby is born, even though it deserves much more than what is possible here.

Often part of the work at this stage focuses on "debriefing" what happened during the birth and bonding time, or what happened during the pregnancy. The principles we discussed previously in this chapter all apply here, especially speaking the truth with loving compassion, and with remorse when parents are sorry about the effect their actions may have had on their child. If you do sessions with parents with the baby present, I believe including the baby and giving priority to the baby's pacing, responses, and emotional state is the best practice. If the baby is crying or increasingly getting fussy or activated, attend to the baby. Slow the pace down, become quiet inside yourself, encourage the parents to do so also, and make contact with the baby. Comment on what you are talking about and how you notice the baby is upset. Don't try to power through the EFT in that case. Be with the baby until the baby is able to be in a calmer state and then explain what you are doing and why. Then continue the EFT process.

For most families and professionals, understanding how conscious babies are is still a newer concept. People often talk about babies, for example, about their birth, without actually including them or acknowledging how that might have been for them. Part of the Integrated Approach is to change that pattern to include babies. To read examples of including babies directly in sessions, I recommend my journal article "The Power of Beliefs: What Babies Are Teaching Us" (McCarty, 2002, also included as Appendix in *Welcoming Consciousness*).

The EFT process then becomes an integral part of the entire Integrated Approach. For example, while a parent talks to the baby about what happened at the baby's birth, we do EFT for the parent and the baby. I recommend doing EFT *for* the baby, rather than *on* the baby. Many babies are sensitive to touch on their head and face as a result of their birth. I prefer that parents tap on themselves with the intention to serve as a surrogate for the baby. In general, I transition from surrogate tapping when children are old enough to tap on themselves. The family field principle applies beautifully here. When parents tap for themselves and their baby, the field changes and the baby's experience and system changes too.

I have evolved much of my practice to do a lot of the work without babies present. Much of my current work with families is done via phone/Skype sessions with mothers, and we have someone care for the baby while we work together. That way mothers can get the full benefit of help for themselves first. We work together for the mothers' own healing, and do surrogate healing for their babies using EFT. I mentor the mothers on how to talk with their babies (or their children, if older) about the authentic truths and subjects *after* we have addressed the issue or event and have done the EFT for them. I also mentor them on incorporating EFT in their daily lives.

Now in the last section of this chapter, let's turn to an EFT session with pregnant Jena and her baby. In this session I use very simple ways of including the baby. Many mothers begin connecting through physical sensation and their baby's movement, like Jena did. I will often move deeper into more mind-to-mind communication with the baby and mentor parents on this as well as in future sessions.

## An Integrated Approach–EFT Session with Pregnant Mother and Her Baby

### Prior to the Session

I was teaching the Santa Barbara Graduate Institute course *Practice with Families During Pregnancy*. I recruited a volunteer pregnant mom from the community for a class demonstration session in how to use EFT during pregnancy from the perspective of an Integrated Approach.

She received my informed consent form that described my practice, my Integrated Model and therapeutic Integrated Approach, and EFT as a leading-edge healing modality. Prior to the class, Jena completed an in-depth questionnaire that included questions about her own prenatal, birth, and infant history; childhood issues or traumas;

her previous pregnancies, births, and parenting experiences; her current pregnancy and relationship to the baby she was carrying; and what she wanted to focus on in the session. In the questionnaire I asked if she would like to learn ways to build her relationship more directly with her baby now. Jena said, "Absolutely," which opened the door for me to bring that focus into the session.

In reading her responses before we met, I learned several important things to consider while we worked together. She was a 33-year-old married professional, and the mother of two young children. She listed the following concerns: "lessening my anxiety about the intensity involved in labor and delivery, raising my confidence in the final stages of delivery and not fearing pushing." Other areas with which she wanted help included: "getting 'I am not enough' out of my head," and how to "let go of the angst from the struggle in my relationship with my mother."

Jena shared that this pregnancy's baby was planned, wanted, and that they were very excited about having this third baby. She was now 28 weeks' pregnant and said she'd had highs and lows during this pregnancy and had experienced a few weeks of unusually volatile emotions. On the 0–10 SUD (subjective units of distress) scale, with 10 being the highest level of emotion, she responded that during those periods, she had experienced level 7 stress, level 8 anxiety, level 8 upset/overwhelm, and level 7 impatience. She wrote, "I've been frustrated that I can't seem to control my emotions for the health of the baby during these times." She described this baby as "*very* active, even waking me at night since 26 weeks... seems very alert and busy." She felt very bonded to this baby but felt she didn't know the baby very well in that she was so busy with her other children.

In terms of her own early history, her mother had been very traumatized by a miscarriage she'd had before Jena. Little was known about Jena's womb and birth experiences other than she was born vaginally without obvious complications. Jena's older sibling had medical problems and her mother was busy taking care of that sibling. She described Jena as being an independent child who "raised herself." In the current life pattern section, Jena had identified "there's no place for me; I'm an outsider; I don't belong" and "feeling I'm not enough; there isn't enough."

From reading her responses, I was already aware of a possible constellation of issues: early

lack of attachment and becoming self-sufficient at a young age, leading to her sense of never being enough; and a pattern of trying to manage herself, rather than being able to genuinely feel safe to relax. Her baby's "*very* active" pattern of movements could be signs of stress. In my experience when babies are very active, they are often "running" the stress they experience chemically and emotionally while they resonate with mom's stress, emotional upsets, and loss of heart coherence. Thus I had this constellation of potential issues to be attentive to in the session.

The transcript of the session (McCarty, 2008, November) is abbreviated. Some language is slightly adapted for clarity. I have included annotated comments. When I speak directly to the baby, as well as speak to the mother, going back and forth between them, I use single quotation marks to indicate when I am speaking to the baby.

## The Session

During a short period of introductions in the class, Jena shares that she had recently watched the DVD film *What Babies Want* several times, which focuses on the consciousness of babies and made her start thinking about babies in a different way.

Wendy (W): "I would like to say hi to your baby, if that is okay with you."

Mom (M): "Absolutely."

W: "We really love including babies and I got in your history how your baby is really interactive, so I especially want to say, 'Hi, baby. I want to include you today.'"

M: She rubs her belly. "Every time I even think of the baby, I feel the baby go thump, thump."...

W: "So as we start our session and what you want to focus on, let's just check in with the baby. See where he or she is. 'Hi, baby.'"

M: "Just slow movements right now. ... At night baby really goes wild, waking me three or four times a night."

W: "Actually, I'm going to slow down in myself a little bit more now, slowing down so the three of us can get in sync. I'm going to just close my eyes for a moment."

M: "That's a good idea." Mom closes her eyes, with her hand on her belly. We remain quiet for a minute or so.

W: "One of the things I find ... see how my voice just dropped." (I've dropped into my quieter inner place.) "I was very surprised when I started working with babies at BEBA how slow I would need to get to match the baby's slowness to help them integrate experiences. Usually we are speedy-speedy and slowing down really helps the baby, and I think it is true during pregnancy too."

M: "Wow."

W: "So as we go through working on issues that may bring up feelings, one of the principles is to ... slow down while we work with possibly intense feelings. ... I'm appreciating that we are going to be talking about your birth with this baby, and comparing it with your previous births with your children and some issues that it brought up thinking about this birth."

We then talk about her very well developed birth plan and her positive feelings about her OB physician who also delivered her first two babies. She felt very supported by both her OB and her husband in those births.

W: "I read everything in your history that you shared. You expressed yourself so beautifully, so clearly. ... I would suggest that we might focus on the fear of intensity during your upcoming birth."

M: "Excellent. It is imminently in my thoughts." ... And she begins to describe more about the intensity she felt during her last child's birth from the moment her cervix was 8 cm dilated to when the baby's head crowned. ...

W: "I'm going to write down some of these things while we go through this. Actually, this is a great way to process at home too. I put a vertical line down the middle of the paper. I let myself go through almost a stream of consciousness and write down on the left side of the paper all the stuff, what am I feeling about it, and I don't have to have it organized. It's just what comes up when I think about having this child and I'm at 8 cm. On the right side, I write down how I would like it to be. Then we'll work with EFT and see what happens. So it sounds like a lot of things came up at once and that was part of the 8 cm to pushing dynamic. Not only the physical intensity, but it went way beyond that. Did I hear that right?"

M: "Perfect."

We spend several minutes exploring this subject and I write down all of the key aspects of the issue for her to take with her. She relates a SUD

of 9+ for the field of experience. For brevity's sake here, I resume the session transcript at the completion of this exploration. I have just finished explaining the EFT process.

W: "Before we start the EFT process, I want to check in with your baby because your baby is going to go through this with us. 'Baby, I'm real aware that you heard all these feelings we were just talking about.'"

M: "Baby's moving a lot more right now." ...

W: "'Yeah, you heard about these really intense things Mom experienced in the past around this pushing part. This is why we are working on this right now so that you and Mom will be freer to have your own experience.' (Mom closes her eyes, smiling with her hand on her belly). And I love that babies learn this EFT healing process even in the womb. You can use this now when you or the baby is stressed, and your baby is already learning how to move from one state into another. Then you can use the EFT process after the baby is born, you and your baby are already familiar with it. ... And what comes up for you while we are saying 'Hi' and checking in with baby?"

M: "It's just nice to have quiet time with this baby ... because it definitely is minimal during the day with the kids."

W: "We are about to focus on some intense feelings, so let's get quiet for a moment so that you and your baby have a moment together. Ask baby, 'Is there anything you want me to know or consider for you?' and see what happens."

M: "There was a total Braxton Hicks contraction. Baby just seems happy to be here focusing on this."

W: "'Baby, we are going to focus on you and Mom the whole way through just like Mom wants to do in labor.' As we go along, let's keep checking in with baby. It's like practicing and learning how to get baby's cues. 'Anything you want us to know, I'll have my antennas up to listen to you, baby.' So, focus on the fear. It is 8 cm and you go to that place, just before the flooded place and the fear of pain."

*I use italics to indicate specific statements we make while EFT tapping, either affirmation statements or rounds of tapping points.*

**EFT process #1.**

W: "I'll say the first one. A sentence that speaks to the heart of the intensity." (I often construct and speak the first EFT affirmation sentence to help clients.) *"Even though I don't know if I can make it and I feel such overwhelm and fear because the intensity is so great and the pain so high, AND I deeply love and accept myself.* Now you say it in whatever way you just talk about that place."

M: *"Even though I feel scared, fearful of being in that place again and having to get through it again, I deeply and wholly love myself."*

W: "And again."

M: *"When I am in this place of fear and just overwhelming intensity, I know I can do it and I deeply and wholly love myself."*

W: "Okay, let's tap around together. We are going to just say words that come to mind out of this place, out of this field of energy."

In my style of working with clients, I often add words during the rounds of tapping, helping to acknowledge what feels closer to the center of the issue, or intuitively feels helpful to say out loud. I sense this may help Jena to be with her authentic feelings and truth more readily. Sometimes I'm tapping on me while she is tapping on her. When a mother has a pattern of trying to do everything herself, I find it is nurturing and a new experience for her to feel we are doing this process together, like a dance between us in the therapeutic field of shared experience, rather than my instructing her to do it all.

W: *"I'm so afraid. This intensity is too much, I can't do it."*

M: *"I'll not be able to do it."*

W: *"What if I can't do it?"*

M: *"Will there be a C-section or will someone else choose something for the baby that I don't want?"*

M: *"I'll lose control. Other people will take over. It won't be what I want."*

W: "This is where I just let myself have a stream of consciousness, all my worries about it. Whatever comes up for you."

M: *"If that happens, what kind of guilt will I feel?"*

W: *"I'll feel so guilty."*

M: *"Because it was my judgment, my decision."*

W: *"I've got to be enough, I'm not enough. This is too much.* Let's go back to the fear. *This is too much.* Just let yourself feel what you felt when you were so overwhelmed." (Both of us are tapping. Mom doesn't have words, so I continue speaking for her.) *"This is too much. I don't think I can do anymore. That's it. That is all I can do."*

M: *"I'm at my limit."*

W: *"I can't take this pain. The whole thing is just too overwhelming. I'm about to be a mother. That crowning sensation."* (We finish two rounds of tapping together.)

W: "How about if we tap around the positives? *I AM enough."*

W: *"I am enough."*

W: *"I've done it twice before.*

M: (Laughs.) *"I've done it twice before."*

W: *"And this one is totally different. A new baby."*

M: *"I have experience."*

W: *"I can do it. I'm going to do it. I have all the support I need.* Is there a hitch with that, with the support?"

M: *"I do have support, but it is still on me."*

W: "Let's put that in our tapping. *It's all on me."*

M: *"I have a lot of support and strength to do this."*

W: "Just picture yourself. *I am empowered. I'm fully empowered. Baby and I are fully empowered going through this moment together. We are going through this moment together."*

M: *"We will be able to do it together with one another's strength. Doing it together."*

We finish one round of tapping positives. Note that she has moved from focusing on her internal fear and disconnecting from the baby in doing that, to now connecting with baby and doing this together.

W: "Let's pause. Let your system take all this in and see where we land. Just think back to the fear at 8 cm and see where you and baby are at."

M: "Right in this moment, I'm not even at all visualizing a pain aspect. It's just a liberating feeling. That isn't even in my visuals, my map, it was just about focusing on the baby and not worrying, not consuming myself with my past fear."

W: "Oh, so somehow things shifted when you focused on the baby." (From her description, the SUD score sounds neutralized, but I do recommend asking for the SUD number.)

M: "Yeah. Definitely."

W: "Great. So, this is one way to check out how things are. When we do EFT, then we check in and ask, 'What is left? What is here now?' One way to do that, like at home, is to go back and challenge it by trying to go back to that old feeling, the old fear, and the old scenario. Usually, what happens is that you don't connect with the original issue the same way and something else emerges like, 'I connect with the baby this time and we do this together.' Oh, that is new!"

M: "Yeah! (Smiling.) That is very new."

W: "Another way to check is to compare the old scenario of fear and the new scenario—baby and I doing it together empowered—and see which one has the most intensity or realness right now."

M: "Definitely the more positive one. And the baby is kicking everywhere just like this (as she raises her arms in a gesture of triumph). The legs and everything are going. So that is really a neat feeling to have."

W: "Triumph."

M: "Yeah and that changes the whole chain of thoughts if I can say that, let me focus on the baby, then I'm not distracted by my even weak subconscious thoughts."

W: "Yes, it is a different focus. For me, when I tap in intuitively, there does seem to be something very special about the two of you doing it together."

M: "Yes."

W: "Like you said the baby is a connector baby, an extrovert ... so the two of you doing it together. Feeling empowered. What an experience for both of you to come from one reality into another, doing it together, feeling empowered even though in the intensity. So, empowered WITH the intensity."

M: "Yeah, and it really makes me think too what a nice metaphor to use as you begin a new parenting track with a new little individual. It says, 'I'm not going to be brought down by these inhibitions, fears, or past things that are blocking my capacity to mother well. Instead, let me focus on you (baby).'"

W: "And us, you with me, and me with you, and us!"

M: "Yeah, that is an excellent place to be practicing that."

W: "While we are right here, what can happen sometimes—it can happen in the moment we are working on it, or it might be that something pops up tomorrow or the next day, or sometime later—is another aspect of this whole thing. So while we are here together, let's search for one and see if we find one. (I look at my notes of what she had said about the issue.) See if you connect with any of them or if they bring up any memory, a thread from your childhood. It might not bring up anything, but let's just check it out. That sense of 'I can't take it anymore. And the intensity

of the pain. And I don't know if I can do this anymore.'"

M: "Yeah, that was just a feeling that I felt many times in childhood."

W: "Oh, really."

M: ... "It's interesting now because if I go home, those feelings will pop up immediately when I walk in the door. But if my family visits me, it is more my territory."

W: "Yeah, so what is at the core of this pattern? Is it that 'I just can't take this. I can't stand going into this. It's too intense or I can't last?' Or would you put it differently? What's the essence of that old pattern?"

M: "I guess it is more that I don't want to choose to put myself through that anymore, maybe as a child I had to. ... That seems unhealthy time and time again. ... I feel just exhausted, depleted, like someone sucked my energy source right out of me."

W: "That feels like the center of it, that someone just sucks me out of me and I'm exhausted."

M: "Totally. Then it is just like I show up like a mannequin or something."

W: "You just push yourself through it. You're good at that, I can tell."

M: "I can still get aspects of that over a phone conversation with my mother."

W: "Would you like to do a little EFT work with that and see how you feel afterward?"

M: "Yeah. I can give you a new recent example."

Jena then talks about a recent phone conversation with her mother that was very upsetting. She felt her mother didn't understand her, was critical and intrusive, and undermined her sense of being a good mother. This was a pattern in which she would shut down and try to escape in some way.

M: "My response was 'Is Dad there?' That's my exit. ... I'm just shut down at that point. I don't have a response. That just seems cruel. I can't imagine telling my daughters that. ... I can't imagine bestowing that kind of heaviness. Then there is the acceptance that it isn't just about me. It includes me, but that is an issue she has to bear on her own. There is a part of 'I am not enough' that is derived from that imprint. But there is a part that is also freed to say, 'I don't have to own it.'"

W: "I don't have to own it, but it sure ..."

M: "Weighs me down. Even a phone conversation can still bring that same place ... keeling over."

W: "And not only are you feeling that, but you and *your baby* are, and your baby is learning all about those kinds of relationships right now."

M: "Poor baby."

W: "So let's help and see what happens."

**EFT process #2.**

W: "So think about that old pattern and this last conversation on the phone. Just go into the middle of the energy, that field of experience that you have replayed over and over again, weights you down. I can't stand it, sucky energy, sucks you out."

M: "Totally."

W: "So just before that place where you cut out. Just be with it."

M: "I just feel like I want to run out of my body. Yuck permeates. So unbelievably heavy, you wish you were anyone else."

W: "On scale of 0–10?"

M: "Yeah, 9+, the same as the crowning was."

W: "So, baby, this is your mom's old pattern with her mom."

M: "Nothing to do with this baby," putting both hands on her belly.

W: "And we are right in the middle of it, baby. This is what it felt like for your mom growing up and still does with her mom. This is part of her experience that you are learning about. I want you both just to feel what it feels like right now." We start tapping the Karate point and I say the affirmation the first time.

W: "*Even though this awful place that I have known for so many years, ever since I can remember, with my mother and family, and it just feels awful, I deeply love and I accept myself.* Just say whatever comes up about that pattern."

M: Tapping on Karate point, "*Even though I haven't been able to get rid of that pattern or not be desensitized to it ...*"

W: "*... and not feel all that yuck.*"

M: "*... and not feel all that yuck, I am working on it, I am really trying to address it and I do deeply love and accept myself, and that is why I want to delete this! It doesn't feel necessary to have in my life. And I would never want to replicate that with anyone.*"

W: "*Even though I have carried this weight all my life,* and I'm going to put a word in and you can change it. *It is so violating to who I am. ...*"

M: "Yeah! Perfect word."

W: "*I deeply love and accept myself.*"

M: "I do."

W: "Tapping around now. *This awful place. So violated.* You pick some words out."

M: "*The me that I am is ignored.*"

W: "*I'm ignored. I'm not seen.*"

M: "*I don't feel heard. ...*"

W: "*I'm not seen. I'm not heard. And this feels awful.*"

M: "*Feels awful.*"

W: "*It sucks the life out of me. It is exhausting.*"

M: "*As a pregnant mother with two children, I just choose to not let it happen.*"

W: "*But it happened to me. It is still happening to me now.*"

M: "*It is still happening. If I withdraw from calling back...*"

W: "*It just feels awful.*"

M: "*It feels awful. I definitely will do what I can to not get there.*"

W: "I'm going to ask for you to drop deeper into the feeling of it. At the core of what it has felt like, at the core of that place with your mother for all those years."

M: She sighs. "I think violating is just perfect because you would expect your mother of all people to get you."

W: "And she doesn't get you."

M: "I don't think so. It's sad." She chokes up with tears and stops tapping on herself as she listens to me speaking the words and tapping on myself for her.

W: "*Yeah, I feel so sad. She doesn't get who I am. So sad. She doesn't see me. I feel so violated. I just can't stand this. It is just so intense. I just can't stand this.*" Her silent soft tears continue. "*It is just so intense.*"

W: "Just tap with me with all those feelings that are right at the core of it. Right there."

M: Silently tapping with tears.

W: "*Such a weight. All those years. Didn't have to be. It's not about who I am. Still doesn't change it. It's about who my mother is. It still feels awful.*"

M: Continues to tap silently and nod with, "*Feels awful.*"

W: "Have any words?"

M: Shakes her head no.

W: "Okay if I say them?"

M: "Yeah." She continues to tap a round with me.

W: "*So violating. I really needed her to see me. I craved her to see me. She's never gotten me. I'm sensitive. It hurts me so deeply. I can't take it. That is really an intense place.*" I conclude my tapping.

M: Silent and nodding.

W: "Let's just see where we are. 'Hi, baby. That was really intense there.'"

M: "The baby really tenses out and that's why I try not to be in that place with her even if I note the conversation could be going in that direction and feel very forced or limited or judged, then I pull out pretty quick, even if it is a totally ridiculous excuse because I just don't want to have that."

W: "Yeah, it's not right for you. ... You said you wanted the choice not to go into that energy."

M: "Yeah, why bring that on, especially when carrying a baby. I thought about it even while nursing. Yuck. The toxins that must be going through your system if you are feeling that kind of emotion."

W: "Yes and energetically."

M: "What is being passed to the baby? There may be other times in life when I have to face up and may be asked to, but I think there is a limit."

W: "Absolutely. So just check in on that whole thing and see how it feels. Already you are talking about it a little differently."

M: "I think if I can remind myself it isn't about me, it's more about choices she made in parenting me, but my focus needs to be on my family, our family."

W: "So let's tap that positive in. You can tap negative things, just tapping while you are in the intensity of the negative things helps your whole system reorganize, letting go of some of the pent-up stuff from over the years. It just dissipates and reorganizes in whatever way supports you in a new way without having to manage or work at it. Then you can just tap in what you want. It's like you are strengthening, saying to your system, 'Yeah. I have a choice.' Whatever those are, let's just tap them." We both start tapping a round.

M: "It reminds me of the movie *What the Bleep*, where you are changing the dendrite pathway."

W: "Yes, that is what we are doing. *Wait a minute, I have choice. I choose to have healthy relationships. I don't want to put myself in something that isn't right for me.*"

M: "*Nor ever place my children in that.*"

W: "*I have my own life with my children.*"

M: "*I have my own culture of family to create.*"

W: "*It's not about me. It is my mother's stuff.*"

M: "*I don't need to carry that.*"

W: "*I like feeling my energy. Who I am.*"

M: "*I like who I am.*"

W: "*I like who I am.*" Said louder, "*I like who I am!*"

M: She laughs and beats on her chest playfully. "*I like who I am. ... It shouldn't be invaded by anyone.*"

W: "*It is good for me to have my boundaries. It's healthy for me to have my boundaries.*"

M: "Yes."

W: "*I am good enough. I'm a good person.*"

M: "*I am good enough.*"

W: "*I am a good mama.*"

M: "*I am a good mom.*"

W: "*I'm a good mama who is a pregnant mama and it is about OUR time.*"

M: "*Building a new path I am proud of. My children will respect, will feel heard and seen genuinely for who they are, not for who I want to morph them to be.*" We stop tapping. "That is huge. That is beyond all parenting wishes. That is the highest for me. Letting my kids be who they are intended to be."

W: "I really got that. Absolutely."

M: "That resounds daily. ... I am pretty protective when people say, 'Why don't you try this? Or, you should do ...' I kind of come in like this cougar mom protecting our space."

W: "And it is okay to be that cougar for yourself?"

M: "Yeah."

W: "Let's check in one more time when you think about your mom and you think about having your own boundaries. See if there is any other trigger place that comes up."

M: "We definitely nailed the core."

W: "On a scale of 0–10, with 10 being the most intense, check in on: *I can't stand it. Sucky energy. I feel like I'm about to break.* Where are you now?"

M: "2." ... She goes on to talk about what a weight it was and how she used to exercise to work off the energy from it.

We begin transitioning to talking about doing EFT at home for follow-up and in general. I talk about processing feelings rather than the old way of trying to manage them. The session resumes here as I am talking about processing using EFT and specifically including her baby.

W: "There is something about you and this baby and doing it together that is just awesome. So, if you are feeling something, like with your mother, talk to the baby, 'Okay, this is that same feeling, this stuff with my mother, and you are feeling it with me. I am sorry. We are in this together. Let's do some EFT.' Then do the EFT and when you feel better, check in and say to baby something like 'Wow. I feel better. You feel better too?'"

M: "Rather than 'This is just me. It doesn't affect you.'"

W: "A lot of moms try to keep hard feelings from the baby, but then what happens is that you get separated."

M: "Totally."

W: "Rather than separating from your baby to keep those feelings away, say something like, 'Hey, look, you are learning. This is part of life. It's a hard part of my life. I know you are feeling it. But let's do something about it together. And then we'll feel better and can go do something else.' Because you see how you can feel better after doing the EFT, don't you?"

M: "Way better."

W: "And those were just two short processes."

M: "Yeah, it was amazing because it went from 10 and 9+ to what I felt afterward. It is like pushing. If I can get from that 9+ to a 2 because I am in charge, not in a beastly way, but that I am strong enough to direct myself in a positive way—that is a whole different way."

W: "So a couple of things on taking it home, if things come up about the birth. Oftentimes when people do a process like this, it just doesn't come back the same way. It is just different. If it does start coming back, I highly recommend, because your system has already shifted on the issue, that if it comes back, right when it comes back, if you can just stop, be with yourself, and say to yourself, 'Okay, here is some more stuff about this, let's process this through.' Then just do the EFT process and it will come down. Gary Craig, who originated EFT, said it is like pulling weeds in a garden. Sometimes you'll have a circumstance that will trigger it and you pull that weed. Pull another weed and all of a sudden—poof!—the whole thing just pops and it is just not there anymore. I think where things might come up more, because there are different aspects, is around your mom. So, each time it comes up, I'd highly recommend doing that process until your whole being just isn't holding it like it used to."

M: "Right. That is a very different way of viewing it."

W: "And it is empowering. Empowering and you two doing it together."

M: "I really value that. It's just allowing yourself to reroute and rewire. Because when I hit the wall, I need something that takes those dendrites to another place. And when you keep repeating that pattern, that pattern gets stronger and stronger."

W: "My hunch is when you process something, you really like to think it through. EFT gives you a great focus to go through and your system just emerges differently. I'd love it if you would e-mail me and when you check in with these issues later, tell me how it feels to you. Okay?"

M: "Yeah, it is amazing how all those pieces wove together. I knew when I was writing the history, there had to be some link."

W: "That's why when you have different aspects at home that come up and you start doing EFT on each aspect, then how they all link up to hold together as a whole old field just starts breaking up."

M: "And that is so important should a few more intense weeks come, because the chemistry of each baby is different, so the chemistry of this baby from the first few weeks and this first part of the third trimester has been like, 'Wow, what is happening?'" (She was referring to those uncharacteristically emotionally volatile weeks she experienced during this pregnancy.)

W: "Okay, if the whole intensity starts building again, first thing I would do is just get quiet and connect with the baby. Talk to the baby about it. 'I don't know what all this is about. I feel rather scared. I'm used to managing things. I'm used to having control and I don't feel that right now. And it is scary.' So, I would just talk to the baby about it, and then just quietly start, *Even though I feel this building and it scares me because I don't feel in control, I deeply love and accept myself.* Tapping around, *all this scary intensity, fear, frustration.* Just name it. I think your system will settle right down. If it starts building again, just do it again."

M: "Back to that quiet place. Slowing down. Not worrying."

W: "With EFT, you don't have to manage as much. Just be with it. Recognize, acknowledge, be with baby and yourself, and do the EFT process. I think you will really like how empowered you feel."

M: "I think so too."

We talk a bit more about intensity and she mentions her baby's pattern of being very intense and moving intensely, especially at night.

W: "... If you have been managing a lot of things during the day, managing in your system during the day and then you let go at night, oftentimes with babies, their nervous system is running off that energy. So sometimes, that active-active can be their way of working out what they felt with you managing stuff. So, if you have been managing, which you are going to do sometimes, then before you go to bed, connect with the baby and tap, *all this stuff I was so wound up about today*, and see if you can bring your nervous system down a little bit. I'm curious to see if that helps with baby."

M: "And that is not unpractical to do at a few points during the day. It's not asking a lot of time. That's smart because I definitely run a high energy ship."

## Post Session

Student to Mother: "You thought your baby's movements were a good thing. Wendy suggested it might mean something else, in response to things. How did that make you feel?"

M: "It was interesting to be aware that not every moment is this gleeful thing. It is more a response to that emotion, that tough emotion. (She makes a gesture like a tense body pose.) So the baby is tightening up and then relaxing. So that same thing happened when I let go of the bad aspect of my relationship with my mother during the EFT; I felt the baby's movement become so much more free. I think many mothers in pregnancy commonly think any movement is great movement. Yet now ... even thinking about the baby's intense movements at nights, yeah, what do they mean?"

W: "Glad we came back to this. I had an insight and idea that might be neat for you guys. Each of us processes in a different way. Movement kinesthetic processors tend to be very emotionally based. They feel things and express things in their body. They take in information and express it many times in movement. 'So, baby, it may be that movement is one of the key ways you express and you have a full range of expression. Just like for us, sometime our movements are hard and choppy and have a lot of tension, and other times they may be very intense, but they are smooth and expressing an aliveness, *hello!*' So it would be really interesting to say to baby, 'Baby, I really want to get to know your full range of movements and get closer that way,' because I think there is a whole range and it is a style of expression."

M: "That's interesting. ... That is a great idea for getting to know the baby."

After this session, the mother wrote me a warm thank-you letter, which included these passages:

> The gift that you gave me, Wendy, was one that will remain with me for a lifetime. You were able to give me the ability to open myself up to new ways of approaching concerns that have weighed on me for some time. I felt a weight being lifted that I had carried for quite some time. Already in mere days since processing with you and your students, I have felt more confident, more directed, and more at ease with simply what life has bestowed my way.
>
> ... I sat with my husband and shared what the experience had been like for me. Most extraordinary I said, is the amount of contractions (Braxton Hicks) I experience while going into my more difficult places of either intensity of delivery or challenging events with my mom. Then I shared with him what surprised me most about the process and essentially how awe striking it has been since. I told him that as you worked with me on EFT to get underneath some of these issues and express them and then change my routes of perception for those previously bogged-down synapses, I literally felt the baby stretch out in the most contenting and large motion I have experienced yet. The baby immediately relaxed into the space that had been freed up, as did my posture and emotional spirit. I told my husband that within minutes, our special baby took that stretch of contented peacefulness and fell fast asleep, as if to say, "That feels better, that feels resolved, that feels so right!"

## Concluding Remarks

Many of the basic EFT steps and techniques you have learned as general EFT practice can be applied during pregnancy, birth, and baby's first years. For example, in working with parents' trauma, fears, unresolved grief, or working to strengthen what one wants to create, such as confidence, you can apply what you would use with adults in general. Yet in this chapter we have moved beyond simply applying EFT generically to work with families during this developmental period. Rather, we now situate EFT practice within the broader landscape of consciousness-based understandings of the beginning of life, clinical findings from prenatal and perinatal psychology, and the integrated lens of early development.

I believe this can transform our work and offer families something much more—a more conscious way of being with their baby and themselves. I find greater intimacy and deeper connection between moms and babies develop when I embed the EFT technique into a broader intention of helping parents perceive, communicate, and consider their baby from the PPN integrated perspective. The first time I experienced Dr. Emerson's communication with the baby in their session and witnessed the baby's response, it changed me. When parents experience that level of communication and possibility with their baby in EFT sessions, the whole family changes and the baby blossoms.

When I reviewed PPN clinical findings to develop my model of early development that reflected the evidence gathered about our multidimensional nature and the themes we were seeing in PPN clinical findings, one theme stood out, above all others—the need to be considered and related to as a conscious being, a person, from the beginning of life.

Emily beautifully expresses this theme as she describes her experience as a newborn during a hypnosis session with Dr. David Chamberlain. "They don't think I'm a person. I *know* I am!" she declares (Chamberlain, 1999, p. 80). Dr. Emerson suggests that the majority of babies born have trauma from the way in which we carry, birth, and treat newborns (Emerson, 1998). I believe even when conditions are not ideal, or birth is difficult, if we relate to the baby as a *sentient being–sensitive being* and stay connected with the baby throughout the experience, we can prevent or mitigate potentially constricting outcomes.

In our EFT work with families we have the opportunity to change how we welcome, communicate, and care for babies in a way that better embraces the whole baby and strengthens family relationships. My healing intention to support multidimensional wholeness, coherence, and right relationship within every person, adult or baby, guides me to relate to that greater SELF in a way that honors each as a person and says to the baby, "I know you are a person and I know you know

you are. Welcome to being human. Let's do this together."

# References

Chamberlain, D. (1999). The significance of birth memories. *Journal of Prenatal and Perinatal Psychology and Health, 14*(1–2), 65–84.

Eden, D. (2012). Quote in front section of *Welcoming consciousness: Supporting babies' wholeness from the beginning of life—An integrated model of early development.* Santa Barbara, CA: Wondrous Beginnings Publishing.

Emerson, W. (1998). Birth trauma: The psychological effects of obstetrical interventions. *Journal of Prenatal and Perinatal Psychology and Health, 13*(1), 11–44.

McCarty, W. A. (2002). The power of beliefs: What babies are teaching us. *Journal of Prenatal & Perinatal Psychology & Health, 16,* 341–360. (Also published as Appendix in *Welcoming Consciousness,* 2012.)

McCarty, W. A. (2005). Nurturing the Possible: Supporting the integrated self from the beginning of life. *Shift: At the Frontiers of Consciousness, 6,* 18–20.

McCarty, W. A. (2006a) Clinical story of a 6-year-old boy's eating phobia: An integrated approach utilizing prenatal and perinatal psychology with energy psychology's Emotional Freedom Technique (EFT) in a surrogate non-local application. *Journal of Prenatal & Perinatal Psychology & Health, 21*(2), 117–139.

McCarty, W. A. (2006b). Supporting babies' wholeness in the 21st century: An integrated model of early development. *Journal of Prenatal & Perinatal Psychology & Health, 20*(3), 187–220.

McCarty, W.A. (2007). *EFT for Mom, baby, and Dad from the beginning of life.* Wondrous Beginnings Publishing: Santa Barbara, CA.

McCarty, W. A. & Glenn, M. (2008). Investing in human potential from the beginning of life: Keys to maximizing human capital. *Journal of Prenatal & Perinatal Psychology & Health, 23*(2), 117–135.

McCarty, W. A. (2008, November). EFT session with pregnant mother [video recording transcript] during graduate course *Practice with Families During Pregnancy,* Santa Barbara Graduate Institute.

McCarty, W. A. (2012). *Welcoming consciousness: Supporting babies' wholeness from the beginning of life—An integrated model of early development.* Santa Barbara, CA: Wondrous Beginnings Publishing. (Originally published as eBook in 2004 under same title.)

McCraty, R. (2003). *The energetic heart: The bioelectromagnetic interactions within and between people.* Boulder Creek, CA: Institute of HeartMath.

McCraty, R., Trevor, R., & Tomasino, D. (2005). The resonant heart. *Shift: At the Frontiers of Consciousness, 5,* 15–19.

Quinn, J. F. (2013). Transpersonal human caring and healing. In B. M. Dossey & L. Keegan (Eds.), *Holistic Nursing: A Handbook for Practice* (6th ed.). (pp. 107–116). Burlington, MA: Jones & Bartlett Learning.

# Chapter 48
# Cross-Cultural EFT

*David MacKay and Puja Kanth Alfred*

**Abstract**

Cross-Cultural EFT, also known as Geo-Specific EFT, aims to unlock the difficulties in presenting EFT to clients from cultures different from our own. Culture and religion play an important role in the development and perpetuation of problems, while language plays a key role in the healing process. Cross-cultural research in the area of emotions, identity, trauma, self-image, individualism-collectivism, and acculturation show that practitioners and therapists who understand these Geo-Specific concepts are able to gain a more comprehensive understanding of clients' problems and thereby better assist them. When working with clients from our own culture, some modifications in the Setup Statement can facilitate faster healing. English, though universally spoken, differs in its expression in each country. As words play an important role in healing, English as a second language can hamper the client's expression. Hence, when working with clients from a culture and language different from our own, we need to consider several factors: We need to be mindful of our own beliefs, encourage usage of native language when required, demonstrate sensitive preframing, use cultural reframes, and watch our verbal and nonverbal communication. In short, an awareness of the cross-cultural differences will make us more sensitive to clients' cultural background and stop us from imposing our sociocultural beliefs on them. We don't have to be experts in diverse cultures; we just need to be mindful of the cultural differences.

**Keywords:** cross-cultural, EFT, acculturative stress, individualism, collectivism, reframes

**David MacKay, BEng**, is president of the Hispanic EFT Association (AHEFT) and a certified EFT trainer. A native of Canada, he has lived in Mexico for 27 years. Send correspondence to David MacKay, Calz. del Bosque 1, Col. San Jose del Puente, Puebla, Mexico 72150, or david@ eftmx.com.

**Puja Kanth Alfred, MA**, is a counseling psychologist and a certified EFT practitioner. She specializes in trauma resolution and works with clients around the globe. Send correspondence to Puja Kanth Alfred, 34/11 Saradha Nagar, Virugambakkam, Chennai 600092, Tamil Nadu, India, or puja@emofreetherapy.com.

# Introduction

As the name implies, Cross-Cultural EFT makes us more mindful of the cultural context of individual clients in the application of Clinical EFT. It is also known as Geo-Specific EFT, emphasizing the significance of the geographical trajectory of the client. As each person carries a unique cultural blueprint that is enmeshed in developing issues, it is important for us to be sensitive to cross-cultural variables: language, culture, and religion. Emotions are universal, but the way they are expressed is not. Culture impacts the development and perpetuation of problems, while language plays a crucial role in healing. In EFT we combine tapping (kinesthetic) and spoken phrases (verbal).

Culture should not be confused with race, ethnicity, or socioeconomic status, which are personal characteristics. There are many factors that are a part of our "subjective culture," such as our values, the way we communicate to others, parenting practices, child-rearing practices, family roles, and "views regarding personal control, spiritual and religious orientations, and a lot more" (Betancourt & Lopez, 1993). Cultures differ in how people perceive happiness, productivity, and many other labels and categories that are used. Despite similarities among cultures, a lot of variability exists. There are cultural beliefs that aid a person in making sense of life, whereas there are some beliefs that hinder. The culture in which a person grows up has a lasting influence on everything a person does.

As technology brings the world closer, we EFT practitioners find ourselves more and more working with people from around the globe. This opens doors for both clients and practitioners, and at the same time creates new challenges to ensure clear communication in the delicate task of emotional healing.

There are two main circumstances to consider in cross-cultural work with EFT:

1. When the practitioner and client are from the same culture, the EFT protocol may benefit from slight modifications to increase its effectiveness. Often, the only adjustment required is to adapt the standard Setup Statement.
2. When the practitioner and client are from different cultures, the practitioner may need to learn the relevant idiosyncrasies and adjust the use of EFT to enhance communication and empathy.

Although the focus in this chapter is on cultural considerations, the ideas are similarly applicable to working with people of a different religion, age group, economic level, or milieu from the practitioner's. As practitioners, we should always take care to "speak the language" of those we want to assist with EFT, in order for it to be as effective as possible for them.

## 1. Cross-Cultural Differences Relevant to EFT

As EFT practitioners we may encounter cross-cultural differences chiefly in these areas: emotions, identity, self-esteem, parenting practices, trauma, and social anxiety.

### 1.1. Emotions

Verbal, emotional, and behavioral expressions differ in each country. When we work with clients from other cultures, there may be difficulty in understanding these expressions. Some behaviors and expressions will seem incongruous to us.

Earlier research suggested that facial expressions are hardwired and do not differ according to culture. However, a study conducted by Jack, Caldara, and Schyns (2012) demonstrates that there is no "universal language of emotion." The researchers found that sad, happy, or angry facial expressions are signaled differently in different cultures. For example, for Chinese participants in the study, the eyes were the primary signalers of facial expression whereas for Western Caucasians the eyebrows and mouth provided the cues.

### 1.2. Identity

The importance of collective versus individual identity varies from culture to culture. EFT was born in a culture in which individuality is generally celebrated, but this is not the case in many other cultures in which the absence of self-importance is highly regarded.

Research on individualism and collectivism is associated mainly with Triandis. Cultures vary in the meaning they give to "private self" and "public self." Private self refers to how the person sees him or herself and public self to how an individual is seen by others (Triandis, 1989). Membership in social groups is part of the collective self. According to Triandis, societies that focus more on individualism such as the United States highlight the private and public selves, whereas collectivist societies such as Asian countries emphasize the collective self while downplaying the private self. For example, Japanese and other Asian cultures tend to feel obligated to their parents for having given birth to them and feel responsible to take care of them; this is seen as respect in the community. Inability to do so can lead to tremendous guilt within the person. Also, in these cultures, children are taught to be obedient to parents and this sometimes develops into fear of authority figures, later in life. In order to understand these problems, we need to know how the cultural concepts differ.

Cousins (1989) and Ross and Nisbett (1991) found that Japanese people related more with others and gave more importance to others' expectations than to their own needs. In a study when they were asked to answer, "Who Am I?" they spoke about where they were employed, whereas Americans used statements that spoke more about personal characteristics. "Social context" was found to be more important for Japanese than for Americans.

The two categories—individualism and collectivism—are not mutually exclusive. The distinction between these categories does not imply that a person from a collectivist culture does not have any sense of "self" or that a person from an individualistic background does not value community. Rather it is a matter of degree.

## 1.3. Self-Esteem

According to Schmitt and Allik (2005), "global self-esteem" is defined as how worthy a person feels. They found that the probability of people in some cultures engaging in self-evaluation was less as compared to other cultures. However, the assumption that self-esteem is higher in individualistic cultures as opposed to collectivist cultures doesn't seem to hold true. In different cultures, different ideas of self-esteem exist. Buddhist followers are required to be selfless and that trait is highly revered. In some cultures, altruism is highly respected. In others, people who are known as pious are seen as having the highest self-esteem.

## 1.4. Parenting Practices

Child-rearing practices and parenting styles differ across cultures. The use of Western models, constructs, and psychological measures to examine practices of non-Western peoples has often led to problems (Jackson, 2006). Although Western constructs and psychological instruments used for studying parenting are highly developed, these tools may not be appropriate to use with non-Westerners. As practitioners we need to take care not to form judgments, in the knowledge that what may seem unacceptable to us may be the norm in another culture.

## 1.5. Trauma

The way trauma is experienced is woven into the culture and personal history of a person. The experience of painful incidents is based on the social, cultural, and political context (Brown, 2008). People from a culture that historically has been oppressed, persecuted, or reviled will likely have hardwired prejudices and survival strategies that form part of their character. Unless it is their explicit desire to change these, or there is obvious damage caused to their well-being, we should proceed cautiously before addressing these with EFT.

Culture affects the meaning we give to trauma, expression of negative feelings, and our expectations for recovery. If we understand trauma from the client's cultural point of view, then we can develop better treatment protocols. Each case of trauma is unique, as it is embedded in unique social roles and cultural context.

For example, Susto, a culture-related traumatic disorder, is common in Latin America and Spanish-speaking communities. Also known as soul loss, it occurs when a frightening event happens such as witnessing an accident, losing someone, or being attacked. The belief is that the event causes the soul to be "dislodged" and leave the body (Jackson, 2006).

## 1.6. Social Anxiety

A study conducted in North America by Hsu et al. (2012) examined the cultural discrepancy hypothesis: whether bicultural East Asian participants had higher social anxiety as compared to unicultural participants. The results showed that EAH (East Asian heritage) participants had more anxiety and depression than WH (Western heritage) participants. Western societies focus more on personal control and responsibility, individual self, and achievement, (Markus & Kitayama, 1991;

Singelis, 1994) giving rise to Western standards of social behavior whereas the East Asian cultural values are more about deference to rank and inter-dependent self (Nisbett, 2003).

Behaviors that are socially valued and appropriate in the Eastern value system such as reserve, averting eye gaze, and displaying humility may, from a Western perspective, be seen as symptoms of social anxiety (Arkowitz, Lichtenstein, McGovern, & Hines, 1975; Baker & Edelmann, 2002; Beidel & Turner, 1999; Spence, Donovan, & Brechman-Toussaint, 1999).

There are culture-related symptoms of anxiety. For example, among Latinos *Ataque de nervios* is a sign of distress. It involves excessive shouting, crying, shakiness, heat in chest, and aggression. Mostly in women, it occurs in family-related stressful events (Jackson, 2006, p.131).

## 2. Adaptations to EFT When the Practitioner Is Familiar with the Client's Culture

When the practitioner is from the same culture as the client, or is sufficiently fluent in the client's language and culture, adapting EFT to the client's needs will be relatively straightforward.

### 2.1. Setup Phrase Wording

EFT and its key component, the spoken phrases, were created in English. The acceptance part of the default Setup Statement in EFT, "I deeply and completely love and accept myself," may not work well with all clients, as it does not have exact equivalents in non-English languages. The English words "love" and "accept" are culture specific. Self-love and acceptance may not be looked upon favorably in certain collectivist cultures in which the self is evaluated in relation to others: family, social group, and so on. In this case it might be better to say, "I can be loved and accepted."

Also, the word "love" has different connotations in different languages. In English, "love" is a universal word used equally for everyone. However, this may not be so for non-English languages. For example in Indian languages, the word is used more in the context of a relationship with someone—"in love with someone." The phrase for "I love you" is used mostly by those in a relationship or marriage. Also, parents do not usually say this to their children, but

rather they say that they are affectionate with their children or care for their children. When parents in India don't say the phrase for "I love you" to their children, it does not mean that they don't love their children, but that the love is not expressed directly through words. (A lot is also dependent on the social strata and influence of other cultures.)

## 2.2. Suggested Translations of the Setup Statement for a Few Languages

**Galician**
Acéptome tal e como son.
Translation: I accept myself exactly as I am.
(Contributed by Noreen Barron)

**German**
Ichliebe und akzeptieremich so wieich bin.
Translation: I love and accept myself just the way I am.
Transliteration: Ichliebe und akzeptieremich so wieich bin.
(Contributed by Gerald Stiehler)

**Hebrew**
אניאוהבומקבלאתעצמיבכללמקרה
Translation: I love and accept myself anyway.
Transliteration: Aniohevvemekabeletatzmibeholmikre. (for men)
Aniohevetvemekabelet at atzmibeholmikre. (for women)
(Contributed by Adi Assodri)

**Hindi**
मैंअपनाख्यालरखनाचाहताहूँ
Translation: I would like to take care of myself.
Transliteration: Main apnakhayalrakhnachahtahoon.
(Contributed by Puja Kanth Alfred)

**Hungarian**
Szeretemeselfogadommagambarhogyan.
Translation: I love and accept myself anyway.
Transliteration: Szeretemeselfogadommagambarhogyan.
(Contributed by Adi Assodri)

**Irish**
Glacaimféin mar atámé.

Translation: I accept myself as I am.
(Contributed by Noreen Barron)

### Italian
Miaccettocosí come sono.
Translation: I accept myself as I am.
(Contributed by Noreen Barron)

### Punjabi
फेरभीमैंअपनेआपनुचंगामनडाहाँ

Translation: I still claim myself to be good.
Transliteration: Pherbhi main apneaap nu changa man da haan.
(Contributed by Satinder Bhalla)

### Spanish
Me amo y me acepto completa y profundamente.
Translation: I love and accept myself completely and deeply.
(Contributed by David MacKay)

### Tamil
நான் என்னை நேசித்து, ஏற்றும் கொள்கிறேன்

Translation: I love myself and I accept myself also.
Transliteration: Naan ennai naesiththu yaetrum kolgiraen.
(Contributed by Alfred Jai)

### Urdu
मैंखुदकोकुबूलकरताहूँ

Translation: I accept myself.
Transliteration: Main khudko Kubool karta hoon.
(Contributed by Puja Kanth Alfred)

## 2.3. Scripts
Simple translations of EFT scripts into native languages may not work because the meaning differs. Translations will lack the impact of unique native expressions. As in regular EFT, the most effective phrases to use will be those that incorporate the client's own words.

## 2.4 Reframes
Reframes generally incorporate an element of surprise and must ring true for the client. For this purpose familiar expressions and proverbs from the client's own culture may strengthen the reframe's capacity to hit home and stick.

## 3. Further Considerations for When the Practitioner Is Unfamiliar with the Client's Culture
To apply EFT with someone from a culture with which you are not intimately familiar, some preparation and precautions are in order. This may not always be possible, so don't be afraid to ask clients what is appropriate for them. The adaptations described previously for applying EFT when the practitioner is already familiar with the client's cultural setting, plus the following, will facilitate the clearing of emotional issues.

## 3.1. Being Mindful of One's Own Beliefs
As practitioners, it is important for us to recognize that our beliefs and attitudes are based on our sociocultural upbringing. That doesn't mean that we need to change them. All of us need a frame of reference, and our beliefs provide that framework. However, that frame of reference can also act as a deterrent. Conscious awareness can accomplish a lot.

Therapy does not take place in a vacuum. There is transference and counter transference. "Staying out of the way" isn't easy, as our beliefs and feelings can get triggered by the client and it may become tough to handle them.

Arden and Linford (n.d.) aptly stated:

After all, the therapeutic relationship is based on the brain's capacity to understand, and to regulate, the emotional states of others. Our ability to acknowledge and mirror these states in others (through the signs of autonomic arousal that underlies another's unhappiness, stress, and anger) is sometimes all that makes human life bearable.

## 3.2. Language
English, though widely spoken all over the world, differs in its expression in each country. Also, English as a second language can pose a considerable barrier for culturally diverse clients; explaining their story in their second language, or through an interpreter, can lead to emotions being expressed inadequately and differently.

The affirmation is an important tool to bring about transformation. Words are the vehicles of expression. Every word in every language has some intensity. The same word spoken by an enemy will have a different intensity than when spoken by a friend.

We are passionate storytellers. So we can only find the hidden core beliefs and other issues by what clients tell, and with the help of tapping and affirmations, we reconstruct the story, making them repeat what they said and tapping on it. So the words of the person are very important. Basically, we are reconstructing the memory with words.

We know that a child learns to make sounds, imitate adult sounds, and associate the sounds with particular sensations. This shows the important role that words play in our lives. We describe, explain, justify, and rationalize our thoughts, feelings, and behavior to ourselves, and we do it through words.

## 3.3. Translation

When working in an emergency situation in a foreign country, for example, it may be that we will have to work through a translator. Here a brief training in the basics of EFT for the translator will be in order. As the practitioner and translator gain experience working as a team, the process can become highly effective.

Experienced EFT practitioners will have noted how a particular turn of phrase can sometimes be the key to releasing emotions. Thus it is particularly important in cross-cultural EFT to invite the translator and client to adjust your phrasing so that it sounds right to them. Also, the significance of native expressions may be lost when translated to your language. If in doubt, ask.

## 3.4. Repetition by the Client

When English-speaking practitioners use EFT with people whose native language is not English, they need to understand that each word has a specific meaning in a certain context. "Some emotion-related words that are learned in a first language may have a deeper level of meaning than the words learned in a second language" (Jackson, 2006).

For this reason it will often be beneficial for clients to say the phrases in their native language. Those who have migrated and now speak a second language fluently may still find it more effective to use their native language when working with events from their past.

## 3.5. Empathy and Rapport

Empathy and rapport with the client is vitally important in applying EFT, or any other psychotherapeutic technique. We need to earn and keep clients' trust so that they can open up and heal their emotional hurts. Our egos can get in the way of healing as our cultural biases and prejudices might prevent us from clearly understanding clients' problems. An attitude of care, loving acceptance, and respect will almost always carry us through any awkwardness in our words, gestures, or behavior when we are working with clients whose cultural upbringing is considerably different from our own. Making the effort to speak the client's language (even if limited to a salutation), gaining some understanding of the client's cultural history and mores, and having patience in clearing any doubts the client may have about EFT will go a long way toward establishing the necessary rapport.

## 3.6. Verbal Communication

If the client's native language is different from yours, speak clearly and a little on the slow side, without exaggerating or raising your voice, as this could be insulting. Especially on first meeting, be aware of how well they understand and adjust your speech to as near normal as possible without losing them. If their meaning or pronunciation is unclear to you, take responsibility and ask for clarification. Relax, tap, and your ear will attune to them.

Keep sentence structure simple. Use shorter Setup and Reminder Phrases. Even when you have the same native language, avoid the use of slang expressions, as these are often culture-specific. Pay attention to verbal cues and look for nonverbal cues—what they say and feel, how they express themselves, and the congruence between words and expressions. Listen carefully so that you can use the expressions of the client and include native expressions from the client's vocabulary.

Many languages distinguish between formal and informal ways of addressing others, such as *usted* or *tu* in Spanish. If you speak the language, but are uncertain of the appropriate form of address, it is usually best to use the more respectful form with adults until invited to use the informal.

## 3.7. Nonverbal Communication

Nonverbal expressions will also differ in the areas of "proxemics (personal space), kinesics (bodily movements), paralanguage (vocal cues, e.g., vocal inflections), and high- and low-context communication" (Jackson, 2006, p. 129). Hence, as EFT practitioners we need to be aware of the subtle changes that can occur in the nonverbal expressions of our clients and ask for clarifications if we don't understand.

We need to research or be aware of how people greet one another, how eye contact is perceived, and in what circumstances physical contact is acceptable or not in our client's culture. A quick Internet search can usually provide these answers; a useful resource for this purpose is www.culturecrossing.net.

## 3.8. Preframing

Begin the EFT session by explaining these key things to your client:

- I am helping you heal, but the healing comes from you and is not being done by me.
- Your choice of words may differ from mine; please feel free to change the words as you like.
- Sometimes you may not understand the way I express things or our nonverbal expressions may differ. It's okay when this happens. Please let me know if you feel uncomfortable or misunderstood.
- The way I pronounce words may be different. Please ask me to clarify when something isn't clear.
- Please ask me to clarify, change, and explain anything during the EFT session that you do not understand.
- If you feel that your religious or spiritual beliefs are not allowing you to do EFT, please talk about this with me. (It's best not to jump in and defend EFT. Help your clients understand how they can heal with EFT in the way that they understand, without directly or indirectly passing judgments about their religious or cultural beliefs.)

## 3.9. Cultural Reframes

Reframing is about changing the perspective for the event. It can be used with the Setup or Reminder Phrases.

**Incorporate healthy cultural beliefs.** Cultural reframes are about changing the frame of reference of the problem at hand by taking the healthy cultural beliefs of the client that can be relied upon to transform these unhealthy beliefs. For example, a client who was very uncomfortable with the

default Setup Statement, used, in keeping with his religious beliefs, *"Even though I feel ____, God accepts me the way I am."* Another client felt that she did not deserve to be compassionate toward herself. We used the phrase "God would want me to be compassionate toward myself" and this was very helpful in the process of dissolving her limiting self-beliefs.

It is often difficult to examine one's hardwired beliefs and transform them, even if they are unhealthy. Therefore, it is important to let clients utilize their healthy cultural frame of reference and connect it to the Setup Statements and reframes, while they try to outgrow their limiting beliefs. Don't underestimate the strength or belittle beliefs that may seem odd to you, even when it may seem to you they could be easily dismissed. Directly targeting hardwired beliefs can feel to the client like a personal attack and may bring about more harm than good.

**Try inverting the original belief.** Prachi had quit her job due to her back pain. During that time, when she had severe back pain, a tantric (a mystic who can remove curses, etc.) scared her by saying that black magic had been done on her and it was the reason she lost her job. We tapped on: *"Even though that tantric said that someone has done some black magic on me, I choose to release this belief about black magic. I choose to believe in myself... in my power to heal."*(This affirmation did not resonate with her. She had resistance to releasing her belief in black magic.)

When asked, "What do you think black magic is?" she said, "It's a negative intention." When asked, "If negative intention exists, then is it possible for positive intention to exist as well?" she said, "Yes! "In answer to the question "What can this negative intention do to you?" she said, "When my immunity is down with back pain, then the negative intention can affect me." Then we tapped on the following statement, which met with no resistance:*"Even though I feel that my immunity was down and the negative intention could have affected me, I choose to reverse the effects of those negative intentions."*

She said, "This is excellent. I feel good already."

"Do you still feel that the tantric's words can affect you?"

She said, "Yes, maybe."

So we tapped on: *"Even though the tantric may have been right that this person who was jealous of me may have done some black magic, I don't know if he did something; that is not important. What is important is that I can reverse the effects of anyone's negative intentions; I can heal myself. I choose to not let these beliefs hinder my healing process."* (Native language was also used.)

Note: "What is important is that I can reverse the effects of anyone's negative intentions" was a reframe that again allowed space for shifting the perspective that was hindering her healing.

**Try taking the collective or individual self into reframing.** For example, in cultures in which the collectivist values are stronger than the individualist values, a reframe might be: *"Even though it didn't work out as I had hoped, my intention was for the greater good."*

## 3.10. Acculturative Stress

This can be defined as the stress faced by an immigrant population due to the conflict between their cultural heritage and the mainstream cultural values of the country in which they are residing.

Acculturation is the cultural modification of an individual, group, or people by adapting to or borrowing traits from another culture ("Acculturation," Merriam-Webster).

Due to immigration, societies have become "culturally plural." Berry's research on acculturation reveals four acculturative strategies based on the following two issues: (a) Maintaining the culture—how much the cultural identity and characteristics hold importance; and (b) "contact and participation"—the extent to which individuals will involve themselves with other cultural groups. The four strategies are: (1) Assimilation is when the nondominant group does not want to maintain their cultural identity and seek greater interactions with the mainstream or dominant culture; (2) separation happens when they wish to hold on to their identity and avoid interactions with the dominant group; (3) integration is retaining cultural identity as well as interacting; and (4) marginalization is complete alienation (Berry, 1997, pp. 8–9).

Acculturation brings about stress if the individuals are not able to adapt to the dominant/mainstream culture. Integration leads to a positive adaptation and enables "mutual accommodation" (Berry, 1997, p. 24).

How much clients have adapted to the dominant culture, the level of understanding the client and the practitioner have about individuality and collectivism, gender roles, and family dynamics will determine how comfortable they are in handling acculturative stress. Anxiety is a major issue for immigrants who have to handle a new environment, language, culture, education, and work system.

## 4. Examples of Geo-Specific EFT

### 4.1. The Importance of Community

"Inge" called me from Indonesia. She was going through a difficult phase in her marriage and a friend had advised her to consider divorce. She was not comfortable with the suggestion and revealed that divorce in her community carried a social stigma. She was very stressed and indecisive. She was anxious that her daughter's life would be negatively affected by a decision of divorce, as her daughter would be teased mercilessly at her school. She and her parents would also face repercussions in their community.

The focus of EFT sessions was to help Inge find ways to resolve conflicts within the marriage and release her anger with her husband. She felt much better after finding a way to work on her problems. Her eventual decision not to seek divorce, based on her cultural beliefs, became a significant factor in her healing process. She was not comfortable with the idea of divorce and attached a lot of importance to her family and her community. Her self-worth was reflected in her "self-other relationships" and her being part of the community. If I had focused on changing her cultural beliefs and downplaying the importance of community, it could have aggravated her situation. Instead, helping her within her cultural framework was more beneficial.

### 4.2. Religion

Some problems are deeply imbedded in a religious context and understanding them in that context is very important.

"Carolina" from South America came to me for issues related with self-image. In the course of the sessions, she told me about her belief in spirits; she could feel them at times. A part of her anxiety and fear was embedded in this specific belief. She also believed, however, that these spirits would not harm her, but she was not able to reduce her anxiety. My first instinct was to challenge her beliefs, but I realized that it would be more helpful to use an EFT reframe for her anxiety in the context of this belief: *"Even though I see apparitions and I get terrified of them, I choose to feel safe when I see them because I know they won't harm me."* This helped in significantly reducing her anxiety.

Ranjitha, a pious person, believed that she had psoriasis because she didn't appreciate her hands and legs and God was punishing her for this. The following EFT statements gave her a lot of solace, and brought about a significant shift in her problems:

> *Even though I have psoriasis because I didn't appreciate my beautiful hands and feet that God has given me...*
>
> *Even though I feel that God gave me psoriasis to make me realize that I did not appreciate my hands and legs, I deeply and completely love and forgive myself for not appreciating what God gave me and ask God for his forgiveness.*

# 5. A Sampling of Suggestions from EFT Practitioners

## 5.1. Greece

Cultural influence comes from instilled beliefs and values, which in Greece are usually related to family relationships, public behavior (especially in small towns), and reduced self-esteem. Families in Greece are rather close communities, which means that bad behavior within the family usually stays within the family and the affected member (usually the child or mother) suppresses reactions. Also, the issue of shame could be considered cultural, again especially in small towns, and that generates a number of issues with clients, often core ones. There are a number of other such issues as well. In general, I respect beliefs originating from a client's culture and don't try to question them or replace them in any way; instead, we usually reframe how the client sees the problem or other people's reactions, in parallel with diffusing the blocked emotions and that works fine. I also use humor from time to time, which is well accepted and is a strong part of our culture.

The default Setup Statement works perfectly with clients, exactly translated in Greek.

Sometimes clients are in strong denial of self-acceptance, so we introduce "maybe" and similar gentle variations. I never use stronger affirmations such as "love" or "forgive" as that may cause additional resistance in clients. I stick with "I accept myself" and it works fine.

With multilingual clients, I ask them to use Greek if that is their native language. In fact, I always ask them to use their native language, even though my guidance is in Greek or English (and they have a different native language). Sometimes, clients prefer to use a specific language for their own reasons, so I let them do so and watch for the results. However, I also check for reasons to do so, as they may reveal additional aspects or issues to work on. I have come to the conclusion that even though native language works faster when resolving issues, the client's preference for a different language should be respected.

—Ypatios Varelas, www.eft.gr, www.eft-help.com, www.change.gr

## 5.2. Iran

In my experience the following guidelines should be followed in tapping on Iranians. Since the majority of Iranians are Muslim, I guess the same applies to other Islamic nations as well.

Some people (especially religious women) do not like to be tapped by the opposite sex. The practitioner should be very careful in this regard. Any kind of touching might be interpreted as a violation of privacy and even some kind of sexual abuse.

On the other hand, some people think that there is a curing power in the practitioner's fingertips. Therefore they insist on being tapped and even refuse to do it by themselves. This kind of behavior may be seen in both the religious and non-religious.

So the practitioner must weigh the situation very carefully before deciding whether to tap on the client or ask him/her to do it.

There are several languages used in Iran. Some people prefer to say the Setup and the Reminder Phrase in their native language even though they are fluent in my language. I have always respected this desire and have never encountered any kind of problem in this regard. So I think that if the client prefers to say anything in his/her language, there is no reason to object.

Various translations of the default Setup and Reminder Phrase have worked very well. I think there is nothing culturally oriented here.

—Farhad Forughmand, forughmand@yahoo.com, www.eft.ir

## 5.3. Poland

Doing EFT among Polish people is pretty standard. I haven't noticed any cultural exceptions that would affect EFT procedure. I do it the same way with Americans and Poles. Sometimes they ask if EFT may be against their faith or religion, but it is more conceptual concern than procedural. After I explain that EFT has nothing to do with any dogma, the session looks standard.

—Kasia Dodd, info@instytuteft.com, www.instytuteft.com/blog

## 5.4. Serbia

I must say that there are no special barriers or prerequisites in doing EFT with clients in Serbia. Tapping is easy to offer as a solution; both children and adults accept it; no need to dramatically change setup phrases; eye contact, even body touch is natural in tapping communication... So, in general, it is okay to do EFT with clients in Serbia.

—Milena Kostic, www.jazzord.com

## 6. Conclusion

Our work as practitioners is to help clients change the beliefs that hinder their growth rather than change their core cultural or religious beliefs. It is important to distinguish between beliefs that hinder growth and cultural beliefs that are supportive. Beliefs that may seem like a block to us may be healthy cultural beliefs in the client that do not need to be changed. Therefore, awareness of our own cultural and religious beliefs is very important before we use EFT on clients from different cultures. This will help us refrain from imposing our sociocultural beliefs on them.

*Note: Please do not form any generalizations about any culture or religion based on the examples given in this chapter. Geo-Specific EFT does not intend to encourage stereotypes, biases, or prejudices.*

## References

Acculturation. (n.d.). In *Merriam-Webster's online dictionary.* Retrieved from http://www.merriam-webster.com/dictionary/acculturation

Arden, J. & Linford, L. (n.d.). The rise and fall of Paxmedica. *Psychotherapy Networker.* Retrieved from http://www.psychotherapynetworker.org/magazine/recentissues/732-the-rise-and-fall-of-paxmedica

Arkowitz, H., Lichtenstein, E., McGovern, K., & Hines, P. (1975). The behavioral assessment of social competence in males. *Behavior Therapy, 6,* 3–13. doi:10.1016/S0005-7894(75)80056-6

Baker, S. R. & Edelmann, R. J. (2002). Is social phobia related to lack of social skills? Duration of skill-related behaviours and ratings of behavioural adequacy. *British Journal of Clinical Psychology, 41,* 243–257. doi:10.1348/014466502760379118

Beidel, D. C. & Turner, S. M. (1999). The natural course of shyness and related syndromes. In L. A. Schmidt & J. Schulkin (Eds.), *Extreme fear, shyness, and social phobia: Origins, biological mechanisms, and clinical outcomes* (pp. 203–223). New York, NY: Oxford University Press.

Berry, J. W. (1997). Immigration, acculturation and adaptation. *Applied Psychology: An International Review, 46*(1), 5–68.

Betancourt, H. & Lopez, S. R. (1993). The study of culture, ethnicity, and race in American psychology. *American Psychologist, 48*(6), 629–637.

Brown, L. (2008). *Cultural competence in trauma therapy: The context of the flashback.* Washington, DC: American Psychological Association.

Cousins, N. (1989). *Head first: The biology of hope.* New York, NY: Dutton.

Hsu, L., Woody, S. R., Lee, H., Peng, Y., Zhou, X., & Ryder, A. G. (2012). Social anxiety among East Asians in North America: East Asian socialization or the challenge of acculturation? *Cultural Diversity and Ethnic Minority Psychology, 18*(2), 181–191.

Jack, R. E., Caldara, R., & Schyns, P. G. (2012, February). Internal representations reveal cultural diversity in expectations of facial expressions of emotion. *Journal of Experimental Psychology: General, 141*(1), 19–25. doi:10.1037/a0023463

Jackson, Y. K. (Ed.) (2006). *Encyclopedia of Multicultural Psychology.* Thousand Oaks, CA: Sage Publications.

Markus, H. R. & Kitayama, S. (1991). Culture and the self: Implications for cognition, emotion, and motivation. *Psychological Review, 98,* 224–253. doi:10.1037/0033-295X.98.2.224

Nisbett, R. E. (2003). The geography of thought: How Asians and Westerners think differently and why. New York, NY: Free Press.

Ross, L. & Nisbett, R. E. (1991). The person and the situation. New York, NY: McGraw-Hill.

Schmitt, D. P. & Allik, J. (2005). Simultaneous administration of the Rosenberg self-esteem scale in 53 nations: Exploring the universal and culture-specific features of global self-esteem. *Journal of Personality and Social Psychology, 89,* 623–642.

Singelis, T. M. (1994). The measurement of independent and interdependent self-construals. *Personality and Social Psychology Bulletin, 20,* 580–591. doi:10.1177/0146167294205014

Spence, S. H., Donovan, C., & Brechman-Toussaint, M. (1999). Social skills, social outcomes, and cognitive features of childhood social phobia. *Journal of Abnormal Psychology, 108,* 211–221. doi:10.1037/0021843X.108.2.211

Triandis, H. C. (1989). The self and social behavior in differing cultural contexts. *Psychological Review, 96,* 506–520.

# Chapter 49
# Tapping for the Highly Sensitive Person
*Rue Anne Hass*

## Abstract

In the national bestseller *The Highly Sensitive Person: How to Thrive When the World Overwhelms You,* author Elaine N. Aron, PhD, defined a distinct personality trait that affects as many as one in five people. According to Dr. Aron (1996), the highly sensitive person (HSP) has a sensitive nervous system, is aware of subtleties in his or her surroundings, and is more easily overwhelmed when in a highly stimulating environment. In addition, illuminating facts about HSP include: high sensitivity is innate (the brains of HSPs function differently from those of non-HSPs); HSPs tend to observe before acting; shyness is not the same as HSP (30% of HSPs are extroverts); and HSPs from cultures that do not value sensitivity tend to have low self-esteem (Aron, 2013). Mainstream psychology has accepted the HSP personality trait. If you are highly sensitive, you will be glad to know that EFT has been exceptionally useful for people with this trait. This chapter explores the highly sensitive temperament, details the advantages and disadvantages, demonstrates how to tap on common HSP issues, and gives a case example illustrating how EFT can help.

**Keywords:** highly sensitive person, HSP, highly sensitive temperament, HST, emotional temperament, EFT

**Rue Anne Hass, MA,** is a spiritual life path coach and intuitive mentor, author, ordained minister, and EFT Master practitioner. She is the author of *EFT for the Highly Sensitive Temperament* and fits the sensitive temperament profile. Her background includes extensive training in psychospiritual philosophy and energy psychology therapies. Send correspondence to Rue Anne Hass, PO Box 17653, Boulder, CO 80308-0653, or rue@intuitivementoring.com. www.IntuitiveMentoring.com.

Have people ever said to you any of the following?

"Oh, you are just too sensitive!"

"You take things so hard!"

"Just let it roll off your back."

"Why can't you just let it go?!"

And maybe even, "What's wrong with you? You are such a cry baby!"

If you've heard such comments often, you have probably come to think people are right—there must be something wrong with you. In fact, you may be what is termed a "highly sensitive person" (HSP), or alternatively, a "highly sensitive temperament" (HST).

For those of us with this temperament, EFT is the perfect tool to learn how to "deeply and completely love and accept" ourselves, instead of continuing to internalize the criticisms we have heard all our lives regarding being "too sensitive." We can learn to say: "I'm not 'introverted'; I am reserved, self-contained, independent. I am not 'shy'; I love and intend to create deep and meaningful interaction." It is remarkable that when we change our perception of ourselves, we automatically change our perception of the world. And then the world changes.

## Being Sensitive Is an Emotional Temperament

The general construct of sensory processing sensitivity, the concept described here, is a normal temperament variation found in 20% of the population (Aron, 2013). Personally, I believe that sensitivity is a kind of awareness that can save the world. I speak as a "highly sensitive person" myself. It has taken me most of my life to understand this temperament and value it for its gifts. In my work as an Intuitive Mentor, I have worked with many people who are extra sensitive to stress, traumatic experiences, and environmental toxins. People with this temperament are also extraordinarily sensitive to beauty and spirituality, and they all have a desire to be a good custodian of the earth.

Being highly sensitive has its blessings and its drawbacks, sometimes both simultaneously. Much of my work has been about how to use EFT to heal the wounds of the sensitive nature so that we are empowered to use our gifts in the service of ourselves, our families, our communities, and the world.

Here are some ways to gather information for tapping with a sensitive person (or with yourself

if you are that person). HSP clients might want to learn more about their trait, and perhaps even tap for the feelings that being "so sensitive" has brought up in them. But help them to keep in mind that everything in a sensitive person's experience will always be more vivid, more intense—a deeper experience of pain or a richer experience of joy.

I have written most of this chapter as if you were working with yourself, but you could equally use it as a guide to helping someone else. (For more detail, see Hass, 2009.)

## How Can I Tell If I Am a Highly Sensitive Person?

If the majority of the following statements describe you, you are likely an HSP (you may wish to tap as you read):

- You feel emotions deeply, and you can't hide what you feel.
- You are always aware of what people around you are feeling.
- Your feelings are easily hurt by criticism or even a look, and you keep thinking about what happened, and what you might have done wrong, and what you should have done instead.
- You feel deeply for other people's suffering. It is difficult to watch the news or to see sad movies.
- Sometimes you can slip easily into feeling anxious or depressed, and once caught in the feeling it is hard for you to move out of it.
- You are not comfortable in large crowds, hectic environments, or around loud music. You get easily overwhelmed when there is a lot going on.
- You are a perfectionist, and you want to be helpful—so much so that you put other people's needs ahead of your own.
- You do your best to avoid conflicts.
- You might feel like an alien in your own family. They are practical, industrious, social, while you are quiet, imaginative, thoughtful, and creative.
- You have a mission to bring peace to the world. You want to save the world from itself. You can see how good things could be, if only...

## The Positive and Negative Aspects of Being Sensitive

When I have asked sensitive people what they like best and least about their sensitive trait, I have gotten answers that reflect the following qualities (again you may wish to tap along as you read).

## Drawbacks to Being So Sensitive

- I notice more details, and when I comment on them, people think I am weird.
- I am too attuned to what feels like impending criticism or disapproval.
- I feel socially awkward because I am not good at small talk.
- I am too empathic—I feel what everyone else is feeling.
- I don't have good boundaries—I seem to become the other person.
- I get nervous easily.
- I try to protect everyone.
- I worry about being a victim.
- I put other people's needs before mine.

## Blessings of Being Sensitive

- I am intuitively aware of what another person may be thinking or feeling.
- Being sensitive is a great early warning system.
- Being so empathic makes me very understanding.
- I am able to sense/see to the heart of a matter.
- I am deeply attuned to beauty.
- The "poetry" of everything comes through.
- I have a deep connection with spirit.
- My sense of humor is deeper, and more readily available.
- I can see the beauty in almost anything.
- I see wholeness, always, everywhere.

## Tapping on Being "So Sensitive"

You might start with tapping on how you experience being a sensitive person:

*Even though...*
> I worry that I am TOO sensitive
> I feel so deeply
> I am so open to others' emotions
> I am easily hurt and upset
> I don't like conflict
> It's hard to stop feeling sad sometimes

> I can't watch the news or sad or violent movies
> I get depressed easily
> I get overwhelmed

*...I deeply and completely love and accept myself anyway.*
> *Even though...*

> I can't stand large crowds
> I can't take loud noise
> I don't like hectic environments
> I wish I were tougher and could let things roll off easier
> I think my sensitivity is a weakness
> I think something is wrong with me. It is my fault.
> I wish things didn't bother me so much
> I wish my emotions weren't so obvious to other people
> I wish I could let things go and not worry so much
> I hide my sensitivity from others

*...I deeply and completely love and accept myself anyway, and I want to find other ways of thinking and feeling about this.*

## Finding the Right Issues to Focus on When Tapping

When working with someone, I find it helpful to hold a kind of map in my mind of the experience of being highly sensitive. It helps me to ask the right questions so I know what we might focus on.

A good way to do this is to write out a stream of consciousness page of thoughts, feelings, and memories that arise in you, as you hold each of the following questions in your mind. Then pull out phrases and sentences that trigger an emotional response. Fit them into your tapping routine. Tap on your answers to the questions in each section.

## We Had Heartbreaking Experiences

Painful experiences are felt more deeply by a sensitive person, especially as a child. The sample answers are all quotes from real people. The next step in EFT will be to find specific events that are examples of what broke your heart.

Question: "What broke your heart?"
Examples of answers:

They told me it was my fault.
I had to put their needs first.

I always believed, growing up, that something was terribly wrong with me.

I never felt safe.

My feelings were not important.

I felt invisible.

I never felt loved or accepted for being me, by anyone.

My childhood was very troubled, traumatic, and lonesome.

I was not wanted.

I was told what was "expected of me," and if I fell short, I was shamed.

I was told, "That is too shameful to talk about."

My father abandoned me.

My mother was cold to me.

They told me repeatedly that I would never be any good.

I grew up with that empty, futile, little-boy feeling that no one cares about you, and that it is somehow your fault and you are worthless.

Living in my family was a tsunami of name calling.

## Those Experiences Led to Beliefs

Those heartbreaking experiences, large and small, can lead to beliefs about who we are and what is possible for us in life.

Question: "What did this experience lead you to believe about yourself or about what it is like to be in the world?"

Examples of answers:

I identified with the upset feelings of my parents more than my own feelings.

I wonder if others love, accept, or want me.

They need me, but do they want me?

I didn't know I was enough.

I didn't know I mattered.

I don't deserve anything.

I am not okay.

It is not okay to take up space.

I didn't know it was okay to breathe.

My only job was to be a servant to someone else.

I had no feelings, wants, desires, or goals except to take care of others.

I have very little belief in myself.

I didn't know I was important!

This is the story my family told, and I believed them.

This is the story my culture tells about people like me, and I never questioned it.

I have to do it all on my own.

I can't ask for help.

I don't value myself enough to ask for support.

I struggle speaking up when in relationships.

I find it hard to speak up and advocate for myself when there is any confrontation or difficult issues.

I have to be perfect.

I have to tough it out and soldier on.

## We Had to Stuff Our Feelings

It may not have been possible or safe to express the powerful anger, sadness, fear, and shame we felt during and after the painful experiences. Those feelings got stuffed or swallowed. Stuffed feelings show up later in life as physical and emotional pain and illness. Most people with chronic physical and emotional pain are highly sensitive. The fear of confronting powerful feelings can stop us from beginning a healing journey.

Question: "What emotions and feelings does this experience bring up in you?"

Examples of answers:

That feeling of abject loss and self-blame.

Sadness, anger, fear, shame, embarrassment, grief and loss, guilt, physical or emotional pain, trauma.

I feel like I'm just one big ball of pain all of a sudden.

My defenses are down and all I do is cry...but I'll be rejected if I cry.

I don't even want to do EFT.

Shutting down has created responses in my body.

Chronic nausea.

A gripping feeling in my center.

A square block of tension.

Feeling so numb.

I know I should be feeling something more.

What is wrong with me?

Everyone else seems to have feelings... where are mine?

I can't feel what I must be feeling.

I want to feel...no I don't.

I never want to feel like that again.

My parents were "soldier on" sorts so they set that example...and expected that attitude.

Feeling is too intense.
I get sick when I feel what is in there.
Pain in my back.
My heart hurts.
My chest and throat ache.
My legs feel weak and I am off balance.
I can't breathe.
Something heavy sitting on my chest.
It's a pain in the neck.
My arms hurt.
I can't reach out for help.
I feel overwhelmed; I don't know where to start.
I had to withdraw, leave my body, live in my own world.
I learned to make myself small, stifle myself; I had to second-guess everything I said and did to avoid rejection and abandonment.
I've been through enough crises to know that I will get through this one too, but there still is a very frightened and lonely child inside.

## Our Families Had Beliefs and Feelings about Being So Sensitive

Our families may have taught us that we had to tough it out, not stand out. They thought they were "making us strong." The people in our families who mistreated us did so because that was how they were treated, and these were the beliefs and feelings they themselves took on from their own family experience. The tendency to replicate these misunderstandings and illnesses gets passed down through the generations of a family.

Question: "What did your family believe about you being 'so sensitive'? Were they trying to 'toughen you up for a tough world'? Did your sensitivity threaten their own carefully covered up or denied sensitivity?"

Examples of answers:

One minute I was getting off the school bus, the next I was told my grandmother was dead. My world had fallen apart.
Once I'd reconnected with my grief I stayed there for days.

My mum told me that I cried for weeks.
Her words were "We didn't know if you'd ever stop."
Mum told me I didn't seem to be getting over it.
She said that everyone else had started to stop grieving by then and had moved on.
I seemed stuck and Mum said they were worried about me.
I could physically feel the pain in my chest.
I was 7 years old again and stuffing down my crying, which had never been released.
I thought other people's feelings and needs come before mine.
I was told that it's selfish to wallow in your own sadness.
Other people didn't like the intensity of my feelings (and didn't know how to deal with it).
The world is not a safe place.
I felt helpless.
My family has a "must prepare for the worst" outlook.
I learned that it's dangerous to be fun loving, spontaneous, and carefree.
Surprises are *not* welcome in our family.
Many of the beliefs I formed at the time had been running my life ever since.
They told me, "You should not take it personally."
They demanded that I allow this behavior or speech to continue; they allowed the behavior to continue or to have taken place; I couldn't say anything because they would tell me "it isn't personal."
It was meant to assert control over me.
It happens over and over, and I'm supposed to continue as though there were no attack, as though there were no wound
It was intended to wound.
They said, "I was just kidding."
I was labeled as the irrational, overemotional person who can't deal with reality like a grown-up.
They said I should toughen up, soldier on, hunker down.
It made me feel all alone in an alien environment.
I struggled with bulimia because I never felt that my feelings were valid.

## Our Personal Healing Can Heal the Whole Family History

Healing our family's history is on the way to healing the world. We just thought we had to *start* with healing the whole world so that it would be a safe place for us. That was pretty exhausting. We left ourselves off our own to-do list.

Question: "How can you take care of yourself and your needs without thinking that you are selfish? How could taking care of yourself first be a *good* thing? (Hint: I like to think of selfish as spelled "Self-ish," meaning "care of the Soul" or "self care.")

Examples of answers:

You were not meant to be here to sacrifice for others.
Treat yourself as worthy.
You are worth being protected.
You can still care for others.
You can live from that knowing of your own worth.
Be empathic, continue to feel deeply, but your first priority is to protect yourself.
When I speak up for others, I am really wanting to speak up for myself.
I know how to walk away now.

## Reframing Sensitive Reactions to Life Events

When a sensitive person chooses a life event to explore with EFT, here is a possible protocol to follow. These questions will be evocative no matter what the issue or how sensitive the individual.

Use the same question-asking process just described. Ask yourself each question, and then write out a page or paragraph in response. Then tap for everything that comes up.

The underlying supposition is this:

*Even though I don't see how I could reframe this event positively, I am open to seeing it differently, and I'm open to seeing purpose and wisdom in the event and in my own and others' response, and I deeply and completely love and accept myself, no matter what.*

Ask questions to elicit tapping Setups and phrases:

- How did you respond to the event itself? (tap)
- What were your emotions, thoughts, and/or your body's response? (tap)
- How did other people respond to the event? (tap)
- How do you feel/think about your (and others') response? (tap)
- What regrets, sorrow, or other feelings do you have about the event and its effect on you and your life? e.g., "If only I had known, I wouldn't have suffered/wasted my life/limited myself." (tap)
- Would things have gone differently if you (and others) had known you are highly sensitive? Now that you understand that you are highly sensitive, what would you (and others) do differently in response to the event? (tap)
- From the perspective of a wise, sensitive advisor to yourself, what wisdom do you see in your (and others') response? (tap)
- What does the event and your response mean about you and your capacity to respond to life now?
- What was the *positive intention* of your (and others') response at the time? What were you trying to get for yourself? (tap)

## Case Example

Here are some of the answers that one person, now in her 50s, gave to the previous questions, as she considered the effect on her life of having been raped in her senior year of high school. An EFT tapping Setup phrase can be created out of each of these answers.

How did you respond to the event? What were your emotions and thoughts?

Trauma, shock, alone, afraid, confused, felt stupid, tricked.
The dreams of my life were shattered.
I identified with the upset feelings of my parents more than my own feelings.
All I wanted to do was protect my father, his reputation.

How did other people respond?

No one knew how to deal with it.
My mother was in shock and couldn't respond.
My father wanted to deal with the situation but keep it quiet because of the effect it would have on his career.
My parents did the best they could.

If I had known I was sensitive, I might have been more aware that:

I come from a family of warriors that have had to hide their identity.

Pay attention to the real me, not the story about me.

I could say—stop—I am the one who was hurt here.

I am not as invincible as I seem.

My mother would have been able to be there for me.

I could ask to be held.

I thought I had to—and could—protect everyone.

I didn't know that I didn't know how to be safe.

I would not have been tricked into the situation to begin with.

I would have found help in healing the trauma at the time, rather than allowing it to shape my whole subsequent life.

What my "Wise Advisor" perspective might have shared:

You were so aware of your father's stresses, and you so wanted to help.

You were not meant to be here to sacrifice for others.

Treat yourself as worthy.

You are worth being protected.

You can still care for others.

You can live from that knowing of your own worth.

Be empathic, continue to feel deeply, but your first priority is to protect yourself.

This experience taught me to stand up for myself.

When I speak up for others, I am really wanting to speak up for myself.

I know how to walk away now.

That experience blasted me out of the shell that had been holding me in place.

The blessing is in understanding my sensitivity trait instead of going to blame, shame, or "I have wasted my life."

## HSP Tapping in Everyday Life

Here is a brief and simple example of how a tapping routine might go for you as a highly sensitive

person encountering the stresses of a normal day. Think of a small incident that happened recently at work, or in your family, or with an acquaintance, something that bothered you and that you are finding hard to let go of.

Think of what really bothered you about the incident. Was it the look on the person's face? The person's tone of voice? What did you think that meant about you?

Examples: "She said _____ and it hurt my feelings" or "He gave me that look and I felt _____" or "That was the last straw—I just can't get all this done."

Give the event a title.

Rate the intensity of the feelings you have about it on a 0–10 scale.

### 1. EFT Setup Statement

Put the phrase that contains what bothered you most into a Setup Statement like this:

*Even though _____ happened, and I am so sensitive to things like this, so it made me feel _____ (use your words), I accept myself anyway.*

*Even though the look on his/her face made me think _____ (use your words), I love and accept myself anyway. I was doing the best I could.*

*Even though I can't seem to let go of all my feelings about this—I am too sensitive! I love and accept myself anyway, and I am choosing to feel as good as I can right now.*

While tapping the Karate Chop point on either hand, repeat these statements out loud (change the words to fit your own situation).

### 2. Tapping Round

Now, tap through the points, using your title and your feelings:

Eyebrow: *She said _____ (use your title here).*

Side of Eye: *She said _____.*

Under Eye: *She said _____.*

Nose: *She said _____.*

Chin: *I feel hurt and misunderstood.*

Collarbone: *It is really my fault. What is wrong with me? I get overwhelmed so easily.*

Under Arm: *I feel sad and angry and all alone.*

Head: *She said _____ and that made me think _____.*

## 3. Check In

Replay your memory of the incident. Notice what is different about your response. Check your 0–10 intensity level.

## 4. Second Round

Do another round with the same Setup Statements as previously, then tapping on the points in this way:

Eyebrow: *I feel so bad. I am too sensitive! Everyone always said that.*

Side of Eye: *Why can't I just let this roll off my back?*

Under Eye: *What he/she did was wrong.*

Nose: *I don't like being treated that way.*

Chin: *That really hurt my feelings*

Collarbone: *I shouldn't be so upset about this! What is wrong with me?*

Under Arm: *It was my fault. I have to tough it out and soldier on.*

Head: *Maybe part of me doesn't want to let go of this issue.*

## 5. Reframing Round

Now do another round, and experiment with creative ways of rephrasing or reframing the story you have been telling yourself about this incident. Here are some examples:

*Even though that happened, I have decided to accept myself anyway. I wouldn't give up my sensitivity—it gives my life richness and meaning.*

*Even though I might like to feel resentful sometimes, I accept who I am and how I feel.*

*Even though that happened, I choose to feel as good as I can right now.*

Try some phrases and questions that gently and respectfully begin to shift your way of thinking about this incident, what it meant to you, and how your sensitive temperament responded. Imagine that you are taking the perspective of a loving wise advisor:

Eyebrow: *Is there a different way I could be thinking about this?*

Side of Eye: *I might be able to let go of this resentment if I chose to.*

Under Eye: *Maybe I have more choices about my feelings than I thought.*

Nose: *I can always go back to this negative feeling later.*

Chin: *What if I am actually right to feel this way? What if I decided to feel good right now?*

Collarbone: *I appreciate all of my feelings and I appreciate that I care so deeply.*

Under Arm: *I choose to feel relieved and peaceful. We were both doing the best we could.*

Head: *I am glad for the relief and the joy I am tapping into.*

## 6. Check In

Notice what feelings and thoughts remain.

Check your intensity level.

If you need to, do some more rounds of tapping for *"This remaining feeling"*

## 7. Self-care Round

Tap on the following phrases as you complete one more round:

*I love knowing that I deserve better.*

*I choose to believe in myself and value my sensitive temperament.*

*I appreciate that harmony is so important to me.*

*I love appreciating myself.*

*I'm grateful for this opportunity to rethink this incident.*

*I am glad to be exactly who I am—being so sensitive could be a gift.*

*I appreciate all the lessons I have learned.*

*I am so grateful for all the goodness in my life.*

*I am grateful to have such a finely tuned guidance system in my feelings.*

## 8. Final Round

End with a tapping round using the phrase "Especially because…"

*Especially because I love that I am so sensitive, I choose to deepen and expand my sensitivity in even more powerful wonderful ways.*

*Especially because I love that I am so sensitive, I hunger for deep and meaningful relationships so I make creating and maintaining a good and satisfying relationship with myself my first priority.*

*Especially because I love that I am so sensitive and I have a mission of bringing peace into the world, I choose a mission of bringing peace into my own life. I deserve this!*

Check in again, and notice how you feel and think about that incident now.

## Conclusion

If you do EFT for just a few minutes on all the little incidents that come up in a day, you will find your life changing dramatically. The sensitivity that seemed like a burden and a flaw before will begin to appear as the gift it is—a precise and finely tuned guidance system that lets you know right away when you are getting off the track of your deepest truth.

## References

Aron, E. N. (1996). *The highly sensitive person: How to thrive when the world overwhelms you.* New York, NY: Carol Publishing Group.

Aron, E. N. (2013). The highly sensitive person: Letter from Elaine Aron. Retrieved from http://www.hsperson.com

Hass, R. (2009). *EFT for the highly sensitive temperament.* Fulton, CA: Energy Psychology Press.

# Chapter 50
# Healing the Cycle of Addiction
*Carol Look*

### Abstract

Addictions of all kinds can ruin our lives, families, careers, and health. When we lose control over the ability to regulate the intake of substances, we have crossed the line into the addictive cycle of using substances to feel better, which ultimately has negative effects on our emotional and physical health. EFT is an effective treatment of choice to address buried emotional traumas from the past that trigger the initial desire to use substances to numb emotions and avoid psychological pain. EFT can also relieve emotional states in the present tense, reduce stress, and help process charged emotional material. In addition, EFT can address the intensity of immediate cravings, which when left unchecked, often cause people who have been previously committed to sobriety to relapse in spite of their best efforts to refrain from ingesting their substance of choice. This chapter demonstrates how using energy psychology and EFT can eliminate the desire to use substances in spite of their negative consequences, eliminate the reasons addicts have such challenges sticking to a plan of sobriety, and interrupt the emotional cycle of substance abuse.

**Keywords:** addiction, healing, cravings, trauma, self-soothing, substances, dependence

**Carol Look, LCSW**, EFT Master, international speaker, and seminar leader, has been a pioneer and leading voice in the EFT community. She has worked for 22 years in the mental health field, including 8 years as a staff counselor at an outpatient treatment facility for addictions. Send correspondence to Carol Look, 5 East 22nd Street, New York, NY 10010, or support@attractingabundance.com.

## The Problem

Addictions of all kinds ruin countless lives, disrupt relationships, and contribute to unemployment, divorce, poor health, and death. Yet in spite of these dire consequences, people continue to use and abuse substances such as alcohol, drugs, cigarettes, and food. The cycle looks like this:

1. Feeling emotionally upset.
2. Using substances to feel better.
3. Using substances creates "trouble" at work and at home.
4. "Swearing off" the substance.
5. Feeling emotionally (or physically) upset.
6. Using substances to feel better.
7. Getting into trouble again.
8. Swearing off drugs and alcohol, again...

Eight years as a staff counselor at an outpatient treatment facility for addictions taught me many important lessons. The most important lesson I learned is that the rhythm of addiction is a repeatable cycle, and if there is no intervention at key moments in this cycle, relapse and addictive behavior are inevitably repeated.

The primary challenge, besides the problem of easy access to alcohol and drugs, is that we haven't taught addicts how to manage their emotions that they are seeking to anesthetize with drugs and substances in the first place. We've only given them temporary solutions that don't relieve the original problem: emotional distress.

When I was an intake counselor, I heard daily from my beginning clients the following stories and excuses:

- "If he weren't so mean, I could get sober."
- "If there weren't so much stress, I could handle it."
- "I'm not as bad as my neighbor."
- "Everyone's a nag; it's not me."
- "I can handle it, I have it under control."

Since they were sitting in my office because they had agreed with a family member to come see a therapist at a reputable institution known for treating alcoholics and addicts, it was obvious that they did *not* have anything under control at all.

After weeks or months of sobriety, the stories were slightly different from those of clients who were considered "beginners":

- "I'm not sure how to hold on."
- "I can't resist the cravings."
- "Too much chaos is coming up; it's easier to relapse."
- "I don't know if I can handle my feelings."
- "Life is too stressful."
- "The past is coming back to haunt me."

Once recovering addicts achieved the more mechanical task of staying away from the bottle for a period of time, the emotional demons would surface and threaten even those people most committed to sobriety. This is the place where EFT and energy psychology can intervene and make dramatic progress.

## Addiction Defined

An addict or alcoholic is described as someone who gets into emotional, physical, or professional trouble as a direct result of drug or alcohol abuse, yet refuses to stop, avoids professional treatment, and continues to deny that his or her life has been negatively impacted by the substance abuse. The addict or alcoholic continues to have difficulty controlling his or her intake of alcohol or drugs, regardless of promises, infractions, family pressure, or commitments.

For an official diagnosis of substance dependence, the following are the *DSM-IV-TR* (American Psychiatric Association, 2000, p. 197) criteria:

A maladaptive pattern of substance use, leading to clinically significant impairment or distress, as manifested by three (or more) of the following, occurring at any time in the same 12 month period:

1. tolerance, as defined by either of the following:
   (a) a need for markedly increased amounts of the substance to achieve intoxification or desired effect
   (b) markedly diminished effect with continued uses of the same amount of the substance
2. withdrawal, as manifested by either of the following:
   (a) the characteristic withdrawal syndrome for the substance...
   (b) the same (or a closely related) substance is taken to relieve or avoid withdrawal symptoms
3. the substance is often taken in larger amounts or over a longer period of time than intended

4. there is a persistent desire or unsuccessful efforts to cut down or control substance use.

5. a great deal of time is spent in activities necessary to obtain the substance…, use the substance…, or recover from its effects

6. Important social, occupational, or recreational activities are given up or reduced because of substance use

7. the substance use is continued despite knowledge of having a persistent or recurrent physical or psychological problem that is likely to have been caused or exacerbated by the substance….

People become addicted or dependent on alcohol, heroin, cocaine, pain medication, anxiety medication, marijuana, and methamphetamines, to name the most common substances. Their behavior is erratic as a result, their family members complain and beg them to get help, yet they continue to deny the problem is "that bad."

When a professional or family member notices and reports three or more of the features listed, then the person is clinically diagnosed as *substance dependent*. Counselors often ask questions to determine how much the substance use has been interfering in the person's life, which is usually minimized by the addict.

## The Drug of Choice

Can someone be addicted to food, work, or sex as well as typical substances such as drugs and alcohol? If food, work, and sex are "used" to avoid feelings and to get "high" or numb their emotions, then yes, in my professional opinion, people can be addicted to food, work, and sex as ways to stay disconnected from their emotional life. Again, family members or friends complain and beg these people to get help for their compulsive, imbalanced behavior.

Though food addiction is not a clinical diagnosis, after having worked with countless people who call themselves food addicts, and after applying the DSM criteria to someone struggling with their food obsessions and eating compulsions, I have concluded that individuals can use food as their addictive substance.

It may be difficult to categorize someone as "addicted" to work, but when you consider the checklist of the impairment resulting from "using"

this substance (spending too much time at the office), it is clear that work can easily be plugged in as a "drug of choice." In addition, there is now more attention paid to the category of "sex addict," with clients seeking help from professionals for similarly debilitating repercussions in their lives as those experienced by drug and alcohol abusers.

For the remainder of this chapter, however, I will be referring primarily to drugs and alcohol as the primary addictive substances.

## Denial

The defense mechanism of denial is an enormous problem in the beginning of the sobriety process and is certainly used as an excuse by addicts and alcoholics to refuse professional help. Addicts insist that their drug use and erratic behavior are "not that bad" and haven't caused as much distress as their family members or boss report. Yet the consequences are obvious: a DUI, a divorce, being put on probation at work, missing important events. You would think the seriousness of such events would be difficult to deny.

Why would something so obvious—that drug and alcohol abuse interferes with a peaceful life of joy, social fulfillment, and good health—be completely obliterated by the addict's argument that "It's _____'s fault" or "If only _____ was different" or "It's not that bad"?

It's important to remember the wise saying: "The problem was once the solution." The key to helping individuals leave their addictive substance and erratic behavior in the past is identifying what problem(s) the drinking or drug use "solve" in their life—or at least in their mind. Though physical addiction appears to be the primary problem, addicts don't start out as addicts; they begin with the desire to numb their emotions or change their state of mind and feelings. It is this purpose—numbing their feelings or changing how they feel—that we must treat if clinicians are going to be effective in reducing addiction and relapse.

Addictions solve a major problem—the distress caused by emotional conflict from early childhood, family stress, and life's challenges. This is how excessive drug or alcohol abuse begins, and this is the point of intervention that clinicians need to explore. When EFT and other forms of energy medicine are applied to addicts' emotional distress in their past, present, or about their future, progress is steady and impressive.

## It's Not about the Substance

By the time someone is diagnosed or has been sent to professional outpatient (or inpatient) treatment for drug or alcohol use, the individual is clearly unable to abstain from using drugs or alcohol and it appears that alcohol and drugs are the main problem. But what is the precipitating conflict(s) that led the person to choose drug use in the first place? Unresolved emotional conflicts—fear, hurt, abandonment, abuse issues, anger, and an inability to regulate or moderate emotions—are the real problems we need to address. Some people have no outlet, others had poor role models, and others were dealt such a bad hand in the first 10 years of their life that it is easy to understand why they cherish using alcohol and drugs to anesthetize their emotions.

The alcohol and drugs must be absent for the process of recovery to begin, but they are the proverbial tip of the iceberg. By this time, personality changes have occurred, the denial has enraged family members and loved ones, and maladaptive behaviors have led others to mistrust the alcoholic and addict.

While cravings for the substance are incredibly challenging for anyone who has tried to quit drinking, drugging, or smoking, or been on a diet, the challenge is even more complicated than simply managing cravings on a daily basis. Underneath the cravings are powerful emotions, conflicts, interpersonal and social challenges, legal tussles, and possibly health worries as well. All of these issues must be faced when the alcohol is no longer blurring the person's outlook or numbing feelings.

## Safety, Safety, Safety

Why is it so difficult to put down the substances and start living a full life? Addicts and alcoholics are afraid to give up their drug of choice because it threatens their emotional safety. If they didn't have to face their emotional conflicts from childhood, the anger and disruption they've caused in their lives as a result of using substances, their current emotional turmoil, and fear over having to piece their lives back together, giving up drugs and alcohol wouldn't be that difficult. But getting sober (abstaining from substances for long periods of time, and using emotional support such as Alcoholics Anonymous and counseling to adjust their attitudes) is extremely challenging in our society because few of us have been given the right tools.

## The "Right" Tools

What if you or someone you love who has been abusing alcohol for 3 decades were given the right tool to eliminate daily cravings to drink?

What if an addict who had ruined his marriage and his relationship with his kids was given the right tool to release his shame and guilt so he could start to repair his relationships and move on?

What if a cocaine addict was given the right tool so she could release the resentment she has over childhood trauma and the spiral of an out-of-control situation in her upbringing?

What if you could release your overwhelm about the level of destruction you have caused in your life and could make good, sober decisions about your future?

Again, the primary challenges for an addict are:

- Cravings
- Managing emotions – guilt, shame, resentment, anger
- Daily stress/worry
- Regret about the past (lost time)
- Fear of the future

EFT is the single most valuable tool I've come across in 22 years in the mental health field to successfully help people deal with all these challenges to getting clean and sober and living the life they want to live. EFT can be and needs to be aimed at the challenges for addicts: cravings, managing emotions, daily stress, regret about the past, and fear about the future. Then, and only then, can someone release the cycle of addictive behavior and enjoy a fully integrated emotional, social, and personal life.

To use EFT effectively, there are simple steps to follow:

1. Choose a target (an emotion, a symptom, a memory of an event, or a belief).
2. Rate the intensity of the emotion/target on the 0–10 scale.
3. Devise a Setup Statement and say it while tapping on the Karate Chop point.
4. Tap the remaining sequence of points while repeating the Reminder Phrase (the target feeling).

## Addressing Cravings with EFT

Physiological cravings for the drug of choice are often intense and obsessive. People complain of cravings getting the better of them, overtaking them, even having a life of their own. When cravings strike, the sober person is at risk of losing months, even years, of sobriety. Addicts report that the cravings are so powerful that they lose all sense of balance and rationality, and resort to denying that their problem was ever that bad: "It's my birthday, a few lines of cocaine won't hurt." Within minutes, the addict is reengaged physically, emotionally, and spiritually with the addiction.

Although cravings feel physiological and physical in the moment, the work we've done with EFT and cravings consistently reveals that strong emotions trigger the cravings, and once the emotional feelings are released, the cravings can subside within minutes. But again, in the moment, the addict is at a very high risk of choosing the substance over sobriety.

I recommend that my clients use EFT on stress and emotional conflicts every day to reduce the incidence of cravings, especially in early sobriety. When a craving hits, however, here is a process that can help:

1. When the strong craving surfaces, measure how high it feels right now on the 0–10 intensity scale.
2. Devise a Setup Statement to use while tapping on the Karate Chop point, such as *"Even though I have this intense craving, I deeply and completely love and accept myself."*
3. Tap the sequence of tapping points while repeating the Reminder Phrase, such as *"these intense cravings."*

Karate Chop point: *Even though I'm having intense cravings right now, I choose to relax and accept how I feel... Even though I'm having terrible cravings right now, I deeply and completely love and accept myself... Even though these cravings feel so strong right now, I accept who I am and how I feel.*

Eyebrow: *I have these intense cravings right now.*
Side of Eye: *Such strong cravings.*
Under Eye: *How am I going to resist?*
Under Nose: *These intense cravings.*
Chin: *I really want to drink/drug.*
Collarbone: *I have these intense cravings right now.*

Under Arm: *How will I resist my cravings?*
Top of Head: *They're so intense.*

Take a deep breath, and assess the craving now on the 0–10 scale. If the craving still feels intense, repeat the tapping round for as many times as necessary. If intense emotions surface while the craving subsides, apply the EFT tapping treatment to the intense emotions that have surfaced.

## Addressing Guilt and Shame

People carry around profound guilt about what they've done wrong in life and shame about who they are. Once clients deal with their guilt and shame, they are better equipped to handle the truth about the damage they've caused as a result of their addiction and are ready to consider repairing their relationships. If they can't tackle the guilt and shame, they will be unable to address the pain they've caused others. If they can't address the pain they've caused others, they will not be trusted, and are in danger of relapsing because of their struggle with denial that their drug or alcohol use was "never that bad."

Some people fear that releasing guilt through a method such as EFT will let them "off the hook." This is not the case. Releasing guilt allows addicts to face the situation squarely and address what really happened, rather than being hyperfocused on feeling like a "bad" person. They still know that what they did was hurtful but can now face the situation with compassion toward themselves and others.

## Sample Exercise for Clearing Guilt

Choose an incident you feel guilty about, and rate the intensity of the guilt on the 0–10 intensity scale. Tap as indicated.

Karate Chop point: *Even though I feel so guilty for what I did, I deeply and profoundly love and accept myself... Even though I feel really guilty for what I did back then, I accept who I am now... Even though I feel so guilty for what I did, I deeply and profoundly love and accept myself!*

Eyebrow: *I feel so guilty.*
Side of Eye: *What was I thinking?*
Under Eye: *I feel so guilty, and stupid.*
Under Nose: *What was I thinking?*
Chin: *I feel so guilty about that incident.*
Collarbone: *They must think I'm terrible.*
Under Arm: *I shouldn't have done it (said it).*
Top of Head: *I feel so guilty.*

Take a deep breath, and measure the intensity of your guilt again on the 0–10 scale. Repeat as necessary for this incident.

There may be multiple events or incidents you feel guilty about. You can safely apply this treatment to each and every one of these incidents when you said or did something you regret. When the guilt is released, you will be able to address the truth of the situation, rather than wallow in the guilt.

Feeling ashamed is quite different from guilt. For that reason, I'm including an exercise to deal specifically with the feeling of shame. Guilt is feeling regret about a particular incident, event, outburst, or action. When people feel shame, however, they feel defective, bad, and rotten to the core. They didn't do something terrible; they just *are* terrible.

## Sample Exercise for Clearing Shame

Tune into your feeling of shame about yourself, and rate it on the 0–10 intensity scale. Tap as indicated.

Karate Chop point: *Even though I feel so ashamed of who I am, I deeply and profoundly love and accept how I feel... Even though I've felt shame for as long as I can remember, I accept who I am right now... Even though I feel so much shame about me and who I am, I accept who I am and how I feel.*

Eyebrow: *I feel so much shame.*
Side of Eye: *I am so ashamed.*
Under Eye: *I feel so much shame.*
Under Nose: *I'm so defective.*
Chin: *I'm the problem.*
Collarbone: *I feel such shame.*
Under Arm: *I feel so ashamed.*
Top of Head: *I am full of shame.*

Take a deep breath, and measure the intensity of your shame again on the 0–10 scale. Repeat as necessary until the intensity is considerably lower than when you started.

## Releasing Resentment and Anger

Having resolved resentment and anger toward others in their life, people's ability to handle conflict in the future greatly improves. Resentments are painful reminders of conflict, and they must be released or the original incident will fester for years, even decades. Old feelings of anger have been proven to exert significant emotional and physical stress on the body and mind.

## Sample Exercise for Releasing Resentment and Anger

Think of a resentment you have toward someone, remember the situation that triggered this feeling, and measure how intense your resentment feels to you on the 0–10 scale. Tap as indicated.

Karate Chop point: *Even though I feel so resentful right now, I accept who I am and how I feel... Even though I feel resentful about what happened, I accept who I am and how I feel now... Even though I've been holding onto this resentment for so long, I accept who I am and how I feel.*

Eyebrow: *I feel resentful.*
Side of Eye: *I'm so resentful.*
Under Eye: *I feel resentful about what happened.*
Under Nose: *I feel so resentful.*
Chin: *I feel resentful.*
Collarbone: *I can't let go.*
Under Arm: *I don't know how to let go.*
Top of Head: *I don't know how to let go.*

Take a deep breath, and measure the intensity of your resentment again on the 0–10 scale. Repeat as necessary. You may feel resentful toward many people who've tried to help you in the past, who called your bluff, or who told authorities you had relapsed. Each incident or memory of resentment can be used as a different target for EFT.

Anger is different from resentment and can lead someone back to drug or alcohol use quite quickly. The emotion itself is powerful and frightens many people, and the knee-jerk reaction to drink or drug is understandable.

Think of something that makes you angry right now, and measure how intense your feeling is on the 0–10 intensity scale.

Karate Chop point: *Even though I feel so angry about what happened, it isn't fair, I deeply and completely love and accept myself anyway... Even though I feel really angry about what happened, I accept who I am and how I feel... Even though I feel so angry it's hard to focus, I accept who I am and how I feel.*

Eyebrow: *I feel so angry right now.*
Side of Eye: *I just want to run away.*

Under Eye: *I feel so angry right now.*
Under Nose: *I just want to drink or drug to feel better.*
Chin: *I feel enraged.*
Collarbone: *I feel so angry.*
Under Arm: *I really want to run away.*
Top of Head: *I feel so angry I can't even concentrate.*

Take a deep breath and measure the intensity of the feeling again on the 0–10 scale. Repeat as necessary on this particular event you chose, or move on to something else you feel angry about, and tap as indicated.

## Daily Stress/Worry

It's nearly impossible to resist temptation when a person has no coping skills for daily stress and anxiety. Whether the person is in early sobriety or has been sober for a long period of time, life presents many opportunities to practice trying to be calm instead of overreactive. But when people feel threatened, automatic reactions trigger feeling scared and stressed. I highly recommend that my clients use tapping to clear away general daily stress, or use tapping at the end of the day to clear out the stressful situations that happened during each day.

In addition, tapping can be used before an interview, before an important meeting, before making a sales call, and so on to clear the anxiety and stress circulating through the body and mind. Tapping is helpful for clearing insomnia, calming nerves, and concentrating at work.

## Sample Exercise for Releasing Stress and Worry

Notice how "stressed out" you feel about a situation in your day or at work. Measure how high the stress feels to you on the 0–10 intensity scale. Tap as indicated.

Karate Chop point: *Even though I feel so much stress in my life, and it's weighing on me, I accept who I am and how I feel... Even though I feel really worried all the time, I accept who I am and how I feel... Even though I feel worried and stressed out, I deeply and completely love and accept myself.*

Eyebrow: *I feel so stressed out.*
Side of Eye: *I feel it all over my body.*

Under Eye: *I feel such stress and strain.*
Under Nose: *I'm so worried about everything.*
Chin: *My mind is always racing.*
Collarbone: *I feel so worried.*
Under Arm: *I feel so worried about everything.*
Top of Head: *I want to calm down.*

Take a deep breath, and measure the intensity of your stress level again on the 0–10 scale. Repeat as necessary. Remember to apply the tapping to additional situations if they are also causing you stress and concern.

## Denial as a Target for Tapping

Denial is a truly frustrating defense mechanism. But until the threat and terror of life without drugs or alcohol is addressed, denial will remain a key element of the addicts' defense of their behavior. Tapping on denial is ineffective, because addicts are unable to address the truth and will be resistant to naming this as their target. With my clients, I continue to use tapping on the emotions from their past, present, or future.

## Regret about the Past

Regret about past conflicts, missed commitments, and embarrassing events haunts many alcoholics and addicts I have worked with in my practice. What amount of damage have they done? How can they ever restore trust and faith? Who would ever believe them again after all the lies? How can anyone recover after that many mistakes? This topic is different from basic guilt about cross words or behavior.

## Sample Exercise for Releasing Regret

Focus on a particular incident over which you feel intense regret, and measure the feeling on the 0–10 intensity scale. Tap as indicated, changing the words to match your situation more exactly if necessary.

Karate Chop point: *Even though I regret that incident that happened in my past, and feel terrible about it, I accept who I am and how I feel... Even though I wish I could have been different, I choose to accept who I am and how I feel... Even though I'm afraid to face my past, I accept all of me right now.*

Eyebrow: *I hate my past.*
Side of Eye: *I regret my past.*
Under Eye: *I wish it wasn't mine.*
Under Nose: *I wish it wasn't my past.*
Chin: *I hate who I was.*
Collarbone: *I'm not sure I can ever get over it.*
Under Arm: *I'm not sure how to get over it.*
Top of Head: *I hate my past.*

Focus again on the incident you regret, or on something as general as "I regret my past." Measure the intensity on the 0–10 scale. If the feeling of regret has not subsided significantly, repeat this tapping exercise. Again, this treatment can be applied to numerous incidents from your past.

## Fear of the Future

Paralyzing fear of the future—getting a new job, starting a new relationship, handling daily conflicts that arise—is another threat to long-term sobriety. The fear causes addicts or alcoholics to think less clearly, make decisions that aren't best for them, and even avoid situations and people they need to face. This fear can also trigger intense cravings for the drug of choice.

## Sample Exercise for Clearing Fear of the Future

Choose an event or task in the future you need to face but feel fear or anxiety about. Measure your fear on the 0–10 intensity scale. How afraid are you of that job interview? That date? That meeting with your ex-spouse? Tap as indicated, changing the wording to fit your situation.

Karate Chop point: *Even though I'm worried about what's going to happen in my future, I deeply and completely love and accept myself anyway... Even though I'm afraid of the future and the unknown, I accept who I am and how I feel... Even though I'm afraid of the future, I deeply and completely love and accept myself.*

Eyebrow: *I'm so afraid of the future.*
Side of Eye: *I'm so afraid of what's next.*

Under Eye: *I'm worried about the future.*
Under Nose: *I'm worried about what might happen.*
Chin: *I have so much fear.*
Collarbone: *I'm very afraid of the unknown.*
Under Arm: *I'm worried about the future.*
Head: *I'm so full of fear about my future.*

Take a deep breath, and measure the intensity of your fear of the future again on the 0–10 scale. Repeat as necessary. Again, you can apply the tapping to several upcoming meetings or situations in your immediate or distant future.

## Summary

EFT is the most comprehensive, effective treatment I have found for addressing addictions in over 22 years as a mental health practitioner. EFT is capable of addressing all the challenges someone faces when trying to maintain sobriety in their life. EFT has the capacity to:

- Address the emotional cause of addictive behavior.
- Release the emotional blocks to sobriety.
- Support the process of sobriety.
- Support emotional strength.
- Provide the right tools.

Teach those suffering with addictions how to address and manage the real causes of addiction, and they will turn their lives around dramatically, live fully and deeply, and serve others by offering strength and hope to countless peers who need them as role models.

## Reference

American Psychiatric Association. (2000). *DSM-IV-TR (Diagnostic and Statistical Manual of Mental Disorder, 4th Ed., Text Rev.* Washington, DC: American Psychiatric Association.

# Personal Performance: Business, Sports, Life

Chapter 51
# Creating a Successful EFT-Based Practice
*Pamela Bruner*

## Abstract
This chapter explores the components of building a successful EFT practice and examines the beliefs (myths) that pose common obstacles to achieving that success. Being a successful EFT practitioner depends not only on having expertise in the modality, but also on understanding the fundamentals of business. Creating your practice based on solid marketing principles, focusing on solving a single challenge or issue, knowing how to attract clients, and having an understanding of money and pricing are all essential to creating success as well as serving the world.

**Keywords:** EFT, business, marketing, networking

**Pamela Bruner**, business coach, EFT Expert, and CEO of Make Your Success Real, has supported thousands of service professionals in creating businesses that make money while making a difference in the world. Send correspondence to 4370 Old US 25, Zirconia, NC 28790, or Pamela@MakeYourSuccessReal.com.

In a fervent desire to benefit others and share the power of EFT, many practitioners set up practice without considering the challenges of building a business. Knowledge of EFT, even being an expert, does not guarantee that one can build a successful EFT practice. You must have an understanding of business fundamentals, and a willingness to learn and grow in your business, just as you learn and grow in your expertise in helping people.

Together we'll look at many of the myths and misunderstandings around creating a successful practice. Dismantling these myths will position you to serve people with your skills, expand your reach, make more of a difference in the world, and be well paid for what you do.

## Myth #1: You Should Open a General EFT Practice

During your training in EFT, it can be very useful to work with a variety of different people on a number of different issues. Because EFT is not yet a widely recognized modality like acupuncture or chiropractic care, however, going into business and announcing "I'm an EFT practitioner" is likely to be met with blank stares. Also, due to the fact that EFT has been shared briefly in many ways by many people—YouTube abounds with EFT tapping videos—if someone has heard of EFT, she may dismiss it as ineffective, having never worked with a skilled practitioner before.

To create a successful practice, you need to create your business based on the following idea: You provide a specific solution to a specific challenge for a specific group of people. The specific group of people is called your "target market," the specific challenge is known as "the pain" or "pain points," and the specific solution is referred to as "the benefits" that you provide.

Now that we have some language to discuss this, let's talk about why this is important.

If you try to sell or market EFT, you have an educational challenge on your hands. While spreading the news of the power of EFT is certainly a worthwhile mission, doing so won't actually grow your business. People aren't looking for a modality or process; they are looking for a solution to a problem.

Here's an example: If you have a flat tire, you want the tire changed. You don't care about the kind of wrench the mechanic uses, as long as it gets the job done. If a mechanic tried to hold a public talk touting the wonders of a new wrench, that talk would be of very little interest (except perhaps to other mechanics.) The mechanic's customers, or potential customers, only care about getting the tire changed, how fast it can be done, how good the work will be, and how much it will cost.

Just like the mechanic, you want to build your business around solving a problem. You may choose to help people with weight loss, relationship issues, chronic pain, fear of public speaking, or any other of a host of specific challenges. However, you must pick one. Although you know, and other EFT practitioners know, that EFT can be used on a wide variety of issues, if you try to market and sell that concept, you end up sounding like a snake-oil salesman. Imagine walking into a networking event where you are going to connect with potential clients, and saying, "I help people lose weight, improve their love life, make more money, get over their fear of heights, and I can even help with your skin inflammation." You sound amateurish at best and, at worst, totally unbelievable. Doing this not only doesn't help you build a business, it doesn't help spread the idea of EFT as an effective modality either.

At this point, most practitioners will say something like "Can I work with people on fear? That's a specific issue." However, most people aren't searching for help getting over general fears. They are searching for help getting over a particular fear. As a rule of thumb, a good question to ask yourself is "Would someone sit down and search for the solution to this problem on the Internet?" If not, it's not specific enough.

Another concern that practitioners have is that there will not be enough clients if they choose a narrow focus. Actually, the reverse is true. When you become known as an expert who helps people in a given arena, people know to come to you for that issue. It makes it easier to refer their friends to you, because they know exactly what you do. You also have the professional standing that comes from being an acknowledged expert in that area.

## Myth #2: If I Am Good at What I Do, I Don't Have to Market Myself

Unfortunately, this myth not only hinders marketing activities, it also creates shame and doubt in the minds of practitioners who don't find themselves flooded with clients without engaging in marketing. Although there are a very few service providers who run their business entirely through word-of-mouth and referrals, most practitioners must share continuously about their work in order to have a steady stream of clients.

The most basic ways to market are also the most effective ways: networking, speaking, and referrals.

Networking is usually thought of as attending a Chamber of Commerce meeting, but networking can occur in many different venues. In order to network successfully, you should seek out locations where your target market gathers. This might be associations, organizational meetings, social settings, large events, or online locations such as forums or blogs. Networking in places in which all the people are not in your target market is frustrating and ineffective. Resist the temptation to "go through the motions" of networking by going to events that aren't a match for your prospective clients.

As you network, two key things to keep in mind are: (1) focus on being helpful to others, and (2) be very clear about the solution that you provide. When you are honestly inquiring into other people's businesses and are willing to help others get what they need, they more willing to help you and you are seen as a good connector and resource. A good phrase to remember is "Be more interested than interesting." A great question to ask someone at a networking event is "What would you like to get out of this event, and who are you looking to connect with?"

Being clear on the solution that you provide allows you to speak clearly and succinctly to prospective clients, and to identify quickly which people are a match for what you provide. This idea ties back to the idea that you don't want to create a general EFT practice, because you would have to spend your time at networking events explaining EFT, how it worked, and so on. Instead if you can deliver a phrase such as "I help professional women overcome their fear of public speaking" or "I help stay-at-home moms get back into shape after having a baby," people will understand the challenges that you help people with, the solution that you provide, and be more able to self-select as a client or refer you to someone they know who needs your services.

The biggest mistake that most business owners make when networking, besides picking a venue that doesn't represent their target market, is not following up after the networking event.

Never assume that someone you met will call you. Instead, when you meet someone who expresses interest in what you do, ask her for her card, and let her know that you will call her to schedule a follow-up conversation. This is especially important because it enables you to be free to connect with others at the event, rather than spending all of your time talking to one person, and because you will have the 100% attention of the other person as well. It's often a good idea to leave some free time in your schedule in the day or two after a networking event so you can schedule appointments immediately.

Speaking is one of the best ways to connect with larger numbers of people at one time, and establish you as an expert. Most organizations and associations need speakers, so asking around about speaking opportunities will often lead to getting in front of dozens of people. In order to shine as a speaker, you'll want to create a signature talk that is of interest to your target market. Think about some juicy information that your people would love to hear, and give your talk a name that gets attention. Examples of talk titles that attract include "3 Mistakes Most People Make When Quitting Smoking" or "5 Secrets to a Great Love Life."

Just as with networking, when you speak to a group, don't assume that any prospective client who is listening will contact you. You must make the initiative to follow up with them. There are a number of ways that you can gather the contact information of the audience for follow-up purposes. One way is to offer a raffle, and collect business cards. Be sure to tell people that you will be "sending them information from time to time" before you put them on a mailing list. Another option is to offer a free gift, such as a special report, audio, or video, that requires you to e-mail it to the recipient. Again, you want to be clear when you gather their contact data that they will be receiving information from you regularly.

If this thought makes you uncomfortable, please consider that the attendees would not have come to the talk or would not be asking for your free gift unless your information was of value to them. When you continually give great information, people want to do business with you. Don't worry about giving away your "best stuff" because people will still want more. That being said, don't offer free hour-long tapping classes every week, because if there is an overwhelming amount of "free," there is no incentive to consider purchasing from you or hiring you.

Referrals are a great way to get business. Research has found that someone who was referred to you is four times more likely to say yes to you than someone you met without a referral ("Referral marketing," 2012). You can get referrals from clients, from friends, from associates or acquaintances, and even from people who you work with as a client. Sometimes you'll even get referrals from people you've met who have not hired you, because they liked or were impressed by you.

The key to getting referrals is to ask for them, and to ask in a certain way. If you say something vague to your clients such as "Be sure to tell people about me," you're unlikely to get results, because you haven't really given them a specific instruction. Instead, ask for the business this way: "I'd like to add a few more clients to my practice, and since you're such a great client, I thought that anyone you know who could benefit from my services would be a great client too. Since you love working with me, I'm sure you'd like to see your friends get the same benefits. Can you come up with two people you could introduce me to? I'd love to offer any of your friends (a gift)." The gift could be similar to the gift you give away while speaking—a report, audio, or video—or a special introductory session, or just a conversation about their challenges.

Many practitioners are uncomfortable with referrals because they feel as though they are imposing on their friends or acquaintances, or that they are begging for business. If you feel confident in the work you do, however, then it's necessary for you to be as successful as possible. Otherwise, there are people out there who need your help who you are not reaching. Don't let your fears about other people's reactions keep you from making a difference in the world. Also, most people enjoy doing favors and offering great resources. This actually makes them feel good, so allow them to be a contribution to you, and to their friends.

Once you have begun attracting clients, or getting people with whom you can discuss the possibility of working with you, you need to overcome myths about sales and money.

## Myth #3: The Cheaper I Price My Services, the More I Serve People

Do you believe that your clients are better served when you charge less? That seems logical, right?

Actually, it's not true, especially when you're offering transformational services and products such as EFT.

This is because people value what they pay for. One of the best ways to have your work disregarded, or have clients not work on their own to support the work that you are doing together, is to give away your services or price yourself too cheaply.

(Please note, I'm not talking about emergency services. If you are providing EFT to victims of recent severe trauma or volunteering your services at a local shelter, that is a gift to your community, and it's great to give in that way. However, that's a charitable contribution, not the way to run a business.)

Think about it this way: If you bought a $10 book, and a $100 book, which would you read first? I'm guessing that you'd read the $100 book first. You'd probably read it several times, memorize portions of it, take notes on it, and really pay attention to everything it had to offer, just because you paid more for it.

When you charge lower fees, you're giving your clients the message "This isn't very important" and "You don't need to pay much attention to it." When you charge more, not only are you saying "This work is important" and "My work is worth it," you're also saying "You, my client, are worth spending money on, you're worth investing in." And that's a very powerful message of transformation.

## Myth #4: I Can't Increase My Rates— No One Will Pay That

There are actually two money misunderstandings going on here. One is that if you're charging by the session or by the month for your work, it's not surprising that you don't feel you can raise your rates. We all have a certain dollar amount that we feel is reasonable to spend for an hour, and if you try to go above that, not only might you struggle to get clients, but you'll also feel out of integrity. So consider the following two offerings. Which of these can you charge more for: three sessions of hypnotherapy, or "A Rapid Results Quit Smoking Program that allows you to get off the nicotine and live smoke free—fast"?

The Rapid Results program is much more appealing, because it allows someone to say, "How much would I pay to quit smoking?' rather than

"How much would I pay for three sessions?" Many practitioners are uncomfortable with this, because they are unsure of how long "transformation" will take. However, creating packages around transformation allows you to focus on results, and you can both serve your client more and charge more for your deservedly transformational work.

The other money misunderstanding has to do with "money set-point." Your money set-point is what you think is a reasonable amount to spend for anything. You have a money set-point for a cup of coffee, for what you'll pay for a hotel room, for what a meal should cost, and so on. So suppose your money set-point for a hotel is about $100, so you'd be comfortable booking and staying in a $100 a night hotel. Then if a hotel room is priced at $500 a night, that will seem like too much to you and you'd say "That's just *too* expensive." But if a hotel room is $25 dollars a night, doesn't that feel a little low? Just hearing that price would probably make you think that it would be not a good place to stay. If so, you've just found your money set-point for hotels. Now imagine if that cheap hotel said, "You don't want to stay for $25 a night? Okay, how about $20 a night?" Given this offer, you wouldn't be more inclined to stay there; you'd be less inclined.

The fees you charge for your services and products are exactly the same as this hotel example. There are people who aren't even considering working with you now, because you don't charge enough to be within their money set-point. When you raise your prices, you'll begin attracting people who have your new, higher money set-point.

The concept of money set-point is also why you may feel uncomfortable raising your fees if you're pricing by the session, rather than pricing for a transformational package. Most people's money set-point for a unit of time varies from $50 an hour to perhaps $150 an hour. Trying to charge more than this for an hour of time will often cause price resistance, and you may feel out of integrity if you try to charge an amount that is greater than *your* money set-point for an hour of time.

However, most EFT practitioners offer EFT-based services because they have gotten incredible transformation from using the technique. Invariably, when the question is posed "Would you accept $1,000,000 to not have heard of EFT, and to not have received the transformation that you received from it?" the answer is always no.

If it was that valuable to you, then consider that it is that valuable to the people you're now serving, and set your fees accordingly.

## Myth #5: Setting Higher Prices Means That Poorer People Won't Get Served

Some practitioners express concern with these money concepts, saying, "What about the people I've been serving? If I raise my rates, they won't be able to afford me, and then they won't get help. That doesn't seem fair."

The truth is that you can't serve everyone. There are only so many people you can serve with your private time. When you raise your rates for your top-level offerings, the ones that take most of your private time, you can also create lower-priced products such as home study systems, group programs, and books that will serve people who can't invest in those top-level offerings.

Here's the powerful reframe: Once you get clear on your target market and start building your fan base, you'll have lots of people who want to get the transformation you offer. They will all have different money set-points. So you serve the new clients, those with the higher money set-points, with your new increased rates, and you serve others, including your current clients, with your other lower-level offerings.

If you're uncomfortable with this, consider that if you don't raise your rates, and you're struggling to survive and not making enough money, you won't have the time or energy to create those lower-level offerings that allow you to serve even more people. This model allows you to share your transformation with thousands, or tens of thousands, rather than just a few dozen.

Apart from learning the basics of marketing, sales, and money management, changing your belief system is the biggest hurdle to creating a successful practice. Because the inclination to give away helping services like EFT is so strong, however, creating new belief systems that help you reframe selling as service, marketing as sharing, and appropriate price-setting as essential to success is a vital part of creating a successful practice. In this chapter, you've been introduced to some of the reframes that will help you build your practice. As you continue to study business-building, you'll need to look for more reframes and new perspectives that allow you to stay in integrity, remain authentic, serve people in accordance with your value system, *and* make the money that you want and deserve.

If you do not have a successful practice, not only do you suffer, but also you're not making the difference in the world that you could be making. People desperately need the transformation that you can provide, so your success is not a selfish pursuit; it is in service to a much greater good. Applying the information in this chapter is only the beginning of creating a successful EFT practice. Successfully applying just these few concepts will allow you to create a practice that is both sustaining and serves the world.

# Reference

Referral marketing. (2012). Retrieved from http://www.marketing-schools.org/types-of-marketing/referral-marketing.html

Chapter 52

# EFT in Performance Enhancement: Bridging Psychotherapy, Coaching, and Positive Psychology

*John Hartung*

**Abstract**

It is suggested that the term "performance enhancement" is best understood as but one example of how we as human beings can deliberately strengthen internal resources. A model is described for assisting individuals in developing positive personal qualities, which can be strengthened with EFT and used for reaching measurable goals. Unlike mainstream coaching and most applications of the principles of positive psychology, the model also involves the use of EFT for the healing of memories that interfere with present and future functioning. The model is intended to be applicable to anyone who seeks to reach an as-of-yet unrealized goal, not just to the so-called high achievers that performance enhancement often connotes. The procedure has been used safely and effectively by coaches, by mental health professionals, and in self-treatment. Support for use of the model with EFT is at the case study level.

**Keywords:** EFT, performance enhancement, coaching, goal setting, positive psychology

**John Hartung, PsyD,** a clinical psychologist, is codirector of the Bodymind Integration Institute of Singapore and Colorado. The institute's teams offer trainings and consultation in 30 countries in coaching, performance enhancement, leadership, and trauma treatment—for professionals and nonprofessionals. Send correspondence to John Hartung, 215 Crown High Court, Colorado Springs, CO 80904, or jhartung@uccs.edu.

The application of EFT to performance enhancement is still being refined. The history of psychology and psychotherapy—then of positive psychology, coaching, and performance enhancement—provides a context for understanding the opportunities and challenges that await EFT practitioners.

Psychology and psychotherapy have traditionally and stereotypically implied a negative focus: on problems, deficits, and pathology, with a bias toward the past. Therapists have concerned themselves with attitudes and emotions, with helping people feel and think better about themselves. Therapists (except for behaviorists) are not usually viewed as expert in helping clients set practical goals and developing relevant skills.

Coaches, by contrast, are focused on the positive and on strengths, with an eye to the present and future. Coaches also favor planning, assessment, practical goal setting and relevant skill development, rehearsal and practice, and specialty training for the coach. A review of the more than 100 coach training institutes in the United States leads to the conclusion that there is wide consensus on this coaching curriculum (Coach U, 2005).

These distinctions largely remain, even as psychotherapists discover positive psychology and move increasingly into coaching specialties, and as coaches realize they use many of the basic qualities and skills of psychotherapists. Popular books still state that coaches do not concern themselves with their clients' past (e.g., Steele, 2011; Williams & Menendez, 2007); if a client encounters an emotional block to success, the coach may well refer to a psychotherapist. Regulatory agencies also reinforce these differences. For example, in Colorado (where I reside), licensed psychologists are presumed to be skilled to work in the field of emotions, with the past, and with troubling memories; coaches, who presumably are not skilled to do so, are not licensed or regulated and it is widely assumed that they will *not* concern themselves with such issues. This breach between psychotherapy/psychology and coaching has been maintained during the growing popularity of *performance enhancement,* a specialty hybrid combining coaching skills and strategies from positive psychology.

As the practice of energy psychology (EP; Gallo, 2000) became popular in the United States and other societies, it might have been expected that

the distinctions just noted would have diminished. After all, the new approaches would seem to offer tools for coaches to help clients safely and efficiently heal the past without presuming a need for extended therapeutic relationships, complex treatments, or esoteric concepts. And the same approaches would seem to allow therapists to move into future-focused coaching without ignoring the importance of resolving traumatic memories that might keep a client locked in the past.

In reality, however, there has been little true integration of coaching and performance enhancement with EP and other brief therapies. An Internet search in November of 2012 for "EFT and coaching" and "EFT and performance enhancement" revealed only three examples where the EFT practitioner explicitly follows a formula that allows EFT to serve as a bridge between coaching and performance on the one hand and psychotherapy on the other hand. One example is Maryam Webster's energy coaching program (Energy Coach Institute) that combines the best of traditional coaching with EFT, other energy psychology tools, and additional innovative strategies. Steve Wells (in Australia; EFTdownunder. com; see Chapter 55), and Greg Warburton (in the United States, under Greg Warburton Inner Liberty) both describe sophisticated approaches to athletic, executive, and organizational success. They attend to the importance of clarifying goals and values, planning, and action-informed skills, and they appear to collaborate with specialty coaches. Their case testimonials are, as a result, credible and likely replicable.

Beyond these three welcomed examples, however, EFT practitioners who market coaching and performance services on websites and through e-books tend to limit their use of EFT to reducing anxiety and other emotional blocks to success, and for building self-confidence. The hard work of performance and achievement goes unmentioned. Additionally, it is not clear whether any *enhancement of performance* per se is ever considered, or whether the interventions are limited to reducing whatever interferes with already-honed performance skills. I am reminded of many occasions when an EFT trainer treated subjects who initially would not speak in public, climb a ladder, or engage in other observable behavior. Following the intervention, the subject would then perform successfully. These are, however, better conceptualized as examples of anxiety reduction, not the enhancement of performance per se. Even when such improvements in performance are studied scientifically (e.g., in overcoming social phobia, Schoninger & Hartung, 2010) it is often not necessary to enhance skills, but rather only to remove blocks to skills the person already has. In other training situations, an EFT subject might state vague goals such as "Increasing my confidence in attracting financial success." Though the subject might indeed report increased confidence post-treatment, it is not shown or known whether increased financial independence follows. This absence of outcome measures is also notably absent in most EFT marketing.

These examples can leave the impression that EFT is somehow magical, and that by using EFT one can ignore the many other factors involved in reaching a goal. This abbreviated intervention is at times appropriate (as in the previously cited examples, and in cases where an athlete or executive is already highly skilled and needs only to eliminate interfering emotions and memories). However, a narrow use of EFT will limit the EFT practitioner when meeting a client who has set vague or unfeasible goals, who is under-skilled or under-practiced, who is hampered by secondary gain issues and dilemmas, and who presents with other issues that are more within the field of traditional coaching. Not everyone who seeks help is already a world-class athlete or an experienced entrepreneur looking solely for confidence-building tools.

The bridge between the various disciplines just cited is still under construction. A model for continuing the bridging, to be summarized next, has been detailed elsewhere (Hartung, 2009). Different aspects of the model have been used in a number of countries in Europe and the Americas. The model was previously investigated and shown to be effective where the intervention was with Eye Movement Desensitization and Reprocessing or EMDR (Grachek, 2010), and where the methodology was a time-series, repeated-measures study of athletic performance. EFT and EMDR may be approximately equivalent in the treatment of trauma (Karatzias et al, 2011); since trauma resolution is part of this protocol, it is hypothesized that employing EFT within the same design will produce similar positive results. Additionally, given that EFT has already been used successfully in the treatment of PTSD by persons who are not mental health professionals (Hartung & Stein, 2012), successful use of the model by EFT coaches could make a serious contribution to the dearth of mental health professionals around the world.

The model is now described according to the design followed by Grachek (2010). From time to time the reader will be advised to **pay attention to** issues that have been noted with certain individuals and that require adjustment of the procedures. As the model has been used by professional psychotherapists as well as coaches, the user will be abbreviated as T/C (for therapist and coach).

## Step 1: The Therapist/Coach Does a Self-Assessment

Before agreeing to work with clients, T/Cs are encouraged to assess their own credentials to ensure that they can appreciate the context in which the client will be working toward a goal. Relevant questions might be: If working with an athlete, how much do you, the T/C, need to know about athletic coaching, specific sports, and sports psychology in general, or is it better to work in tandem with an athletic coach? If assisting an executive, is it expected that you understand leadership, decision-making practices, and relevant psychological measurements? If offering services to addicted persons, do you understand how addiction and relapse are multi-determined? Since many clients of all types may require processing of traumatic memories that interfere with meeting their goals, are you sufficiently familiar with how the past meddles with the present and future and how it cannot be simply willed away? Is a trauma background also necessary for effective EFT targeting of triggers? Space does not allow for responses to these questions; they are raised only to point out that effective performance coaching may require specialty knowledge, training, and experience. "Not practicing outside one's area of competence" is a key ethical guideline in mental health professions.

**Pay attention to** your own level of confidence and optimism as a T/C EFT practitioner. It may be already obvious that this model can be used by the T/C to develop positive attitudes and confidence in the use of EFT. The EFT practitioner is encouraged to practice resilience and other virtues that can help when facing the criticisms, doubts, and skepticism that traditional coaches and potential clients have been known to exhibit.

## Step 2: History-taking, Goal Statements, Strengths Inventory

**Client history** is often given short shrift in EFT, perhaps because the benefits are so often rapid and can usually be realized with safety even in the absence of a complete history. In performance enhancement a detailed history is recommended. Past attempts to reach a goal, along with information about (partial) successes and (partial) failures, will be essential in the design of a program more likely to be effective.

At some point the client will state the **goal** of the intervention. Recall that any realistic, feasible goal that is as-of-yet unmet is appropriate. "Performance enhancement" has, unfortunately, become too closely associated with so-called "high achievers." Though the present model serves persons who are already successful and who wish to increase their achievements (world-class athletes or executives), it has been used with equal benefit with individuals who recall relatively few positive memories, who report deficiencies regarding their internal resources, who confess to difficulty regulating strong emotion (both negative and positive), and who admit to being habitually pessimistic.

An **inventory of resources and strengths** is also conducted at this point, both the more intangible sorts (attitudes, emotions, beliefs, imagery) and the more practical skills.

**Pay attention to** the *feasibility* of the stated goal, including whether the person has the skills necessary to reach it. Example: One man wanted to develop confidence in moving his office to a distant geographic location even though he had not researched the site to see if there was a market for his discipline; subsequent discussions revealed that he was primarily trying to escape from interpersonal conflicts at his present site, so his goal changed dramatically. Note that you can accept the initial goal while allowing that it may well change during EFT intervention. This model provides an opportunity to revisit goals to see if they have been colored or encouraged by others, rather than being the sole domain of the client.

## Step 3: Identify Triggers

It is important in this step to identify the **next opportunities** for approaching the goal again, which in this model are called *triggers*. Triggers can be in the future ("The next time I sit with my boss for my annual review," "I am standing on stage in front of a large audience of people rooting for my competitors in this athletic contest") or the present ("The smell of the gym makes me too anxious to do well," "The smell of tobacco causes me to light up and then to drink alcohol.") Space limitations do not allow adequate discussion of triggers except to note at this point that a trigger is both in the future or present, *and in the past*. It is for this latter reason that it can be targeted with EFT until it becomes neutralized or "desensitized" (Wolpe, 1969).

The previous examples are all acceptable triggers, they have all been identified by clients of mine, and in each case the power of the trigger was reduced. When triggers are first identified in history taking, however, they still have their power. Many T/Cs use a variation of the 0-to-10 subjective units of discomfort (SUD) scale to measure the strength of the trigger and to establish a base line.

**Pay attention to** the wide variety of triggers than can cause a client to stumble. Generally, it will be *the next time* the client attempts a goal. *Present* triggers are also potent treatment targets, however. Some triggers can be brought to the office, such as a barbell (for an athlete), a script (for an actor), or a bottle of Jim Beam (for a person working to overcome an addiction). Some triggers are not so portable so you may need to accompany the person to the site of the trigger: the auditorium where s/he will talk or the gym where s/he will perform. The value of these *in situ* experiences is that some people cannot visualize sufficiently well to feel the impact of a trigger in your office. When real life cannot be replicated in this way, the alternative is to go to where the trigger will produce its effect in real life.

## Step 4: Identify Positive Qualities and Other Resources

Here is where the T/C, in collaboration with the client, identifies the internal and external qualities, skills, and other resources that are required for achieving a goal. Such resources are necessary whether the goal involves leading a high-performance cycling team, developing executive presence, strengthening a relationship with one's adult children, or enjoying life without depending on alcohol to do so. Once the qualities are identified, they can be *enhanced* with EFT in Step 5.

In my experience, T/C practitioners who use EFT in performance enhancement struggle most with this task of *identifying and enhancing* positive qualities. Often insufficient attention is paid to whether the qualities are actually relevant to the goal. And subsequently, the enhancement portion of the task can be haphazard, and often little measurement is done to see whether the procedure is having any impact or not. How does one set out identifying relevant resources? Several guides are now summarized. The first is the BASIC I.D. developed by Arnold Lazarus. Three other examples will also be described.

**(4.1) The BASIC I.D.** is from the multimodal therapy approach of Lazarus (1989) and was the guide used in the original study of the model described in this chapter. The acronym refers to behavior, affect, sensation, imagery, cognitions, interpersonal, and drug/diet/biology, said to be a comprehensive checklist that accounts for everything necessary for working with a client, in this case one seeking to enhance performance.

Given space limits, only a few examples will be provided (further examples are found in Hartung, 2012). An example of *B,* or behavior, might be teaching coherence breathing, a very important part in performance success. Given that many hundreds of breathing models are in use, no sides can be taken here. However, the biofeedback-informed breathing tool pioneered by the HeartMath Institute (McCraty, Atkinson, Tomasino, & Bradley, 2006) has been found to be very powerful and is recommended as one "best practice." Another example of behavior might be actual practice in public speaking, or actual study skills for taking an exam.

The *A* in BASIC I.D. reminds us that positive affect/emotion varies from one goal to another; perhaps excitement would fit an athletic pursuit, whereas abundance and freedom may be more suitable for someone seeking the positive side of sobriety. The *C* (for cognitions) reminds us to focus on how the client talks to him- or herself. Positive words, phrases, concepts, and stories can be further strengthened with EFT.

**(4.2) The list of positive emotions and attitudes associated with acupoints** is an alternative to the BASIC I.D. Many EFT practitioners refer to this list of 14 positive terms and attitudes. The person simply reflects on the positive quality while tapping or touching the points, thereby trusting the body to identify those that are particularly salient. The list that I follow relies on many sources. Only one term for each acupoint is listed next; the reader may wish to add to or otherwise modify this list, as many variations are in print.

> Eyebrow (or tear duct): mindfulness
> Side of eye: forgiveness
> Under the eye: peace
> Under the nose: hope
> Under the lips: self-worth
> Under collarbone: look to the future
> Under the arms: sufficiency, abundance
> Ribs: joy
> Thumb: tolerance
> Index finger: self-forgiveness
> Middle finger: generosity
> Pinkie: forgiveness
> Back of hand: acceptance
> Side of hand: acceptance

With vulnerable persons whose sense of the positive is closely linked to negative contamination, even these words may need fine-tuning. If possible, a person could say, for example, "I am here" while stimulating the eyebrow or tear duct point. A person with fewer internal resources, however, might benefit first from learning grounding strategies such as simply attending to (being mindful of) feet on the floor or the aroma of a freshly peeled orange while stimulating the point. The person then might be able to say only, "I can feel my feet on the floor and smell this orange." When this person moves on to the side-of-the-eye point, instead of stating "I forgive," s/he may only be able to say, "I wish you could know how you hurt me." *Dosage* and *pacing* are working principles here.

This may appear similar to the concept of interoception, called the sixth sense by Siegel (2012), the becoming aware of one's internally driven experiences.

**(4.3) The list of virtues** from the Seligman group (Seligman, Steen, Park, & Peterson, 2005) is a third way to identify relevant resources. They enumerate a list of virtues widely endorsed around the world and in use in cognitive therapy. The published list is organized by category (and paraphrased) as follows:

- Wisdom and knowledge (I am creative, original, curious, and interested; I am open to new experiences; I love to learn; I have ingenuity.)
- Courage (I am brave, persistent, industrious, honest, authentic, enthusiastic, and energetic.)

- Humanity (I am loving, kind, generous, nurturing, caring, compassionate, and pleasant.)
- Justice (I am socially responsible, just, loyal, and fair, and I am a good leader.)
- Temperance (I am forgiving, merciful, humble, modest, and prudent, and I have self-control.)
- Transcendence (I appreciate beauty, excellence, awe, and wonder; I am grateful, hopeful, optimistic, and future-minded; I am playful and humorous; I am spiritual; I have a sense of purpose.)

Borrowing from the Seligman group, the EFT practitioner invites the person to identify desired virtues, then to visualize and feel the virtue while stimulating each of the 14 acupoints. Some people will be able to think back to an example of when they experienced practicing the virtue in real life; others may have to imagine such a case. Again, guided by the concept of *dosage* (see Step 5), the T/C will slowly introduce the person to the concept and gradually help the client to enhance the experience.

**(4.4) The client's personalized checklist,** a fourth option for identifying resources, is an informal but empowering intervention at this level (and one that is recommended throughout performance enhancement work). The T/C listens carefully to and observes the client for positive expressions, then points those out to the client who can then tap on them. Catching the client showing a smile, expressing a positive word, or breathing coherently can be followed by the T/C saying, "Did you notice what you just did/said?"

Often unaware of these detours into the positive, the client might say, "No, what?" The T/C can say: "I think you said something about, what was it, 'I can …'" or "You did something with your breathing. Can you say/do that again?" The client can be empowered in this way by repeating, practicing, becoming aware of, and owning what was expressed. Stimulating the EFT acupoints along with the practice may further enhance the positive expression.

**Pay attention to** the possibility that positive-sounding qualities may have become contaminated for a particular person, and that when positive expressions are brought more clearly into the person's conscious awareness, they can provoke negative reactions.

Sometimes a person will find it easier to manage the positive emotion by *thinking* or *writing down* or even *drawing the expression or concept,* rather than stating it explicitly. For example, what may appear to be matter-of-fact breath training can paradoxically cause *more* anxiety, rather than *less*. Some persons seem to live in a fairly constant state of readiness or alarm, breathing shallowly as if needing to be on guard against an inherently dangerous world. When they begin to breathe more deeply and rhythmically, they can experience full-blown panic, as when, in the words of one client, "I felt like I let my guard down."

Likewise, the word "success" might sound fine on paper, but might remind someone quite paradoxically of failure or doubt, or be a source of a superstition. While preparing this chapter, I was observing a group of coaches working with one another in a training course in a European country. During practicum one asked another to practice breathing while saying the words "I am grateful" and touching EFT points. These two simple suggestions appeared to be perfectly sensible and justified, given the professional formation and experience of this group, and the T/C in this case was later supported by the group as having proceeded appropriately. However, the client who was asked to breathe and to make the positive statement began to turn white, then tearful, clearly frightened. The simple words "I am grateful" and deliberate deep breathing had triggered the client back to age 3 where she recalled that there was nothing for which she could feel grateful.

Though it may seem that only persons with few resources and success stories are at risk for being triggered in these ways, there are also cases where an apparently high achiever is unexpectedly shaken. In a leadership program in which I participated as executive coach, a role-play had been designed to test resilience. During a group exercise, one person would be randomly selected out as a "low performer." Even though the selection had nothing to do with the person removed, it was found that some of the otherwise extremely competent junior executives were triggered into past memories of failure, and that this disrupted the entire training program. Changes were made to the exercise so that a person would be selected on the basis of being a "high performer," rather than low. This too had to be scrapped when it was found that even being singled out for this apparently *positive* reason could trigger participants into memories of self-doubt and inadequacy. How can this be? Though leadership folklore might imply that all leaders are tough and privileged, the fact is that many carry unfinished emotional baggage, which can be triggered when the situation is just so—and "just so" can be either an apparently positive experience or a negative one.

When you, the T/C, know from history that you are working with such a person, or when you happen to learn from making a mistake in thinking that you were actually working with someone with greater resources, simply dose the exposure as suggested previously so that the client gradually becomes accustomed to increasingly more negative (or positive!) challenges.

## Step 5: Enhance the Qualities and Resources with EFT

EFT is then used to strengthen qualities that the client has identified as relevant to meeting the next performance challenge. A recommended measure is 0–100% so clients can report on how close they feel to experiencing that quality (100% being optimal). This strengthening is done in the abstract, separate from any attention given to the goal, so that any negative thought or emotion related to the goal is less likely to be triggered. The purpose is to continue with the strengthening of the positive qualities until the person can report a total, purely positive experience. (One hypothetical neurological mechanism of action is that at this point the person's parasympathetic branch of the autonomic nervous system is being strengthened so that it, in antagonistic fashion, can interfere with the sympathetic hyperarousal that so often frustrates optimal performance.)

Quite obviously, the relationship with the T/C is paramount, as the T/C will provide the safety that clients may not have experienced in their families of origin or from other early childhood experiences. Trust, confidence, and accurate listening are essential. It seems clear from the HeartMath literature that the heart of the client can detect whether the heart of the T/C is in a state of love or disgust, so the T/C is always encouraged to enter coherence and respect prior to initiating contact (McCraty, Atkinson, Tomasino, & Bradley, 2006).

**Pay attention to** the same potential issues cited in Step 4: Fragile persons can retreat from a positive focus and find themselves in a traumatic memory when being exposed to potential resources that have been contaminated by shame, doubt, and failure.

An advantage with EFT is that often the negative aspects that appear at such times can be simply treated with continued EFT acupoint stimulation, albeit to neutralize the negative rather than strengthen the positive. In this case, ensure that the person is able to handle the negative symptoms. It is possible that such symptoms had previously been dissociated, and so may be particularly surprising when they appear. It may be useful to invite the person not to continue with the symptoms, but rather to pay attention to a positive alternative. The T/C can suggest, "Notice that it is something that happened a long time ago" or "Notice where you are right now, here, with me" or simply, "It's over."

The concept of *dosage* may also be helpful, in that the T/C can invite the person to attend to only a fragment of a feeling or sensation, rather than the entire experience. EFT can then be used to desensitize that fragment, and only then will the person be encouraged to recall or feel more and more of the experience, desensitizing each new aspect as it appears. This is relevant whether the person works bit by bit on a negative, or on a positive: If "love" is too strong a term, start with "acceptance" instead. If saying a word is intolerable, ask the person to write it, or draw it, at first. At each progressive step, the EFT acupoints are stimulated. Repeat at each step until the person can make the statements, or feel the emotions and sensations, with calm and acceptance.

It may seem to be minimal progress until we reflect that the process has actually been one of resolving a series of phobias—learned fears to objects (words) that have no inherent power to pose threat.

## Step 6: Link the Positive Qualities with the Trigger

The purpose of this step is to *test the power of the positive qualities* as compared to the relative power of the trigger. The positive qualities or positive state are linked—usually through imagined visualization—with a trigger. If necessary and feasible, the linkage can be made *in vivo,* either in a real-life setting or when a physical trigger is available that represents the real-life challenge, as when the weight lifter brought a small barbell into the office in order to experience the triggering scent of metal and talcum power.

Using an agreed-upon measure, the person is asked to rate the power of the trigger (i.e., the next opportunity); visualizing (or being in) the place of the next opportunity will produce either a positive, neutral, or negative feeling. A common goal is to feel totally tranquil, or at least neutral, during this test. At times, however, a slightly negative—or at least some level of activation—is preferred; for example, an athlete may *not* want to experience a neutral or totally positive feeling, but rather may have an optimal level of activation, nervousness, or arousal of some kind that is motivational for the person. Here is where specialty training may help, as it would be the client's preference, not the T/C's bias, that would direct the next step.

**If the reported emotional level of arousal is acceptable**, it would be presumed that the person is ready to try things out *in situ,* in which case plans would be made for the next opportunity to reach the goal, and relevant coaching would be offered.

**If the client reports an unacceptably high level of activation** or arousal during this test, several options are considered.

- Individuals may note that they are **not ready skill-wise** and may need to learn or rehearse further. Trying to meet the goal at this point is likely to ensure failure.

- Some persons decide at this point to **modify their goal** so that it feels more realistic and attainable. Changing goals is frequently found using this protocol.

- **Secondary gain** (what might be lost if the goal is actually met) is frequently discovered at this point. There is no sense in proceeding until this is resolved. A physician-in-training could not continue with taking her medical exam until she resolved her reluctance to please her father, who shared the same goal with her.

- Other issues with **motivation** may appear, and may or may not be targeted with EFT. A professional skater decided to stop competing because the hard work involved was creating intolerable imbalance in her life.

- If the first options are cleared, it may be sufficient to return to Step 4 and repeat the **strengthening** sequences, then Step 5 to revisit the next opportunity.

- Some people experience **ambivalence or a dilemma** at this point. To some degree dilemmas can be simply talked through, but not always, as they may reflect unconscious conflicts. In this case, ask the person to place each side of the dilemma in separate hands, close the hands, notice the *sensory* experiences in the hands, and continue with EFT until the dilemma is resolved. This may be as simple as it sounds. Then repeat Steps 4 and 5.

- Others may find that the negative experience is due to a specific **trigger**. In this case, target the trigger with EFT until it neutralizes. A person addicted to cigarettes held a cigarette while doing EFT until he no longer felt the urge to smoke, and was able to move on with his goal of becoming more physically fit.

- Some people will recall a specific event, with its image, time, place, age, and so forth. **Traumatic memories** of this kind can be targeted directly with EFT until resolved. Review Steps 4 and 5 afterward.

**Pay attention to** the value of inviting the client to begin here with a mildly or moderately challenging goal at first. Sometimes a person who asks for assistance on reaching a high-level goal reports a sparse history of having worked toward lower-level goals. An example is the executive in leadership training who set what appeared to be the feasible goal of "I will speak to the executive committee with calm and enjoyment." He might first need to identify the various qualities that go into meeting the goal, and then practice each one. If courage is one component, he could visualize putting this virtue into action, and actually do something courageous later that day. A second example is the person addicted to substances who first needs to practice alternative ways to experience good feelings naturally. A third is the father who asked for help to learn to embrace his adult sons, but who had not yet asked why his sons seemed to be as afraid of him as he was of them. A final case relates to emergency responders (EMTs) who have only infrequent opportunities to put their *resilience* into action during disasters; in this case, they can practice elements of resilience several times a day so that they are more ready when a life-threatening emergency tests them.

Sometimes the same adjustments need to be made because the ultimate goal cannot be easily tested in real life. I worked with a group of police psychologists to teach resilience (Bonanno & Mancini, 2012) to soldiers assigned to manage crowds of protesters. The history had been bloody, as the soldiers were easily triggered into overreactions. As an example of the training experience, the participants bumped into each other (to stimulate a sympathetic response of anger/fight and fear/flight). They would then recover by tapping EFT points and, when necessary, would maintain eye contact with their colleagues while recalling that they were in a safe place. Sometimes they would need to extend a hand while saying, "Hello, Partner." The goal was to teach pendulation between the alarm state (making rough-and-tumble physical contact) and calm (that is, ventral vagal parasympathetic responses, as described by Porges [2012]). This would allow for rehearsing of psychophysiological responses important for the goal of maintaining calm in the face of threats and, presumably, strengthening relevant neural circuits. The clients would then visually visit "the next time" and continue their resilience practice.

## Step 7: Action Plan and Real-Life Tryouts

Once the person can report a positive experience while only *visualizing* the next opportunity, or *being in the place* where the next opportunity will occur (without yet actually engaging in the goal), an action plan is developed so that the person can try things out in real life. A time and date are set, and coaching focuses on logistics. In the last example cited, the soldiers would be ultimately tested in a real-life challenge with real protesters.

## Step 8: Debriefing

A further meeting is arranged in which the event is debriefed. If successful, plans are made for continued setting and reaching of goals. If not successful, information is gathered with an eye to good news: What went well, and what has the person learned? Notice that any failure is an *opportunity to learn*. At this point one can revisit the options in Step 6 to identify where the best intervention might be focused.

**Pay special attention to** triggers that only appear in the real-life situation, and the opportunity to learn from both success and failure.

## Intermittent Coaching

Clients are sent on their way as soon as is feasible. The practitioner is encouraged to keep an open-door policy so that the clients know they can always ask for additional help. Clients are reminded that future challenges will be other learning opportunities: Successes point to virtues and other qualities deserving even more attention; failures are ways to learn about the power of the environment, and of their own internal triggers. All future experiences will teach clients about the internal and external factors that shape their behavior, and where they might have more to learn to regain mastery of their lives.

## References

Bonanno, G. A. & Mancini, A. D. (2012). Beyond resilience and PTSD: Mapping the heterogeneity of responses to potential trauma, *Psychological Trauma: Theory, Research, Practice, and Policy, 4*(1), 74–83.

Coach U. (2005). *Coach U's essentials, foundation, and resources set.* New York, NY: Wiley.

Gallo, F. (2000). *Energy diagnostic and treatment methods.* New York, NY: Norton.

Grachek, K. (2010). *Evaluating the efficacy of EMDR as an athletic performance enhancement intervention* (Doctoral dissertation, University of the Rockies, Colorado Springs, CO). Retrieved from ProQuest Dissertation Publishing (UMI order no. 3433356).

Harper, M., Rasolkhani-Kalhorn, T., & Drozd, J. F. (2009). On the neural basis of EMDR therapy: Insights from qEEG studies. *Traumatology, 15*(2), 81–95.

Hartung, J. (2009). Enhancing positive emotion and performance with EMDR. In M. Luber (Ed.). *EMDR scripted protocols: Basics and special situations* (pp. 339–375). New York, NY: Springer.

Hartung, J. (2012). *Innovative practices—from the East and West—for bodymind health.* Singapore: BII Press.

Hartung, J. & Stein, P. (2012). Telephone delivery of EFT (Emotional Freedom Techniques) remediates PTSD symptoms in veterans: A randomized controlled trial. *Energy Psychology: Theory, Research, & Treatment, 4*(1), 33–42.

Karatzias, T., Power, K., Brown, K., McGoldrick, T., Begum, M., Young, J., Loughran, P., Chouliara, Z., … Adams, S. (2011). A controlled comparison of the effectiveness and efficiency of two psychotherapies for posttraumatic stress disorder: Eye Movement Desensitization and Reprocessing vs. Emotional Freedom Techniques. *Journal of Nervous and Mental Disorders, 199*(6), 372–378.

Lazarus, A. (1989). *The practice of multimodal therapy.* New York, NY: McGraw-Hill.

McCraty, R., Atkinson, M., Tomasino, D., & Bradley, R. T. (2006). *The coherent heart: Heart-brain interactions, psychophysiological coherence, and the emergence of system-wide order.* Boulder Creek, CA: Institute of HeartMath.

Porges, S. W. (2011). *The Polyvagal Theory: Neurophysiological foundations of emotions, attachment, communication, and self-regulation.* New York, NY: Norton.

Schoninger, B. & Hartung, J. (2010). Changes on self-report measures of public speaking anxiety following treatment with thought-field therapy. *Energy Psychology, 2*(1), 13–26.

Seligman, M. E. P., Steen, T. A., Park, N., & Peterson, C. (2005). Positive psychology progress: Empirical validation of interventions. *American Psychologist, 60,* 410–521.

Siegel, D. J. (2012). *Pocket guide to interpersonal neurobiology: An integrative handbook of the mind.* New York, NY: Norton.

Steele, D. (2011). *From therapist to coach: How to leverage your clinical expertise to build a thriving coaching practice.* New York, NY: Wiley.

Williams, P. & Menendez, D. S. (2007). *Becoming a professional life coach: Lessons from the Institute for Life Coach Training.* New York, NY: Norton.

Wolpe, J. (1969). *The practice of behavior therapy.* New York, NY: Pergamon Press.

# Chapter 53
# Group Energies and Sports: Some Preliminary Speculation and Research

*Eric Leskowitz*

## Abstract

People everywhere are moved by the power of groups, whether it's at a concert, in a congregation, or at a political rally. The maturing science of consciousness research has proven that invisible energies are the key to this power, and the preeminent laboratory for studying these forces is an unexpected location: at the ballpark. This chapter describes how my love of the Boston Red Sox baseball team helped me discover that the principles of energy medicine and intentionality research explain the intangibles in sports: the home field advantage, the electricity in the crowd, team chemistry, and the prayers of fans. Computer studies using the random number generator approach developed at Princeton's famous PEAR Lab have measured fan energy at Fenway Park, and live lab tests (with me as the guinea pig) have shown that positive emotions are contagiously spread by the mechanism of coherent electromagnetic fields. Energetically savvy fans can learn how to enhance their team's performance by using their own enthusiasm and heart coherence to get their team into "the Zone" of peak performance.

**Keywords:** sports, baseball, energy, intangibles, the Zone, heart coherence, random number generators

**Eric Leskowitz, MD**, heads the Integrative Medicine Task Force at Spaulding Rehabilitation Hospital in Boston, and is a member of the Department of Psychiatry at Harvard Medical School. For more information about the documentary film discussed in this chapter, visit www. TheJoyOfSoxMovie.com. Send correspondence to Eric Leskowitz, 23 Tolman Street, Needham, MA 02492, or rleskowitz@pol.net.

Sports fans in New England are a strange breed, sharing as they do a devotion to their favorite team that borders on religious fervor. Perhaps they're aware that the word "fan" is a shortened version of "fanatic" (not a surprise), which itself comes from the Latin word *fanaticus,* referring to possession by the deity or spirit of a particular temple or shrine. And there's probably no more popular sports shrine around than Fenway Park, home of the Boston Red Sox. That ballpark has seen plenty of satisfied worshippers since the amazing come-from-behind road to the team's World Series victory of 2004. Many baseball commentators talked about "Fenway magic"—the home field advantage (HFA)—as a key component of the team's successes (including the 2007 championship as well), but few are aware of emerging research from the field of energy medicine that documents the key role that subtle energy plays in the all-important HFA.

Studying the HFA involves obvious factors such as friendly faces and positive cheers from the crowd, home cooking, and comfortable beds, not to mention jet-lagged opponents. But it also opens the door to a whole range of unusual, if not downright mystical and paranormal, phenomena that have previously been known only to an inner circle of researchers in the esoteric field of subtle energies, members of groups with acronyms like IONS, PEAR, ISSSEEM, and ACEP (translations: Institute of Noetic Sciences, Princeton Engineering Anomalies Research, International Society for the Study of Subtle Energy and Energy Medicine, and the Association for Comprehensive Energy Psychology).

However, baseball has the potential to bring these critical insights right into the cultural mainstream as part of an emerging 21st century social transformation, because the same energy processes that underlie such holistic healing methods as acupuncture, energy psychology (EFT, TAT, WHEE, and the like), intercessory prayer, and Reiki also impact sports performance. I have been investigating this overlap in recent years in my dual roles as a holistic psychiatrist at Spaulding Rehabilitation Hospital in Boston and as a lifelong Sox fan. More recently, my filmmaker cousin and I recorded interviews with players, fans, and researchers in order to make a documentary film about this topic called *The Joy of Sox: Weird Science and the Power of Intention.* We also conducted lab and field research to investigate the assertions of our interview subjects.

Belief in these mysterious forces is widespread in America today, despite the arcane-sounding jargon associated with consciousness research: heart rate variability, group electromagnetic fields, interpersonal coherence, and random number generators. However, these concepts are not as elusive as these terms sound and may explain the so-called intangibles in sports. For example, the common idiom "team chemistry" describes how interpersonal coherence (mediated by resonant electromagnetic fields) can enhance mind-body coordination and enable a group of people to function more effectively than a group of randomly assembled individuals who haven't bonded (one reason why American Olympic basketball or baseball teams lose to foreign teams with fewer star players—the Americans haven't played together as a team for months or years as the Europeans typically do). Boston area fans still remember the so-called "lovable idiots" of the 2004 Red Sox because they were fun to watch, obviously enjoyed each other's company and inspired the affection of their fans. In 2012, we watch San Francisco Giant fans fill their stadium with thousands of waving orange banners in support of a team that exhibits positive interpersonal bonding as it captivates their fans. Science shows that all those shared emotions can have a positive impact on sports performance, above and beyond the impact that a happy mood will have on decreasing stress levels.

The Institute of HeartMath reports that mind-body coordination is enhanced when people enter a unique state of psychophysiologic balance and heart rhythm called "heart coherence." This state of high heart rate variability (HRV) occurs when the heartbeat becomes less like a metronome and more like a slowly undulating wave in its variations of the interval between successive heartbeats. Emotions such as appreciation and joy engender this variable rhythm by balancing the competing arms of the autonomic nervous system in a way that simple muscle relaxation doesn't accomplish (Tiller, McCraty, & Atkinson, 1996). HRV training helps research subjects enter "the Zone" of peak athletic performance by sharpening reflexes and heightening concentration. It has long been suspected that these emotions (and their beneficial effects) are literally contagious, and can spread from person to person without words or sounds, seemingly via the impact of forces that originate in realms beyond the five physical senses. A rich folklore exists in all cultures describing the power of joyful groups, especially when ceremonial or intentional in nature (Ehrenreich, 2007).

In a laboratory test we performed at the Institute of HeartMath, a research subject was blindfolded and earplugged while his HRV was being monitored via pulse readings measured by an earlobe plethysmograph and fed to a computer with proprietary analytic software. The readings indicated that the subject, while in a state of nonspecific relaxation, could only attain a very low level of coherence. But when a group of HeartMath practitioners quietly entered the room and began their silent heart coherence practice (which consists of remembering feelings of appreciation, and focusing on the heart region where those sensations arise), the monitored subject's HRV rose dramatically, as if his nervous system was literally being entrained into the group's stronger state of coherence (Leskowitz, 2009). This finding implies that a group of people who share a state of happiness can literally spread positive vibrations (presumably of an electromagnetic nature, given that the heart's magnetic field is stronger than that generated by any other organ) that affect other people in their vicinity. A similar process may be at work in situations of teammate-to-teammate interactions and fan-to-player cheering, and may constitute the mechanism of "team chemistry" and fan power.

Stanford physicist William Tiller noted that positive emotions generate standing waves of a higher order resonant energy, which can easily be dissipated by negative emotions like angry booing. In other words, if fans are shouting "Yankees suck!" (a popular Boston chant), they are liable to cancel out the benefits that might be simultaneously accruing from other fans cheering "Go Sox!" Cheering works better if all the fans are on the same page, though Boston's Yankee-bashing fans may not be ready to make this major shift in consciousness. And vice versa for New Yorkers booing the Red Sox. Americans seem to enjoy booing more than they love cheering, presenting a spiritual challenge wherein one's chances for victory are improved by transcending the emotions of aggression and rivalry.

Boston baseball fans share the experience of mass enthusiasm with sports fans the world over, as well as fans of music and other mass events. This energy is palpable, memorable, and, not incidentally, highly addictive. We measured this effect by building on work done at Princeton University over the past 30 years. The PEAR (Princeton Engineering Anomalies Research) lab has documented that seemingly random events (such as a random ball cascade, a stochastic robot, or a randomized stream of computer-generated ones and zeroes) can be affected by the human mind (Jahn & Bunne, 2005). RNG devices are essentially electronic coin-flippers, creating a continuous stream of random heads or tails (actually, binary ones or zeroes). Human intention subtly alters the stream of random numbers, and moments of nonrandomness are detected when the RNG output diverges from true 50/50 randomness by more than two standard deviations, to reach the 0.05 level of statistical significance. Even though there are no physical connections between the people and the machines, these mind-machine interactions are real and reproducible.

We took a modified version of Princeton's RNG software (Wilber, 2006) to Fenway Park during a Boston Red Sox baseball game and were able to detect several clear moments of high nonrandomness during the game. Far more RNG spikes were observed during the game than would be expected to occur randomly (the odds against this happening purely by chance were 100,000 to 1). These RNG spikes happened at the same moments as game events or actions that had a strong emotional significance for the crowd. The game's largest peak effect—an unlikely swing of 3.40 standard deviations—came not during a play on the field, but during the "Sweet Caroline" sing-along that has become a regular eighth-inning ritual, compelling proof of the power that music has on human emotions (Leskowitz, 2011). Noteworthy in this research design is the fact that the computer didn't have a microphone, electrode, or vibration detector; it was just a laptop whose software was generating a steady stream of thousands of ones and zeroes per second from its perch above the right-field grandstand. Through some as yet undetermined mechanism, collective human attention can be detected by physical instrumentation.

Players confirm the positive effects of being bathed in this atmosphere of support. Former outfielder Gabe Kapler called Fenway's crowd support "the ultimate amphetamine." Pitcher Mike Timlin described how the crowd energy can help him get so deeply into the zone that he can sometimes know exactly what the opposing batters are thinking ("It's like ESP, or whatever you want to call it.") Sportscaster Jerry Remy also noted the edge that Fenway gives the Sox because this fan intensity "not only boosts the Sox, but it also intimidates the other players."

Iconoclast Bill "Spaceman" Lee, however, remarked how brawls between players could help spark team energy as effectively "as any of that touchy-feely stuff could" (he was particularly fond of sparring with Hall of Fame teammate Carlton Fisk). The Spaceman is also skeptical that Fenway Park has any special aura of its own that would make it what Stanford physicist William Tiller calls a "conditioned space." Dr. Tiller has documented that chemical properties such as the pH (acidity level) of water samples can be altered if the samples are placed in a room that has hosted an ongoing series of regular group meditations (Tiller, Dibble, Shealy, & Nunley, 2004). Even when obvious variables such as temperature and humidity are controlled, chemistry experiments unfold differently in spaces that have been "conditioned" by this sort of earlier human mental activity.

This finding implies that shrines such as Lourdes and Chartres (and Fenway?) could have been conditioned by thousands of people pouring out intense emotions for decades, if not centuries. Perhaps there is an imprinting from the resonant and coherent electromagnetic fields (EMFs) to which these locations are exposed. If that's true, then it should be possible to detect something "in the air" at these sacred spaces even when no one is present. PEAR's RNG readings at the Great Pyramid in Egypt show this imprinting effect (Nelson, 1997), and preliminary readings at Fenway during the offseason and during the lull before a game suggest that a modest but measurable effect seems to linger at Fenway even after the fans have gone home.

Related scientific studies support the hypothesis that "fan power" brings the home team advantage to life. Noted prayer researcher Larry Dossey has described how so-called intercessory or distant prayer can boost the health of patients in the intensive care unit (Dossey, 1997). We suspect that distant prayer for players can boost their performance in an analogous way, though the barriers to rigorous research in this area would be daunting, if not impossible. From a practical perspective, it looks as though fans can have a very beneficial resonant impact on their favorite players, and when they band together intentionally, the impact may be even greater.

Some professional ballplayers have begun to explore the use of energy modalities to optimize their performance, though this practice is still generally conducted outside the public eye. In the documentary film *The Joy of Sox,* however, one Boston Red Sox player describes how he used the energy psychology modality called Emotional Freedom Techniques (EFT) to overcome his performance anxieties. Also, the MVP of the College Baseball World Series is shown on camera administering self-EFT during a lull in the game (Hampton, 2012). These examples suggest that the coming era of energy medicine may be ushered in by athletes and sports fans (SEC Group, 2013), with a few celebrity endorsements of energy techniques potentially having a greater impact than a dossier full of research studies, and with our national addiction to group sporting events infecting us all with the energy bug, thereby opening the cultural doors to awareness of other realms of consciousness and new ways of being.

# References

Dossey, L. (1997). *Healing words: The power of prayer and the practice of medicine.* New York, NY: HarperOne.

Ehrenreich, B. (2007). *Dancing in the streets: A history of collective joy.* New York, NY: Holt.

Hampton, K. (2012, July 27). When the yips affect athletes, they call Greg Warburton. *Corvallis Gazette-Times.* Retrieved from http://www.gazettetimes.com/sports/community/when-the-yips-afflict-athletes-they-call-greg-warburton-for/article_00e9dcc2-d93c-11e1-9bec-0019bb2963f4.html

Jahn, R. & Bunne, B. The PEAR proposition. *Journal of Scientific Exploration, 19*(2), 195–245. 2005.

Leskowitz, E. (2009). The influence of group heart rhythm on target subject physiology: Case report of a laboratory demonstration, and suggestions for further research. *Subtle Energies and Energy Medicine, 18*(3), 77–88.

Leskowitz, E. (2011, January). Random number generators at the ballpark. *International Journal of Healing and Caring, 1,* 1–11.

Nelson, R. D. (1997). FieldREG measurements in Egypt: Resonant consciousness at sacred sites. Technical Note PEAR 97002, Princeton Engineering Anomalies Research, Princeton University, School of Engineering/Applied Science.

SEC Group (Sports, Energy and Consciousness Group). (2013). Retrieved from http://www.SportsEnergyGroup.com

Tiller, W. A., Dibble, Jr., W. E., Shealy, C. N., & Nunley, R. N. (2004, April). Toward general experimentation and discovery in conditioned laboratory spaces: Part II. pH-change experience at four remote sites, 1 year later. *Journal of Alternative and Complementary Medicine, 10*(2), 301–306.

Tiller, W., McCraty, R. and Atkinson, M. (1996). Cardiac coherence: A new non-invasive measure of autonomic nervous system order. *Alternative Therapies, 2*(1), 52–65.

Wilber, S. A. (2006). Machine-enhanced anomalous cognition. Retrieved from http://psigenics.com/research/Papers/PRD_Whitepaper.pdf

# Chapter 54
# EFT and Sports Performance

*Tam Llewellyn-Edwards*

**Abstract**

This chapter discusses the use of EFT in enhancing sports performance. A number of examples are presented to show how EFT has succeeded in this area together with the methods used to produce the desired result. It outlines a number of academically viable research projects that show statistically the positive effect of EFT in sports performance. Examples are given in the sports of baseball, basketball, rugby, soccer, horse riding and golf. Attention is drawn to the dangers of unthinking application of EFT in inappropriate areas of sports injuries. References where the reader can find more detail are provided.

**Keywords:** sports performance, rugby, baseball, basketball, golf, soccer, horse riding

**Tam Llewellyn-Edwards, PhD**, EFT Master, is an EFT trainer and practitioner, and professor of homeopathy and energy therapies at Calamus University in London. He also runs a complementary medicine clinic where he sees clients and teaches various therapies. Send correspondence to Tam Llewellyn-Edwards, Ty Goch Clinic, 4 St. Mary's Mews, Tickhill, South Yorkshire, DN11 9LR UK, or TLlewellyn@aol.com.

## How EFT Can Help

EFT cannot improve sports performance beyond the capabilities of certain structural limitations. For instance, I am about 1.65 meters (5' 5") tall, and no matter how much I tapped, I would never become a basketball star. Many sports, or particular playing positions in sports, demand specific physical attributes and it is counterproductive to try to place a player who does not have those attributes into one of those sports or positions if you are expecting that player to become a top-class player. Though I will never be a top-flight basketball player, I was a professional rugby league player and was even trialed as an American football player, but as a kicker not a linebacker

So how, then, can EFT help with sports performance? It never helped me because I had given up on professional sports long before I found EFT, but I do wish EFT had been around when I was actively playing.

EFT will not make a purse out of a sow's ear (nor a linebacker out of a kicker), but it can remove the blocks preventing people playing sports from becoming the best their physical makeup allows them to be. It is even more useful when players who have achieved success lose their edge. This use of EFT has been well researched and documented, as we shall see.

## Success in Baseball

The improvements that can be achieved when using EFT to improve sports performance have been reported for some years. One of the earliest was that of Pat Ahearne, a baseball pitcher. It was in 1999 that Ahearne, then a pitcher in the Australian Perth Heat team, first encountered EFT. After learning to use EFT, he moved up the leagues and played baseball around the world. His earned run average (ERA) dropped from a poor 33.3 to a surprisingly low 0.87 (Craig, 2010, pp. 113–116). Craig (2010) also quotes a number of outstanding examples of the improvements made in sports after using EFT. These are reports of individual cases and failures, however, so it is difficult to use these academically to show that EFT improves sports performance in general.

## Rugby Goal Kicking

Research by Sam Smith of Australia (Craig, 2010, pp. 122–123) demonstrates how a simple trial can measure the effect of EFT on performance. This trial was done on a group of rugby players but would be equally valid for American football kickers. Smith was at a rugby event and took the opportunity to demonstrate the effectiveness of EFT. He did this by setting up a goal-kicking practice in which 37 volunteers, aged 12 to 54 years, kicked a rugby ball through the rugby goal posts; each performed 10 kicks from 20, 25, 30, 35, and 40 meters directly in front of the goal. (A top-class goal kicker would score nearly 100% success from these distances, but the volunteers were by no means expert goal kickers.) After completing the 10 kicks, each participant was given a short session of EFT based on the things they saw as spoiling their performance.

They then repeated the same 10 kicks. The average score rate in the first 10 kicks was 19%. After EFT, the success rate had risen to 24%. It was also noted that in the first test, 15 of the misses hit the woodwork and bounced out of the goal; in the second test, 163 of the misses hit the woodwork and bounced out of the goal. This showed that even the misses were closer to being goals after EFT.

This trial demonstrated how a short session of EFT can improve performance and was particularly useful, as a large number of subjects were used in a controlled test to demonstrate a consistent result. Such trials are easy to arrange and all EFT practitioners are urged to undertake such work and report results. However, trials of this sort, although useful demonstrations, are not academically acceptable, as they do not use control groups or statistical analysis.

In another rugby setting, I had a client who had lost his ability to kick goals. He had previously been a good goal scorer but had recently "lost it." Discussion of the history of the problem disclosed the root cause. In the final minutes of a close game, his team was one point behind and had gained a penalty from an easily kickable position that would have given them two points to win the game. My client missed the goal and the team lost the game. What followed was the actual or perceived contempt of his teammates and the supporters at his missing such an easy kick and his own loss of confidence in his ability to score. The result was he became a poor kicker and was dropped from the first team.

This problem of loss of confidence is common in sports therapy when a player who previously was proficient loses his or her edge. EFT will handle this problem, though it may not be easy. There are often layers of events and/or ideas that lead to this loss of confidence and self-respect, together with a series of later events that "prove" the player was no good. All of these aspects must be dealt with. In the case of my client, we had to deal with the actual event—missing that vital kick—together with all the resulting events. These included the reaction of his teammates and supporters (real or imagined), the loss of his first team place, and all the subsequent failed kicks.

We tapped away each event one by one until no more problem events surfaced. Happily, the player regained his confidence, his ability to kick goals, and his first team place.

Loss of confidence and self-esteem are the two most common problems we face in sport psychology. EFT deals with both simply and easily and the effects seem to last. A number of academically sound research projects have recently demonstrated this improvement in statistically valid trials with control groups (Church & Downs, 2012).

## Research into Soccer Performance

Mary Llewellyn-Edwards, my wife, another EFT Master practitioner, and I have acted as "psychological trainers" for two women's soccer teams in the United Kingdom—one an under-16 years of age team and the other an open age team. Both teams did very well in their respective leagues. In fact, the under-16 teams won every match in the league and consequently were declared league champions after the half point of the season. They also scored a record number of goals. The open age team came a very creditable second in their league.

There is a problem in assessing this type of success, as there are many factors that contributed to it—too many uncontrolled variables. The girls and older women may just have all been exceptionally skilful soccer players, and I cannot forget that there were others training the teams who must have some credit for the success. To claim even part of the success for EFT, we must first reduce the variables and provide a control group that did not use EFT. Only then can we demonstrate the statistical effect of the use of EFT. This we did. The full description of our research and its statistical analysis is available in Llewellyn-Edwards and Llewellyn-Edwards (2012), but it is worth outlining the research here. Participants in this study were players of Keepmoat Stadium Ladies,

a group of female soccer teams for which we provide psychological coaching. Thus the participants were familiar with EFT and had had some earlier experience in its use and advantages, which made a blind test impossible.

The study was carried out during normal practice sessions at the Keepmoat Stadium in Doncaster, United Kingdom, using a small five-a-side outdoor pitch where the teams usually trained. Informed consent had been obtained prior to the trials, which were undertaken with the support of the team management who provided two trainers to work with the control group.

A total of 26 players took part from the open and under-16 teams. Fifteen players from the senior team took part (eight of these made up the control group). The age range of this group was 15 to 30. Eleven under-16 players made up a separate active group, all aged 14 to 15. The two age groups were studied separately, but the results are shown both individually and pooled. The control group was drawn only from the senior team, being judged to be those who would best benefit from the standard coaching procedures, whereas the under-16 girls were considered less likely to benefit from such a short standard coaching session. Thus the investigation could be described as being in two parts: a randomized controlled trial with the open team members and a supporting uncontrolled trial with the under-16 team members.

All participants performed their usual warming-up period and then had the process of the trial explained to them. The test involved taking two sets of five dead-ball kicks at goal from a distance of 13.5 meters. The goal was the standard five-a-side goal (5.0 meters wide by 1.2 meters high). There was no goalkeeper employed (to reduce the uncontrolled variables), but only kicks that entered one of the two outer thirds of the available goal area were counted as scoring. Those that entered the center third of the goal were considered as would have been saved by a goalkeeper.

After the first 10 kicks, the players were given a short coaching session and then 10 more kicks were taken. The trial was to assess if the coaching sessions served to make a significant improvement in performance, not to assess the performance of the individual players.

The 15 senior players were randomly divided into two groups: active and control. The control and active groups were sent to opposite ends of the pitch but were intentionally allowed to watch the attempts of others to score. The under-16 group undertook the trial at a different time but under identical conditions, except that there was no under-16 control group.

Each player was allowed five kicks at the goal, a short rest, and five further kicks. The total of two attempts of 10 kicks was decided after the participants' trainers had judged that 20 kicks would not tire the players unduly. The trainers' estimate was halved to remove possible fatigue as an uncontrolled variable.

The scores of the active teams were recorded by the two researchers and those of the control group by two of the trainers.

Once the initial 10 goal shots had been taken, the groups were given coaching in an attempt to increase their score rates. The active groups were give a coaching session by the researchers, which consisted of a group "Borrowing Benefits" EFT session. This involved a group tapping session while they each considered what might have hindered their scoring in the earlier session, as well as hearing the reasons expressed by others in their group.

The control group had a group session with their normal trainers, which was aimed at increasing their score rate. This involved the trainers commenting on the players' earlier efforts at scoring and advising on actions to improve their technique in shooting. No actual shooting practice was allowed during this intervention.

After the coaching sessions, the groups were again given two sets of five kicks at the goal under identical conditions to those used pre-treatment. Again the scoring level was recorded.

The score rates before and after treatment for each group were compared and statistically assessed to judge if any improvement following treatment was significant and to compare the significance of any difference between the active groups and the control group. The scoring rates in the first and second series of penalty kicks were calculated to determine the amount of improvement before and after coaching with EFT (active groups) and normal coaching (control group).

With this small sample, it was not possible to test the results to see if they were normally distributed. Consequently, the significance of the results was first assessed with a simple sign test, using the null hypothesis that the EFT process did not significantly improve the players' performance when compared to the improvement from standard coaching. As the experiment produced numerical values for the performance change, the Wilcoxon signed-rank sum test was used to increase the power of the testing. To facilitate comparison of the results with an earlier study by Church (2009), two-tailed t-tests were also undertaken.

The results of the sign test showed that the difference between the performance before and after coaching/EFT was significant in the "Ladies Open" active group, but not significant in the control group. As the under-16 sample size was larger, this was not assessed using the sign test, but only using a t-test.

All three groups—control, Ladies Open, and under 16—were assessed using a t-test to judge if there was a significant difference before and after coaching against the null hypothesis that there would be no significant difference in performance. This assessment showed:

**Control Group**
T-value = 2.10,
Calculated T-value = 0.31
Null hypothesis not rejected

**Ladies Open**
T-value = 2.10,
Calculated T-value = 2.20
Null hypothesis rejected

**Under 16**
T-value = 2.10,
Calculated T-value = 2.68
Null hypothesis rejected

**Pooled**
T-value = 2.10,
Calculated T-value = 2.95
Null hypothesis rejected

Thus it was shown that the active groups all had a statistically significant improvement after EFT, whereas the control group, which had not had the benefit of EFT, did not.

## Research on Basketball Performance

A basic requirement of good research is that the research is reproducible; that is, a similar piece of research conducted at a different time by different researchers under different conditions would produce similar results. Our soccer research did, in fact, confirm the reproducibility of an earlier study, as did other research published in the same year as ours (Baker, 2010).

The earlier investigation was conducted by Dawson Church (2009). In his study, he tested the effect of EFT on the performance of a basketball team in the United States. His research measured performance on free throws and vertical jump height. The time frame of data collection and treatment simulated an actual basketball game. A statistically significant difference between the two groups was found for free throws (p < .03). On posttest, players who received the EFT intervention improved an average of 20.8%, while the control group decreased an average of 16.6%. There was no difference between treatment groups in jump height. When performance was analyzed separately by gender, trends toward significance were found for the women's team on both performance measures, with better results for the EFT intervention group. This indicated that EFT increased performance.

Church's basketball investigation showed a statistically significant improvement after EFT, and the soccer research my wife and I conducted replicated these results. The active groups showed an increase in scoring rate. We modeled our soccer research on the earlier basketball research so that the results could be compared to show reproducibility. This they did, helping validate both research projects.

## Other Research

There is a mass of other research showing the effectiveness of even a short application of EFT on sports performance. Craig (2010) outlines a large number of research projects with copious references to full reports.

## EFT in Practice

Along with formal academic research, there is a growing mass of anecdotal evidence accrued from the clinical practice of EFT practitioners who specialize in sports psychology. Reports of clinical success abound across a host of sports. While this may not be acceptable academically, it is still valuable as evidence that changes can be made with EFT. In this chapter, I will restrict my examples to successful outcomes achieved in our clinic at Tickhill, South Yorkshire, UK.

## The "Yips"

"The yips" is a term used when a sports person freezes at some critical point in the action in the sports process. In sports such as archery, darts, and billiards/snooker/pool, it occurs when, at some point in the action, the player has to take a decisive

and irrevocable action such as releasing the arrow or striking the ball. The problem is basically one of fear that the time or aim is not right to take the action. In many of these sports, an overlong wait time increases the chances of a poor shot, which only confirms the player's belief that it was taken too soon. This produces more and more hesitation until the player becomes simply unable to take the action.

A client of mine was an archer. As an archer draws the bow, the tension on the arm and back muscles increases until at the time the arrow must be released the strain on those muscles is at its greatest. If the arrow is not released immediately, the arm begins to shake and the aim moves off target, causing a bad shot. In the case of this client, his hesitation had caused a number of bad shots, including one that had missed the target completely. The result was that he had found it impossible to release and had exceeded the time limit, disqualifying his team. So he looked to me for help.

The first problem we looked at was his causing the disqualification of his team. This proved to be a problem simply handled using EFT and it was soon cleared. When I accompanied the client to the archery range, however, he was still unable to release his arrows. The deeper problem remained.

We dealt with the deeper problem using the "Choices" extension of EFT (Carrington, 2012). We removed the target completely and had the client simply draw his bow and release an arrow randomly into the back net immediately he achieved full draw. The drawing of a bow produces great muscle tension and the release provides a welcome relaxation and calm (Herrigel, 1989). With the stress of having to hit the target removed, my client was able to draw and release without problem. We then used EFT with the Setup Statement:

*"Even though I cannot release the arrow, I am a good archer anyway."*

After a few rounds, we introduced the "Choices" phrase:

*"I choose to release the arrow and enjoy the relief it brings."*
*"I am delighted to wallow in the joy and relaxation of the release."*

It is not possible to tap while drawing a bow, so I asked the client to imagine tapping and saying the phrases mentally while at the stand. The target was then reintroduced but I advised the client not to try to score high marks, but just to hit the target somewhere and enjoy the feeling of relaxation on release. It was soon clear that the client was hitting the target easily and obtaining high scores. Some months later, the archer was still using EFT mentally while shooting and was obtaining high scores without any sign of the yips.

A similar approach has been used successfully on other "yips plagued" competitors, and research into the effects of EFT on "the yips" has been conducted (Rotherham et al., 2012).

## Animals

EFT will work on animals. I once treated a horse who was afraid of heights. This particular horse hesitated to walk along tracks that led to narrow mountain trails, and actually refused by rearing dangerously if turned onto one of those trails.

Horses are large animals and can be dangerous if afraid. Consequently, I chose to tap on myself for the horse, using remote (surrogate) EFT. Naturally, the horse (I'll call him Guy—not his real name) could not tell me his problems nor the roots of those problems, but his rider could give me that information. Just before the problem started, Guy was being ridden on a narrow hill trail with a steep drop on one side. Suddenly, another horse came toward Guy at full gallop from up the trail. The other rider reigned in in time, but there was some contact between the horses and the other horse bit Guy.

The initial treatment was standard EFT, except that I tapped on myself rather than on the horse and it took the form of telling the story of the initiating event while tapping. Since it was not possible to obtain a SUD (subjective units of distress) rating from the horse, the test was to see that the rider could ride Guy onto the trail that led to the narrow mountain track. The rider was able to do this while I watched and tapped on myself for the horse, and all was well.

Unfortunately, that was not the solution to the problem. A week or so later the rider contacted me, reporting that Guy would happily go down the low tracks but simply refused to turn onto the high tracks. He simply froze. This problem occurred on all high trails, not only on the one where the earlier incident had occurred.

Before the second session, I rode Guy myself toward the high track, with the rider behind us on a second horse. With me on his back, Guy turned happily onto the high track and trotted up it. The problem was not with the horse but with the rider. It was not that Guy was afraid of the high track, but that the rider was afraid to ride him up the high track and was transmitting this fear to Guy.

Thus the second session was on the rider not the horse. Again using the EFT Story Technique, I took the rider through the incident. There were a number of high SUD level sub-events: the sight of the horse galloping down the narrow track toward them, the sight of the drop-off on one side of the track, the collision, and the horror the rider felt when Guy was bitten. All these were dealt with one by one. Also a little work was done on the later incidents when Guy had reared dangerously when turned onto the high track again after the original event.

Following the second session the rider reported that there was no longer a problem and she had resumed her riding with her horse along the spectacular high tracks.

## Golf

Golf is a relatively simple game, but the requirements for a top-class golfer and the detailed action to produce a good shot are complex and detailed. Any small error at the point of the swing can destroy the shot and the round. It is a fertile area for small problems to ruin performance, and an ideal ground for EFT.

A good way to approach building up one's golfing ability with EFT is to start treatment at a practice putting green. This is usually in sight of the golf course clubhouse and other players will be intrigued.

A routine I have used a number of times is to have the client golfer place a number of balls around the hole on the practice putting green at the greatest distance from the hole at which he is sure he can hole-out most of them. I then double the distance and have the client try to hole-out each ball. I record the number holed-out.

Then the EFT session takes place. I ask clients why they think they did so badly in our trial. Typical reasons are: "I cannot putt from that distance," "My friends in the clubhouse were watching," and "This new putter is no good."

I then do a standard EFT process using whatever excuse/problem the particular client voiced as the first half of the Setup Statement.

Once I have dealt with all the problems voiced, and any others that came up during the rounds, I take the clients back onto the practice green and have them putt again from the greater distance, counting the successful putts. Invariably after EFT, they are more successful than they were before EFT. This give the clients confidence that I can help them with other aspects of their game, and incidentally often produces new clients from those watching from the clubhouse.

Golf is a mental game rather than a physical one. Basically, it is easy. All that is necessary is to use the same swing for all long distance shots each time and to choose the right club. Why then do so many of our shots end up in the rough? It is a mental thing.

One client of mine was a good amateur club level golfer but had never won his club's championship, although he was certainly one of the best golfers in his club and had won other competitions. His grandfather had founded the club and had won the club championship many times, as had his father. Both grandfather and father were looking forward to the time when he would win it and the third generation would be added to the names on the trophy.

The client reported that a number of times he had been ahead toward the end of his round in the championship but had played poorly on the final holes.

During his EFT session, he claimed that there was no pressure on him to win from his father or grandfather, or from himself, as he "knew" he could win. Early in the session, it was clear that this was, in fact, the case. Neither did there seem to be any bad memories of his failing toward the end of previous competitions. He claimed to feel excitement and joy each time he neared the end, as his name would soon be added to the trophy.

What, then, was the problem? His excitement and relief in coming toward the end of the competition and winning was spoiling his concentration and his swing. EFT quickly resolved the problem using the "Choices" addition. We tapped on:

*"As I come toward the winning of this competition, I choose to hold my concentration and relax so I can wonder at how easy it has been."*

He was able to use EFT with this Choices statement and to win the next club championship, to the delight of his father and grandfather.

## How EFT Can Do Harm

Many people say that EFT can do no harm, but this is simply not so if it covers up danger signs. This is especially true of sports injuries and so it would not be right to end this chapter without some warning.

Pain is usually considered "bad," but it can be good. Pain is there to warn us that something is amiss and we should heed its call. When a sports person leaves the field of play with an injury, there may be a temptation to use EFT to remove the pain and return the player to the field. This is also the case when an old injury is slow to heal and the player is eager to return to playing after an injury layoff. EFT is easily capable of removing the pain in these cases, but I advise care.

Pain warns us that the body has been damaged, or stressed beyond its limits. Removing the pain may allow the player to return to the field, but once returned to the fray more damage can occur at the site of the previous injury. This is not a problem restricted to EFT, as the warning applies equally to the use of analgesics and pain-reducing sprays in conventional medical practice.

How, then, should the EFT practitioner act? Clearly, if the injury and its cause are obvious and the pain slight, such as following a minor knock or kick, EFT can easily be used. If a conventional medical physiotherapist has assessed the injury and recommended only pain-killers, then EFT is equally a useful choice.

The problem lies when conventional medical advice is not available and there is no obvious reason for the pain or the pain is incapacitating. EFT can be used to reduce the pain and the stress on the injured and, indeed, should be used to ease the effect of the event on the player. However, we should be careful and hesitant before returning the player to the field before the injury has been medically assessed. Certainly, if any reduction in the player's movement is noted, the player should be recalled from the game; this should also certainly be done if the same problem reoccurs.

Be safe, not sorry. Avoid removing pain so the player resumes action and aggravates the injury.

## Conclusion

It is clear that EFT alone cannot make top sports persons, but it can remove blocks and worries and thus allow the true performance to come through for success. A good EFT sports psychologist will not be attempting to create a top-flight performer but will be trying to make the best possible performer out of the client, by removing blocks and memories of previous poor performance that are obstacles to success.

# References

Baker, A. H. (2010). A re-examination of Church's (2009) study into the effects of Emotional Freedom Techniques (EFT) on basketball free-throw performance. *Energy Psychology: Theory, Research, & Treatment, 2*(2), 39–44.

Carrington, P. (2012). EFT choices manual. East Millstone, NJ: Pace Educational Systems.

Church, D. (2009). The effect of EFT (Emotional Freedom Techniques) on athletic performance: A randomized controlled blind trial. *Open Sports Sciences Journal 2,* 94–99. doi:10.2174/1875399X00902010094

Church, D. & Downs, D. (2012). Sports confidence and critical incident intensity after a brief application of Emotional Freedom Techniques: A pilot study. *Sport Journal, 15,* 2012.

Craig, C. (2010). EFT for sports performance. Fulton, CA: Energy Psychology Press.

Herrigel, E. (1989). Zen in the Art of Archery. New York, NY: Vintage.

Llewellyn-Edwards, T. & Llewellyn-Edwards, M. (2012, Spring). The effect of EFT (Emotional Freedom Techniques) on soccer performance. *Fidelity: Journal for the National Council of Psychotherapists, 47,* 14–19.

Rotherham, M., Maynard, I., Thomas, O., Bawden, M., & Francis, L. (2012). Preliminary evidence for the treatment of type I "yips": The efficacy of the Emotional Freedom Techniques. *Sports Psychologist, 26*(4), 551–570.

# Chapter 55
# Cultivating Peak Performance in Business
*Steve Wells*

### Abstract
This chapter provides guidelines on how Emotional Freedom Techniques (EFT) and meridian tapping generally can be used to cultivate peak performance in business, whether in building your own business or assisting others to achieve peak performance. It begins by outlining some basic principles of peak performance and how tapping can be used to facilitate this. Some personal tapping protocols are provided, along with basic guidelines for using tapping within a personal peak performance program and for coaching others. The author outlines a seven-step teaching process he has researched, refined, and modified over 15 years to help entrepreneurs and people in business achieve peak performance and explains how tapping is used within this process to help people overcome their emotional barriers and internal resistance. Also included are important details on the author's "Connecting with Success" process, which involves the use of intention combined with tapping to create an energetic connection with important business or personal goals. Protocols and advice for using tapping to cultivate peak performance within the corporate sector are also provided along with specific examples from the author's experience.

**Keywords:** peak performance, success, tapping, EFT, coaching, business, corporations

**Steve Wells**, is a psychologist, international peak performance consultant, leadership coach, and cocreator of Simple Energy Techniques (SET). He regularly consults worldwide with business achievers and conducts unique personal and business success programs. Send correspondence to Steve Wells, PO Box 54, Inglewood, Western Australia, 6052, or steve@eftdownunder.com.

eak performance does not happen by accident. It is usually the result of a powerful vision and a workable plan put into action over time. However, there are some definite strategies and mental/emotional patterns that can accelerate your success and leverage and enhance your performance. Emotional Freedom Techniques (EFT) and Simple Energy Techniques (SET) are two of the newest and most exciting tools to be applied in the area of peak performance, and I have had significant success in applying them to boost performance, both in sport and business.

This chapter focuses on how you can use EFT and meridian stimulation generally ("tapping") to promote peak performance in business, whether that is building your own business or assisting others to achieve peak performance. It includes important steps I have developed over time in using tapping when coaching people in business—to help them, and the business as a whole, achieve peak performance. We'll look at the basic principles of peak performance, the key elements of a peak performance program, and how you can utilize tapping within that program to facilitate this goal. Of all the elements in such a huge subject, the most important are addressed in this chapter, as an overview.

## Basic Principles of Peak Performance

*Peak performance begins with a commitment to an important vision or goal.*

The impetus for peak performance is a typically a definite, committed decision to achieve something great. You can't achieve a vision if you don't have one! Decide what success is to you and commit to being successful.

Arguably the biggest thing that a business needs to succeed is a compelling vision. This is an image of the business in the future being a peak performing business. What would that look like, what would that feel like to work in, and to work for? What would it be like? What are the important values, goals, and strategies?

There will be blocks and barriers to realizing that image. First there will be an attachment to current reality—all the reasons why you can't change, and why change will be difficult. Essentially, all change begins as a personal issue, whether we are talking about you as a business owner, CEO, or employee in a business. You can apply tapping to these "objections" in context.

Tapping, in short, can be used to help people:

1. Gain clarity
2. Create their vision
3. Release emotional barriers to achieving it
4. Connect emotionally with that vision, and
5. Go for it!

*Action is the difference that makes a difference.*

The decision to become a peak performer, or to create a peak performing business, must be backed by action. When peak performers in all fields are analyzed, it is *the difference in their actions,* not their intelligence, sex, race, or another factor, that makes the most difference in explaining their results. Getting into action can be challenging, and a crucial use of tapping protocols is that of overcoming fears and other emotional barriers to taking action.

*Commitment and persistence is king.*

Research from Swedish psychologist K. Anders Ericcson and colleagues (Ericcson, Krampe, & Tesch-Römer, 1993) indicates that 10,000 hours of practice is associated with becoming a world-class expert in a wide range of areas. In summarizing this research in his book *Outliers,* Malcolm Gladwell (2008) states: "The thing that distinguishes one performer from another is how hard he or she works" (p. 39).

The key distinction for tapping is that "hard work" need not be associated with "hard feelings." In order to persist to the degree required to achieve peak performance, the end result must be associated with an individual's highest values. Tapping can be used to help people to get clear on exactly what their key values are, since values are (at their core) emotional drivers of behavior.

*Peak performers work harder at improving.*

Blind persistence and hard work won't by themselves bring success; results, feedback, and adjustments based on learning from feedback on results are crucial. Peak performers' commitment to ongoing improvement leads them to constantly strive to go beyond where they were before. In business, the return on any investment of energy, time, and resources is crucial. This requires feedback about the results of the actions, using measures of success that are important, and sources of feedback that are helpful.

Jim Loehr and Tony Schwartz (2003) in their book *The Power of Full Engagement* state: "We grow at all levels by expending energy beyond our normal limits, and then recovering…. Expanding capacity requires a willingness to endure short-term discomfort in the service of long-term reward" (p. 44). "We must systematically expose ourselves to stress beyond our normal limits, followed by adequate recovery" (p. 47).

Tapping can help with the discomfort of moving outside our comfort zone, to reduce or ameliorate the negative effects of pushing beyond our normal limits (going from the known to the unknown induces apprehension), and also increase our resilient capacity to recover.

## Business Peak Performance

Napoleon Hill, author of *Think and Grow Rich,* coined the term "Mastermind Principle" to describe the leverage power of a number of committed individuals coming together to focus on achieving a definite objective. His definition of his term is "coordination of knowledge and effort in a spirit of harmony, between two or more people, for the attainment of a definite purpose" (1960, pp. 168–169).

The added dimension in business is that of people and their complexities: businesses achieve peak performance by engaging people in collective action toward an agreed goal or vision. There is leverage potential when people come together to achieve a result. Challenges come when there is lack of clarity or agreement about the vision and resistance to achieving it. Much energy in business is wasted on resistance. These are all issues with emotional roots that can be helped by tapping.

Resistance may be internal. Parts of us are pulling in different directions. We might fear having the success or doing what we think it will take to get to success. Success might conflict with our identity belief (Cialdini, 2008). People within the business may be pulling in different directions. Resistance can also be external; there may be people who object to or oppose our personal or business growth (including competitors) and provide obstruction or barriers we need to go through, over, or around.

These resistances are experienced as emotional issues or values conflicts. Dealing with and desensitizing them requires a technique that can provide an *emotional shift*—such as the tapping techniques. Clarity of values and alignment of values may in fact be the most important factors for peak performance in business. Tapping enhances this process enormously.

Finally, goal setters do better in all areas of business and life. If managers regularly set goals and encourage staff to do the same, the company develops a success identity. With feedback comes encouragement and personal development. The underlying catalyst for this process is managing emotional difficulties. This is the province of tapping for many reasons; it is portable, effective, efficient, and quick. Thus it is ideal as self-help in the daily life of the people in the business.

## Personal Tapping Protocols

The most practical way to utilize the effects of tapping when dealing with complex, multilevel issues is to tap on any available points during the process of exploring and inquiring about the problems. Use at least three points, or your favorite group of points; order and sequence of tapping is not important—just tapping is. At once you have the relaxation of meridian stimulation, and the possibility of addressing difficult issues without overreacting. More important, Dr. David Lake (see Chapter 39) and I have found that when a complex issue or belief is identified, the processing of the associated negative and excessive emotion continues after the tapping session, sometimes for many days.

A habit of regular daily tapping, from a few minutes daily to up to one hour can also lead to more of the "generalizing effect" of EFT. This type of tapping involves simply tapping on the points without any requirement to focus on a problem or issue. We also recommend tapping for "first aid" while the problem is present.

This simplification of using EFT (called Simple Energy Techniques, or SET) means that you are using only the tapping part of EFT, without worrying about the words. You are free to roam around the issue while it is being desensitized at the same time since tapping "works" only with the negative. (Many practitioners use tapping to install the positive after clearing the negative, but I do not believe that anything is installed, merely that the blocks to that belief are released.) Note that you can also add tapping to your preferred coaching or therapeutic strategies to enhance the results.

Tapping can help you overcome doubt and transcend negative perceptions and false connections caused by "current reality" and past failure experiences. Using tapping to help you through that doubt may be the greatest use you find for these techniques.

In general you are actually tapping on the manifestations of:

- Problems
- Blocks
- Barriers

There is always a part of you that objects to a goal, often because there is an immediate conflict with a preferred value. It might also be true that you don't—and can't—*feel successful* at present. You might have objections to getting started, to getting into business in general, to becoming the sort of person you think is associated with success. You might not like setting goals or anything about that. You might feel inadequate, unable, incapable or just plain undeserving. Or you might have a negative emotional association with the process of becoming successful.

In the next section are specific techniques you can use with tapping to overcome these negativities. It is often more personally productive to work with a coach, and it is unlikely that you will uncover all your unconscious blocks in a single tapping session, either by yourself or with a coach. Typically, a good coach is also a peak performer and is action oriented. Ideally, the work is with both the levels of energetic issues and the task/action ones. This is a holistic approach.

I define real success as inner satisfaction and achievement of your values through real action and results in the world.

## The Steps to Becoming a Peak Performer

Over the past 15 years I have researched, refined, and modified a teaching process that is designed to help entrepreneurs and people in business achieve peak performance. It has seven steps:

Step 1. Decide to Be a Peak Performer
Step 2. Break Through the Barriers
Step 3. Clarify Your Values
Step 4. Set Inspiring Goals
Step 5. Build Commitment
Step 6. Engage in Organized Planning
Step 7. Take Action and Persist

Tapping can assist at each step since there is inbuilt resistance and negativity throughout. In this chapter, given the confines of length, I concentrate on steps 1–3. They are the most important.

## Step 1. Decide to Be a Peak Performer: Decide What Success Is to You and Decide to Make It Happen.

All the true peak performers I have met decided to be there. Even though many used different approaches to get there, they all at some point decided that was what they were going to do. Peak performance begins with the decision to do or create something. In business, this means creating a vision of success, deciding to create a peak performing business, deciding what that will look like and deciding to make it real.

In their book *Built to Last,* Collins and Porras (2002) looked at success habits of visionary companies and found that they are committed to core values and enduring purpose. Though their operating practices and business strategies may change over time, their core values don't. In looking at even very large businesses, the importance of an inspiring original vision to enduring success becomes clear.

At the point of creating a vision, at that very moment you set out to create it, you will experience resistance. This takes the form of doubts, fears, and worrying objections. Tapping can be very helpful in dealing with these negative emotions. Because a belief is an emotional attachment to an idea, it is natural that your negative beliefs will rise up when you set yourself a big goal.

## Step 2. Break Through the Barriers

This step is about breaking through mental-emotional barriers to peak performance. Many of the blocks and barriers to success are unconscious on the part of the business owner, CEO, and others in the business. They are typically based on negative emotional associations to the achievement of the goal itself or to the process of getting there.

One of the best ways to identify the unconscious blocking beliefs is to identify goals for change. At that time the blocks will come to the surface in the form of objections, resistance, and emotional distress, which is stirred into action. This then becomes potent material for tapping.

The minute you set a goal to change something, there will be resistance. At the personal level, the goal will trigger all your unconscious blocking beliefs and objections. Then you also have to deal with the triggered reactions of others, who will try to influence you—usually triggered by their own fears.

At the business level, when you decide to change something, there may be resistance triggered by the fact that people fear the change—usually a result of a conflict of basic values, often, for example, involving security. Most of these barriers are related to fears such as fear of failure, fear of success, fear of self-promotion, and so on.

*Question: What are the things in your job that cause you the greatest challenges, and what is the biggest problem they cause you?*

The reality is that the greatest problem those problem people, events, or things cause you is, ultimately, how they make you *feel*. Emotions are typically what underlie all internal resistance and the resistance of people within businesses to take action. People are strongly influenced by how they feel and whether they perceive that certain actions, certain goals, certain directions, and certain changes will lead them to feel good or feel bad. Obviously, if they feel bad or expect that they will feel bad as a result of change, there is conflict at once.

This is where tapping comes into its own: helping the processing of negative emotion triggered by negative beliefs.

Tapping on **goals** and **objections to goals.** Here are four strategies that are very productive for individuals.

(i) Treating negative beliefs

Ask: *What prevents you from having that (vision, goal, success) right now?*

This brings up the person's blocking beliefs and issues immediately. Then apply tapping and monitor the path of his or her reactions.

Example: One business owner who was initially embarrassed mentioned that he had a goal of building $40 million in personal wealth through his business. I asked him to imagine having that money. He was not able to visualize it clearly and felt "blocked off" from it. I then had him do a few minutes of tapping on his objections and then tap while holding the intention to connect with the feeling. He excitedly exclaimed that he could really feel and believe that he could have this, and went away excited to put his plans into action.

(ii) Detaching from the effects of the emotional "push-pull"

Individuals are often conflicted—part of them is pulling emotionally one way and part of them is pulling another way.

The best approach is:

- Identify the pros and cons of each course of action.
- Tap while focusing on the aspects of each in turn.

This can lead to greater clarity about the direction forward, or trigger the creative search for additional win-win alternatives. Presumably, the mechanism involves a reduction in the felt intensity from the internal struggle of beliefs.

(iii) Taking action

The major difference between people who are successful and those who are unsuccessful is the actions they take. Those who are successful are able to get themselves to take action, despite any fear and negative associations. This is where tapping can help, by working directly on the fear or the "disliking" of the action.

Use tapping to:

- Treat your "objections" and ambivalence to taking action.
- Treat your desire for inaction or alternate action.
- Treat yourself for feeling bad when you are not taking action, or for procrastinating.
- Treat yourself for your fear of taking the wrong action (perfectionism).

(iv) Getting into an expansive, free-flowing mental-emotional state

I believe we need to be expansive in the initial stages of thinking about goals, thinking without limits. I am most interested in getting to the big goals that people have been harboring inside but holding back on. I want them to get into that *free-flowing state* where they can explore new realms and generate new possibilities. When most of us try to do this, our current reality interferes. We tend to see the future only through the present, and even if we do see advancement, we tend to do so in an additive fashion rather than seeing our true potential for exponential growth. So the perfect time to tap is during the early stages of goal setting. This allows us to access more free-flowing and expansive states by settling down our conscious judging mind and its associated negative emotional states.

**Tapping in a group or larger business.** Two things are required for peak performance: (1) collective action; and (2) alignment with a common goal, vision, or purpose. All peak performance could be said to depend on aligning with important goals. In larger business, that alignment includes many people. In a business involving just one person, the issue of *internal alignment* is crucial. This also applies to the key leaders in any business— business owner and CEO being the most important.

Tapping can be used strategically with individuals to deal with emotional blocks to "seeing" success; this facilitates goal setting of the best kind. Some people are reluctant to take the actions essential for success, for example, making sales calls, doing presentations to get business, inspiring employees and others to act, and confronting problem behavior and poor performance.

Helping an organization to rebalance is a similar process. There is often a push-pull going on between those who want to go in one direction and those who want to go in another direction, between those who are championing corporate changes and those who are resisting them.

Tapping can help align the two camps if they are willing to participate. It is inherently relaxing and reduces the tension of emotional confrontation. At the simplest level, tapping can be used to deal with fear, which is the number one factor holding most people back from achieving their goals and performing at their peak.

## Step 3. Clarify Your Values

Values are particular types of beliefs that are crucial to all goal achievement. At their core, they are our beliefs about what is *most important* to feel and experience. As such, they represent our strongest emotional drivers, and are crucial to all of our decisions. If you are unclear about your goals and your values, you need to access these and find a way to:

- Clarify what each really is
- Connect with each
- Align with your highest values

The fascinating process of how to clarify your values is beyond the scope of an overview. In essence, it starts with finding your most important values and then humbly putting them through the process of reality testing. For example, you may feel that connection is your number-one value, but if you actually spend most of your time on the road, year after year, then that value cannot be at the top in the real world. Likewise, if you fancy yourself as a risk-taker and entrepreneur but cannot ever act because you fear losing money, then security might just be your number-one value (or near the top of the list)!

Using tapping while ordering such a list is essential to avoid the paralysis of logical impossibilities. All values are important, but some are more important than others. Finding one's true high values is defining for one's identity. This is a core part of my work with individuals and businesses.

## The Process of "Connecting with Success"

One of the key strategies of goal achievement for many high achievers is to be able to see and feel themselves from the position of having achieved their goal. Tapping can help you do this by removing the barriers to accessing this feeling. Spending some time each day imagining having already achieved your goal, while tapping continually can be very productive indeed. Of course, you can also conduct more specifically targeted EFT sequences focused on the specific objections that come up for you when you attempt to connect with the success feeling. As you do this process daily, however, you will find that your success visualizations become more and more real to you, until the achievement of the goal is not only possible, it is also inevitable.

Connecting with Success is a simple process in which you form the intention to connect with the feeling you will have when you have achieved your goal—when you are successful—and use tapping to assist you in creating a stronger, more meaningful connection. As you do this, your energy and motivation to achieve your goal, your "vibration," as it is often called, will increase. Connecting to your goals in this way draws you toward them energetically and emotionally, and it could be argued, draws them toward you as well! This process can also be used to help you connect with wellness when dealing with physical issues or illness, to bring the feeling and energy of being well into your mind-body.

The basic process of Connecting with Success is: (1) Define what success is to you; (2) step into success; (3) keep going; and (4) ignore objections for now (treat them separately).

1. **Define what success is to you.** Think about what it will be like when you have achieved your goal.
2. **Step into success.** Think of that success in the future that you are seeking, then "step into it" (if you visualize, you can "step into the image" in your mind) and allow yourself to feel how it will feel. Keep tapping while holding the intention to connect with the success feelings.
3. **Keep going.** As you persist with this process, you will likely find it easier and easier to connect with the success feelings, as the negative associations and feelings are naturally desensitized by tapping.
4. **Ignore objections for now (treat them separately).** When doing this process for the first time, you will almost certainly find that negative objections arise in your mind and tension arises in your body. These objections and tensions will likely aim to distract you from your intention to connect with success. Although it can work to focus in on those objections and tensions and apply tapping to them, I highly recommend separating that kind of "remedial work" into a separate tapping session. So in most cases, it is best if you continue tapping while maintaining the intention to connect with the real feelings of success, *despite your negative objections.* Typically, the continued tapping will ultimately settle down the intense thoughts and feelings, allowing you to connect progressively with the real feelings of success.

## Tapping Protocols for the Corporate Sector

The principles for applying EFT and tapping generally to enhance peak performance in business are largely the same as building peak performance in any area, with some specific additional aspects for business. Work with the business owner or key managers and help them clarify their vision and values and goals. Use tapping to help them break through the emotional barriers to achieving it, and use it to connect with success.

I believe that managing negative emotions is the essential business skill for the new millennium. This is what I say to corporate leaders. The biggest stopping factor for business owners is their own belief system: their limiting ways of thinking about what is possible for them and their business. And what holds those negative beliefs in place are emotions (which tapping can release).

*Key individuals in a business have a significant impact on results.*

I consider that using tapping can confer a considerable advantage on corporations and businesses in the following ways:

**Stress management.** When the potential for excessive stress can be eliminated by a simple technique, then the incidence of stress-related accidents and illnesses must decline. As well, imagine a workplace with a higher degree of emotional harmony.

**Emotional resilience.** Emotions influence people and drive behavior, and management of emotions has never been more needed than in today's turbulent times of economic uncertainty. Learning to manage your own emotions is one of the most powerful ways to influence the emotions of your clients and customers. Employees who can influence people's emotions positively are highly valued, as are managers and leaders who can inspire people with enthusiasm. Consider the effects of grumpy, upset staff in terms of their interactions with customers. What if people were able to deal with these emotional reactions as they occurred, modify their response to emotional triggers, clear the negative effects of talking with an angry customer, and negotiate such situations from a position of calm?

**Improving productivity.** How many salespeople and managers are being held back by fear, indecision, and the procrastination and "call reluctance" they cause? How many decisions are not being made because the person who has the authority to make the decision is fearful of change, fearful of the consequences of failure, or even fearful of success? Potentially, tapping can facilitate the removal of much of the effects of these fears from the workplace. Staff would not be reluctant to make phone calls, conduct presentations, or confront issues if they all felt more comfortable in dealing with problems, changes, and adopting new technologies.

**Clear corporate vision.** Many managers and CEOs who drive the future vision and set the direction of the company are also working hard to avoid emotional pain. Fear of failure often drives lack of clarity, inertia, and slow or no decision-making on their part. If they overcame the emotional tension associated with their role in getting things to happen (or their fear about what might happen), everything would be different.

## Tapping Appears Weird, But It Really Helps

It is important to keep in mind that tapping "as is" is too "way out" for the average corporate manager to accept so you must give a great deal of consideration to pacing. Pacing means fitting it in with their belief systems and their views of the world—*and* their view of what is important and useful. It does not matter how good tapping is; it's their perceptions that are important. Even those managers who do accept tapping because they have been to a workshop often need help in structuring proposals so that others in the organization will be prepared to accept it. The key is not to emphasize the technique, but instead focus on the results that the technique can achieve. And that requires you to fit tapping into a program that focuses on solving problems and achieving goals that are important to those to whom you are introducing it.

I have typically integrated tapping into a presentation on stress relief, conflict resolution, and/or change management, or alternatively, and most frequently, within a peak performance program. These are the sorts of things that corporate people can identify with because issues of stress, conflict, and resistance to change are perennial challenges in the workplace, and motivation and enhancing performance are also important to them. So this is often where we need to start.

When marketing tapping to corporations, we need to focus on what we can do for them in terms of solving their problems, rather than focusing on telling them about the technique, at least initially. If you are not able to discuss the impact your work will ultimately have on improving productivity, boosting profits, or bottom-line results, then in my experience you will be shown the door (or not even allowed to enter it in the first place).

Unless you can do the following, you will never be able to apply tapping in the corporate sector! You must be able to:

- "Get a foot in the door" initially
- Structure a proposal

- Meet key people
- Work in the world of business
- Gain rapport within the corporate system
- Focus on results that are important to them
- Know how to apply the techniques of tapping with people on real issues
- Leverage your results
- Get paid what you are worth

There are many different models of delivery: individual coaching, group programs, corporate training, and consulting. The main issue is to work with the people who can make the most difference. These are the "influencers," decision makers, business owners, CEOs, and managers. Pace their understanding and adapt your approach to them. Working with these people and helping them change will cascade that change through the organization. Here is the approach that I have found will have greatest leverage: (1) Work first on vision, values, goals; then (2) deal with the emotional issues preventing them from moving forward.

1. **Work first on vision, values, and goals.** Apply tapping to objections and blocking beliefs, as in the individual work. Have them visualize succeeding, stepping into the image and feeling how that will feel. Then help them to realize this vision by translating it to goals and strategies and using tapping to treat anything that is aiding resistance. This resistance is both personal and also applies to their employees.
2. **Deal with the emotional issues preventing them from moving forward.** Typically, these include: presentation fears, fear of confronting people, financial fears and worries, and dealing with the "people issues" of conflict, resistance to change, and lack of emotional intelligence.

Most work is on breaking through blocking beliefs. I have found over years that many key people in corporations are very cognitive, which means they are used to focusing on concepts rather than emotions. They are often low on emotional intelligence and have low levels of emotional self-awareness. Therefore starting with emotions as a focus can be confronting. Consider simple methods of tapping here, emphasize scientific facts, and start with negative thoughts rather than feelings. I also typically start with problems and challenges and move toward goals.

My experience tells me that I must focus on results that have meaning to the person.

In order to get a corporation to succeed, you need to get everyone aligned with a goal. The challenge truly is getting people to align with one common vision and do the things necessary to achieve that goal.

My own corporate approach requires me to:

1. Gain rapport and empathize with current situation.
2. Focus on the problems, needs, and goals.
3. Present myself and my techniques (including tapping) as a possible solution.
4. Start small and build.

I like when possible to work mostly with key people (individual coaching work) and also to set up group programs. In groups, you can teach tapping for general stress relief then build from there, or introduce peak performance concepts. I often introduce tapping on less emotionally challenging issues and "get some runs on the board." Then I apply tapping on deeper issues, working individually where necessary.

## Practical Coaching Examples
### Individual

I once worked with a business owner who was faced with having to take the lead role in his business due to his partner becoming pregnant. I started by asking about his challenges and then sought to identify the negative beliefs and barriers to him being able to be successful. I'm particularly interested in identity beliefs. In this man's case, he had negative beliefs about not being "smart enough" and not being "strong enough" to manage and lead the business on his own. I taught him the tapping and we began to apply it to these beliefs and the emotions they provoked. I asked him to identify how true these beliefs felt to him, as well as the emotions they triggered. Then after a few rounds of tapping on each belief I checked to see how true they felt. Within just a few minutes of tapping, the beliefs started to feel less true to him and he was much calmer.

Next I asked him to identify the opposite beliefs, which were quite simply "I am strong enough" and "I am smart enough," and we did some tapping on those statements. Then we tapped interchangeably on both the negative and positive belief statements. This is important because both sides can feel "true" and "not true" to the person, and spending too much time on one side stirs up the other. Tapping on both sides of the continuum releases the attachment to the entire belief concept. Alternatively, trying to make one side win sets up a resistance to acknowledging the inner emotional "truth" of the other side, and leaves the person stuck with an emotional attachment to a constricting self-concept. It can be just as constricting to have to continually prove that you "are smart enough" as it is to believe you are "not smart enough."

Tapping interchangeably on both positive and negative sides ultimately frees up a lot of energy that can be used for goal achievement, as it did in this man's case. I then sought to identify significant emotional events in which he'd learned to evaluate himself in terms of smartness and strength, and we applied tapping to those emotional experiences using the Movie Technique. Each time we did this, it freed up a lot of energy. We then moved into some heavy-duty goal setting and I was able to ask him about his "ultimate" goals for his business and his life. This is typical of my approach: starting with the problems, freeing up some energy, and *then* moving to goals. Moving to goals too quickly can be a trap with such individuals, and hamper progress. The key is always to start from where the person *is*. When energy is freed up, the person tends to set bigger, more inspiring, and more congruent goals.

With this gentleman, we worked through a values clarification and goal-setting process. If goals do not relate to high values, there will be no energy and power for their achievement, so we tested his goals against his important values to ensure alignment and congruency. Once we were clear that his goals would take him and his family to where they really wanted to be, I then worked on helping him access and build commitment to those goals. He identified some big, exciting goals for the business, and we applied tapping to the resistance and objections to achieving them. In this case, apart from a little remaining self-doubt, he had a lot of fear of the unknown. After applying tapping to this fear, it was replaced by excitement, resolve, and confidence in his abilities. Not only was he able to take the helm of his business with ease, his newfound focus and confidence led him to create an ambitious plan for expansion that resulted in the creation of several new centers and a period of massive growth for the business.

## Corporate Example 1

A CEO of an engineering firm contacted us because he wanted to train his senior management team in presentation skills. This was just after the global financial crisis and the company had decided that they wanted all senior managers to assume responsibility for internal training in their respective areas as a cost-saving measure. They also desperately needed to build new business and wanted to learn how to conduct more effective presentations to potential clients in order to secure the work.

We designed a program that incorporated training in presentation skills and included tapping as a tool for overcoming presentation fears and allowing the presenters to focus on their audience's needs and objectives. I also followed up with some individual tapping sessions with key managers to address their specific aspects.

The tapping was warmly embraced by many of the senior managers, including the CEO and the COO (chief operating officer) who had previously been quite anxious over their presentations, both internal to employees and external to potential customers. Each manager was videotaped doing a presentation before and after the training and the before-and-after results were profound. Many of the managers reported great success in using the tapping to overcome their presentation fears and all were able to transition to conducting successful internal and external presentations.

The scope of the program was expanded to include some consulting regarding overall direction of the company, and included some individual tapping coaching programs with key executives including the CEO and COO on their goals within the company as well as life goals.

Shortly after this, the COO secured a multimillion dollar contract through a successful client-focused presentation, the results of which he attributed to the combination of tapping and basic instruction on how to design an effective presentation. This contract safeguarded the future of the company and allowed them to come through a difficult financial period with a positive balance sheet.

## Corporate Example 2

I introduced tapping to one organization as part of a training series a colleague and I were conducting for a government department. The main aim of the program was to develop a positive customer-focused culture within a department that had previously focused on enforcement with a very authoritarian approach. We worked with about 75 participants in four groups of 15–20 participants, which included managers, supervisors, and employees. Two members of the senior management also participated, which was one factor contributing to the success of the program.

We were able to identify quickly that many employees were very anxious about restructuring within the department, which had been threatened for several years. In addition, their working environment typically involved interaction with people who usually did not want to be there, and often involved verbal abuse and resistance from their "customers."

We designed a five-module training in change management and incorporated tapping in one of the modules focused on stress management. I presented tapping as one of several approaches they could use to reduce stress. It has been my experience that when tapping is presented in this way rather than as the only approach, people are more readily able to accept it. In this introductory session, I simply introduced them to the tapping and demonstrated how to apply it to general emotional issues and stress.

The response to the initial sessions was so positive that the management, several of whom were participants in the program, requested a separate tapping session be conducted focusing on specific work-related issues. This of course was my aim. I should point out that a key to getting this second round of training approved was that the most senior manager had experienced personally the benefits of tapping from the initial sessions. This was particularly important because the programs were conducted at a time when the department was at a real crisis point and there had been several instances of conflict between employees and their depot supervisors and managers over work timetables and shifts.

In these follow-up sessions, I had the employees identify all of the work situations that were causing them emotional stress, and then we systematically applied tapping to their emotional reactions to those situations. We focused interchangeably on issues shared by the group and then focused on individual reactions that were intense and specific to certain employees.

For example, one employee, who had started out threatening physical harm to his supervisor because of a shift dispute, left expressing willingness to approach him and talk it through calmly, which he subsequently did. He was astounded at how well the discussion went, and all the issues regarding his timetable were resolved amicably. This sort of result was typical.

The level of frustration and anger when these groups of employees began to list their challenges was replaced with calmness, focus, and openness by the end of each of the 4-hour tapping sessions. They took this back to the workplace and were able to come through a very difficult period for that department with flying colors. The senior manager was excited to report improvements in all areas of service delivery and significant improvements in customer service ratings. He was particularly impressed at the shifts in attitude, which enabled the department to confront the challenges they faced and "sail through" them, and were reflected in a newfound positivity across the entire section. This department became a "poster child" for positive change management, and led to further change management work for us in several other sections in the department. A large part of that fantastic result was due to tapping on the specific emotional issues affecting people in their daily work.

## Conclusion

Corporations all over the world are desperately in need of the results that tapping can effect in reducing work-related stress claims, dealing with conflict, battling internal resistance, overcoming anxiety and confidence challenges, and myriad other issues currently preventing businesses and their employees from achieving their highest potential. When energy is freed up from the emotional resistances that are currently blocking progress, the way will be open for individuals and the businesses within which they operate to achieve their peak performance.

## References

Cialdini, R. (2008). *Influence: Science and practice.* London, UK: Pearson.

Collins, J. & Porras, J. I. (2002). *Built to last.* New York, NY: Harper.

Ericcson, K. A. (Ed.). (1996). *The road to excellence: The acquisition of expert performance in the arts and sciences, sports and games.* Mahwah, NJ: Lawrence Erlbaum Associates.

Ericcson, K. A., Krampe, R. T., & Tesch-Römer, C. (1993). The role of deliberate practice in the acquisition of expert performance. *Psychological Review, 100*(3), 363–406.

Gladwell, M. (2008). *Outliers: The story of success.* New York, NY: Little, Brown.

Hill, N. (1960) Think and grow rich (Rev. ed.). Greenwich, CT: Fawcett Publications.

Loehr, J. & Schwartz, T. (2003). *The power of full engagement.* New York, NY: Free Press.

# Chapter 56
# The Nature and Treatment of Impediments of EFT
*Robert Pasahow*

## Abstract

Emotional Freedom Techniques (EFT) is an effective psychotherapy for psychological problems and symptoms. There are, however, impediments that limit the efficacy of EFT. Neurological disorganization causes disturbances in thought processes, learning, and behavior. Neurological disorganization is quickly remedied by a procedure called "collarbone breathing." This is a procedure that includes a five-step respiration pattern while stimulating the collarbone meridian (Kidney 27) point and the Gamut point. Psychological reversal is a different impediment; it prevents natural healing and is usually accompanied by self-defeating behaviors and negative attitudes and mood states. Psychological reversals limit otherwise effective treatments. The successful treatment of a psychological reversal is confirmed when the correction for that reversal is completed and the very treatment that did not work a moment before now has the therapeutic effect. This chapter specifies treatments for different types of Psychological Reversals and explains the purpose of the Setup phase. It also explores the impediment of energy toxins, which are substances that cause an imbalance in the energy system precluding or limiting the effectiveness of EFT. A neutralization technique from the Thought Field Therapy's algorithm treatment model to neutralize energy toxins is described, along with how it can be applied in EFT. The treatment procedures for these impediments can be easily incorporated into EFT's Basic Recipe. An EFT psychotherapy session is most effective when it can treat the important aspects of a problem and bring the SUD level of each aspect and the original problem to 0. This is maximized when the treatments for the impediments are included. Increasing the efficacy of EFT will increase the probability that future research can demonstrate that this treatment is safer, more expedient, and comprehensive in its therapeutic results in comparison to traditional psychotherapies.

**Keywords:** impediment, neurological disorganization, collarbone breathing, psychological reversal, energy toxins, Thought Field Therapy, TFT

**Robert Pasahow, PhD**, is a clinical psychologist who has published numerous articles in the peer-reviewed journal *Energy Psychology: Theory, Research, and Treatment*. He is on the research committee for the Association of Comprehensive Energy Psychology and the Thought Field Therapy Foundation. Send correspondence to Robert Pasahow, 600 New Road, Northfield, NJ 08225, or affiliates600@aol.com.

An impediment to Emotional Freedom Techniques (EFT) is an energetic force or substance that precludes or obstructs this therapeutic modality from being optimally effective. Such factors limit the effectiveness of EFT by an estimated 20% (Craig, 2008/2011). Psychotherapists previously trained in other therapeutic models such as psychoanalysis and cognitive behavior therapy hypothesize that these impediments contribute to the slowness and limited effectiveness of these traditional forms of psychotherapy (Callahan, 1985; Callahan & Callahan, 1996; Diepold, Britt, & Bender, 2004; Gallo, 2000; Feinstein, Craig, & Eden, 2004; Mollon, 2008). This chapter is written with the assumption that the therapist has or is going through an EFT certification program, attended workshops, and has obtained clinical training and supervision in psychotherapy and EFT. This chapter is about difficulties caused by impediments and the treatments to eliminate their effect.

## Neurological Disorganization

Neurological disorganization leads to disturbances in thought processes, learning, and behavior. Examples of neurological disorganization affecting thinking and behavior include: verbalizing words in a sentence in the wrong order, impaired information processing, deterioration in concentration and memory, sense of being in a fog or fuzziness, contribution to learning disabilities, confused behavior (i.e., putting silverware in the microwave and food in the dishwasher), sense of equilibrium being off, and clumsiness.

## The Fight-Flight Response as a Cause and Effect of Neurological Disorganization

A pattern of easily and frequently becoming angry, nervous, and sad can contribute to and/ or be a consequence of neurological disorganization. Frequent fight-flight experiences cause a vulnerability to chronic anxiety and susceptibility to panic attacks. Such reactions start with a conscious or unconscious misperception of danger leading to the release of adrenaline and stress-related chemicals that activate the sympathetic autonomic nervous system to engender preparation for intense protective physical action. The fight-flight response evolved from prehistoric times to protect against frequent and pervasive danger, as when a caveman was suddenly faced with a dangerous animal, which could also be a source of food for his family. In the response, the adaptive nervous system releases chemicals that cause bodily changes optimizing survival. Very quickly, pupils dilate, increasing visual acuity (which, in the example of the caveman, enabled him to perceive the potential danger of the animal and decide whether to kill or take flight). Blood is pumped from the heart for greater strength, respiration changes enable greater endurance for long fights or flights, blood vessels constrict to minimize bleeding, and perspiration prevents overheating. The defensive and adaptive responses contributed to survival and have been evolved into our current autonomic nervous system.

Although necessary to respond to potential danger during prehistoric times, most fight-flight responses in current society are false alarms when there is, in fact, no danger. Being late for a meeting and being stuck in a traffic jam or seeing a police car suddenly come up behind you with flashing lights on certainly does not constitute a threat to survival. However, rapid heartbeat, breathlessness, and perspiration are experienced as anxiety or, worse yet, as a panic attack. A pattern of such reactions causes a susceptibility to neurological disorganization, resulting in neurophysiological changes in the limbic system that interfere with optimal judgment, reasoning, planning, and information processing. A self-perpetuating cycle occurs between shifting into neurological disorganization and the distressful consequences of the fight-flight response.

## Neuropsychological Disorganization, Applied Kinesiology, and Energy Psychology

Roger Callahan, PhD, is credited with being the father and pioneer of energy psychology (Gallo, 2000). He developed Thought Field Therapy (TFT; Callahan, 1985), which was based on incorporating acupressure point (acupoint) stimulation as a psychotherapeutic intervention to facilitate rapid, safe, and comprehensive improvement. Gary Craig was an early student of Callahan and the basic structure of an EFT psychotherapy session that Craig developed is based on Thought Field Therapy.

Callahan (1985) used applied kinesiology as a diagnostic procedure. As will be described later, this is a method to assess and confirm treatment effects related to neurological disorganization, psychological reversals, and energy toxins (Callahan & Callahan, 1996). Applied kinesiology is a method that assesses muscle strength under different health-related conditions (Callahan & Callahan, 1996; Diepold et al, 2004; Eden & Feinstein, 2008; Gallo, 2000). In applied kinesiology, the therapist applies a consistent amount of force to a specific muscle of the client (indicator muscle) while the client resists movement of this muscle with the same amount of strength at all times. The weakening of the indicator muscle, even though the client is given the same resistance, provides diagnostic information. Beardall (1995), Walther (1981), Goodheart (1987), and Eden and Feinstein (2008) have explained this diagnostic procedure as a biphasic process in which strength and energy are affected by different conditions and stimuli. Lin, Hsu, Chang, Chien, and Chang's (2008) review of 12 randomized control trials demonstrates the reliability and validity of applied kinesiology. Neurological disorganization interferes with the accuracy of applied kinesiology. Whereas differential strength is expected when comparing two responses, neurological disorganization can cause no such difference, precluding obtaining diagnostic information. For instance, the indicator muscle should be stronger when a person accurately says his or her name versus when lying about his or her name. This should also be true when the muscle is tested after saying "pure water" versus saying "poison." The presence of neurological disorganization can result, however, in the indicator muscle staying at the same strength no matter what the person verbalizes.

Walther (1981) attributed neurological disorganization to a dysfunction of the cranial sacral primary respiration mechanism. He hypothesized that neurological disorganization results from afferent receptors sending mixed information to the central nervous system, which limits the accuracy of applied kinesiology. Neurological disorganization can also be caused by chemical and nutritional imbalances. The concept of switching applies to neurological disorganization. When discussing switching, Gallo (1990) writes "Think of this as a DC current that travels from a positive to a

negative pole. In this respect, there are three areas in which polarity can be switched: left-to-right polarity, front-to-back polarity, and top-to-bottom polarity." Callahan found in some cases that distress decreased slowly or not at all, even though TFT was applied correctly. From his studies with Dr. John Diamond (1985), Callahan was aware that neurological disorganization can make applied kinesiology unreliable and cause TFT to be ineffective in reducing distress in the session and in symptom reduction. Even though applied kinesiology would be expected to find different strengths in the indicator muscle, none would be found. For example, true statements did not result in greater strength than false statements. For example, in polarity testing, greater strength is found when one's palm is directly over the head compared to the back of the hand, a phenomenon known as non-polarization. Neurological disorganization can result in not obtaining this effect. This also occurs when applied kinesiology reveals that a massive energetic reversal exist, providing evidence of the close relationship between the neurological disorganization and psychological reversals, an additional impediment to EFT that will be described later.

To test for the existence of neurological disorganization, Callahan had clients follow alternating and sequential steps. While doing applied kinesiology, two fingertips and then knuckles of the same hand were placed on the left and right collarbone treatment point (Kidney 27 [K-27]). This also occurred with the opposite hand and knuckle touching the two K-27 points. Neurological disorganization is diagnosed if the indicator muscle not touching the body tests weak while the fingertips or knuckles of the other hand are touching the collarbone acupoint.

Energy medicine tests for neurological disorganization by comparing muscle strength before and after walking forward (Eden & Feinstein, 2008). Greater strength in applied kinesiology is expected by walking forward. Neurological disorganization is revealed when the indicator muscle becomes weaker. Eden and Feinstein also found that healthy energetic states exist when there is a crossing of energy flow between the left and right side of the body. It is less expected that greater muscle strength will occur when looking at an *X* compared to parallel lines. Neurological disorganization causes the opposite effect in the indicator muscle.

*Energy Medicine* (Eden & Feinstein, 2008), *Psychoanalytic Energy Psychotherapy* (Mollon,

2008), and *Evolving Thought Field Therapy* (Diepold, Britt, & Bender, 2004) have proposed a number of methods to correct neurological disorganization. TFT and EFT, however, use a procedure that Callahan developed and labeled "collarbone breathing." There are eight sequential steps in collarbone breathing. Each of these eight steps follows this respiration pattern: (1) A normal breath in and out, (2) a deep breath in and hold for 5 seconds, (3) breathe halfway out and hold for 5 seconds, (4) a deep breath out and hold for 5 seconds, and (5) breathe in halfway and hold for 5 seconds. The fingertips and then the knuckles of one hand touch the collarbone meridian end point on both the left and right sides, providing for four tapping sequences. One then switches hands and repeats the same tapping and respiration pattern, making a total series of eight steps. Callahan would then use the applied kinesiology procedure described previously to ensure that collarbone breathing eliminated the neurological disorganization.

EFT implements collarbone breathing in the treatment session similarly to how it is done in TFT, but EFT does not use applied kinesiology to test for and confirm the effect of collarbone breathing. When distress is reduced at too slow a pace and is not due to the emergence of new aspect, collarbone breathing is administered. The client then thinks of the psychological problem and resumes the Basic Recipe. Therapeutic effects are expected to then occur unless other obstacles are present. One such obstacle can be a psychological reversal.

## Psychological Reversals

A review of energy psychotherapists indicate that they generally think of psychological reversal as an energetic force that is self-defeating and precludes one from reaching conscious goals (Callahan, 1985; Diepold et al., 2004; Gallo, 2000; Mollon, 2008). Callahan and Callahan (1996) wrote: "Psychological reversal is a state or condition that prevents natural healing... usually accompanied by negative attitudes and self-sabotage that leads to self-defeating behaviors. ... Psychological reversals are usually confined to a particular area of one's life, but may occur in any areas such as personal relationships, athletics, love, sex or health" (p. 221). Examples of psychological reversals include an obese person bingeing when trying to lose weight or a client consciously fighting a disease but taking the wrong medication. These actions are the opposite of their conscious wishes. It leads to self-castigation and makes others doubt the person's sincerity or commitment. Callahan observed this odd and incongruous behavior early on, especially with those trying to lose weight. For instance, an individual's indicator muscle will go weak when the person verbalizes, "I want to lose weight" versus "I want to gain weight." There is reversal of the amount of energy and strength such that the individual's conscious goal has less power and energy. Callahan originally tested clients' muscle strength when they were verbalizing positive and negative statements, such as "I want to be happy" versus "I want to be miserable." Clients need to be told before hand that their muscle strength is not a reflection of their conscious desire but of their unconscious energetic state. With psychological reversals, greater muscle strength occurs when the negative statement is verbalized. Thus, in this case, the weakening of the muscle with the verbalization "I want to be healthy" would represent what Callahan labeled as a "massive reversal" (Callahan & Callahan, 1996). Although their initial reaction may be to be upset, clients can now better understand that there is an underlying force that is interfering with improvement that is out of their conscious control.

In reference to treatment progress, Callahan & Callahan (1996) states that a psychological reversal "blocks otherwise effective treatment from working... The presence of psychological reversals is confirmed when the correction for the reversal is done and the very treatment that did not work a moment before now works" (p. 221). I contend, however, that the TFT literature has used the term "psychological reversal" too loosely. Consider the following: In some TFT sessions, applied kinesiology will not show differential strength when the client verbalizes, "I will be over this problem" versus "I will keep this problem." Thus there is no observable manifestation of a reversal, but the desired outcome that applied kinesiology will reveal greater strength when the client verbalizes the healthier statement does not occur. When this is combined with no change in the SUD (subjective units of distress) level, these two occurrences could best be described as a "psychological blockage" (Pasahow, 2013). Whether a psychological reversal or blockage, such an occurrence limited or precluded TFT from reducing SUD levels during the treatment session.

## Types of Reversals

Callahan originally focused on three psychological reversals and employed applied kinesiology to detect and treat their existence.

*Massive Reversal:* The client's indicator muscle is tested while he or she is verbalizing, "I want to be happy" versus "I want to be miserable." If the individual tests stronger on the negative statement, the treatment Callahan applied was for the person to tap the side of the hand and verbalize three times, "I deeply and profoundly accept myself, with all my problems and limitations."

*Specific Reversal:* "I want to be over this problem" versus "I want to keep this problem." If the individual tests stronger on the negative statement, the treatment Callahan applied was for the person to tap the side of the hand and verbalize three times, "I deeply and profoundly accept myself even though I have this problem."

*Reoccurring Reversal:* "I will be over this problem" versus "I will continue to have this problem." If the individual tests stronger on the negative statement, the treatment Callahan applied was for the person to tap the side of the hand and verbalize three times, "I deeply accept myself even if I never get over this problem."

When the SUD level reduced to about 60%, but additional treatment did not bring it to 0, Callahan attributed this to mini reversals. Thus a client might tap the side of the hand while verbalizing, "I deeply accept myself even though I still have some of this problem." In recent years, Callahan has indicated that these verbalizations are not needed. Tapping on the correct acupoints is sufficient to remove this hindrance to treatment (2008). However, Mollon (2008) and I have found that the reversals sometimes only correct when the affirmation is verbalized. Verbalizations can also be more closely related to the problem.

Gallo (1990), Diepold et al. (2004), and Mollon (2008) have identified additional reversals or belief-related blocks regarding the issues of safety, deservedness, and incorporate verbalizations. Although outside the current TFT protocol, a person suffering from problems with intimacy could treat this by tapping on the Karate Chop point of the hand and say, "I deeply accept myself even though I am scared of getting hurt." Deeper therapy work might reveal that such fearful expectations stem from early abandonment by the individual's mother. It might then be necessary to verbalize, "Even though my mother abandoned me, it does not mean that I am unlovable."

In reference to EFT, there are a number of important points to consider. The only reversal that EFT has addressed is TFT's specific reversal. EFT's treatment for a possible reversal is to use a Setup Statement in which the client first states the problem and then makes a self-accepting statement. An example of this would be: "Even though I am angry, I deeply and completely accept myself." Since EFT does not use applied kinesiology, there could not be any confirmation of the existence and elimination of a psychological reversal. This is important because therapists would not know if the Setup Statement failed to eliminate the obstacle to effective treatment. Though there is debate about the existence of psychological reversal, EFT still uses the Setup Statement, the goal being to acknowledge one's problem and to accept oneself in spite of having that problem. Although there has not been any formal survey about EFT therapists' and energy psychotherapists' beliefs about the existence of psychological reversals, their writings indicate that the vast majority believe it is a very powerful impediment and needs treatment in meridian-based energy psychotherapies. Research clearly has demonstrated that EFT is effective when including the Setup Statement, no matter how its effect is being interpreted.

## Energy Toxins

*The EFT Manual* advises practitioners that "if you have repeatedly tried EFT with little or no success and have exhausted or addressed all aspects of the issue and you have applied EFT to the specific events that may be underlying the problem, then a possible culprit is some form of energy toxin that is irritating your energy system and thus competing with these procedures" (Craig, 2011, p. 196). Thus, only after EFT has not had the desired effect and the therapist has exhaustively applied the treatment, including collarbone breathing, does one conclude that individual energy toxins have limited or precluded that EFT session from being effective. However, at such moments, there is a high probability that the time in a normal therapy session has been used up. Although the client may have been somewhat helped, bringing the SUD level down to 0 would have engendered greater therapeutic results.

The following list of toxins includes potential individual energy toxins. It is in no way exhaustive. The reader should keep in mind that each person has his or her own individual energy toxins. The list includes items that are used in everyday life and are therefore more commonly found to be individual energy toxins.

## Potential Energy Toxins

| | |
|---|---|
| Tobacco smoke | Makeup |
| Perfume | Cologne |
| Hairspray | Aftershave |
| Harsh laundry | Aerosol sprays |
| detergents | Dry-cleaned clothes |
| Alcohol | Grains (wheat, corn, soy) |
| Medications | Food coloring |
| Supplements | Artificial sweetener |
| Coffee | |

Energy toxins are different from allergens. Energy toxins are substances that have a deleterious effect and cause or intensify an imbalance in the bioenergy system and can interfere with progress in energy psychotherapies. In contrast, physicians label an allergen as a substance that the immune system misidentifies as foreign or deleterious to health but that may not cause such reactions in others. The immune system's reaction is essentially a false alarm because the object does not jeopardize one's health. Energy toxins do not necessarily cause allergic reactions.

Energy psychology clinicians recommend that clients avoid the substances on the potential energy toxins list (Craig, 2011; Gallo, 2008). If an energy toxin is impeding a treatment session, however, avoidance is often impossible. Even if the energy toxin is properly identified, it often cannot be readily removed. For instance, certain foods may have been eaten before the session. An individual may have showered that morning with highly scented shampoo and soap. The EFT therapist does not know in advance that an energy toxin will limit the effectiveness of a session. If the SUD level decreases very little and is not attributable to there being a new aspect to the issue at hand, this is an indication that an energy toxin may be interfering with the treatment. There could be one or a number of energy toxins interfering with the reduction of the SUD level.

One way to overcome an energy toxin in a session is to treat it within the Setup Statement. The following are examples of how this could be worded:

*"Even though this cologne makes me sneeze, I deeply and completely accept myself."*

*"Even though coffee interferes with my treatment, I deeply and completely accept myself."* However, there has not been any research to indicate that this step neutralizes an energy toxin.

Thought Field Therapy's algorithm treatment model provides an intervention that EFT therapists can use to minimize the obstructive effects of an energy toxin. As with EFT, the TFT algorithm treatment model does not use applied kinesiology. When the SUD level is not going down after treating psychological reversals and applying collarbone breathing, it is concluded that an energy toxin is interfering. The treatment for an individual energy toxin in the TFT algorithm model is to tap the inside of the index finger 15 times and then tap the side of the hand 15 times. This tapping sequence is interesting. Tapping on the index finger is the intervention to neutralize the individual energy toxin. With the energy toxin neutralized, the tapping of the side of the hand is to eliminate any possible psychological reversal that may be present; it can now be corrected since the energy toxin has been eliminated. It is also noteworthy that these tapping points are end points of the large and small intestine meridian pathways (Callahan, 1996; Eden and Feinstein, 2008). Thus an EFT therapist would have the client tap the inside of the fingernail of the index finger 15 times and then 15 times on the Karate Chop point when suspecting that an energy toxin is interfering with progress.

## Concluding Comments

When discussing impediments to treatment, the issue of optimal effects becomes relevant. Research has clearly demonstrated that EFT effectively decreases a number of psychological and physiological disorders (Craig, 2011; Feinstein, 2012). Why then be concerned about impediments? Improving the effects of any therapeutic modality is important.

Learning to treat impediments is consistent with the goal of improving the efficacy of EFT. Any EFT psychotherapy session is most effective if it can treat important aspects of a problem and reduce SUD levels related to these aspects down to 0. The brief interventions to quickly overcome neurological disorganization, psychological reversals, and energy toxins can easily be applied between rounds and when desensitizing different aspects of a problem, enabling more rapid collapsing of the table legs that hold up the table top of the psychological problem.

Research clearly demonstrates the efficacy of TFT and EFT (Feinstein, 2012). Many energy psychotherapists report that their therapies are safer, expedient, and more effective than traditional studies. There have not yet been any series of research studies comparing the efficacy of an energy psychotherapy to a conventional therapy model, such as cognitive behavior therapy. It should be noted that demonstrating that EFT has greater efficacy than established psychotherapies is not easy to demonstrate statistically. For instance, cognitive behavior therapy has been found to significantly reduce a number of anxious and depressed symptoms (Clark & Beck, 2010). Science requires that such experiments demonstrate that therapeutic effectiveness is greater than a control or placebo group. It is generally required that the results are 95% certain that these improvements are not due to chance or are random. Statistical tests would have to show a $p < .05$. To conclude that EFT is significantly more effective than cognitive behavior therapy, symptom reduction on any psychological test would have to be substantially greater in order to show an additional statistical effect at the $p < .05$ level. Thus EFT's therapeutic improvement would have to be at the $p < .0025$ level (.05 multiplied by .05), a result not easily obtained. This might only or more easily occur if these therapeutic procedures to overcome the impediments are utilized.

# References

Beardall, A. G. (1995). *Clinical kinesiology laboratory manual.* Portland, OR: Human Bio-Dynamics.

Callahan, R. J. (1985). *Five minute phobia cure.* Wilmington, DE: Enterprise Publishing.

Callahan, R. J. (2008). *Callahan Techniques Thought Field Therapy: Basic diagnostic training, Steps A & B.* Indio, CA: Callahan Techniques.

Callahan, R. J. & Callahan, J. (1996). *Thought Field Therapy (TFT) and trauma: Treatment and theory.* Indian Wells, CA: Thought Field Therapy Training Center.

Callahan, R. J. & Callahan, J. (2000). *Stop the nightmares of trauma.* Chapel Hill, NC: Professional Press.

Callahan, R. J. & Callahan, J. (2012). *Sensitivities, intolerances, individual energy toxins: How to identify and neutralize them with TFT.* Indio, CA: Callahan Techniques.

Clark, D. A. & Beck, A. T. (2010). *Cognitive therapy of anxiety disorders: Science and practice.* New York, NY: Guilford Press.

Craig, G. (2008/2011). *The EFT Manual.* Santa Rosa, CA: Energy Psychology Press.

Diamond, J. (1985). *Life energy.* St. Paul, MN: Paragon House.

Diepold, J. H., Britt, V., & Bender, S. S. (2004). *Evolving Thought Field Therapy: The clinician's handbook of diagnoses, treatment, and theory.* New York, NY: W. W. Norton.

Eden, D. & Feinstein, D. (2008). *Energy medicine.* New York, NY: Penguin.

Feinstein, D. (2012). Acupoint stimulation in treating psychological disorders: Evidence of efficacy. *Review of General Psychology, 16,* 364–380.

Feinstein, D., Craig, G., & Eden, D. (2004). *The promise of energy psychology.* London, UK: Penguin.

Fleming, T. (2011). About Tapas Fleming and TAT. Retrieved from http://www.tatlife.com/about

Gallo, F. (2000). *Energy diagnostic and treatment methods.* New York, NY: Norton.

Goodheart, G. J. (1987). *You'll be better.* Geneva, OH: Author.

Lin, H. T., Hsu, A. T., Chang, J. H., Chien, C. S., & Chang, G. L. (2008). Comparison of EMG activity between maximal manual muscle testing and cybex maximal isometric testing of the quadriceps femoris. *Journal of the Formosan Medical Association, 107*(2), 175–180. doi:10.1016/S0929-6646(08)60131-X

Mollon, P. (2008). *Psychoanalytic energy psychotherapy.* London, UK: Karnac Books.

Nims, L. (n.d.). Be Set Free Fast—BSFF. Retrieved from http://www.feelingfree.net/energy_psychology/bsff.htm

Pasahow, R. *Psychological freedom therapy: An integration of energy psychotherapies.* Manuscript in preparation.

Walther, D. S. (1981). *Applied kinesiology, Vol. 1: Basic procedures and muscle testing.* Pueblo, CO: Systems DC.

Wolpe, J. (1958). *Psychology by reciprocal inhibition.* Stanford, CA: Stanford University Press.

# Innovations in EFT

# Chapter 57
# EFT, Change, Forgiveness, and the Positive Pressure Point Techniques

*Philip H. Friedman*

## Abstract

This chapter first discusses ways to track clinical change empirically in order to establish a practice-based evidence approach to psychotherapy in general and EFT in particular. Various bar graphs are used to show marked changes over 5, 10, 15, and 20 sessions in distress levels (overall stress, depression, anxiety, anger, interpersonal sensitivity, and obsessing) as well as in well-being, flourishing, forgiveness, self-compassion, emotional stability, joy, happiness, positive affect, positive beliefs, and cognitive-affective balance. This assessment approach is shown to be cost effective and easy to administer, score, and track in a clinical practice. The chapter then demonstrates with pictures and words a variant of EFT called the Positive Pressure Point Techniques (PPPT) and discusses in some detail the first five levels of PPPT, troubleshooting, and the value of including powerful forgiveness approaches with PPPT. In reexamining the discovery statement of EFT and in particular the "disruption" in the flow of energy phrase, I found that the "disruptions" were generally caused by unforgiveness and/or judgments toward oneself, others, or life circumstances. Finally, I present three clinical cases to show how the five levels of PPPT work in real life.

**Keywords:** EFT, change, practice-based evidence, forgiveness, Positive Pressure Point Techniques, integrative, well-being

**Philip H. Friedman, PhD**, is a clinical psychologist and psychotherapist, director of the Foundation for Well-Being, assistant professor at Sophia University, and the author of two books, *Creating Well-Being* and *The Forgiveness Solution*, as well as the Friedman Assessment Scales and the Creating Well-Being and Forgiveness Solution audiotapes. Send correspondence to Philip Friedman, Foundation for Well-being, PO Box 627, Plymouth Meeting, PA 19462, or integrativehelp@aol.com.

# EFT, Change, and Practice-Based Evidence

This opening section will map out a method for measuring and tracking change in psychotherapy in general and EFT in particular. In order to know that change takes place during the clinical practice of psychotherapy, we need tools to assess our effectiveness. Evidence-based practice evaluates psychotherapeutic interventions using controlled, empirical studies of two or more treatment interventions. Practice-based evidence, on the other hand, permits clinicians to evaluate the success of their interventions in their own unique psychotherapeutic practice (Friedman, 1982a, 1982b, 2002, 2006, 2010).

The assessment tools used in the clinical study described in this chapter are: Friedman Well-Being Scale (1992) and three subscales (emotional stability, joviality, and happiness); Friedman Belief Scale (1993); Friedman Affect Scale (1998); Friedman Self-Worth Scale (1997b); Friedman Meaning Scale (1997a); Diener et al. Satisfaction with Life Scale (1985); Diener et al. Flourishing Scale (2010); short form of the Neff Self-Compassion Scale (Raes, 2011); Transgression-Related Interpersonal Motivations Scale, or TRIMS (McCullough, Fincham, & Tsang, 2003); Heartland Forgiveness Scale (Thomson et al., 2005), and the Hopkins Stress Symptom Checklist (Derogatis, Lipman, & Covi, 1973) and five subscales (depression, anxiety, anger, obsessive-compulsive, and interpersonal sensitivity). Each of these scales is short, easy to administer, and easy to score and track over time. They can be administered in the therapist's waiting room before the psychotherapy session and scored at the beginning of the therapy session. The scales can be given every session or at various intervals, such as every five sessions, to track client change. Generally, clients are asked to fill them out for the past week.

Although subjective units of distress (SUD) measures, first used by behavior therapists Joseph Wolpe, MD, and Arnold Lazarus, PhD, are useful in-session measures of change, the aforementioned scales are measures of between-sessions change and are much better to use for tracking change over time.

In this practice-based evidence study, all clients seen in an outpatient psychotherapy practice were administered all the scales at intake before the initial consultation session. Fifteen clients who had Hopkins Stress Symptom scores of at least 50 at intake were included in the study, that is, at session 1 (there were 15 clients at session 5, 14 clients at session 10, 12 clients at session 15, and 6 clients at session 20). There were nine males and six females with an average age of 33.4 (range 21 to 62) and an average individual income of $62,000. All clients experienced either EFT or an off shoot of EFT referred to as PPPT (Positive Pressure Point Techniques) as one of the major interventions.

Tables 1 and 2 show the changes in both the Total Hopkins Stress Symptoms score and the Total Negative Affect score over 5, 10, 15, and 20 sessions.

Previous research on the Hopkins Stress Symptom Inventory (HSSI) has indicated that an average client at intake has a score of 90 to 110 and an average population score is about 22. Table 1 indicates that at intake these 15 clients started with a HSSI total score of 109; by session 5 their HSSI total score was 35, and by session 10 it was 27, which was in the average range for the HSSI total score. On the Friedman Affect Scale, the negative affect (NA) total score (the sum of 25 items covering hostility, sadness, fear, guilt, and fatigue) was 52 at intake. It dropped to 22 by session 5, and 18 by session 10, which was in the normal range.

Tables 3 and 4 show that not only do the Total Stress Symptoms decrease substantially using the Hopkins Stress Symptom Checklist over the psychotherapy sessions, but there are also marked drops in the following five subscales; depression, interpersonal sensitivity, obsessive-compulsive symptoms, anxiety, and anger. This confirms that overall negative affect/distress is decreasing consistently over the course of the psychotherapy sessions across a range of distress subscales.

Table 5 shows changes over time in overall forgiveness using the Heartland Forgiveness Scale while Table 6 shows the changes in the three subscales of the Heartland Forgiveness Scale (Forgiveness of Self, Forgiveness of Others, and Forgiveness of Circumstances) over the course of the psychotherapy sessions. The bar graphs show substantial increases in all three subscales indicating that the clients were able to forgive themselves, forgive others, and forgive the circumstances in their lives over time using these short, easily administered and scored, self-report measures.

This also means that the 15 clients were able to let go of anger, guilt, and negative thoughts and

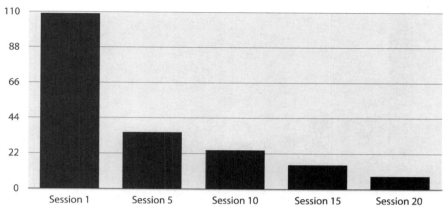

■ **Total Stress**

**Table 1.** *Changes in Total Stress Symptoms Over Time*

beliefs toward themselves, others, and their life situations more effectively over time.

The previous scales were general scales while the scale presented in Table 7 is specific toward one person. The McCullough TRIMS Scale (Unforgiveness Toward One Person) has 18 items and three subscales (avoidance, revenge, and benevolence) that refer to degrees of unforgiving feelings directed toward one person who previously hurt you. Table 7 shows that there are steady decreases in unforgiving feelings on the first two subscales combined (avoidance and revenge) over the course of the psychotherapy sessions.

Table 8 shows the changes that took place in three measures of happiness, well-being, and joy over time, using the Friedman Well-Being Scale.

A low score on these three measures is in the 40s and an average score is around 65. As you can see, on all three measures of happiness, well-being, and joy the 15 clients shifted from a low score at intake (in the 40s) to an average score in the mid 60s soon after session 5.

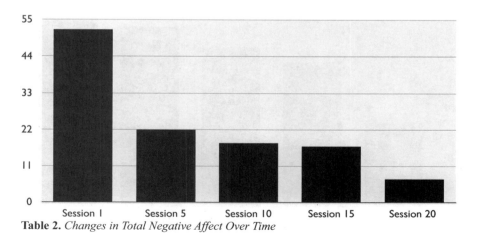

■ **Tot. Neg. Affect**

**Table 2.** *Changes in Total Negative Affect Over Time*

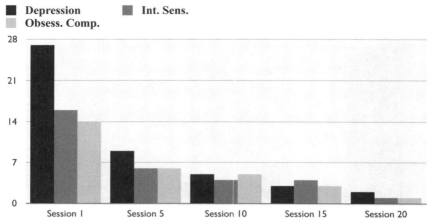

**Table 3.** *Changes in Depression, Interpersonal Sensitivity and Obsessing over*

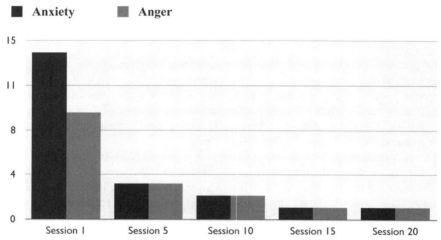

**Table 4.** *Changes in Anxiety and Anger Over Time*

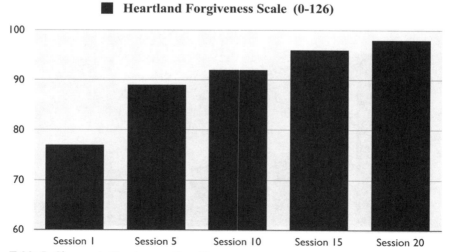

**Table 5.** *Changes in Forgiveness Over Time*

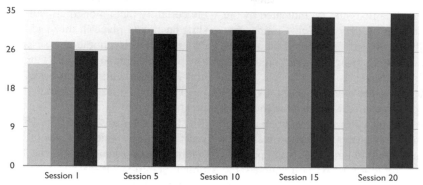

**Table 6.** *Changes in 3 Subscales of Forgiveness Over Time*

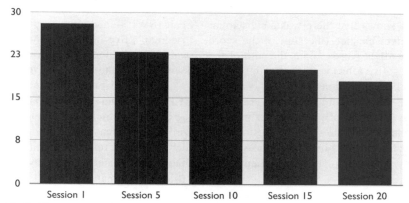

**Table 7.** *Changes in Unforgiveness Toward One Person Over Time*

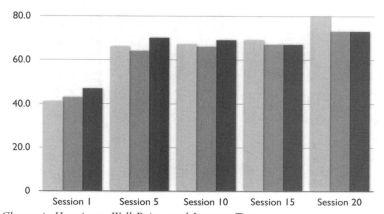

**Table 8.** *Change in Happiness, Well-Being, and Joy over Time*

Table 9 indicates that not only did clients show more forgiveness of self and others in the course of the psychotherapy sessions, they also showed more self-compassion, as indicated by the short form (12 items) of the Neff Self-Compassion Scale. In addition they demonstrated significant increases in flourishing using the short, eight-item Diener Flourishing Scale.

Table 10 shows the changes that took place in the total positive affect score and the total positive belief score using the Friedman Affect and Friedman Belief scales. On these measures a low score is around 40 and an average population score is in the low 60s. As you can see, the 15 clients in this study substantially increased their overall positive affect (a sum of joy, attention, love, peace, and self-assurance) and also increased their positive beliefs (a sum of 20 positive beliefs) over the course of the first five psychotherapy sessions.

Tables 11 shows that there was a substantial increase in affect balance (the sum of the score on 25 positive affect words minus the sum of the score on 25 negative affect words) over the course of the psychotherapy sessions.

There was also a significant increase in cognitive balance (the ratio of the score for positive beliefs over the ratio of the score for positive beliefs plus negative beliefs) over the course of the psychotherapy sessions for these 15 clients (see Table 12).

Because previous clinical research has shown very high correlations between affect balance and cognitive balance, it can be said with reasonable certainty that an energetic affective-cognitive shift has taken place in these 15 clients over the course of the psychotherapy sessions. Moreover, any psychotherapist using EFT or, for that matter, non-EFT interventions can easily use this tracking system to measure change in their clinical practice.

Table 13 shows that the 15 clients in this practice-based evidence study also showed substantial positive changes on the Friedman Emotional Stability subscale (10 questions) and the Friedman Self-Worth Scale (also 10 questions) over the psychotherapy sessions, indicating major increases in emotional stability and self-worth.

In addition the 15 clients showed marked improvement in satisfaction with life using the five-item Diener et al. Satisfaction with Life Scale (SWLS); meaning, purpose, and goals using Friedman's five-item scale (MPG); and gratitude using the six-item McCullough, Emmons, and Tsang GQ6 Gratitude Scale (see Table 14).

One could even make a case for renaming EFT (Emotional Freedom Techniques) EST or the Emotional Stability Techniques, as there is no well-known measure of emotional freedom and there are short, reliable emotional stability scales that easily measure change over time such as the 10-item Friedman Emotional Stability subscale.

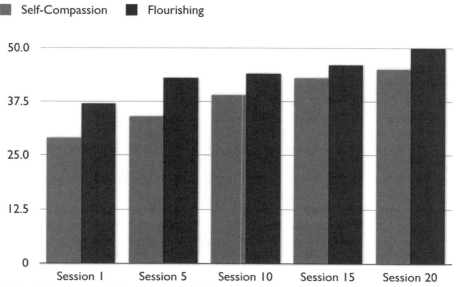

**Table 9.** *Change in Self-Compassion and Flourishing*

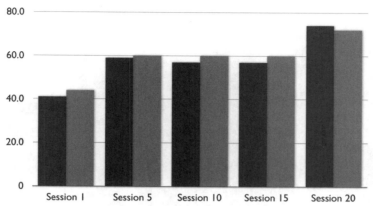

**Table 10.** *Change in Positive Affect and Positive Beliefs*

■ **Affect Balance**

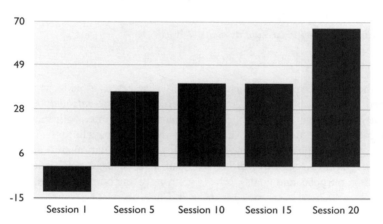

**Table 11.** *Changes in Affect Balance (Positive minus Negative Affect) Over Time*

■ Cognitive Balance Ratio

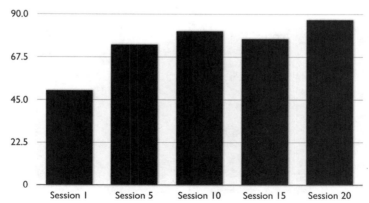

**Table 12.** *Change in Cognitive Balance (Positive Beliefs Divided by Positive and Negative Beliefs) Ratio*

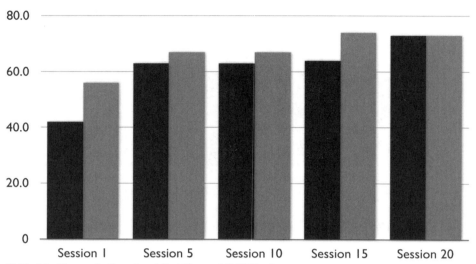

**Table 13.** *Change in Emotional Stability and Self-Worth*

In any case, these short, easily administered, and easily scored measures show that clients change significantly in positive affect and beliefs, well-being, life satisfaction, flourishing, happiness, forgiveness, self-compassion, self-worth, emotional stability, gratitude, cognitive-affective balance, and meaning, purpose, and goals.

I selected a wide variety of measures to demonstrate the various possibilities for tracking change over time, both increases and decreases, in important psychological variables. With couples, short relationship and marital measures can also be used. EFT and other clinicians are strongly encouraged to use these and similar

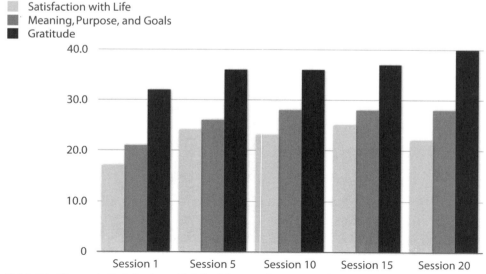

**Table 14.** *Change in Satisfaction with Life; Meaning, Purpose, and Goals; and Gratitude*

scales in their practice to track change over time and to establish for themselves effective practice-based evidence.

## Summary of EFT, Change, and Practice-Based Evidence

A wide variety of easily administered, scored, and recorded scales were used to measure change over time in a clinical psychotherapy sample of 15 clients. One of the major interventions used was either EFT or a spinoff of EFT called PPPT (Positive Pressure Point Techniques). These scales can be used effectively by any EFT or other clinician to provide both the client and the psychotherapist immediate access to tracking measures of change. These tracking measures serve collectively as practice-based evidence for the effectiveness of the psychotherapy such as EFT.

The scales can be administered at the beginning of the psychotherapy sessions and over the course of treatment at various intervals (session by session; every 5, 10, etc. sessions). All of the scales used in this study are either free or low cost to the clinician. I selected a wide variety of measures to demonstrate the various possibilities for tracking change over time, both increases and decreases, in important psychological variables.

## Five Levels of the Positive Pressure Point Techniques (PPPT)

I have developed my own integrated psychotherapy approach called Integrative Psychotherapy (Friedman, 1980, 1989, 2001, 2002) and an integrated evolved version of EFT called the Positive Pressure Point Techniques or PPPT (Friedman, 2006, 2010). These techniques are designed to facilitate well-being, happiness, quality of life, healing, forgiveness, gratitude, and peace and reduce emotional distress (Friedman, 1989, 2001, 2010; Friedman & Toussaint, 2006; Toussaint & Friedman, 2009; Piedmont & Friedman, 2011). The following information is adapted slightly from my recent book *The Forgiveness Solution* (Friedman, 2010) with permission of my publisher, Conari Press. PPPT is an offshoot or kissing cousin of EFT. The Pressure Points in the PPPT name refer to acupressure meridian pressure points. There are eight levels to PPPT. The first five are discussed in this chapter.

## Positive Pressure Point Techniques Level 1 (PPPT-L1): Use of Pressure Points and Tapping with No Affirmations

1. Select one area of emotional distress, such as anger, hurt, guilt, sadness, or fear that you experience when you think about the person, circumstance, or self that you are having a challenging time with. Rate it on a 10-point scale, with 10 being very distressed (i.e., experiencing a lot of anger, hurt, guilt, sadness, or fear) and 1 being not distressed at all. That number is your SUD (subjective units of distress) level. (Note: I don't include 0 on the SUD scale I use with clients. As long as the meaning attached is clear, 0 or 1 can be the no-distress rating.)

2. Briefly think about the particular form of emotional distress you are feeling. This is called attuning to the negative feelings. Do not dwell on it, however. Just briefly think about it.

3. Using the index and middle fingers of your right hand, rub continuously on the neurolymphatic point, also called the "sore point, or spot" because it often feels weaker or sorer than other points on the chest, while repeating the Psychological Uplifter (explanation follows). You will find the "sore point" on Diagram 1 and Figure 1. Within reasonable limits, the louder you say the Psychological Uplifter, the better. Find a quiet place to do this where you won't be disturbed. If it is impossible to say it out loud, say it to yourself.

## Psychological Uplifter

a) Repeat the following three times. *"Even though I have this problem or negative emotion* (name the emotion, e.g., fear, anxiety, hurt, anger, depression, sadness, frustration, guilt, shame, low self-esteem, or marital, family, relationship, or work problems, etc.), *I accept myself deeply and profoundly, and I am a good and magnificent person."*

b) Now, three times, while rubbing continuously on the sore point, say, *"I love and forgive myself unconditionally, despite my problems, limitations, and challenges."*

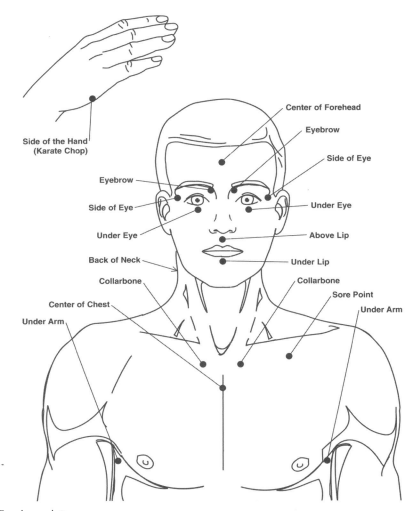

*Diagram 1.* Tapping points.

*Figure 1.* The "sore point."

c) Now, while rubbing on the sore point, say three times, *"I am entitled to miracles."* If at all possible, say this louder and with more conviction each time. Many people find it beneficial to write the Psychological Uplifter on a card, their cell phone, their computer, an organizer, or something else of their choosing and post it in various places at home, at work, etc.

4. With two fingers tap gently on the fleshy side of your other hand (see Figure 2). This is conventionally called the Karate Chop point because it is the place with which you would deliver a karate chop. Say the following phrases:

*Figure 2.* The Karate Chop point.

*Point 1.* Center of the forehead. Use one hand and two fingers.

*Anything is possible.*
*I am entitled to miracles.*
*Miracles are happening.*
*Miracles come from love.*
Repeat this step two times.

5. Using two fingers, continue tapping on the Karate Chop point (Figure 2) and say, *"I release this* (fill in the name of the emotional distress or limiting belief here, such as, anger, hurt, guilt, disappointment, judgment, grievance, attack thoughts) *and all of its roots and causes and all of its effects on me and everyone else in my life."* (Repeat two times.) Then say, *"Instead, I choose to feel calm, relaxed, at peace, and confident."* (Repeat two times.)

6. Again, reflect briefly on the one area of emotional distress, such as anger, hurt, guilt, sadness, or fear, you feel when you think of the person, circumstance, or self that you are having a challenging time forgiving. Again, rate it on a 10-point scale with 10 being very distressed (i.e., experiencing a lot of anger, hurt, guilt, sadness, or fear) and 1 being not distressed at all.

7. Attune to the emotional distress. Briefly think about the emotional distress, anger, hurt, guilt, sadness, disappointment, fear, etc. Do not dwell on it, however. Just think about it briefly.

Using two fingers of either hand, tap gently and consistently 15 to 20 times on each of the following eight pressure points.

*Point 2.* Inside corner of the eyebrows, just below the eyebrow. Using two fingers of both hands is preferable.

*Point 3.* Just outside the side of the eye. Using two fingers of both hands is preferable.

*Point 4.* Under the eye on the bony part of the eye in the center. Using two fingers of both hands is preferable.

*Point 5.* Above the lip. Using two fingers of one hand is preferable on this pressure point.

*Point 6.* Below the lip and above the chin. Using two fingers of one hand is preferable on this pressure point.

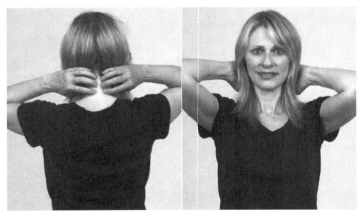

*Point 7.* Behind the neck. When tapping behind the neck, use all the fingers of both hands. Tap up, down, and all around 35 times on the back of the neck points, as this area is especially beneficial. Make sure when tapping on the back of the neck to go down the center, up, and around while covering all the muscles, arteries, and veins in the back of the neck.

*Point 8.* The collarbone-chest area. Using two or more fingers of both hands is preferable on these pressure points.

After tapping on the first four points, stop briefly and give yourself another SUD rating from 1 to 10. In most cases, the numbers will have dropped as many as 2 to 6 points, and very occasionally all the way to 1. After tapping on all eight pressure points, give yourself another SUD rating. In many cases, the SUD rating will have dropped to 1. If the SUD rating has not dropped to 1, repeat Level 1. If you are having difficulty, read the troubleshooting instructions at the end of PPPT Level 4.

See Figures 3 and 4 for typical pictures of before (distressed) and after (happy) doing PPPT.

*Figure 3.* Before PPPT.

*Figure 4.* After PPPT.

## Positive Pressure Point Techniques Level 2 (PPPT-L2): Pressure Points with Holding and Breathing with No Affirmations

Follow the instructions for the seven steps of PPPT Level 1.

8. Using two fingers of either hand, hold each pressure point while breathing in slowly through the nose and breathing out slowly through the mouth. Breathe in and out slowly through the nose and out through the mouth three times for each of these eight pressure points (the first six are the same as in Level 1).

    Point 1: Center of the forehead.
    Point 2: Inside corner of the eyebrows.
    Point 3: Just outside the side of the eye.
    Point 4: Under the eye on the bony part of the eye in the center.
    Point 5: Above the lip.
    Point 6: Below the lip and above the chin.
    Point 7: Behind the neck (new). Put one hand on the back of the neck and one hand on the forehead. Do the holding and breathing as usual.
    Point 8: The collarbone-chest area (same as level 1).

9. After holding and breathing on the first four pressure points, stop briefly and give yourself another SUD rating. In most cases, the numbers will have dropped as many as 2 to 6 points, and occasionally all the way to 1. After holding and breathing

on all eight points, give yourself another SUD rating. In many cases, the SUD rating will have dropped to 1. If the SUD rating has not dropped to 1, repeat Level 2 and retest yourself. If you are having difficulty, read the troubleshooting instructions at the end of PPPT Level 4.

## Positive Pressure Point Techniques Level 3 (PPPT-L3): Pressure Points with Tapping, Holding, and Breathing with No Affirmations

Level 3 of the Positive Pressure Point Techniques is identical to Levels 1 and 2 except that you alternate a round of tapping on the eight pressure points with a round of holding and breathing.

Start with the seven steps of PPPT-L1.

8. Using two fingers of either hand, tap gently and consistently 15 to 20 times on each of the eight pressure points. After you have tapped on the pressure point 15 to 20 times, again using two fingers of either hand, hold each pressure point while breathing in slowly through the nose and breathing out slowly through the mouth two times for each of the following eight pressure points.

   Point 1: Center of the forehead.
   Point 2: Inside corner of the eyebrows, just below the eyebrow.
   Point 3: Just outside the side of the eye.
   Point 4: Under the eye on the bony part of the eye in the center.
   Point 5: Above the lip.
   Point 6: Below the lip and above the chin.
   Point 7: Behind the neck. When tapping behind the neck, use all the fingers of both hands. Tap up, down, and all around 35 times on the back of the neck points, as this area is especially beneficial. Make sure when tapping on the back of the neck to go down the center, up, and around while covering all the muscles, arteries, and veins in the back of the neck. Then, when you hold and breathe, put one hand on the back of the neck and one hand on the forehead. Do the holding and breathing as usual.
   Point 8: The collarbone-chest area.

9. After both tapping, holding, and breathing on the first four pressure points, stop briefly and give yourself another SUD rating. In most cases, the numbers will have dropped from 2 to 6 points, and occasionally all the way to 1. After tapping and holding and breathing on all eight points, give yourself another SUD rating. In many cases, the SUD rating will have dropped to 1. If the SUD rating has not dropped to 1, repeat Level 3 of the Positive Pressure Point Techniques; that is, do the tapping, holding, and breathing again on all eight points, giving yourself a SUD ratings after four points and again after all eight points. In most cases the SUD level will have dropped to 1. If you are having difficulty, read the troubleshooting instructions at the end of PPPT Level 4.

I encourage you to practice Levels 1, 2, and 3 of the Positive Pressure Point Techniques 10 to 20 times a day, or as often as you can, for a few weeks before learning the next levels and experiment with using the method on all kinds of distress.

## Positive Pressure Point Techniques Level 4 (PPPT-L4): Pressure Points with Tapping, Holding, and Breathing with Affirmations

Level 4 of the Positive Pressure Point Techniques is identical to Level 3 except that you alternate a round of tapping on the eight pressure points with a round of holding and breathing and also add certain affirmations.

Start by doing the seven steps of the Positive Pressure Point Techniques Level 1. Then, using two fingers of either hand, tap gently and consistently 15 to 20 times on each the eight pressure points (same points as in Level 1).

8. When tapping on each pressure point, say the following generic affirmation formula two to three times (best to say it three times at first):

   *I release X, I want Y. I release X, I choose Y. I release X, I am Y.*

   More specifically, say:
   *"I release anger, I want to be at peace. I release anger, I choose to be at peace. I release anger, I am at peace";* or

*"I release guilt, I want to be at peace. I release guilt, I choose to be peace. I release guilt, I am at peace";* or

*"I release hurt, I want to be at peace. I release hurt, I choose to be at peace. I release hurt, I am at peace."*

This set of affirmations focuses on what you want to release, what you want to experience—empowerment (I choose) and acknowledgment/remembrance of one's true nature (peace). In general, it reinforces what you have been learning in other ways; that is, releasing darkness and choosing/acknowledging light. Sometimes it is also beneficial to add "I release X, I intend Y" and "I release X, I focus on Y" after you say, "I release X, I choose Y," where X is the anger, guilt, hurt, or other distressing emotion, and Y is "be at peace."

9. After you have done the tapping with the affirmations on each pressure point, I encourage you to practice the holding and breathing process two times on each pressure point, with the idea that you are breathing in peace on the in-breath and breathing out whatever distress you are attuned to on the out-breath. For example, you want to imagine that you are breathing in peace and breathing out anger or guilt or sadness or fear or hurt. Sometimes you may find it beneficial to use more than one word while doing the tapping. For example, you may want to say, "releasing anger, hurt, and disappointment," instead of releasing only anger. You may want to say, "I want" or "I choose to be calm, relaxed, and at peace" rather than "I want" or "I choose to be at peace." The main point is that you are reducing or releasing the negative distress and increasing or strengthening the positive feelings and attitudes.

You may find that you prefer either the tapping method or the hold and breathe method, and you may find after practicing them both that you prefer doing the Positive Pressure Point Techniques process with or without affirmations. Everyone is unique, and there is no right or wrong way to do it. I do, however, encourage you to try the different versions on all kinds of issues, both small and large, and to practice it frequently, such as 10 to 20 times a day. Practicing even a few times a day, however, can bring great relief for many people. It is often very beneficial to write the affirmations or the whole process on note cards, your computer, or PDA or in a journal.

## Troubleshooting

If you get stuck using any of the previous Positive Pressure Point Techniques, I have two recommendations. Most of the time it won't be necessary to use these, but if you do run into trouble, they can be very helpful.

1. Tap the Karate Chop point with two fingers of the other hand, tapping continuously while repeating: *"Even though I still have _____ (this problem; fill in the blank with anger, hurt, resentment, guilt, sadness, fear, anxiety, etc.), I accept myself deeply and profoundly and I am a good and magnificent person."* Do this three times and then return to whichever of the Positive Pressure Point Techniques you are using.

2. Access an earlier or deeper upset/feeling. In this approach, which I find is the most powerful, you close your eyes and look within until you find an earlier or deeper feeling inside you that you didn't notice before, one that was underneath the feeling you were working on. For example, suppose you were using PPPT to release hurt and the SUD number came down from 10 to 8, then 8 to 6, and then became stuck; that is, the number either didn't get any lower or moved very slowly from 6 to 5 and 5 to 4. Close your eyes and look inside. You might then discover that there were some strong angry feelings underneath the hurt feelings. Switch over to the angry feeling, give it a SUD number (for example, a 9 out of 10), and then do the Positive Pressure Point Techniques on angry feelings. When the SUD rating on the angry feelings has come down to 1, check back to see what the SUD number was on hurt feelings. Sometimes the SUD number on the hurt feelings will also have come down to 1 (the hurt will be gone). At other times, some of the hurt will still be there. At that point, give it a new SUD number from 1 to 10. Then do the Positive Pressure Point Techniques you are using for hurt feelings until it comes down to 1.

*Figure 5.* The under the arm point.

## Positive Pressure Point Techniques Level 5 (PPPT-L5): Use of Pressure Points with Tapping, Holding, and Breathing with Forgiveness Affirmations

In Level 5, we add forgiveness affirmations. After doing all the steps of Level 3, you then tap continuously about a hand's width beneath your armpit, first under the right arm and then under the left (Figure 5). Finally, you tap on the center of the chest (no figure). The forgiveness affirmations are used to further emphasize that forgiveness is a key to happiness, to strengthen your connection with the path of light, and to further connect you with your true identity.

### Forgiveness Affirmations

This group is used while tapping under the right arm:

> *I forgive myself for my contribution to this problem.*
> *I forgive myself, I am doing the best that I can.*
> *I forgive myself, I release all judgments against myself.*
> *I forgive myself, I release all grievances against myself.*
> *I forgive myself, I release all attack thoughts against myself.*
> *Forgiveness is the key to happiness.*

Then while tapping under the left arm, repeat these phrases:

> *I forgive _____ (use the person's name) for his/her (pick one) contribution to the problem.*
> *I forgive _____ (use the person's name). He/she is doing the best that he/she can.*
> *I forgive _____. I release all judgments against him/her.*
> *I forgive _____. I release all criticisms against him/her.*
> *I forgive _____. I release all attack thoughts against him/her.*
> *Forgiveness is the key to happiness.*

Now, while tapping in the center of the chest, repeat these phrases:

> *Forgiveness is the key to happiness.*
> *There is forgiveness in my heart for myself and for _____. (Use the person's name and say this twice.)*
> *There is love in my heart for myself and for _____ (Use the person's name and say this twice.)*
> *Deep down, I am the Presence of Love. (Say twice.)*
> *I thank God or the Universe (choose one) that I am at peace, and all my problems have been solved.*
> *I thank God or the Universe (choose one) that I am healed and at peace.*
> *I thank God or the Universe (choose one) that I am at peace and healed.*
> *I thank God or the Universe (choose one) that I am out of the darkness and experiencing light.*

Now put your hand on your heart and close your eyes. Then say silently and slowly to yourself:

> *I am grateful for all the experiences in my life in the last month, the last three months, the last six months, and the last year.* (Say three times and reflect on those experiences.)
> *I am at peace.* (Say two times slowly.)
> *I am calm, relaxed, and at peace.* (Say two times slowly.)

Take three more slow, deep breaths. Gradually, very gradually open your eyes and bring your consciousness back into the room. Give yourself a SUD number. If it isn't down to 1, repeat the PPPT Level 5 from the beginning.

## Forgiveness and the Positive Pressure Point Techniques

PPPT Level 5 introduced the powerful role of forgiveness in the healing process. In my book *The Forgiveness Solution* (2010), I elaborate on how forgiveness works and its catalytic influence on healing and change. There are many forgiveness processes and exercises other than PPPT presented in that book.

In *The Forgiveness Solution,* I define forgiveness as:

1. Releasing the negative emotions of anger, resentment, bitterness, indignation, hurt, irritation, and guilt toward not only others and circumstances but also oneself, God, and groups of people.
2. Giving up the beliefs that generate these emotions such as the grievances, judgments, "shoulds," and attack thoughts behind them.
3. Shifting one's perceptions toward the person or circumstance that triggered the unpleasant or negative feeling so that you learn to see things differently.
4. Choosing and deciding to forgive.
5. Developing positive or benevolent feelings and attitudes toward the person or circumstance that was previously perceived as hurtful, including oneself; these include feelings of compassion, kindness, warmth, and love.
6. Developing a sense of peace and contentment when thinking about the person or situation previously perceived as hurting or harming you.

7. Giving up the desire for retribution, punishment, or harm to another person.
8. Discovering that the events or circumstances that were perceived as harmful or hurtful were learning experiences that existed for the personal and spiritual growth of all the parties.
9. Discovering eventually at a deeper more profound level that the person you perceived as harming or hurting you is your savior.

## The EFT Discovery Statement and Unforgiveness

The EFT Discovery Statement is: "The cause of all negative emotion is a disruption in the body's energy system." However, the question arises: Where does the disruption comes from? In *A Course in Miracles* (1975), which strongly influenced my writing of *The Forgiveness Solution* (2010), it says there is only one core problem (a judgment, grievance, unforgiveness, condemnation) and one core solution, which is forgiveness.

So the disruption comes from a judgment, grievance, unforgiveness, condemnation toward ourselves, others, or circumstances.

In other words the disruption/blockage in the energetic flow of love comes from a judgment, grievance, unforgiveness, or condemnation (these are essentially the same). The energetic river of love then is blocked/disrupted by a judgment/unforgiveness, which dams the energy flow (of love, peace, joy, well-being, etc.) So look for the blockage/disruption by discovering where the judgment/unforgiveness is. Then tap it away or hold and breathe it away or use another process or exercise described in *The Forgiveness Solution* to release the blockage/disruption.

## New Case Examples
## Case 1: Anxiety Attacks

Carol was a 24-year-old college student who came to see me because she was having uncontrollable anxiety attacks. She used to be able to talk herself down from the anxiety, but could no longer do so. She couldn't concentrate on her school work and her grades were deteriorating. I taught Carol PPPT. She rated her SUD level for anxiety at a 9 and then attuned briefly to the anxiety. She repeated the Psychological Uplifter: *"Even though I have this anxiety, I accept* myself deeply and profoundly and I am a good and magnificent person. I love myself unconditionally despite my problems, challenges, and limitations. I am entitled to miracles." She said this three times while rubbing on the sore point. Then while tapping on the Karate Chop point, she said, *"Anything is possible. I am entitled to miracles. Miracles are happening. Miracles come from love"* (3 times) and then *"Releasing this anxiety and all the roots and causes (known and unknown) and all its effects on me and everyone else in my life. Instead I choose to feel calm, relaxed, and at peace"* (2 times).

After these steps Carol's SUD level came down to 7.

Then we did the PPPT Level 1 (tapping without affirmations) and her SUD level decreased from 7 to 3. Finally, using just a few pressure points with PPPT Level 2 (hold and breathe without affirmations), Carol's SUD level came down to 1. She practiced these PPPTs diligently between sessions in addition to reading *The Forgiveness Solution*. Carol reported that within 2 months she was able to control her anxiety and concentrate on her schoolwork. Moreover, within a very short time her grades had improved so much that she was getting all A's in her courses. She reported that the PPPT techniques, in addition to what she learned about forgiveness, helped her greatly improve her relationships with members of her family.

## Case 2: A Draining Life—Guilt and Fear about the Future

Robert, a 50-year-old interior designer and engineer, had owned and operated his own company with two employees for 20 years. With the lagging economy, financial stressors were mounting. In addition, his 89-year-old mother was no longer able to drive, shop, clean, or cook. Repeated visits to her home were draining him emotionally and financially. One day the stock market dropped markedly and he started to panic, out of intense fear. He was unable to cope, socialize, or focus on his work tasks. He could barely speak with his wife. He lost 25 pounds and felt like a zombie with his "life blood drained out of his body." A member of Robert's family who had previously seen me referred Robert to me.

After filling out a battery of questionnaires on stress, well-being, forgiveness, compassion, beliefs, affects, and flourishing, I taught Robert

PPPT, especially Levels 3 and 4, and assigned *The Forgiveness Solution* book and its exercises. Robert first chose to work on "guilt," for putting his mother in a nursing home. His SUD level was a 10. He attuned to guilt and practiced the Psychological Uplifter: *"Even though I have this guilt, I accept myself deeply and profoundly and I am a good and magnificent person. I love myself unconditionally despite my problems, challenges, and limitations and my guilt. I am entitled to miracles."* He said this three times while rubbing on the sore point. Then while tapping on the Karate Chop point, he said, *"Anything is possible. I am entitled to miracles. Miracles are happening. Miracles come from love"* (3 times) and then *"Releasing this guilt and all the roots and causes (known and unknown) and all its effects on me and everyone else in my life. Instead I choose to feel calm, relaxed, and at peace"* (2 times). His SUD level had decreased by that point to a 7.

We then did PPPT Level 3, using the tapping and holding and breathing on the eight main pressure points without affirmations. The first round through, without the affirmations, his SUD level on guilt decreased quickly to 4 and then to 1. Then Robert realized he had anger and resentment at his mother for making him feel guilty. His SUD level here was an 8 on anger/resentment. Using PPPT Level 4 with the affirmations, his anger/resentment dropped from an 8 to a 5 to a 2 to a 1. He started feeling much better after these early sessions.

In the next session we worked on his intense fear and dread about the future, especially regarding his financial situation—his ability to sustain his business and support two employees of many years. We used PPPT Level 4. After using the Psychological Uplifter, his SUD rating decreased just a little from 9 to 8. After the first four pressure points using tapping, holding, and breathing and affirmations, the SUD level only dropped to a 7. At that point, I moved into troubleshooting. I asked him to close his eyes, go within, and check for any other emotion he was feeling. Immediately, he said, "Sadness," and his eyes became moist. I asked him for a SUD number and he said 10.

We again did the Psychological Uplifter, using sadness as the emotion and his SUD level decreased from 10 to 7. Then we went through all the steps of PPPT Level 4 and his SUD level decreased quickly from 7 to 4, 4 to 2, and 2 to 1. When I asked him to return to the fear and dread, he said his SUD level was now 4. After using a few additional pressure points with PPPT Level 4, his SUD level on fear and dread dropped to 1.

Robert consistently practiced the PPPT exercises and some other affirmations he learned and liked from *The Forgiveness Solution* over the next few weeks between sessions. His despondency dissolved. His confidence came back. He found that he could cope with both his financial fears, his mother (who eventually died peacefully in the nursing home after a year), and his employees. His mood, attitude, and overall well-being improved dramatically from then on. In fact, he decided he wanted to teach part time at a university and within 4 months was able to arrange that, which brought him great enjoyment. His business survived, thanks to some wise decisions he made to develop new business ventures, and he didn't have to lay off either of his long-time employees. Even Robert's relationship with his wife improved, as his energy and enthusiasm for life returned and he started to flourish again. All his scores on the questionnaires showed dramatic improvements.

## Case 3: Out-of-Control Rage

Bill, a gym teacher in his early 30s, came in because he was experiencing a great deal of anger at his wife and three children. He had started to pound walls to keep himself from hitting someone. His wife was very concerned about him but threatened to leave if he didn't get some help. In addition, he sometimes got into verbal arguments with his supervisor at work and almost got into a fistfight with his older brother. Needless to say, Bill was angry, resentful, fearful, and guilty.

We worked mainly with PPPT Levels 4 and 5, though I introduced Bill to the first three levels to familiarize him with the method. At first we focused on his anger at his children, which was most evident. His SUD level was 8. He felt his kids were disrespectful to him and often didn't listen to him. We did the Psychological Uplifter on anger: *"Even though I have this anger, I accept myself deeply and profoundly and I am a good and magnificent person. I love myself unconditionally despite my problems, challenges and limitations and my anger. I am entitled to miracles."* He said this three times while rubbing on the sore point. Then while tapping on the Karate Chop point, he said, *"Anything is possible. I am entitled to miracles. Miracles are happening. Miracles come from love"* (3 times) and

then *"Releasing this anger and all the roots and causes (known and unknown) and all its effects on me and everyone else in my life. Instead I choose to feel calm, relaxed, and at peace"* (2 times).

His SUD level dropped to a 6. We then did the first four pressure points of PPPT Level 4 with the affirmations and his SUD level decreased to 3. When we did the last four pressure points, his SUD level decreased to 1.

Next we tackled his guilt over screaming at his kids and pounding walls. His SUD level here was 10. We used PPPT Level 5 with the forgiveness affirmations. First we did the Psychological Uplifter, using guilt as the key emotion. His SUD level dropped to 7 after doing this while rubbing on the sore point. So out of curiosity, I decided to switch directly to using the forgiveness affirmations while having him tap under his armpits (bypassing the eight main pressure points) to see what would happen. After briefly thinking about shouting at his kids, pounding the walls, and his guilt, he repeated the first set of forgiveness affirmations while tapping under his right arm:

> *I forgive myself for my contribution to this problem.*
> *I forgive myself, I am doing the best that I can.*
> *I forgive myself, I release all judgments against myself.*
> *I forgive myself, I release all grievances against myself.*
> *I forgive myself, I release all attack thoughts against myself.*
> *Forgiveness is the key to happiness.*

Then while tapping under the left arm, he repeated these phrases:

> *I forgive my kids for their contribution to this problem.*
> *I forgive them. They were doing the best that they could.*
> *I forgive them. I release all judgments against them.*
> *I forgive them. I release all criticisms against them.*
> *I forgive them. I release all attack thoughts against them.*
> *Forgiveness is the key to happiness.*

Then while tapping in the center of his chest, he repeated these phrases:

> *Forgiveness is the key to happiness.*

*There is forgiveness in my heart for myself and for my kids.* (2 times)

*There is love in my heart for myself and for my kids* (using their names and saying it 2 times).

*Deep down, I am the Presence of Love.* (2 times)

*Deep down, they are the Presence of Love.* (2 times)

*I thank God that I am at peace, and all my problems have been solved.*

*I thank God that I am healed and at peace.*

*I thank God that I am at peace and healed.*

*I thank God that I am out of the darkness and experiencing light.*

Now I had him put his hand on his heart and close his eyes. Then I had him say silently and slowly to himself:

*I am grateful for all the experiences in my life in the last month, the last three months, the last six months, and the last year.*

*I am at peace.* (2 times slowly)

*I am calm, relaxed, and at peace.* (2 times slowly)

He then took three more slow, deep breaths. Gradually, very gradually, he opened his eyes and brought his consciousness back into the room. He then gave himself a SUD level of 1.

Basically, we did the same PPPT procedures for his anger and guilt at his wife, where his SUD levels were 8 and 9, respectively. A few rounds of PPPT Levels 4 and 5 and his SUD levels were down to 1. However, some deep sadness surfaced around his wife when his SUD level dropped to 1. His SUD rating on sadness was 10. Working slowly and carefully using PPPT Levels 4 and 5, his SUD level on sadness came down from 10 to 8, 8 to 5, 5 to 2, and 2 to 1. Then he felt very relaxed and at peace.

Although a great deal of progress was made after dealing with his strong feelings toward his wife and kids, there was more to do. In particular his feelings toward his brother were even more powerful than his feelings toward his wife and kids. He felt continuously put down and disrespected by his oldest brother. He was clearly insecure around him and easily threatened. Once he almost came to blows with him and had to withdraw to prevent this. There were many childhood scenes with his

brother and family of origin that he felt hurt by. Anger, resentment, fear, shame, hurt, and guilt would surface, depending on the situation. After using PPPT Levels 4 and 5 plus some other exercises from *The Forgiveness Solution* over a period of 2–3 months, his high level of emotional distress with his brother and family diminished dramatically. He was able to talk calmly to his brother without anger or withdrawal.

Eventually, Bill's happiness and well-being improved so much that he consistently scored high on the well-being, happiness, flourishing, forgiveness, and self-compassion scales, with very low levels of emotional distress (anger, guilt, sadness, fear, anxiety). His wife was very pleased with the positive changes and he and his kids were getting along well. He was even asked to resolve difficulties at work between his supervisor and other teachers, and received compliments from his teaching colleagues for the marked change they saw in him. In particular, they said he was so much calmer and cooler now in general and when under pressure.

## Summary

In this chapter I have taken an integrative, multidimensional approach to "EFT, Change, Forgiveness, and the Positive Pressure Point Techniques (PPPT)." I have drawn from both Eastern and Western approaches to healing. I have used body-centered approaches and energy therapy (meridian-based acupressure points), attitudinal healing, and *A Course in Miracles* (forgiveness, positive attitudes, blessings, inner worth and inner light), cognitive therapy, and positive psychology (well-being, flourishing, gratitude, strengths, positive beliefs), the law of attraction (wants, choices, intentions, focus), humanistic psychology (the expansion of human potential, growth, openness, self-worth, empowerment), relationship therapy (healing conflicted relationships both current and past), emotion-focused therapy (awareness of, owning, taking responsibility for, and shifting emotions), spiritual psychology (mindfulness, awareness, self-compassion, peace, joy, inner goodness, compassion, love), and an empirical approach to assessment, tracking, and change first learned from behavior and multimodal therapists. This powerful and highly effective approach to healing and change still leaves room for further exploration, integration, and change itself. In particular, it leaves room for the current movement toward awakening and oneness in our lives, our relationships, and the world, which is the next great step for humankind.

# References

*A course in miracles*. (1975). Temecula, CA: Foundation for Inner Peace.

Derogatis, L. R., Lipman, R. S., & Covi, L. (1973). The SCL-90: An outpatient psychiatric rating scale. *Psychopharmacology Bulletin, 9,* 13–28.

Diener, E., Emmons, R. A., Larsen, R. J., & Griffin, S. (1985). Satisfaction with life scale. *Journal of Personality Assessment, 49,* 71–75.

Diener, E., Wirtz, D., Tov, W., Kim-Prieto, C., Choi, D., Oishi, S., & Biswas-Diener, R. (2010). New well-being measures: Short scales to assess flourishing and positive and negative feelings. *Social Indicators Research, 97,* 143–156. doi 10.1007/s11205-009-9493-y.

Friedman, P. (1980). Integrative psychotherapy. In R. Herink (Ed.), *The psychotherapy handbook*. New York, NY: New American Library.

Friedman, P. (1982a). Assessment tools and procedures in integrative psychotherapy. In A. Gurman (Ed.), *Questions and answers in the practice of family therapy*. New York, NY: Guilford Press.

Friedman, P. (1982b). An integrative approach to the assessment and outcome of psychotherapy. Paper presented at the NCCMHC Conference, New York.

Friedman, P. (1989). *Creating well-being: The healing path to love, peace, self-esteem, and happiness*. Saratoga, CA: R&E Publishers.

Friedman, P. (1992). *Friedman Well-Being Scale and professional manual*. Plymouth Meeting, PA: Foundation for Well-Being/Menlo Park, CA: Mind Garden.

Friedman, P. (1993). *Friedman Belief Scale and research manual*. Plymouth Meeting, PA: Foundation for Well-Being.

Friedman, P. (1997a). *Friedman Meaning Scale*. Plymouth Meeting, PA: Foundation for Well-Being.

Friedman, P. (1997b). *Friedman Self-Worth Scale*. Plymouth Meeting, PA: Foundation for Well-Being.

Friedman, P. (1998). *Friedman Affect Scale*. Plymouth Meeting, PA: Foundation for Well-Being.

Friedman, P. (2001). *Integrative healing manual*. Plymouth Meeting, PA: Foundation for Well-Being.

Friedman, P. (2002). Integrative energy and spiritual therapy. In F. Gallo (Ed.), *Energy psychology in psychotherapy: A comprehensive sourcebook* (pp. 198–s215). New York, NY: Norton.

Friedman, P. (2006). Pressure point therapy. In P. Mountrose & J. Mountrose, *The heart and soul of EFT and beyond*. Sacramento, CA: Holistic Communications.

Friedman, P. (2010). *The forgiveness solution: The whole-body Rx for finding true happiness, abundant love, and inner peace*. San Francisco, CA: Conari Press.

Friedman, P. & Toussaint, L. (2006a). The relationship between forgiveness, gratitude, distress, and well-being: An integrative review of the literature. *International Journal of Healing and Caring, 6*(2), 1–10.

———. (2006b). Changes in forgiveness, gratitude, stress, and well-being during psychotherapy: An integrative, evidence-based approach. *International Journal of Healing and Caring, 6*(2), 11–28.

McCullough, M. E., Fincham, F. D., & Tsang, J. (2003). Forgiveness, forbearance, and time: The temporal unfolding of transgression-related interpersonal motivations. *Journal of Personality and Social Psychology, 84,* 540–557.

Piedmont, R. & Friedman, P. (2011). Spirituality, religiosity and quality of life. In K. C. Land, A. C. Michalos, & M. J. Sirgy (Eds.), *Handbook of social indicators and quality-of-life research* (pp. 313–330). New York, NY: Springer.

Raes, F., Pommier, E., Neff, K. D., & Van Gucht, D. (2011). Construction and factorial validation of a short form of the Self-Compassion Scale. *Clinical Psychology and Psychotherapy, 18,* 250–255.

Thompson, L. Y., Snyder, C. R., Hoffman, L., Michael, S. T., Rasmussen, H. N., Billings, L.S., … & Robert, D. E. (2005). Dispositional forgiveness of self, others, and situations: The Heartland Forgiveness Scale. *Journal of Personality, 73,* 313–359.

Toussaint, L. & Friedman, P. (2009, December). Forgiveness, gratitude, and well-being: The mediating role of affect and beliefs. *Journal of Happiness Studies, 10*(6), 635–654. doi 10.1007/s10902-008-9111-8.

# Chapter 58
# Energy Frequencies Promote Optimal Health

*M. Marie Green*

### Abstract

Tapping therapies work well in combination with other modalities. These combinations essentially enhance results in the shortest amount of time. The modalities covered in this chapter are: chelated minerals nutrition to restore health and brain health; Transcendental Meditation; light frequencies found in the pRoshi, a specialized set of light goggles that deliver hundreds of frequencies to the brain to facilitate the brain's following response; Scenar and Cosmodic, frequency devices created by the Russians along the lines of a TENS machine, but 30 years further along in development, to increase brain coherence, relieve pain, spasms, headaches; and other natural remedies for conditions such as depression, anxiety, stress, headaches, backaches, restless legs, asthma, diabetes, chest pain, cerebral allergies, inflammation, and more. Eight essential steps bring EFT into the position of ushering in a return to robust health. The eight steps are: (1) maximizing rapport, (2) applied psychophysiology, (3) tapping traumas and each aspect within the trauma, (4) EFT as homework, (5) optimizing nutrition, (6) recognizing substance sensitivities and toxins, (7) teaching the benefits of meditation, and (8) reviewing self-help resources.

**Keywords:** meditation, microcurrent devices, lasers, nutrition, chelation, natural remedies

**M. Marie Green, DSW, LCSW, BCD**, is a clinical social worker, neurotherapist, and pioneer in energy psychology and complementary therapies. She is currently adjunct faculty in gerontology/social work at Weber State University in Utah, and has a private psychotherapy and pain management practice focusing on complementary approaches. Send correspondence to M. Marie Green, 1276 South Wall Avenue, Ogden, Utah 84404, or DrMMGreen@yahoo.com. www.GreenTherapyCounseling.com.

You are probably reading this chapter because you have experienced the miracles that come from EFT. The good news is that there are more. Combinations such as pRoshi and Scenar or Cosmodic along with nutritional corrections and elimination of toxins essentially enhance results in the shortest amount of time. This provides welcome relief to clients. Nutritional deficiencies, pain syndromes, and trauma can be quickly resolved with combination strategies. As an example, PTSD often takes months or years to resolve and yet, with combination approaches adding Scenar, chelated mineral nutrition, and the elimination of toxins, the resolution of layers of trauma can come in days or weeks.

## 8 Steps for Optimizing Client Health

The eight steps optimize client health through: (1) maximizing rapport, (2) applied psychophysiology (the use of pRoshi light goggles to calm the brain and Scenar or Cosmodic to help alleviate pain at the body level), (3) tapping traumas and each aspect within the trauma, (4) EFT as homework, (5) optimizing nutrition, (6) recognizing substance sensitivities and toxins, (7) teaching the benefits of meditation, and (8) reviewing self-help resources. Each step of the work deals with the brain, body, and emotions and, when applied in combination, facilitates a more robust improvement. Let's look at each one in detail.

## Step 1: Maximizing Rapport

The powerful first task is to listen carefully to the client's story and gather information on what in the story triggers symptoms. Listening is a vital component in establishing rapport.

The essentials of rapport are best explained with neuro-linguistic programming (NLP). Training in this specialty encourages you as the practitioner to match, pace, and lead. This means you match the client's tone, tempo, voice modulation, vernacular, and postures. Then you lead the client from what may be an unresourceful tone, tempo, content, or posture into a more resourceful state and this often includes reframing. Reframing is a method to help the client see some benefit in the experience rather than seeing only angst or difficulty. NLP training will enable you to understand eye accessing cues, language

patterns, submodalities, and communication strategies. The eye accessing cues are essentially watching the movement of the client's eyes. Looking up may indicate that the client is accessing visual memories, whereas looking down may indicate accessing states of emotion or feelings. Looking sideways toward the ears may indicate accessing auditory information or talking to oneself. This kind of information helps you more effectively understand how clients are processing their experience. For instance, you may not want to talk about feelings if the person is mainly processing experience through her own visual pictures of an event. Likewise, you would not want to talk about how things looked if the person is processing the experience in terms of feelings or sound. As you identify the client's preferred method of processing information, you will be more able to gain and maintain rapport effectively.

## Step 2: Applied Psychophysiology

Applied psychophysiology is a biofeedback process through which you can train a client to shift their body's processes into a better state. In addition to standard biofeedback, techniques in this field include neurofeedback and the use of the pRoshi, Scenar, and Cosmodic devices. These devices essentially do an automatic training of the body-brain interaction. The client does not have to do anything but have the instrument applied to his or her head or body. The devices then create a biofeedback loop and the brain entrains to the new information. This information causes the brain to do self-corrections. Training in psychophysiology is available through the Association for Applied Psychophysiology and Biofeedback, an international society for mind-body research, health care, and education (www.appb.org). Of the numerous interventions in this field, the ones that I have found easiest to implement are the Scenar/Cosmodic and pRoshi followed by training clients in what I call heart rate variability (HRV) breathing.

**The pRoshi device.** The pRoshi device (see Figure 1) was developed by Chuck Davis in Los Angeles, California, more than 20 years ago. He studied with several neurofeedback experts and arrived at an interesting conclusion. Why not give the whole brain a retraining rather than just two sites, which is common in regular

*Figure 1.* pRoshi light goggles.

neurofeedback? He looked at the brain maps of meditating monks who have wonderfully healthy brain waves after 40 plus years of meditating. He decided to train the brain to follow the frequencies that are visible in optimally healthy brains. He programmed the pRoshi light goggles to deliver over 2,040 frequencies to the brain via the flashing lights. The brain attends to those frequencies and self-corrects, which creates a mind that is at its optimal resting pace. The result is a feeling of calm and peacefulness.

Davis explains that the lights in the pRoshi glasses create what he calls an "LED and MagStim flicker." He continues: "This presents the brain with a complex set of phase instructions that it must accurately follow, in order to correct its own internal phase vector errors—true linear to non-linear transformation, in real-time. It is with this unique method that the brain performs its own neurofeedback duties, without any outside human intervention" (Davis, n.d.).

The brain is well equipped to self-correct. The pRoshi, sometimes referred to as Roshi, calms the brain to a peaceful state and enhances coherence or the ways different parts of the brain communicate with each other.

I tried for years to help my mother overcome chronic migraine, back and neck pain, and associated depression. I searched high and low for answers. Her pain was intractable. We visited every kind of healing practice and several pain clinics with poor results. It was an extremely discouraging process and, with each year of her aging process, the pain grew worse. Finally, she just needed higher level pain control and the only way to get pain control was through hospice care. She was put on hospice and within three months she died at age 80. Sadly, shortly after her death, I found the pRoshi and the Scenar (see later), which would have stopped her pain. I have clients wear the pRoshi light goggles for a few minutes to help them relax before I begin taking their history.

The device is very helpful during therapy and you can actually tap around the goggles to reduce traumatic stress while the lights in the pRoshi recalibrate aberrant brain waves and reduce or eliminate pain. I typically have people wear the goggles while they are tapping. The tapping helps reduce the emotional charge on the issue while the light goggles recalibrate the frequencies that are changing secondary to the tapping. It's an amazingly effective combination approach. This is extremely helpful for people with headaches or pain elsewhere. Blood perfusion in the brain is enhanced with the pRoshi and causes migraines to stop or greatly reduce in frequency and severity. The pRoshi has also been used to stop intractable seizures by improving perfusion and preventing the cascade into seizure.

Research indicates a link between brain EEG activity and the experience of pain. "Specifically, this research suggests that the subjective experience of pain is associated with relatively lower amplitudes of slower wave (delta, theta, and alpha) activity and relatively higher amplitudes of faster wave (beta) activity. Second, there has been a recent increase in interest in interventions that impact the cortical neuromodulation of pain, including behavioral treatments (such as self-hypnosis training and neurofeedback) and both invasive and noninvasive brain stimulation" (Jensen, Hakimian, Sherlin, & Fregni, 2008).

This is where EFT, pRoshi, and Scenar come in. The combination is astoundingly effective in the shortest amount of time with severe post-traumatic stress disorder and conditions such as depression, anxiety, stress, and pain. I continue to be amazed by the outcomes secondary to this combination. Currently, I treat a lot of Spanish-speaking victims of domestic violence who have suffered extreme beatings, rapes, and head injuries as well as the severe emotional trauma that accompanies such battery. Before EFT it would take weeks or months to get the clients relief using talk therapy alone. Now with EFT, TFT, BSFF, or other tapping protocols, relief occurs quickly.

When the pRoshi is added, the relief seems even better because it helps prevent retraumatization while working on the trauma, which is extremely important. With the EFT and pRoshi combination, many clients experience feeling much better after their first session than they have since the trauma occurred.

**Q1000 laser.** Using a soft laser light creates another interesting outcome. The soft laser, known as the Q1000 Laser (see Figure 2), transmits frequencies in the form of light and these can be very helpful in combination with EFT.

Janie had episodes when she was very depressed and inconsolable. She was in one of those states when she came in one day. She has a history of not tolerating any psychotropic medications, which has left her out of mainstream medication protocols. Essentially, laboratory studies validated that as part of a PMS picture, her serotonin drops off and she feels terrible. We placed the Q1000 Laser on her abdomen as we did EFT on several issues. Within 10 minutes, she felt the stress and depression reducing.

Certain light frequencies delivered by the Q1000 Laser stimulate the production of serotonin. The Scenar also has a protocol that stimulates the production of neuropeptides, which enhance overall calmness and stimulate healing. "Neuropeptides are small protein-like molecules (peptides) used by neurons to communicate with each other. Different neuropeptides are involved in a wide range of brain functions, including analgesia, reward, food intake, metabolism…" (Fricker, 2012, p. 11). Essentially, neuropeptides are messenger or signaling molecules that link to specific receptors. When people are stressed, there is an overactivation of the sympathetic nervous system. When they are calm, the parasympathetic nervous system is activated. What is needed is balance.

Most people who are stressed are out of balance. The neuropeptides work to send messages to the receptors to activate the balance, but this is often compromised by the person continuing to stress. The Q1000 Laser, Scenar, Cosmodic, and pRoshi all help to modulate this overactivation of the sympathetic nervous system. Neuropeptides are increased in production when these tools are applied and the system then has more resources to apply to balancing the sympathetic and parasympathetic nervous systems. Most of the clients you will likely see will have excessive stress and benefit greatly from these combination applications. Without them, the clients continue adding stress daily.

**Scenar and cosmodic devices.** The Scenars and Cosmodics (see Figures 3 and 4) are frequency devices, each of which is the size of a television remote control. The Scenar device is an advanced form of TENS (transcutaneous electrical nerve stimulation) unit that far outperforms the simpler TENS. The Scenar in comparison to TENS can be likened to a Learjet in comparison to a roller skate. There are a series of Scenar instruments that recalibrate the body's energy frequencies through the C fibers in the skin. Scenar devices work in a way similar to the pRoshi in that they cause the brain to do self-corrections on the body level. When homeostasis is regained, pain stops! This is a powerful approach indeed and is exceptional when it comes to alleviating myalgias and other physical pain, muscle spasms, anxiety, stress, headaches, and more.

The Scenar or the Cosmodic are applied to the body where there is pain or dysfunction. The instrument is placed on the area of pain (e.g., on the head or stomach in the case of headache or stomachache) and left there until it signals that it has "dosed." This means that it is finished

*Figure 2.* Q1000 Laser.

*Figure 3.* The Scenar device.

*Figure 4.* The Cosmodic device.

communicating and recalibrating the body to homeostasis, that is, to a more normal or pain-free state. The frequencies are interchanged between the body and the device and the device changes it frequencies automatically based on the reaction it induces in the body. This creates a constant biofeedback loop with changing information that accomplishes the recalibration of the body. These devices constantly change the form and power of their signals according to what is needed to achieve calibration as the body makes self-corrections. This constant changing of frequencies and power prevents the brain and body from accommodating to the signals and in turn pushes the body to increase production of neuropeptides—those essential elements that enable the body to heal itself and return to homeostasis.

The Scenar and Cosmodic devices are extremely helpful during therapy to assist in reducing stress in the client. When people have high stress, there is a point at which they are no longer able to relax normally and need help to regain that ability. Or they have so much stress that muscle spasms set in; these spasms are often in the upper back area and move up to the neck and head, causing headaches. The devices can be placed on the body and held into place with wraps or small beanbag weights while the EFT tapping protocols are completed. The combination amounts to bringing into awareness the issue that is stressful while at the same time using the tapping and frequency modulation devices to restore healing. Note that there are myriad cases in which only EFT or other tapping protocols work sufficiently. For highly complex and chronic issues, however, the extra frequencies from pRoshi, Scenar, or soft laser are extremely helpful in reducing symptoms and bringing relief in the shortest amount of time. EFT is the first-line choice for many issues because it is so quick and effective. When it does not reduce or eliminate the symptoms or

the symptoms return, one would typically try more rounds of EFT, TFT, BSFF, or other tapping protocols. One would also attend to issues of reversed polarity and toxic exposures, which create reversals, and treat these reversals related to symptom chronicity. When symptoms persist after treating the reversals, then is the time to move forward with the added frequencies.

Scenars and Cosmodic devices help reset the body's neurological signals that control pain. With the combination of the pRoshi and the Scenar, you can stop a headache in about 10 minutes. Most migraine sufferers have a severe magnesium deficiency that must be corrected with the *chelated* magnesium in order to obtain long-term relief. If they self-treat with another form of magnesium such as magnesium oxide or magnesium sulfate, they will usually get diarrhea before their stores of magnesium are replenished; this will sabotage the effort and results will not follow. The chelates do not precipitate diarrhea as profoundly as other forms and these chelates absorb quickly into the muscles where they are so desperately needed.

One day my elderly mentor, Lorraine, who was living in a nursing home called me and said, "Marie, will you come and treat Ricky? He is so depressed and needs the Roshi." Lorraine knew the power of the Roshi because we had used it on her several times and she was highly impressed. A psychologist and social worker, she had quite an adjustment to nursing home living, which brought on intermittent depression. Ricky had come to the nursing home at age 52 after having suffered a hemiplegic stroke. I used the pRoshi and Scenar in combination. I did not use EFT. I did use EFT on Lorraine, however, to treat the traumas associated with living in a nursing home, such as having several roommates die in the night and waking to an empty bed where the roommate had slept. EFT was very effective on the multiple aspects of this trauma and vicarious trauma for her. But her focus remained on helping others rather than focusing on her own difficulties and Ricky, she knew, was struggling and could be helped.

When we started, he could not walk but was in a wheelchair that he could not operate himself. He had been moved from the Veterans Hospital and placed at the nursing home for rehabilitation physical therapies. I worked on him three evenings a week for an hour each session. At the end of the fourth week, he met me at the door without any assistive equipment and with a huge smile on his face. I asked him to check with his physical therapist to see how long it would "normally" take to rehab from a stroke of this type. He checked and was told by his physical therapist that it would normally take about 18 months! Ricky walked out of the nursing home about a week later and back into a more normal life for a 52-year-old. We were both astounded.

Over the years I have treated many different conditions including some symptoms of Parkinson's disease, asthma, arthritis, knee pain, back and neck muscle spasms, migraines/ headaches, stomachaches, menstrual cramps, phantom pain, and peripheral neuropathy using EFT, pRoshi, chelated minerals (see Step 5), and Scenar as combination modalities. Each of these conditions was either resolved or improved substantially and the clients were delighted. The anxiety, depression, and insomnia that go with these conditions is often also reduced substantially. EFT helps them to help themselves and they love that ability to address symptoms.

One client, Jerry, came in for treatment of PTSD and addiction. He had tried to climb onto a moving train when he was drunk and fell under the train, amputating his leg above the knee and cutting off portions of his other foot. The physical wounds had healed, but he continued to suffer from the addiction, physical and emotional trauma, pain, and phantom pain. He was especially bothered by the phantom pain, so I applied the Scenar to his leg stump. His pain went down from 8 to 0 on a 10-point scale. During a second visit we treated the stump again and the pain again went from 4 to 0. Several weeks later he reported that he had no pain in this stump and was able to stop taking the gabapentin prescribed for his phantom pain. With the pain alleviated, we could much more easily go to work on treating his PTSD and addiction using EFT. I also referred him to a nutritionist to discuss balanced nutrition and correcting the alcohol-induced malnutrition. He began supplementing with chelated zinc to stop the cravings. This strategy is helping him as he goes through recovery this time, unlike his previous attempts.

Susan has Parkinson's disease accompanied by depression and anxiety. Intermittently, she gets severe constipation in which her abdomen swells up and she is unable to get relief. I did a home visit and used the Scenar on her abdomen. Within 20 minutes, she was able to clear the blockage that had stopped her up. As a nurse, Susan knows what works and how to apply cathartic remedies for constipation, but none of these had worked so she was delighted with the Scenar results. As a nurse, Susan knows too much about the course of Parkinson's and her anxiety was high, so I taught her EFT. She uses it often to lower her anxiety and restore peace.

Shanna had restless leg syndrome that kept her awake at night. When she came to me, the problem was severe. I used the Scenar to treat the top of the spine at C7 and the bottom of the spine. That was 3 years ago. She gets a recurrence of this restlessness about every few months and we treat it again and get her relief. It simply works. A local neurologist's research indicates that this condition is often precipitated by low iron. She knew she had a problem with low iron intermittently and began taking the *chelated iron*. She notes that when she has adequate stores of iron and a normal hemoglobin, she does not experience restless legs.

Shanna also has a condition called oculogyric crisis in which her eyes roll up into the upper plane of her eye orbits and she is unable to see in the normal plane of vision. We have used Cosmodic on this condition with good results, treating her around the eye orbits, and the pRoshi with the magstims over her eyes brings her quick relief. We treated her initially in 2004 when the oculogyric crisis would last 30 to 60 minutes and leave her with a terrible migraine headache. Now she has an event only when she has a high level stress or forgets to eat or lacks sleep. She is also on the chelated minerals to support her nerve conduction. Shanna has intermittent episodes of alopecia areata as well. She had seen a dermatologist who gave her a special ointment to apply to regrow hair. During the last episode, instead of the cream, we applied the Q1000 Laser light to the bald spot. The hair regrowth took only 2 weeks, whereas with the ointment it takes about 3 months to get the hair regrowing. We were both pleasantly surprised by this. Shanna simply has a high-stress job. She uses EFT often and has been an assistant as I taught classes in EFT and TFT, and these have been very useful to her in her work. She used to be painfully shy. After she assisted me in a training and went through the whole training herself, she was brave enough to walk up to famous country singer Mickey Gilley in the airport and request his autograph, something she wouldn't have attempted before. She laughs about it now but uses EFT frequently for stress and anxiety.

Molly is a dwarf who has had 19 back surgeries. She has chronic pain and difficulty sleeping. She comes in for Scenar and pRoshi treatments. The treatment takes her pain completely away and she falls sound asleep, which is an excellent outcome considering that she did not sleep well prior to treatment due to the pain. I taught her EFT to help her cope with difficult situations in her life and this has helped her too.

**Heart rate variability breathing.** Clients can be taught to improve their heart rate variability (HRV) through breathing. An increase in HRV increases heart and brain coherence. One becomes more peaceful and calm, overall health improves, and anxiety and stress are reduced. Karavidas and colleagues (2007) documented these HRV treatment benefits in subjects suffering from depression.

In HRV breathing, you teach clients to slow their breathing, which helps balance the sympathetic and parasympathetic nervous systems. When asking clients to slow their breathing, I usually ask them to breathe through their noses and not through their mouths. Many people who are mouth breathers have an aberrant $O_2$:$CO_2$ ratio, which by itself increases stress and anxiety. Mouth breathing raises $CO_2$ levels. This negatively impacts the autonomic nervous system and overactivates the sympathetic nervous system, which is the picture of hyper stress and the fight-or-flight response. I instruct my clients to do HRV breathing for 15 minutes twice a day.

To accomplish HRV breathing, inhale through the nose slowly to the count of 10 and then exhale through the nose slowly to the count of 10. Do this until a rhythm forms and relaxation ensues. This improves heart rate variability and over time improves health in a variety of parameters.

There is a simple instrument called the Em-Wave (available from the Institute of HeartMath, www.heartmathstore.com), a desktop version, and a newly released I-Phone application that provide visual images that help clients train their breathing and brain wave coherence.

## Step 3: Tapping Traumas and Each Aspect Within the Trauma

Take notes on your client's trauma and be sure to record all the red-flag elements (aspects) of the trauma. Then tap each red-flag element, proceeding through all the layers within each trauma in the story.

Tammy's husband beat her as he screamed at her in drunken rage and slugged her in the face. He grabbed her by her ponytail and flung her against the wall, then threw her to the floor and kicked her in the ribs. She kept thinking he would kill her and then he grabbed a pillow and started to suffocate her. As everything began to go black, she was beyond frightened. He finally relented, then left her and disappeared.

While listening to the story, it is important to note each piece of the trauma: (1) screaming obscenities, (2) slugged in the face, (3) thrown against the wall and floor, (4) kicked in the ribs, (5) fearing he would kill me, (6) suffocation and blacking out, and (7) betrayal. It is of *utmost importance that you as the therapist tap along with the client to avert vicarious trauma* in yourself. This will also keep you in a more resourceful state with lower anxiety and facilitate the therapeutic alliance. Often the issue of domestic violence and other relationship compromises has huge elements of betrayal that precipitate grief. The trust, relationship, and connection that were believed to be solid disappear. It is very important to treat betrayal as a specific issue.

I greatly appreciate the energy psychology technique Be Set Free Fast (BSFF) as a process for eliminating grief and trauma. Dr. Larry Nims' website (www.BeSetFreeFast.com) provides the details of how to do BSFF. It can be used when there are layers and layers of trauma to dispel the distress efficiently and effectively. I've found that the older BSFF process is most helpful with layers and layers of trauma.

## Step 4: EFT as Homework

This step involves teaching clients how to do the EFT protocol on their own so they can use it between sessions. It is most important that clients have an EFT handout to assist them when they feel stressed. We used a special handout while working with survivors of the World Trade Center destruction in 2001. It was a great help to the survivors. Most clients benefit from doing daily or several times daily EFT sessions on themselves. This helps reduce stress, fear, sadness, grief, trauma, and more. And the EFT process is additive, meaning that the more they do the tapping, the more calm and able to cope they feel. I usually assign clients to do EFT three times per day until our next session. They might do once a day with that kind of assignment. Some get to feeling so good that they begin teaching their family members how to do EFT and use it on their children and pets too because it is so easy and so effective.

## Step 5: Optimizing Nutrition

Many of us see clients who have very poor diets and rarely eat foods that contain sufficient minerals, or they eat foods or consume drinks that cause them to dump minerals. Many clients come in for high levels of stress, depression, anxiety, pain, and/or trauma. What a therapist must understand is some basic nutritional information. When a person has high stress, they dump their minerals and this sets up a cascade into ill health that is often misdiagnosed as mental illness. For instance, when a woman is highly stressed, she dumps magnesium and thus her serotonin gets depleted. She can replenish this by taking tryptophan, but if the root of the problem, high stress with attendant loss of magnesium, zinc, and other minerals, is not addressed, she will experience further deficiencies that cause further problems. With low magnesium, calcium is also altered and muscle spasms usually occur. These can be very painful, cause back and neck pain, and precipitate headaches. Due to the pain, sleep is often impaired, which further increases stress and sends one precipitously cascading into the depths of illness. It is a chain reaction that exacerbates when not corrected with chelated minerals. These problems are epidemic and easily correctible with highly bioavailable nutrients, and not so correctible with nonchelated minerals.

When this scenario of symptoms is presented to a conventionally trained health care provider, what follows is often a prescription of several drugs, which may include antidepressants, anxiolytic meds, pain medications, muscle relaxants, and even sleeping pills. If the patient has good insurance and sufficient income, these drugs become standard refills over time. Gradually, the person gets sicker and more dependent on these drugs. The drugs sedate the brain and the gut and this exacerbates illness. If you cannot process foods due to a sedated gut and mineral depletion, you begin craving because your physiology drives you to consume foods in hope that you will ingest necessary nutrients. Your cravings increase, and with some medications there is a health-destroying weight gain. Symptoms increase and with each new symptom comes a new drug. After a while, these drugs steal the person's health. Sometimes patients recognize that they need to withdraw from the drugs. When they try, however, their symptoms worsen and they realize that they have become addicted to or reliant on something they thought was not harmful because a physician prescribed it. Harm escalates with each dose!

In *Nutrient Power*, biochemical researcher William J. Walsh, PhD, describes the science behind diagnosing nutrient depletions and then restoring the deficiencies or balancing overload to restore mental health. This kind of science focuses on the ecology with greater precision. Dr. Walsh reports on his research that classifies, for example, six different types of depression related to nutrient deficiencies. When corrective targeted action is taken with nutrients, the client improves dramatically and can often be weaned off the drugs. Dr. Walsh explains:

> [N]utrient imbalances or toxic exposures can alter gene expression rates and may be the root cause of numerous psychiatric disorders. It's not a coincidence that methylation is a dominant factor in epigenetics, and methylation abnormalities are common in mental illnesses. Recent advances in the science of epigenetics provide a roadmap for nutrient therapies that have potential for overcoming mental disorders and eventual elimination of the need for psychiatric medications. (Walsh, 2012, pp. 724–727)

People with schizophrenia and other forms of mental illness often have excess copper. High levels of copper deplete dopamine, which decreases motivation. Excess copper also increases norepinephrine in the brain and, as Dr. Walsh reports, "Imbalances in these important neurotransmitters have been associated with paranoid schizophrenia, bipolar disorder, postpartum depression, ADHD, autism, and violent behavior" (Walsh, 2012, p. 725). Unfortunately, conventional psychiatry does not often address the issue of excess copper. The result can be a series of misdiagnoses followed by drugging rather than correcting nutritional aberrations.

Further, when there is high copper, there is often low zinc. When there is low zinc, the consequence is low levels of neurotransmitters. "In two separate animal studies, a diet that lowered blood copper levels by 75% had a massive effect on norepinephrine and dopamine levels in the brain" (Walsh, 2012, pp. 33–34).

I teach my clients about optimizing their nutrition and obtaining a nutritional consultation with a nutritionist trained in amino acid chelated mineral nutrition. Dr. Janeel Henderson, a nutritionist, is my teacher and a great resource. Here she describes the benefits of amino acid protein chelated nutrition:

When taking a multiple vitamin mineral supplement, if the following is part of the supplement formula you may end up in a *negative* nutritional balance in spite of your supplementation and eating the appearance of a healthy diet.

- Minerals that are in the form of mineral salts, citrates, gluconates, sulfates, carbonates, polynicotinates, and alpha-ketoglutarates are subject to ionization in the gastrointestinal system and not readily available for use by the body.
- Eating a diet high in fiber from fruit, cereals, breads, whole grains, and vegetables will latch onto ionized minerals to form complexes that are *nonabsorbable* in the body and can't be used.
- Dietary phosphates present in whole grains, milk, dairy, and cereal also block the absorption of all the ionized minerals.
- Phosphoric acid found in soft drinks, fizzy beverages, and fizzy water block absorption of ionized minerals.
- Antioxidants that contain high amounts of polyphenols from green tea, coffee, and herbs are attacked by the harsh ionized minerals, rendering them inactive and causing even more nonabsorbable mineral complexes.
- The bottom line is that in spite of taking a multiple vitamin mineral supplement you go into a negative balance for the very minerals you are supplementing.
- The solution to avoiding the pitfalls of intestinal mineral dietary interactions with each other and with ingredients from your diet is to take patented amino acid chelated minerals…
- These patented amino acid chelated functional minerals do not ionize in the

gastrointestinal system the way other mineral forms do. In fact they will not negatively react with medication and sensitive prescription drugs… (Henderson, 2012).

A popular nutritional supplement is calcium carbonate, which the body does not absorb well, and yet many women take this form. Calcium carbonate is like eating rocks and expecting the minerals to be bioavailable. The amino acid chelated minerals are highly absorbable, as Dr. H. DeWayne Ashmead (2012, p. 221) states: "[N]ot only is their absorption from the gastrointestinal tract increased, but also the bioavailability of the minerals from those amino acid chelates is greater when compared to the ingestion of non-chelated minerals."

Although amino acid chelates have been used in both human and animal nutrition after 50 years of research, this is an area that is not well known to the medical community. It seems odd that owners of million-dollar racehorses and prize champion livestock will provide the amino acid chelates in their animal feed and optimize performance, but people do not. These added nutrients in animals increase healthy birth weights, increase litter size, decrease fetal demise, and result in healthy livestock production, and in the case of the dairy industry, greater milk production and higher quality products (Ashmead, 2012).

Perhaps the most critical piece of information coming out of Dr. Ashmead's research as it applies to physical and mental health is that the chelated zinc catalyzes enzymes that transform amino acid proteins into neurotransmitters. Most neurotransmitters are calming neurotransmitters and that is what brings us our sense of happiness and peace. Sugar and simple carbohydrates as well as grains can cause the body to dump zinc and other minerals. When we are highly stressed, many of us consume more donuts, candy, soda, and chips. This increases the zinc dumping, which can raise copper and can cause the neurotransmitter deficiencies that trigger the negative emotional states known as depression and anxiety.

Ashmead and Graff (2006) reported a profound piece of information after research replicated the results of studies in the 1980s and 1990s, though the information is still not being acted upon in treatment programs. The study gave one group of adult male alcoholic rats supplemental zinc and copper amino acid chelates while a second group received no supplements. The supplemented group decreased their alcohol consumption by 96%. The group receiving no supplements "drank themselves to death."

Now I've worked with many families over the years that have a member addicted to alcohol. The families would do anything to help this person recover. Many alcoholics relapse over and over again and many programs see recidivism rates as high as 75%. It makes one wonder what would happen if chelated zinc were part of the treatment, along with the Peniston-Kulkosky Protocol for alpha-theta brain-wave training. This training has been shown to reduce relapse by about 75% but is likewise not incorporated into most drug treatment programs. In my experience, the pRoshi goes beyond alpha-theta brain-wave training and aids the brain in recalibrating many more brain waves, thus calming anxiety and enhancing mood while helping to reduce cravings.

In addition to its role in mental health, zinc is required for the human body to make DNA. "With an absence of DNA, the cells in your body can't reproduce themselves….If this happens in a younger person, or a young animal such as your puppy, growth is retarded. In the adult there may be a vast number of medical problems all stemming back to the body's inability to grow new organ and tissue cells to replace the millions of cells that are continuously dying." (Ashmead, 1981, p. 81)

What if the addicted person were actually treated according to the research, indicating the role of brain training and the need for proper nutritional corrections. The answers have been available for over 20 years! Beyond the treatment of addictions is the treatment of the mentally ill, or perhaps one might call it the mistreatment of the mentally ill. The more outrageous protocols include moving a patient from one addiction such as opiates to another addiction such as methadone or Suboxone. What these drugs do to the body and brain makes their prescription unconscionable and yet prescriptions are written every day.

Whitaker comments on what he calls the "psychopharmacology revolution":

[W]e should expect that the number of disabled mentally ill in the United States, on a per-capita basis, would have declined over the past 50 years. We should also expect that the number of disabled mentally ill, on a per-capita basis, would have declined since the arrival in 1988 of Prozac and the other second-generation psychiatric drugs. We should see a two-step drop in disability rates. Instead, as the psychopharmacology revolution has unfolded, the number of disabled mentally ill in the United States has skyrocketed. (Whitaker, 2010, p. 5)

Many of the issues that are labeled according to the *Diagnostic and Statistical Manual of Mental Disorders (DSM)* would respond nicely to proper treatment with amino acid chelated mineral nutrition, brain training, and energy psychology interventions for trauma. Insurance does not cover that combination, however. So, the poor especially, who are covered by Medicaid and Medicare, are given drugs and more drugs. These drugs themselves deplete vitamins and minerals, and we've seen what happens when just one mineral, zinc, gets depleted: Many chronic illnesses result. Patients and taxpayers are both victimized in this scenario. The nationwide drug bills for the poor in county mental health systems amount to millions of dollars each month.

Dr. Daniel Amen (2013, p. 19) states, "By failing to look at the brain's function in complex cases, psychiatrists miss important information, which leads to erroneous diagnoses and missed opportunities for effective treatment." Brain aberrations are sometimes precipitated by nutritional deficiencies and not always benefitted by drugs.

Drugs deplete vitamins and minerals, leaving a person at a lower level of health and well-being. Drug-induced nutrient depletion has created a modern plague that goes completely unrecognized, except by alternative and integrative practitioners. Dr. Pieczenik, a board-certified psychiatrist, and Dr. Neustadt, a naturopathic doctor, have documented how medications can damage the mitochondria, the cells' energy production sites. The mitochondria send signals to the DNA and the DNA repairs itself to maintain a proper blueprint for the body. When mitochondria are damaged, serious problems arise. And these problems are occurring in the people who are receiving psychotropic and other drugs. This needs to become common knowledge or we are fighting a losing battle in terms of returning someone to optimal health. Drs. Neustadt and Pieczenik describe the problem specifically and powerfully:

Damage to mitochondria is now understood to play a role in the pathogenesis of a wide range of seemingly unrelated disorders such as schizophrenia, bipolar disease, dementia, Alzheimer's disease, epilepsy, migraine headaches, strokes, neuropathic pain, Parkinson's disease, ataxia, transient ischemic attack, cardiomyopathy, coronary artery disease, chronic fatigue syndrome, fibromyalgia, retinitis pigmentosa, diabetes, hepatitis C, and primary biliary cirrhosis. Medications have now emerged as a major cause of mitochondrial damage, which may explain many adverse effects. All classes of psychotropic drugs have been documented to damage mitochondria, as have stain medications, analgesics such as acetaminophen, and many others. (Neustadt & Pieczenik, 2008, p. 783)

Those of us who have worked with the chronically mentally ill see the damage done by the drugs. The psychotropic medications documented to damage mitochondrial function include antidepressants (amitriptyline, amoxapine, citalopram, fluoxetine), antipsychotics (chlorpromazine, fluphenazine, haloperidol, risperidone, quetiapine, clozapine, olanzapine), dementia medications (galantamine, tacrine), seizure medications (valproic acid), mood stabilizers such as lithium, Parkinson's disease medications such as tolcapone, and benzodiazepines (Chan et al., 2005; Fromenty & Pessayre, 1997; Modica-Napolitano et al., 2003; Balijepalli et al., 1999, 2001; Maurer & Moller, 1997; Ezoulin et al., 2005; Lambert et al., 1999; Mansouri et al., 2003; Xia et al., 1999; Yousif, 2002; Brinkman & ter Hofstede, 1999; Chitturi & George, 2002; Beavis, 1989; Berson et al., 1998; Brown & Desmond, 2002; Souza et al., 1994; Sarah & Poonam, 1998).

After one becomes aware of the issues of damaged mitochondria and worsening health, the practice of EFT and other effective therapies increases in importance in terms of intervention quality. EFT does not cause injury or exacerbate illness. EFT and other non drug therapies can effectively reduce or eliminate illness. And that means all kinds of illness!

**More about drugs and mental health.** It's important for clinicians to have a scope of knowledge that supports the client's return to health. *Most of all, the clinician needs to have a conviction that the client can return to health!* My eight-step approach makes possible true healing at the body, mind, and spirit levels and helps improve

the ecology of the occupants on Mother Earth. The mainstream approach to mental illness and drugging has abandoned ecology and ethics in favor of profit and the pharmaceutical industry.

The carnage in terms of lost lives, lost livelihoods, and chronic physical and mental illness triggers in me a desire to show others how to help clients and families escape the iatrogenic plague. I try to help people understand the toxic elements of the drugs they are prescribed and teach them about the negative long-term and, in many cases, short-term consequences of these drugs. I am about helping clients regain robust health, which they are often not able to do while under the influence of drugs.

In *Fire in the Belly: The Surprising Cause of Most Diseases, States of Mind, and Aging Processes,* author Keith Scott-Mumby (2013, p. 30) states: "Any disease requiring constant medication is, by my terms of reference, not properly diagnosed and being treated ineffectively. The only definition of cure I respect is 'no symptoms' (no disease) and 'no treatment' (no further medications, etc. needed). Chronic medication, just keeping trouble suppressed, solves nothing and is a failure! Chronic doesn't mean it won't heal."

Similarly, brain impairment requires specific rectifications that go beyond talk therapies. Dr. Amen uses SPECT scans to visualize brain problems. I teach my students that when they see an odd behavioral pattern to remember that these behaviors may not be under the client's control.

Dr. Amen's research (Amen Clinics, n.d.) indicates that there are at least three different types of behavior problems that can be detected in brain scans and which require different treatments:

- Impulsive issues (often from low activity in the prefrontal cortex)
- Compulsive tendencies (usually due to high activity in the anterior cingulate gyrus)
- Irritability or having memory issues (may be associated with temporal lobe problems)

Dr. Amen uses single-photon emission computed tomography (SPECT) brain scans to identify the type of brain pattern so appropriate treatment such as neurofeedback techniques can be implemented. Unfortunately, insurance companies do not often cover SPECT scans or neurofeedback to diagnose and treat specific conditions. Insurance plans also rarely cover nutritional supplements but will cover numerous drug prescriptions. The outrage here is that many of the sickest patients are on Medicare and Medicaid and neither of these plans will pay for neurofeedback or amino acid chelated mineral nutritional supplements, but these plans will cover $500 to $1000 or more per month in prescriptions drugs. The effective treatments that are available are not usually accessible by the disabled on fixed incomes. This guarantees their ongoing disabilities and chronic drugging until their health is destroyed. It also contributes to the massive profits of the pharmaceutical industry.

## Step 6: Recognizing Substance Sensitivities and Toxins

If one does not understand the impact of toxins and sensitivities, one might miss the true precipitator of illness in clients. Some reactivities can be effectively treated with EFT, TFT, and other energy therapies, but it may be necessary for the client to avoid ingestion of or contact with the source of the sensitivities and eliminate toxins where possible.

Research shows that cancer and neurological and autoimmune diseases occur at a higher rate among celiacs, suggesting that gluten/gliadin may be a contributing factor (Lindeberg et al., 1994). Those who suffer from celiac disease have a reactivity to gluten and gliadin, which are contained in wheat, rye, and barley and cause inflammation in the body. Celiac disease presents sometimes as a gastric problem affecting digestion, and other times it affects the brain or other organs. Yet this area of research seems to have been ignored in the identification of clinical issues. One must wonder at the cause of this neglect of such an important possibility. In practice my colleagues and I have the theory that those clients with alcohol addiction are actually severely gluten/gliadin reactive and the alcohol represents liquid gluten/gliadin, which to them is highly toxic. It also sets up neurological effects that can be exacerbated by simple food items like breads, cookies, yeast, and sugar.

Depression is perhaps the most common symptom people express when seeing a therapist. With prescriptions of SSRIs increasing substantially, there is obviously something very wrong. The identification of toxins is an important element in a good therapist's assessment.

Research links depression to gluten intolerance (Hoggan, 1996). Gluten essentially erodes the gastrointestinal tract, causing the dumping of minerals. Previously, we have seen how important minerals are in terms of making possible the production of neurotransmitters from amino acid proteins. When minerals are depleted, there is a serious problem with absorption as well as processing since there is not enough zinc to catalyze the enzymes that transform proteins into neurotransmitters

Other substances that may be affecting your clients' health include aspartame, fluoride, sucralose (Splenda), benzoate, soy, and genetically modified organisms in corn and other crops. Depression or anxiety can be triggered precipitously with exposure to specific toxins. Neurotoxic substances may be in the paint or the glue under new carpeting; formaldehyde is found in a range of products, including fragrances. Fluoride can be found in prescription drugs, water, salt, bottled and canned drinks, and some foods including baby foods. Fluoride damages the body and brain and knocks out the thyroid function, which of course can precipitate chronic depression, extreme fatigue, and many other problems. Much information is available on the hazards of fluoride (see www.thegreatculling.com; Parents of Fluoride Poisoned Children, http://poisonfluoride.com/pfpc).

Other toxins laced into the food supply are called excitotoxins, a category that includes monosodium glutamate (MSG) and aspartame. These substances overstimulate neurons in the brain until they die. Neuronal death can't be tapped away. A client who eats a lot of fast foods and processed foods that are loaded with these toxins will be prone to depression, anxiety, and difficulty in coping with life's stressors. In a study of 505 aspartame reactors, aspartame exposure precipitated headaches, dizziness, confusion, memory loss, convulsions, drowsiness, paresthesias, severe slurring of speech, hyperactivity and restless legs, severe depression, irritability, anxiety attacks, personality changes, severe insomnia, decreased vision, eye pain, blindness, tinnitus, impaired hearing, and more (Roberts, 1988). Many clients drink diet soda and don't make the connection between their various symptoms and their ingestion of the neurotoxin-containing beverage. In the body, one of the substances aspartame transforms into is methyl alcohol. That was what folks were drinking during Prohibition—wood alcohol. It made people go crazy, dumb, and blind.

I've seen two dramatic cases in which aspartame (methyl alcohol) poisoning irretrievably damaged the individuals' health. Both cases involved excessive ingestion of diet soda. In one, the poisoning caused bleeding in the woman's lungs. Physicians were likely unaware that she was consuming only a couple pieces of toast per day and drinking diet soda. The woman was anorexic so there were many other variables, but the methyl alcohol in her system was an important piece of information that her physician did not understand. In the other case, the poisoning damaged the optic nerves to the point that the man is now blind. The physicians treating these two people did not discuss aspartame (methyl alcohol) poisoning with them and they continued to drink a six-pack or more of diet soda daily!

A therapist needs to be aware of these issues and review with the client potential exposures. EFT, TFT, BSFF, TAT, and other energy psychology modalities can be used to treat substance sensitivities. If reactions are severe, however, it is important to educate the client about the complex potentials for physiological and neurological problems if exposure continues. It is best to help the client avoid the toxins. Helpful resources on these issues include the YouTube videos of Dr. Doris Rapp, the SPECT scans of toxins on the brain on Dr. Amen's website (www.AmenClinics.com), and a video by Dr. Russell Blaylock (www.RussellBlaylockMD.com).

## Step 7: Teach the Benefits of Meditation

A few years ago I was introduced to Transcendental Meditation and have made it a daily practice since. What I have noticed is that doing this special form of meditation, which is easy to learn and effortless to do, has transformed my life into a fairly peaceful experience throughout each day. I recommend this to clients to help them in a variety of ways.

Dr. Norman E. Rosenthal (2011, pp. 1221–1222) provides a very good description of the practice of meditation in terms of its impact in psychotherapy: "When emotions are working badly—too much, for too long, or inappropriately expressed or directed—they can be disastrous. That is why I embrace any new approach that can help alleviate emotional pain and dysfunction, especially one like TM that is essentially free of side effects."

Numerous research studies have demonstrated the benefits of meditation. Research by Newberg et al. (2010) demonstrated cerebral blood flow (CBF) differences between long-term meditators and non-meditators, with the CBF of long-term meditators significantly higher ($p < .05$) than that of non-meditators in the prefrontal cortex, parietal cortex, thalamus, putamen, caudate, and midbrain, brain structures that "underlie the attention network" and "relate to emotion and autonomic function."

A meta-analysis of 146 independent studies found that TM is more effective at reducing trait anxiety when compared with other techniques such as progressive relaxation, EMG biofeedback, and various forms of meditation. TM had a "significantly larger effect size" ($p < .005$), and meditation involving concentration had a "significantly smaller effect" (Eppley, Abrams, & Shear, 1989).

James Krag, MD, medical director of Liberty Point, a residential treatment program in Virginia for adolescents with psychiatric problems, states:

> Just as there are many kinds of medication, there are also many approaches that are termed "meditation." The vast majority of the research on meditation has been on Transcendental Meditation—and the findings clearly indicate that TM works better than other researched mental techniques to promote health. If research shows that a specific medication helps treat a disorder, it would be irresponsible and illogical to conclude that all medications help treat that disorder. In the same way, research on TM should not be generalized to include other techniques also called "meditation." We should intelligently choose what works and what is supported by research. Therefore I strongly support the introduction specifically of Transcendental Meditation into our nation's schools and health care systems." (Krag, n.d.)

The research on the effectiveness of TM is prolific, with volumes of studies validating the powerful improvements secondary to the practice of TM. A small sampling of the research shows:

- Cortisol reduction secondary to acute stress (MacLean et al., 1994).
- Stress reduction (Knight, 1995).
- Decreased emotional stress and cardiovascular events (Medical College of Wisconsin, 2009).
- Prevention of cardiovascular disease (Barnes & Orme-Johnson, 2012).

- Reduction in blood pressure (Goldstein et al., 2012; Paul-Labrador et al., 2006).
- Improvement in cardiac autonomic nervous system tone (Paul-Labrador et al., 2006).
- Enhanced brain-wave functions (Rubik, 2011; Travis, 2011; Travis & Arenander, 2006; Travis et al, 2010; Yamamoto et al., 2006).
- Improved academic performance (Wallace et al., 1984).
- Improved brain reactivity to pain (Orme-Johnson et al., 2006).
- Improved marital adjustment (Aron & Aron, 1982).
- Improved quality of life and longevity (Alexander et al., 1989; Wallace et al., 1982).
- Improvements in health (Rasmussen, 2002, 2007).
- Improvements in psychological well-being (Schoormans & Nyklíček, 2011; Hjelle, 1974, Yunesian et al., 2008).
- Improvements in type 2 diabetes (Bay & Bay, 2011).
- Improved insulin resistance (Paul-Labrador et al., 2006).
- Reduction in health care costs (Herron, 2011).
- Reduction in negative school behaviors in adolescents (Barnes, Bauza, & Treiber, 2003).
- Reduction in psychological distress and improved coping (Nidich et al., 2009; Gelderloos et al., 1990; Lintel, 1980).
- Reduction in symptoms of posttraumatic stress (Rosenthal, Grosswald, Ross, & Rosenthal, 2011; Hankey, 2007).
- Reductions in substance abuse/addictions (Clements, Krenner, & Mölk, 1988).
- Therapeutic effectiveness in anxiety disorders (Krisanaprakornkit et al., 2006).

These studies were published in peer-reviewed journals, which demonstrates the quality and validity of the measures and methodologies of the studies. In addition to the research, there are countless anecdotal reports of dramatic improvements in people's lives and behaviors after they learn TM.

Essentially, the Transcendental Meditation experience is an exercise in optimizing vibrations within oneself. TM simply balances the vibrational currents that enhance life. EFT is a powerful tool in terms of helping one decrease stress sufficiently to be able to begin TM and stick with it. High-level stress is often a huge distraction in life and the use of EFT daily can greatly decrease stress and anxiety. This process can be a readying process to prepare one for the profound experience of Transcendental Meditation.

## Step 8: Teach about Self-help Resources

The self-help methods I share with my clients most often are Bach Flower Remedies, homeopathy, essential oils, and nutrients that are highly bioavailable and easily absorbed, all of which help balance mind-body ecology. Providing basic information on how to use each method and where to obtain further information and products allows clients to remain their own best resource.

One day a fellow name Gary came in for therapy. He was in intense grief after being evicted from his family on Father's Day. Gary loves his children but his wife said she was done and told him to leave. He was deeply depressed and very anxious. He had no place to go and did not want to be away from his family. He left and was referred to me. I used the pRoshi, EFT, and some other approaches, but no matter what I did and no matter what issues we addressed, there was little improvement after several sessions. I referred him to a homeopath for a remedy for intense grief. The homeopath suggested Aurum Metallicum. Gary took it with near instant excellent results.

Essential oils can also be helpful in practice and for clients to use at home. I often put a drop of an essential oil on the palm of someone's hand as we are beginning work. This helps with the calming and facilitates a more peaceful state that is conducive to therapy.

Bach Remedies can likewise be helpful for clients for various symptoms, such as: worried with a brave facade, apprehension, critical of others, exploited, self-doubt, irrational thoughts, inattentive, feeling overwhelmed, despondency, and discouragement (see www.FeelBach.com for more information). The remedies really do work and can help a client feel better in a very short amount of time, sometimes in minutes.

## Case Example of Integrating Modalities

Elaine was kept in isolation for 8 years, physically and mentally abused as a hostage sequestered in her own home by her husband. She was leery of everyone and afraid to go anywhere, but knew she needed to escape. Finally, fearing for her life, she escaped when her brother came and rescued her. Eventually, she sought my help.

We began working on layers of trauma in a process more simple than one might imagine. At our first session, before beginning to take her history, I had her put on the pRoshi light glasses, using the clear lenses so that she could see everything that was going on. The history taking is important but must be done very carefully with someone like Elaine, due to the risk of retraumatization. We had a simple chat to allow the pRoshi about 10 minutes to calm her brain and reduce her anxiety, to enable her to recount her difficult story.

After about 10 minutes on the pRoshi, she became visibly calm. As she took a deep relaxing breath, she began to realize that she might be able to get some relief. She told her painful story over two sessions. With a lesser degree of trauma, one could do this in one session.

As she told me her story, I had her tap the edge of her hand, the Karate Chop point, to avert retraumatization. It was difficult for her, but she needed to talk after all those years. As her story unfolded, I made notes red-flagging specific elements of each trauma.

At the end of her story, I had her history and a list of many, many red flag elements of many traumas. I also had a history of the consequential physical impairments that elicited pain in her back, shoulders, and neck along with frequent headaches. It is common for most clients who seek therapy for help with a psychological or emotional issue to have a physical pain problem as well.

During the first session with a client like Elaine, it is important to begin doing the tapping on the different elements of the trauma in order to alleviate her suffering and thus give her hope that the traumas could be dealt with and she could regain happiness and peace. Like so many clients, Elaine had worked with several therapists and gotten minimal results. On this day, I wanted her to get results like she had not gotten before.

I asked Elaine, "What was the worst part of all of this?" She cited a specific trauma with many elements. And that is where we began tapping. Treat the worst first! Dr. Roger Callahan taught that if you work on the worst first few traumas, many sub-traumas will collapse along with those major ones. That has been true in my experience.

At that first session, Elaine learned how to do EFT and I taught her how to use it between sessions. I also drew up a simple EFT points diagram for Elaine. I do this when clients are so overwhelmed that they have trouble remembering and processing information.

In later sessions, we used Thought Field Therapy (I go with the method that will alleviate suffering for the particular individual) and Be Set Free Fast, due to the power of the forgiveness process in the latter protocol. I also went through my eight-step education process. Elaine proceeded through various steps successfully. During her therapy she continued in isolation for many weeks, until one day she called and said, "Marie, I'm not coming in today because I'm going to the mall with my girlfriends." To me it was the ultimate sign of success. Her paranoia about being around others had vanished. She had started trusting enough to build friendships. Elaine recovered very well. She came in rarely after that because she had become her own best resource with the help of EFT, pRoshi, and Scenar.

## Conclusion

Preventing illness is the most economical and ecological approach to health care. It behooves us to share this approach with clients and help them regain and retain robust physical and psychological health. Tapping combined with the methods described in this chapter will make a very great difference in terms of outcomes. EFT is a key element in helping clients overcome symptoms. It works on physical, emotional, mental, and spiritual symptoms and often brings excellent results. Clients greatly enjoy the rapid results. When symptoms persist, as they do in complex or chronic problems, it is necessary to add the combination approaches. Each device is powerful alone or in combination with EFT. The most powerful device, however, is the clinician's energy of compassion and belief in a positive outcome along with a belief in the client's ability to heal. When all is said and done, there is much we do not know about energy fields. The consciousness of the client and therapist are the active ingredients. The tools that work for the client are essential to the therapist for self-care too. Enjoy the journey.

# References

Alexander, C. N., Langer, E. J., Newman, R .I., Chandler, H. M., & Davies, JL. (1989, December). Transcendental meditation, mindfulness, and longevity: An experimental study with the elderly. *Journal of Personality and Social Psychology, 57*(6), 950–964.

Amen, D. (2013, March–April). It's time to stop flying blind: How not looking at the brain leads to missed diagnoses, failed treatments, and dangerous behaviors. *Alternative Therapies, 19*(2). Retrieved from http://www.alternative-therapies.com/openaccess/ATHM_19-1_Amen.pdf.

Amen Clinics. (n.d.). Behavior problems. Retrieved from http://www.amenclinics.com/index.php/conditions/behavioral-problems

Aron, E. N. & Aron, A. (1982, December). Transcendental Meditation program and marital adjustment. *Psychological Reports, 51*(3 Pt 1), 887–890.

Ashmead, D. (1981). *Chelated mineral nutrition.* Huntington Beach, CA: Institute Publishers/International Institute of Natural Health Sciences.

Ashmead, H. D. (2012). Amino acid chelation in human and animal nutrition. Boca Raton, FL: Taylor & Francis.

Ashmead, H. D. & Graff, D. J. (2006). Decreasing ethanol consumption in ethanol-dependent rats through supplementation of zinc and copper amino acid chelates: A preliminary study. *Journal of Applied Research, 6,* 19–27.

Balaji, P. A., Varne, S. R., & Ali, S. S. (2012, October). Physiological effects of yogic practices and transcendental meditation in health and disease. *North American Journal of Medical Sciences, 4*(10), 442–448.

Balijepalli, S., Boyd, M. R., & Ravindranath, V. (1999). Inhibition of mitochondrial complex I by haloperidol: The role of thiol oxidation. *Neuropharmacology, 38,* 567–577.

Balijepalli, S., Kenchappa, R. S., Boyd, M. R., & Ravindranath, V. (2001). Protein thiol oxidation by haloperidol results in inhibition of mitochondrial complex I in brain regions: Comparison with atypical antipsychotics. *Neurochemistry International, 38,* 425–435.

Barnes, V. A. Bauza, L. B, & Treiber, F. A. (2003, April 23). Impact of stress reduction on negative school behavior in adolescents. *Health and Quality of Life Outcomes, 1,* 10.

Barnes, V. A, & Orme-Johnson, D. W. (2012, August). Prevention and treatment of cardiovascular disease in adolescents and adults through the Transcendental Meditation program: A research review update. *Current Hypertension Reviews, 8*(3), 227–242.

Bay, R. & Bay, F. (2011, September). Combined therapy using acupressure therapy, hypnotherapy, and transcendental meditation versus placebo in type 2 diabetes. *Journal of Acupuncture and Meridian Studies, 4*(3), 183–186.

Beavis, A. D. (1989, January 25). On the inhibition of the mitochondrial inner membrane anion uniporter by cationic amphiphiles and other drugs. *Journal of Biological Chemistry, 264*(3), 1508–1515.

Berson, A., De Beco, V., Lettéron, P., Robin, M. A., Moreau, C., El Kahwaji, J., … Pessayre, D. (1998). Steatohepatitis-inducing drugs cause mitochondrial dysfunction and lipid peroxidation in rat hepatocytes. *Gastroenterology, 114,* 764–774.

Brinkman, K. & ter Hofstede, H. (1999). Mitochondrial toxicity of nucleoside analogue reverse transcriptase inhibitors: Lactic acidosis, risk factors and therapeutic options. *AIDS Reviews, 1,* 140–146.

Brown, S. J. & Desmond, P. V. (2002). Hepatotoxicity of antimicrobial agents. *Seminars in Liver Disease, 2,* 157–168.

Callahan, R. & Trubo, R. (2001). Tapping the healer within: Using Thought Field Therapy to instantly conquer your fears, anxieties, and emotional distress. New York, NY: Contemporary Books. See also the Roger Callahan YouTube video: http://www.youtube.com/watch?v=y3u6gR3BEZg HRV

Chan, K., Truong, D., Shangari, N., & O'Brien, P. J. (2005, December). Drug-induced mitochondrial toxicity. *Expert Opinion on Drug Metabolism & Toxicology, 1*(4), 655–669.

Chitturi, S. M. D. & George, J. P. D. (2002). Hepatotoxicity of commonly used drugs: Nonsteroidal anti-inflammatory drugs, antihypertensives, antidiabetic agents, anticonvulsants, lipidlowering agents, psychotropic drugs. *Seminars in Liver Disease, 2,* 169–184.

Clements, G., Krenner, L., & Mölk, W. (1988). The use of the Transcendental Meditation programme in the prevention of drug abuse and in the treatment of drug-addicted persons. *Bulletin on Narcotics, 40*(1), 51–56.

Cooke, W. T. & Holmes, G. K. T. (1984). *Coeliac disease.* New York, NY: Churchill Livingstone.

Davis, C. (n.d.). Retrieved from http://www.roshi.com

Davis, W. (2011). Wheat belly. New York, NY: Rodale Books.

Eppley, K. R., Abrams, A. I., & Shear, J. (1989, November). Differential effects of relaxation techniques on trait anxiety: A meta-analysis. *Journal of Clinical Psychology, 45*(6), 957–974.

Ezoulin, M. J., Li, J., Wu, G., Dong, C. Z., Ombetta, J. E., Chen, H. Z., Massicot, F., & Heymans, F. (2005). Differential effect of PMS777, a new type of acetylcholinesterase inhibitor, and galanthamine on oxidative injury induced in human neuroblastoma SK-N-SH cells. *Neuroscience Letters, 389,* 61–65.

Fleming, T. (2011). *TAT for a stressful event.* Redondo Beach, CA: TATLife. See also the YouTube channel for TAT: http://www.youtube.com/TATLifeVideos

Fox, M. (2009, August 4). Antidepressant use doubles in U.S., study finds. Reuters. Retrieved from http://www.reuters.com/article/2009/08/04/us-antidepressants-usa-idUSTRE5725E720090804

Fricker, L. D. (2012, June). Neuropeptides and other bioactive peptides: From discovery to function [Colloquium Series on Neuropeptides, Lecture transcript]. doi:10.4199/C00058ED1V01Y201205NPE003. Retrieved from http://www.morganclaypool.com/doi/abs/10.4199/C00058ED1V01Y201205NPE003

Fromenty, B. & Pessayre, D. (1997). Impaired mitochondrial function in microvesicular steatosis effects of drugs, ethanol, hormones and cytokines. *Journal of Hepatology, 26,* 43–53.

Gelderloos, P., Hermans, H. J, Ahlscröm, H. H, & Jacoby, R. (1990, March). Transcendence and psychological health: Studies with long-term participants of the transcendental meditation and TM-Sidhi program. *Journal of Psychology, 124*(2):177–197.

Goldstein, C. M., Josephson, R., Xie, S., & Hughes, J. W. (2012). Current perspectives on the use of meditation to reduce blood pressure. *International Journal of Hypertension, 2012,* 578397. doi:10.1155/2012/578397

Haaga, D. A, Grosswald, S., Gaylord-King, C., Rainforth, M., Tanner, M., Travis, F., Nidich, S., & Schneider, R. H. (2011, March 21). Effects of the transcendental meditation program on substance use among university students. *Cardiology Research and Practice, 2011,* 537101. doi: 10.4061/2011/537101

Hankey, A. (2007, March). CAM and post-traumatic stress disorder. *Evidence-Based Complementary and Alternative Medicine: eCAM, 4*(1), 131–132.

Henderson, J. (2008). The influence of zinc and copper amino acid chelates on ethanol addiction (Unpublished doctoral dissertation). Clayton College of Natural Health. Birmingham, AL.

Henderson, J. (2012, November 3). Why chelation is so important. Retrieved from http://lifezoneliving.wordpress.com/author/lifezoneliving

Herron, R. E. (2011, September–October). Changes in physician costs among high-cost transcendental meditation practitioners compared with high-cost nonpractitioners over 5 years. *American Journal of Health Promotion: AJHP, 26*(1), 56–60.

Himelstein, S. (2011, June). Meditation research: The state of the art in correctional settings. *International Journal of Offender Therapy and Comparative Criminology, 55*(4), 646–661.

Hjelle, L. A. (1974, August). Transcendental meditation and psychological health. *Perceptual and Motor Skills, 39*(1 Pt 2), 623–628.

Hoggan, R. (1996, June 4). Depression. Retrieved from http://gluten-free.org/hoggan/depr.txt

Jensen M. P, Hakimian, S, Sherlin, L. H, & Fregni, F. (2008, March). New insights into neuromodulatory approaches for the treatment of pain. *Pain, 9*(3), 193–199.

Karavidas, M. K., Lehrer, P. M., Vaschillo, E., Vaschillo, B., Marin, H., Buyske, S., King, M. S., Carr, T., & D'Cruz, C. (2002, February). Transcendental meditation, hypertension and heart disease. *Australian Family Physician, 31*(2), 164–168.

Knight, S. (1995, March 23–April 12). Use of transcendental meditation to relieve stress and promote health. *British Journal of Nursing, 4*(6), 315–318.

Krag, J. (n.d.). Benefits of transcendental meditation. Retrieved from http://www.davidlynchfoundation.org.uk/scientific-evidence-that-the-program-works.html

Krisanaprakornkit, T., Krisanaprakornkit, W., Piyavhatkul, N., & Laopaiboon, M. (2006, January 25). Meditation therapy for anxiety disorders. *Cochrane Database of Systematic Reviews, 1,* CD004998.

Lambert, P. D., McGirr, K. M., Ely, T. D., Kilts, C. D., & Kuhar, M. J. (1999). Chronic lithium treatment decreases neuronal activity in the nucleus accumbens and cingulate cortex of the rat. *Neuropsychopharmacology, 21,* 229–237.

Lindeberg, S., Nilsson-Ehle, P., Terént, A., Vessby, B., & Scherstén, B. (1994, September). Cardiovascular risk factors in a Melanesian population apparently free from stroke and ischaemic heart disease: The Kitava study. *Journal of Internal Medicine, 236*(3), 331–340.

Lintel, A. G., III. (1980, February). Physiological anxiety responses in transcendental meditators and nonmeditators. *Perceptual and Motor Skills, 50*(1), 295–300.

Lipton, B. H. (2008). *The biology of belief: Unleashing the power of consciousness, matter, and miracles.* New York, NY: Hay House.

MacLean, C. R., Walton, K. G., Wenneberg, S. R., Levitsky, D. K., Mandarino, J. V., Waziri, R., & Schneider, R. H. (1994, November 30). Altered responses of cortisol, GH, TSH and testosterone to acute stress after four months' practice of transcendental meditation (TM). *Annals of the New York Academy of Sciences, 746,* 381–384.

Malinovsky, I., Radvanski, D., & Hassett, A. (2007). Preliminary results of an open label study of heart rate variability biofeedback for the treatment of major depression. *Applied Psychophysiology and Biofeedback, 32*(1), 19–30.

Mansouri, A., Haouzi, D., Descatoire, V., Demeilliers, C., Sutton, A., Vadrot, N., … Berson, A. (2003). Tacrine inhibits topoisomerases and DNA synthesis to cause mitochondrial DNA depletion and apoptosis in mouse liver. *Hepatology, 38,* 715–725.

Maurer, I. & Moller, H. J. (1997). Inhibition of complex I by neuroleptics in normal human brain cortex parallels the extrapyramidal toxicity of neuroleptics. *Molecular and Cellular Biochemistry, 174,* 255–259.

Medical College of Wisconsin. (2009, November 17). Transcendental Meditation helped heart disease patients lower cardiac disease risks by 50 percent. *Science Daily.* Retrieved from http://www.sciencedaily.com/releases/2009/11/091116163204.htm

Modica-Napolitano, J. S., Lagace, C. J., Brennan, W. A., & Aprille, J. R. (2003). Differential effects of typical and atypical neuroleptics on mitochondrial function in vitro. *Archives of Pharmacal Research, 26,* 951–959.

Neustadt, J., & Pieczenik, S. R. (2008). Medication-induced mitochondrial damage and disease. *Molecular Nutrition and Food Research, 52*(7), 780–788. doi:10.1002/mnfr.200700075

Newberg, A. B., Wintering, N., Waldman, M. R., Amen, D., Khalsa, D. S., & Alavi, A. (2010, December). Cerebral blood flow differences between long-term meditators and non-meditators. *Consciousness and Cognition, 19*(4), 899–905.

Newbury, C. R. (1979, June). Tension and relaxation in the individual. *International Dental Journal, 29*(2), 173–182.

Nidich, S. I., Fields, J. Z., Rainforth, M. V., Pomerantz, R., Cella, D., Kristeller, J., Salerno, J. W., & Schneider, R. H. (2009, September). A randomized controlled trial of the effects of transcendental meditation on quality of life in older breast cancer patients. *Integrative Cancer Therapies, 8*(3), 228–234.

Nidich, S. I., Rainforth, M. V., Haaga, D. A., Hagelin, J., Salerno, J. W., Travis, F., … Schneider, R. H. (2009, December). A randomized controlled trial on effects of the transcendental meditation program on blood pressure, psychological distress, and coping in young adults. *American Journal of Hypertension, 22*(12), 1326–1331.

Nims, L. P. & Sotkin, J. (2003). Be Set Free Fast!: A revolutionary new way to eliminate discomforts. Santa Fe, NM: Sotkin Enterprises.

Orme-Johnson, D. W., Schneider, R. H., Son, Y. D., Nidich, S., & Cho, Z. H. (2006, August 21). Neuroimaging of meditation's effect on brain reactivity to pain. *Neuroreport, 17*(12), 1359–1363.

Paul-Labrador, M., Polk, D., Dwyer, J. H., Velasquez, I., Nidich, S., Rainforth, M., Schneider, R., & Merz, C. N. (2006). Effects of a randomized controlled trial of Transcendental Meditation on components of the metabolic syndrome in subjects with coronary heart disease. *Archives of Internal Medicine, 166*(11), 1218–1224. doi:10.1001/archinte.166.11.1218

Pole, N. (2007, September). The psychophysiology of posttraumatic stress disorder: A meta-analysis. *Psychological Bulletin, 133*(5), 725–746. doi:10.1037/0033-2909.133.5.725

Rasmussen, L. B. (2002, January 20). [Medical effects of transcendental meditation]. *Tidsskr Nor Laegeforen, 122*(2), 220.

Rasmussen, L. B. (2007, Mar 1). [Transcendental meditation and health]. *Tidsskr Nor Laegeforen, 127*(5), 624.

Rasmussen, L. B., Mikkelsen, K., Haugen, M., Pripp, A. H., Fields, J. Z., & Førre, Ø. T. (2012, May). Treatment of fibromyalgia at the Maharishi Ayurveda Health Centre in Norway II: A 24-month follow-up pilot study. *Clinical Rheumatology, 31*(5), 821–827.

Rees, B. (2011, November). Overview of outcome data of potential meditation training for soldier resilience. *Military Medicine, 176*(11), 1232–42.

Roberts, H. J. (1988). Neurological, psychiatric and behavioral reactions to aspartame in 505 aspartame reactors. In R. J Wurtman & E. Ritter-Walker (Eds.), Dietary phenylalanine and brain function (Chapter 45). Boston, MA: Birkhaüser.

Rosenthal, J. Z., Grosswald, S., Ross, R., & Rosenthal, N. (2011, June). Effects of transcendental meditation in veterans of Operation Enduring Freedom and Operation Iraqi Freedom with posttraumatic stress disorder: A pilot study. *Military Medicine, 176*(6), 626–630.

Rosenthal, N. E. (2011). *Transcendence: Healing and transformation through transcendental meditation* (Kindle edition). New York, NY: Penguin.

Rubik, B. (2011, February). Neurofeedback-enhanced gamma brainwaves from the prefrontal cortical region of meditators and non-meditators and associated subjective experiences. *Journal of Alternative and Complementary Medicine, 17*(2), 109–115.

Sarah, M. & Poonam, K. (1998). Diazepam induced early oxidative changes at the subcellular level in rat brain. *Molecular and Cellular Biochemistry, 178*, 41–46.

Schoormans, D. & Nyklíček, I. (2011, July). Mindfulness and psychologic well-being: Are they related to type of meditation technique practiced? *Journal of Alternative and Complementary Medicine, 17*(7), 629–634.

Schwartz, B. G., French, W. J., Mayeda, G. S., Burstein, S., Economides, C., Bhandari, A. K., Cannom, D. S., & Kloner, R. A. (2012, July). Emotional stressors trigger cardiovascular events. *International Journal of Clinical Practice, 66*(7), 631–639.

Scott-Mumby, K. (2013). *Fire in the belly: The surprising cause of most diseases, states of mind, and aging processes.* Reno, NV: Mother Whale.

Sedlmeier, P., Eberth, J., Schwarz, M., Zimmermann, D., Haarig, F., Jaeger, S., & Kunze, S. (2012, November). The psychological effects of meditation: A meta-analysis. *Psychological Bulletin, 138*(6), 1139–1171.

Souza, M. E., Polizello, A. C., Uyemura, S. A., Castro-Silva, O., & Curti, C. (1994, August 3). Effect of fluoxetine on rat liver mitochondria. *Biochemical Pharmacology, 48*(3), 535–541.

Swinehart, R. ( 2008). Two cases support the benefits of transcendental meditation in epilepsy. *Medical Hypotheses, 70*(5), 1070.

Travis, F. (2011, September). Comparison of coherence, amplitude, and eLORETA patterns during transcendental meditation and TM-Sidhi practice. *International Journal of Psychophysiology, 81*(3), 198–202.

Travis, F. & Arenander, A. (2006, December). Cross-sectional and longitudinal study of effects of transcendental meditation practice on interhemispheric frontal asymmetry and frontal coherence. *International Journal of Neurosciences, 116*(12), 1519–1538.

Travis, F., Haaga, D. A., Hagelin, J., Tanner, M., Arenander, A., Nidich, S., … Schneider, R. H. (2010, February). A self-referential default brain state: Patterns of coherence, power, and eLORETA sources during eyes-closed rest and transcendental meditation practice. *Cognitive Processing, 11*(1), 21–30.

Travis, F., Haaga, D. A., Hagelin, J., Tanner, M., Nidich, S., Gaylord-King, C., … Schneider, R. H. (2009, February). Effects of transcendental meditation practice on brain functioning and stress reactivity in college students. *International Journal of Psychophysiology, 71*(2), 170–176.

Van Wijk, E. P., Lüdtke, R., & Van Wijk, R. (2008, April). Differential effects of relaxation techniques on ultraweak photon emission. *Journal of Alternative and Complementary Medicine, 14*(3), 241–250.

Vaschillo, E. G., Vaschillo, B., & Lehrer, P. M. (2006). Characteristics of resonance in heart rate variability stimulated by biofeedback. *Applied Psychophysiology and Biofeedback, 31*(2), 129–142.

Verma, I. C., Jayashankarappa, B. S., & Palani, M. (1982, December). Effect of transcendental meditation on the performance of some cognitive psychological tests. *Indian Journal of Medical Research, 76*(Suppl), 136–143.

Wallace, R. K., Dillbeck, M., Jacobe, E., & Harrington, B. (1982, February). The effects of the transcendental meditation and TM-Sidhi program on the aging process. *International Journal of Neurosciences, 16*(1), 53–58.

Wallace, R. K., Orme-Johnson, D. W., Mills, P. J., & Dillbeck, M. C. (1984, November). Academic achievement and the paired Hoffman reflex in students practicing meditation. *International Journal of Neurosciences, 24*(3–4), 261–266.

Walsh, W. J. (2012). Nutrient power (Kindle edition). New York, NY: Skyhorse Publishing.

Whitaker, R. (2010). *Anatomy of an epidemic* (Kindle edition). New York, NY: Random House.

Xia, Z., Lundgren, B., Bergstrand, A., De Pierre, J. W., & Nassberger, L. (1999). Changes in the generation of reactive oxygen species and in mitochondrial membrane potential during apoptosis induced by the antidepressants imipramine, clomipramine, and citalopram and the effects on these changes by Bcl-2 and Bcl-XIA X(L). *Biochemical Pharmacology, 57*, 1199–1208.

Yamamoto, S., Kitamura, Y., Yamada, N., Nakashima, Y., & Kuroda, S. (2006, February). Medial profrontal cortex and anterior cingulate cortex in the generation of alpha activity induced by transcendental meditation: A magnetoencephalographic study. *Acta Medica Okayama, 60*(1), 51–58.

Yousif, W. (2002). Microscopic studies on the effect of alprazolam (Xanax) on the liver of mice. *Pakistan Journal of Biological Sciences, 5,* 1220–1225.

Yunesian, M., Aslani, A., Vash, J. H., & Yazdi, A. B. (2008, November 1). Effects of transcendental meditation on mental health: A before-after study. *Clinical Practice and Epidemiology in Mental Health, 4,* 25. doi:10.1186/1745-0179-4-25

Zuroff, D. C. & Schwarz, J. C. (1978, April). Effects of transcendental meditation and muscle relaxation on trait anxiety, maladjustment, locus of control, and drug use. *Journal of Consulting and Clinical Psychology, 46*(2), 264–271.

Chapter 59

# Matrix Reimprinting: Rewrite Your Past, Transform Your Future

*Karl Dawson and Sasha Allenby*

### Abstract

Matrix Reimprinting, developed by EFT Master Karl Dawson, is based on the classic EFT techniques, but it significantly advances and furthers what is possible to achieve within a client session, including easy access to early traumatic memories, quick resolution of the most intense traumas, creation of positive new beliefs, overcoming of issues around dissociation, and more client-led work, resulting in less therapeutic leading and projection. In 2006, a shift in awareness enabled Karl to gain new understanding behind the causation and resolution of trauma. This new awareness, gained from extensive observation and experience with myriad different cases of emotional trauma and physical disease, opened the door to the development of Matrix Reimprinting. The method is based on the understanding that we hold in our energy fields the stressful life events that have gone before, not just as memories but as specific energy bodies, which Karl has named "Energetic Consciousness Holograms," or ECHOs. Similar current life experiences reactivate the old memories, bringing the thoughts, feelings, and emotions of the original trauma flooding back into the body, causing stress. With the Matrix Reimprinting techniques, we can work directly with these ECHOs, not only resolving the negative energetic charge around them, but also creating positive memories in their place. This changes our relationship to our past, and affects our emotional and physical health in the present.

**Keywords:** Matrix Reimprinting, EFT, stress, emotions, memory, belief

**Karl Dawson**, one of only 29 EFT Masters worldwide, is the creator of the Matrix Reimprinting method and coauthor of *Matrix Reimprinting Using EFT*. As an EFT trainer for the past 10 years, he has taught EFT to thousands of people, including doctors, scientists, counselors, and therapists. Send correspondence to Karl Dawson, 2 Popes Meadow, Astwood Bank, Worcestershire, B966DR, UK, or karl28dawson@yahoo.com.

**Sasha Allenby** coauthored *Matrix Reimprinting Using EFT*, a Hay House book published in nine languages. She has presented at the Hay House "I Can Do It" conference and taught EFT worldwide. She currently works with pioneers in the personal development and transformation industry to help them share their message authentically. Send correspondence to Sasha Allenby, 2 Landsdowne Crescent, Suite 73, Bournemouth, Dorset, BH1 1SA, UK, or matrixreawakening@gmail.com. www.sashaallenby.com.

## What Is Matrix Reimprinting?

Matrix Reimprinting is an energy psychology technique created by EFT Master Karl Dawson. It involves a unique and creative way of working with and resolving past traumas. It draws on much of the research from the new sciences, including the understanding that we are all connected by a unified energy field and that our beliefs affect our biology. Matrix Reimprinting is also grounded in popular psychotherapeutic theory about trauma. When we experience a trauma, part of us splits off and blocks the memory so that we are protected from it, and another part of us experiences it over and over again. It has been assumed that these parts are buried deep within the brain. But from our experience, the part that splits off to protect us from the trauma and the part that relives it over and over again are one and the same. Furthermore, we believe that this part of our consciousness goes directly into a different dimension in the Matrix, and we can work with it there to release the trauma that it is holding for us. In Matrix Reimprinting, we call these parts that have split off due to a trauma "Energy Consciousness Holograms," or ECHOs.

## Exploring ECHOs

For trauma to occur, all we need is a situation in which we feel powerless and there is a threat to our survival. This threat to survival is relative to our age and our ability to deal with the specific situation. For an adult it may take a major event like a car crash or physical or sexual abuse to create an ECHO. For a young child, being told by a parent that he or she is bad, stupid, ugly, lazy, and so on also has the potential to traumatize. Although these events may not seem vastly traumatic to us as adults, anything that threatens a child's sense of safety and security is potentially traumatic.

Furthermore, adults that have experienced such trauma in childhood are more susceptible in later life to experiencing seemingly lesser events as more traumatic. Their resilience to trauma is often lowered.

## Fight, Flight, *or* Freeze

Whatever our age, at the moment a trauma occurs, if we can't fight, we can't take flight, we feel isolated, and there is no way out, we simply freeze.

The effect of the freeze response is less widely recognized than that of fight or flight, yet it can have the biggest impact emotionally and physiologically. Our chemical responses protect us biochemically from being emotionally and physically overwhelmed. As our consciousness freezes, part of us splits off energetically. At this point, the ECHO is created.

When the ECHO splits off, it is held in the Matrix. The ECHO contains all the information of the traumatic event. It creates the effect of amnesia. The event is numbed out from consciousness as if it never happened. But it lives on in the images of our subconscious and dictates our response to future situations.

## Your Subconscious Isn't Working Against You

Creating an ECHO is one of nature's amazing programs. It has two main functions. The first is to help us deal with the overwhelm of the trauma at the time the event occurs. The second is to warn us subconsciously to avoid similar events in the future.

## When It Becomes Problematic

The problem is that, unlike some tribal cultures or animals in the wild, we do not learn how to dispel the trauma after it has occurred. Instead, we continually perceive any further seemingly similar experiences as threats, retriggering a similar biochemistry as when we experienced the original event, and taking us into a stress response. And as long as the ECHO is holding the trauma, similar events will trigger a similar response. In these circumstances we suffer stress, anxiety, phobias, and so on, which affect our interactions in everyday life and eventually take their toll on our physiology, constantly increasing our cortisol (stress hormone) levels and, in turn, decreasing our DHEA (the "anti-aging" hormone).

## Long-term Effect of Having Unresolved Trauma

It also takes a lot of energy to hold all this information in the Matrix, especially for people with multiple traumas from childhood and adulthood who get triggered often by everyday life. Being constantly triggered like this has a cascade effect, often attracting more and more of the similar events, with repeated stressful or traumatic outcomes. This pattern is fortified as time goes on, making it more difficult to keep the energy of the trauma at bay, and making it more a feature of daily life.

## The Time Frame of the Subconscious Mind

Another issue is that, on a cellular level, the traumatic memory pictures are real-time events, happening now. This is because the subconscious mind is not time framed and does not know the difference between past and present events. You may have past traumas that you perceive as old events, but if they still hold a charge, you will be experiencing them subconsciously as though they are happening in the present. This is why you may not have been able to let go of past events, because, to your subconscious mind, they are still happening in real time.

## Rewriting the Memory

With Matrix Reimprinting we can dialogue with ECHOs back at the time of the trauma. When we help the ECHO release the energy of the trauma and help the client move safely through the memory, the subconscious can let go of the trauma.

The way we work with these ECHOs is to use conventional EFT to tap on the recipient and the ECHO simultaneously. We'll detail how to do this later in the chapter.

## History and Origins of Matrix Reimprinting

In 2006, Karl was teaching EFT in Australia. Working with one of the course participants, he was making little progress. So he asked her, "Can you see that little girl, your younger self, as a picture in the memory?" The woman replied, "I can see her so clearly, I could tap on her." In a moment of inspiration Karl encouraged her to tap on the little self in the memory while he continued to tap on the adult before him. The woman had amazingly quick resolution, and Matrix Reimprinting was born!

## Beliefs and Biology

Matrix Reimprinting also grew out of the research that emerged from the "new sciences" such as

quantum physics and epigenetics (Church, 2007). Bruce Lipton's *The Biology of Belief* (2008) highlights how our beliefs create our biology. In Matrix Reimprinting we connect how the negative life traumas, especially in the early years, form our beliefs in the present day. The part of ourselves that has split off to protect us from the pain of the trauma is not only holding the trauma for us, but is also holding the beliefs about life that were created in that moment. And, in turn, these beliefs are affecting our biology. When we rewrite these beliefs, the body can heal accordingly.

When we find out what was learned about life on the day the belief was formed, we can also rewrite what happened, changing the belief accordingly. So if you learned you were worthless, what do you need to experience in the memory in order to learn that you are worthy? The tapping releases the old belief and changing the picture installs the new one. This is not denying that the past event happened. It is simply transforming the information held in the energy field about what happened, as the picture is what creates the negative feeling in the body when the subconscious repeatedly tunes back into it.

## Matrix Reimprinting and the Law of Attraction

Matrix Reimprinting is also founded on research on the Law of Attraction, such as that detailed in *The Field,* by Lynne McTaggart (2008), and *The Divine Matrix,* by Gregg Braden (2008). The memories that we work on with Matrix Reimprinting also change your point of attraction. If you hold these pictures of your life experiences in your field, you will keep attracting more of the same. This is because as you continually resonate with them, you will keep vibrating at the same frequency and attract other experiences of a similar frequency. As you start to change the pictures in your field, your life experiences start to transform accordingly.

## HeartMath Research

Matrix Reimprinting also draws upon the research from the HeartMath Institute (Childre & Martin, 2000). The research shows how the heart's fields can be measured 10 feet from the body in all directions, and how the heart communicates with the Matrix. In Matrix Reimprinting, the heart is therefore utilized to send out new pictures into the Matrix.

## META-Medicine

Matrix Reimprinting was also influenced by META-Medicine, a diagnostic tool developed by Rob van Overbruggen, PhD, for pinpointing the exact emotional cause for a physiological illness (van Overbruggen, 2006). With confirmation from META-Medicine that each disease is caused by specific trauma conflicts, in locating the ECHOs and helping them resolve trauma at the time of the conflict, physiological healing is accomplished.

## Research of Dr. Robert Scaer

Further influence came from the work of trauma specialist Robert Scaer, MD, and his research around the freeze response (Scaer, 2007). Of particular significance in his findings is the fact that most humans, unlike other animals, do not discharge the freeze response. When we help the ECHO to discharge the freeze response, healing can occur.

## Developing the Techniques

Karl developed the Matrix Reimprinting techniques over a number of years while working with thousands of practitioners and workshop participants worldwide. Although he had been used to getting exceptional feedback from his trainees about the effects of EFT, and life-changing experiences were commonplace, the results that his trainees experienced with Matrix Reimprinting were tenfold, and even more far-reaching and remarkable than Karl had ever witnessed with EFT alone. Many trainees reported that, during almost every EFT session, there was a call to use Matrix Reimprinting, and the results for practically all trainees were consistently phenomenal.

## Matrix Reimprinting Worldwide

One such trainee was Sasha Allenby. Having overcome chronic fatigue syndrome (CFS)/myalgic encephalomyelitis (ME, also known as myalgic encephalopathy) and bipolar affective disorder using Matrix Reimprinting, Sasha was working intensively using Karl's technique in the field of serious disease and childhood trauma, and witnessing amazing results. Despite an array

of qualifications and a career that had included lecturing in colleges and teaching therapeutic drama to teenagers with severe behavioral difficulties, Sasha put all this aside to focus on Matrix Reimprinting, coauthoring the book *Matrix Reimprinting Using EFT* (Dawson & Allenby, 2010), which has been published in multiple languages by Hay House and can now be found in Chinese, Japanese, Spanish, German, and French, to name a few. Matrix Reimprinting has since become a global phenomenon and there are now thousands of Matrix Reimprinting practitioners and a host of trainers worldwide.

## The Difference Between Matrix Reimprinting and Conventional EFT

Matrix Reimprinting is an energy psychology technique that involves the meridians, as both EFT and TFT do. The difference is that while with EFT we clear the charge from past traumatic events, with Matrix Reimprinting we actually transform what happened.

## Tapping on ECHOs

One of the main differences between traditional EFT and Matrix Reimprinting is that EFT doesn't involve working with ECHOs, whereas Matrix Reimprinting does. With Matrix Reimprinting it is the same tapping principle, but with a new and important client, the ECHO. Traditional EFT also does not tend to view the past memories as being held in the Matrix. Instead they are seen as being held in the body-mind.

## Filling the Void

For a number of people, simply clearing the negative energy and not replacing it with anything positive using EFT can leave a void. To fill this void, some EFT practitioners have developed visualizations as an addition to the protocol. Others have filled it with Reiki or other energy techniques. With Matrix Reimprinting there is no need to employ another modality to fill this void, as it is filled with the new picture.

## Benefits of Matrix Reimprinting

The Matrix Reimprinting techniques are easy to use. They are also very gentle. They enable resolution on a whole range of traumatic experiences without retraumatization. The following outlines the further benefits of Matrix Reimprinting.

## Resolving Core Issues and Instilling Positive Beliefs

With Matrix Reimprinting you can quickly find and resolve core issues. In traditional EFT when someone expresses a belief such as "I must be perfect to be loved," you would find the earliest memories relating to this belief and resolve them. With Matrix Reimprinting you not only resolve the memories that contributed to the core issues, you can also instill new supporting beliefs and experiences. This, in turn, affects and transforms the belief system in the present moment.

## Preconscious Trauma

Matrix Reimprinting also locates preconscious trauma, even trauma that has occurred before the first 6 years of life. A limited number of therapies or practices have tools for working with preconscious memories, yet the research of cell biologist Bruce Lipton (2008) indicates that this is when most of the damage is done to our perceptions of self. With Matrix Reimprinting you can interact with yourself as far back as in the womb, and access and resolve preconscious traumas, even ones that the subconscious mind cannot recall.

## Reframes and Cognitive Shifts

Another benefit of Matrix Reimprinting is that it commonly produces reframes and cognitive shifts. If you are working with this technique as a therapist, one of the great benefits is that most of the work comes from the client (although if the client gets stuck at any point, guidance is needed from the practitioner). As clients lead the process, they decide what is best for them, in order to resolve the energetic disruption around the trauma. As the power is with clients, they are much more likely to reframe the situation themselves or emphasize their cognitive shifts. As practitioners we are well aware that these shifts indicate that resolution and therefore healing has taken place.

## Forgiveness

Similarly, Matrix Reimprinting often leads to a place of forgiveness, particularly of the perpetrator of the traumatic experience. A number of schools of thought hold that the purpose of any therapeutic intervention is to reach the point of forgiveness. This is not something to be forced or feigned, and there is often a sticking point in traditional therapeutic practices when clients will feel (on a conscious level) that they have forgiven their perpetrator, but will not have forgiven the perpetrator on a subconscious level. Matrix Reimprinting leads the recipient naturally to a place of true forgiveness.

## Psychological Reversal and Secondary Gain

Matrix Reimprinting also elegantly locates psychological reversal (subconscious holding onto the problem). By interacting with the ECHO we can begin to understand exactly why we are holding onto a problem or an issue that is keeping us stuck in an old pattern of thinking or behavior. The ECHO is most often trying to protect us, or filtering its understanding through the perceptions of a child. As adults we continue to respond to our own worlds through those same childlike perceptions, until the energy around the memory is resolved. This creates more self-understanding when we can trace the current self-destructive behaviors to early memories, and replace them with more supportive beliefs and behaviors.

## Dissociated Clients

Another great benefit is that Matrix Reimprinting is effective for dissociated clients who have no SUD (subjective units of distress) levels, that is, clients who have no feelings or emotions about issues that are still unresolved for them. For EFT practitioners this client group is one of the most challenging to work with. And if you fall into this category, you may not have had any positive experiences with EFT as yet. Matrix Reimprinting works well for people in this group because, in working with the ECHO, the technique is even more effective when the client is dissociated (or in other words, doesn't bring the feelings of the ECHO into his or her body).

## Trauma Resolution

Matrix Reimprinting is very valuable in its ability to send a message to the body that the trauma is over. It ends the trauma cycle in which the trauma is constantly replayed in the Matrix. This enables the body and the cells to respond in heal thier ways, and begin to heal.

## Resolving the Irresolvable

With Matrix Reimprinting you can also resolve issues that have previously been irresolvable. This is particularly beneficial if you have lost family members or loved ones and not had a chance to say good-bye or resolve your differences. Using Matrix Reimprinting you can release the emotions around unresolved relationships and let go of the ties that hold you in the past.

## The Law of Attraction

A further benefit of Matrix Reimprinting is that it utilizes the Law of Attraction. As mentioned earlier, when we have traumatic experiences and hold them in the Matrix, we continue to attract similar experiences. With this technique, once we resolve the trauma, we change our point of attraction and begin to draw more fulfilling and life-sustaining experiences.

## Tipping Point

When we collapse lots of images or memories, there is a tipping point. Just like the generalization effect in EFT, when we start to change the pictures in the Matrix, we sometimes only need to change a small number before similar pictures no longer hold any resonance for us. The positive pictures are many times more powerful in resonance than the negative pictures (just as your positive thoughts have a higher vibration than your negative thoughts). So placing new pictures in the field can create a tipping point of attracting positive experiences in your life, even if you haven't changed all negative pictures on the same theme.

## Summary of the Matrix Reimprinting Protocol

These instructions are written as though you the practitioner are addressing the client (additional instructions for the practitioner are in parentheses):

1. Begin with a scene from the past.
2. Close your eyes (if you are comfortable doing so).
3. Is it okay for me to tap on you?

4. Can you see the younger version of yourself? (This is to check that the client is disassociated—looking at the picture from the outside and not in the body of the ECHO.)
5. Describe the image you see—what you are wearing, where you are, what or who else is in the picture, and so on. This younger version of you that you see is your ECHO.
6. Explain to your ECHO that you have come to help them let go of the negative emotions they are experiencing—use language appropriate to the ECHO's age.
7. *You* are going to tap on your ECHO. Ask your ECHO if you have permission to do so. Imagine tapping on your ECHO as I tap on you, or as you tap on yourself if you are more comfortable doing so.
8. Converse with your ECHO, ask what the ECHO is feeling, where the energy is, what the ECHO is thinking, and so on.
9. Use EFT to release the ECHO's negative emotions, release negative energy, reframe beliefs formed from the event. (This can be in silence between the client and the ECHO or out loud, depending on which the client is most comfortable with.)
10. (If the client gets stuck, help facilitate the dialogue and the EFT process.)
11. Ask your ECHO if there is anything it would like to do to resolve this situation. This can include:
    a) Bringing in new resources
    b) Changing what happened
    c) Inviting somebody or something else in for help and guidance
    d) Doing what you didn't do or wished you had done in that situation.
       (This is all usually done in silence. Offer help if needed but, most important, give the client time and space to complete this step).
12. Come back to the present and open your eyes.
13. Try to replay the original scene. (If there is any intensity remaining, go back to the ECHO to see what else needs to be resolved).
14. Reimprint the final image by taking it in through the top of the head, sending it around the body, taking it into the heart, making it bigger and brighter, and then

sending it from the heart out into the Matrix.

15. Test the original image. (Go back in if any aspects have been missed).

# References

Braden, G. (2008). *The divine matrix: Bridging time, space, miracles, and belief.* Carlsbad, CA: Hay House.

Childre, D. & Martin, H. (2000). *The HeartMath solution: The Institute of HeartMath's revolutionary program for engaging the power of the heart's intelligence.* New York, NY: Harper One.

Church, D. (2007). *The genie in your genes: Epigenetic medicine and the new biology of intention.* Santa Rosa, CA: Energy Psychology Press.

Dawson, K. & Allenby, S. (2010). *Matrix Reimprinting using EFT: Rewrite your past, transform your future.* Carlsbad, CA: Hay House.

Lipton, B. H. (2008). *The biology of belief: Unleashing the power of consciousness, matter, and miracles.* Carlsbad, CA: Hay House.

McTaggart, L. (2008). *The field: The quest for the secret force of the universe.* New York, NY: Harper Perennial.

Scaer, R. C. (2007). *The body bears the burden: Trauma, dissociation, and disease* (2nd ed.). New York, NY: Haworth Medical Press.

Van Overbruggen, R. (2006). *Healing psyche: The patterns in psychological cancer treatment.* North Charleston, SC: BookSurge.

# Chapter 60
# The Dream to Freedom Technique: Integrating EP and Dreamwork

*Robert Hoss and Lynne Hoss*

## Abstract

Dreams are an expression of the unconscious, which can quickly reveal deep unresolved emotional issues that leave us stuck. But understanding our dreams alone will not necessarily remove the emotional barriers to healing. EFT can augment dreamwork with a powerful tool for reducing those barriers by diminishing the anxious stress response once the problem is identified. The Dream to Freedom technique (DTF) integrates both disciplines into a healing protocol, drawing from a unique combination of energy psychology, Gestalt therapy, Jungian psychology, and the neuropsychology of sleep and energy work. It is a three-part protocol that: (1) uses the dream to explore the often traumatic emotional memories and conflicts with which the unconscious is dealing; (2) employs EFT to reduce the stress response brought up by the memory, thus reducing the emotional barriers to progress; and (3) returns to the dream for guiding cues present in the dream story to refine decisions, beliefs, and behavior to progress beyond the problem. This chapter provides a detailed description, along with the full script used to administer the protocol. It is divided into functional sections so that lifting some of the core dreamworking elements, such as the scripted Gestalt, color exploration, or closure tools for a quick application with an energy tool of your own choice can be easily accomplished. A downloadable worksheet for administering a complete session can be found at www.dreamscience.org (Energy Psychology button).

**Keywords:** dreams, dreamwork, energy psychology, EFT, stress response, emotional conflict, Gestalt therapy, Dream To Freedom

**Robert Hoss, MS**, is a director of the International Association for the Study of Dreams and directs the Dream Science Foundation. A scientist with Gestalt training, he has been teaching dreamwork for over 30 years, authored *Dream Language*, and coauthored (with Lynne Hoss) *Dream To Freedom: A Handbook for Integrating Dreamwork and Energy Psychology.*

**Lynne Hoss, MA, CEHP**, is a clinical psychologist, and formerly a substance abuse counselor, counselor for women sheltered from domestic violence, and energy psychology program director for Innersource. Certified by the Association for Comprehensive Energy Psychology, she teaches energy psychology in public forums and private sessions. Send correspondence to Bob and Lynne Hoss, 40104 N. Old Stage Road, Cave Creek, AZ 85331, or bob@dreamscience.org.

Welcome to the Dream to Freedom technique (DTF), an easy method in which you use dreamwork to quickly identify an unresolved emotional issue you are subconsciously dealing with and then apply an energy psychology "tapping" technique to clear your stress regarding the issue. A detailed description, along with the script used to administer the protocol, is provided in this chapter. A downloadable worksheet for recording a session can be found at www.dreamscience.org (Energy Psychology button).

## Why Dreams and Energy Psychology

The psychological healing process often starts with surface-level problems, and then proceeds to peeling away emotional layers until the core issue surfaces. When integrating energy psychology with dreamwork, however, it is possible to begin at a deeper level. Dreams focus on the more salient unprocessed emotional issues of the day. Dreamwork can therefore quickly bring to consciousness an issue with which a person is unconsciously dealing. On the other hand, dreamwork alone—in the absence of other therapies—is not necessarily designed to reduce the emotional stress that may surface, nor help the individual move through the emotional barriers it reveals. Energy psychology (EP), in turn, complements dreamwork by providing a method for reducing the stress and emotional barriers to healing, once an issue is identified. Combining the two disciplines integrates the primary benefits of each into one technique, which is useful for self-help or in a therapeutic setting.

Although the approach in this chapter describes an impressive tool for dreamwork and stress reduction, it is not a substitute for training in psychology or psychotherapy, nor is it intended to treat all conditions or replace qualified medical advice. The techniques used here in rely on recall of emotional incidents, visualization, and role-play and, as such, should not be attempted with individuals who have severe disorders that might be perturbed by such techniques. Practitioners are urged to provide clients with an informed consent to make sure they fully understand and agree to the practice. Refer to Hover-Kramer (2011) and Feinstein and Eden (2011) for guidelines on ethical practices as well the Dreamwork Ethics statement on the International Association for the Study of Dreams website (www.asdreams.org).

Although this chapter is written from the perspective of the practitioner, it can be applied just as readily in self-help by adjusting the terminology a bit for personal work. Because the persons to whom the protocol is applied can range from clients or subjects to individuals and groups, we have used the all-encompassing term "the dreamer," as the protocol begins with a reported dream.

## DTF Design Principles

There are three parts to the protocol: Part 1, which explores the dream using a Gestalt-based approach for discovering the unconscious emotional issues with which the dream and the dreamer is dealing; Part 2, in which we apply energy work, specifically tapping, in order to reduce the anxiety surrounding the issue that stands in the way of progress; and Part 3, in which, once the emotional barriers are reduced, the dream is once again used as an aid in defining what action the person can now take to progress beyond the situation.

The basis for the dreamwork design can be found in *Dream Language* or *Dream to Freedom* (Hoss, 2005; Hoss & Hoss, 2013) or on the website www.dreamscience.org. It is designed to work with dreams in the natural way your dreaming brain works with a dream: beginning with the discovery of important unresolved emotional conflicts; using the insight within the dream to compensate for misconceptions that contribute to the conflict; and following the cues in the dream to test potentially rewarding solutions that can help you move beyond the problem.

The DTF protocol was designed to adapt dreamwork to any of a number of energy psychology techniques aimed at reducing emotional stress. The standard DTF protocol, however, suggests a variation of EFT modified so as to align with dreamwork. For review of traditional EFT approaches, see *Energy Psychology Interactive* (Feinstein, 2004), *The EFT Mini-Manual* (Church, 2012), and www.eftuniverse.com.

## DTF Part 1: Problem Exploration Phase

The protocol begins by exploring the dream to reveal underlying emotional issues that might not be readily apparent on the surface. It often begins with the practitioner asking the client (the dreamer) if he or she has a recent dream or the client brings up a dream, which was either disturbing or felt significant.

The origins of the dreamworking approach lie in: the theoretical work of Carl Jung, the eminent Swiss psychologist and founder of analytical psychology; the practice of Gestalt therapy codeveloped by Fritz Perls; and recent findings in the neuroscience of REM (rapid eye movement) sleep that suggest a conflict resolution and adaptive learning model for dreaming.

Carl Jung, the eminent Swiss psychologist and founder of analytical psychology, stated that "dreams are the most readily accessible expression of the unconscious" (Jung, 1971, p. 283). In the last decade, brain scans (Hobson, Pace-Schott, & Stickbold, 2003) have supported this, showing that the centers that are active during REM dreaming are mostly those that process information below our threshold of awareness or before the outcome becomes conscious. One highly active region is the limbic system, the "emotional brain." This has lead researchers to understand that dreams selectively process unresolved emotional issues and threats, helping us adapt to waking life (Seligman & Yellen, 1987; Stewart & Koulack, 1993; Revonsuo, 2000; Coutts, 2008). From a psychological perspective, this is an important observation in understanding just how valuable dreams can be for quickly revealing the deeper inner issues that a person is struggling with, issues that might be difficult to reveal using cognitive dialogue-based approaches.

Jung (1964, p. 5) also stated that "dreams reveal the unconscious aspect of a conscious event. As you explore dreams, you may notice that, although the dream appears to relate to some event in the dreamer's waking life, the event itself does not appear in the dream. This phenomenon may be a result of our episodic memory (ability to recall episodes) being deactivated during REM. However, the active limbic system is able to readily recall and processes the associated emotional memories and concerns. This ability to focus on the emotional threat and process the appropriate emotional response may have been by evolutionary design.

Furthermore, according to Jung, the unconscious aspect of an event appears as an "emotionally charged pictorial language" (Jung, 1964, p. 30). Ernest Hartmann, MD, researcher and professor of psychiatry at Tufts University, has a similar observation. He states that the dreaming brain is "hyper-connected," weaving new information into existing memory based on what is emotionally important to us. These new connections are presented as picture-metaphor, picturing emotional similarities and revealing new perspectives (Hartmann, 1996, 2011). He further stated that the dream images contain the "feeling-state" of the dreamer. The highly visual and associative nature of our dreams is likely due to the activity in the visual association cortex, along with other REM active areas that associate sensory experience with meaning. They create visual images that are picture representations of the feelings, memories, and concepts being processed within.

Fritz Perls, best known for his work in developing Gestalt therapy (Perls, 1976), provided us with the tools for revealing the emotions contained in dream imagery. Perls considered all the things that populate our dreams to be fragments of our personality (Perls, 1969, pp. 71, 72). They are out there in the dream, rather than integrated into the dreamer, because they are "alienated" (representing feelings that are hurtful or threatening to our self-image). In order to become "whole" we need to reown these parts by allowing them to express themselves and to accommodate them in some manner. This is accomplished in a role-play exercise whereby the dreamer "becomes that thing in the dream" and gives it a "voice" (Perls, 1969, p. 74). In so doing, the emotions that created the dream image surface and are verbalized.

Gestalt therapy is a clinical therapeutic approach that goes much further than is required in the DTF protocol. For this reason we use a simple "scripted Gestalt," which is a series of questions designed to guide the dreamer through a brief role-play session. It takes the dreamer only deep enough to reveal the nature of the emotional conflicts underlying the issue with which the dream is dealing. The dreamer is asked to "become" that "thing" in the dream and, once in that role, is guided through the role-play by answering a group of six to seven questions as they imagine how that "thing" would answer them. These questions are popularly known as the "six magic questions."

The first six questions were designed in pairs to reveal three different emotional connections between the dream and waking life: (1) The first two questions—"What are you?" and "What is your purpose?"—explore the role of the dream element as it might relate to the role the dreamer sees for her or himself in waking life; (2) the next two—"What do you like…" and "What do you dislike.." about being that "thing" in the dream—are designed to reveal potential conflict; and (3) the final two questions—"What do you fear most?" and "What do you desire most?—are designed to reveal fears and desires that motivate the conflict. An optional seventh question—"What would you like to tell the dreamer?"—can be revealing when that "thing" in the dream is interacting or is in conflict with the dreamer in some way (Hoss, 2005, p. 206). In traditional Gestalt work, or other therapeutic approaches (Wakefield, 2012), this question would initiate a longer dialogue between the dream ego and that dream element, but for the DTF protocol, further dialogue is not always necessary.

Throughout the exploration process, the key element is that the dreamer be able to relate the discoveries to waking life feelings and situation. Much of what is discovered either in the dream narrative or the role-play exercise is metaphor and must be related by analogy to the dreamer's life. It is important to feed back the statements and phrases to the dreamer and have the dreamer listen to them, not as having come from something in the dream, but as if each came from the dreamer, describing a feeling or situation from his or her own waking life.

The following example illustrates the principle that the dream reflects the unconscious aspect of an event as a picture-metaphor, from which the emotional contents can be revealed through role-play. This woman was in a relationship that was being undermined by traumatic memories from an earlier divorce. She felt the need to be strong and nurturing for her new boyfriend who was having an operation, but she also felt such anxiety that she was about to end the relationship. The dream was a short scene that took place in her ex-husband's home, where she was looking out at a tree containing dark things. She was trying to determine if the things were birds or bats. The image she picked was of a lone bird's nest. When she "became" the birds nest (role-play), she stated: *"My purpose is to provide a safe landing spot and what I desire is to be there and strong when needed; what I dislike is getting crapped on and what I fear is getting blown out of the tree."* We can see that this was not just an imagined bird's nest speaking, but the dreamer's own unconscious speaking through that bird's nest, expressing conflicting feelings between the painful memories and her desires

in this present situation. Note that the conscious event that triggered the dream was her boyfriend's pending operation, which did not show up in the dream at all. The unconscious impact, the unresolved emotional conflict between wanting to nurture and fear of getting hurt again, was the focus of the dream and drove the dream plot. The picture-metaphor of the lone bird's nest represented the emotional conflict.

## DTF Part 2: Tapping to Reduce Emotional Barriers

Part 2 of the DTF protocol applies a "tapping" technique to reduce the emotional stress brought to mind by the situation revealed in the dreamwork. The idea is that once the stress and emotional barriers are reduced, it becomes easier for the dreamer to explore the dream further and define next steps for progressing beyond the problem.

Some of the common features of TFT and EFT, which we have adapted for use with dreams in the DTF protocol, are: a) mentally activating and picturing a scene from a specific problematic incident; b) rating the stress level; c) making verbal statements and/or affirmations that hold the scene in mind while tapping; d) tapping on a "standard" set of acupoints; and e) continuing until the self-reported stress level reduces to at or near 0. While the DTF protocol is not dependent on any particular energy method, our standard approach uses an adaption, by permission, of Clinical EFT, described in *The EFT Mini-Manual* (Church, 2012) and www.eftuniverse.com, with influence from *Energy Psychology Interactive* (Feinstein, 2004).

There are four important variations required of traditional energy psychology or EFT protocols to adapt them for use with dreamwork in the DTF protocol. The emphasis is on relying on the unconscious where possible to guide the approach, avoiding rational distortions as much as is practical. This means using the dream to help define the problem to be worked on, and using what comes from the dreamwork to create any affirmations to be used in setting up the tapping procedures. These are the variations:

1. Most EP sessions begin with the client reporting a symptom or problem they wish to work on. In the DTF protocol we let the dream (the unconscious) define the problem to be worked on.

2. We attempt to bypass the surface symptoms by beginning at a bit deeper level. We do this by employing a Gestalt-based dreamwork technique that reveals some of the deeper inner conflicts, fears, and motivating factors closer to the core of the issue.

3. We rarely use the standard Setup Statements suggested in the various applications of EFT, but rather create an affirmation that pairs the negative feelings from the specific situation that surfaced from the dreamwork with a positive intention that might also come from the dreamwork.

4. Rather than simply ending the session with a reduction in stress (a wonderful achievement in itself), we turn back to the dream for help in defining next steps in moving forward and perhaps for dealing with the situation if and when it arises again. The reduction in stress provides a new slate, a fresh new beginning to build on, so it is important to take advantage of that at the moment.

## DTF Part 3: Dream Guidance and Closure

Now that the anxiety or emotional barrier surrounding the issue is reduced, we can focus on examining the dream for clues as to how best to gain closure and move forward. Dreams attempt to resolve problems whether we recall them or not. So returning to the dream for guidance might reveal a more natural approach than you might otherwise arrive at.

Jung stated that the general function of dreams is to "restore psychological balance by producing dream material that reestablishes psychic equilibrium" (Jung, 1964, p. 34). He called this the "transcendent function" of dreaming (Jung, 1971, p. 279). It works by "compensating" or correcting for misconceptions that stand in our way, such that we can transition from one state of mind to another. The dreaming brain may indeed have the capacity for this activity. Although the rational thinking part of the brain is inactive in REM sleep, there are many centers active in REM sleep (Hobson, Pace-Schott, & Stickbold, 2003) that are involved in the unconscious or preconscious processing of decisions (among them the anterior cingulate, basal ganglia, insula, and medial prefrontal cortex).

In the waking state they provide such mental function as: detecting that something is wrong; initiating and mediating a resolution; imagining, planning, and testing "what if" scenarios; providing cues (with a "sense of knowing") to guide our actions; monitoring the consequences of our actions; selecting a scenario that is judged to lead to a rewarding outcome; and adapting our behavior in order to achieve that outcome (Hoss & Hoss, 2013). So if we can observe these activities taking place in the dream state, they may indeed provide us with natural clues as to how best to approach the problem in waking life.

From a practical sense, however, it is difficult to recognize and track all these actions in any one dream. In the DTF protocol we have, therefore, reduced the task to looking for four revealing activities: surprise, guidance, reversal/acceptance, and emotional reinforcement:

1. Surprise—something in the dream that was unexpected by the dreamer. This often occurs when the brain detects an anomaly or conflicting perceptions, an inconsistency between our conscious experience and our inner view of reality or our sense of self. The surprise captures the attention of the dream ego and pictures the misconception in a new context in an attempt to correct it.

2. Guidance—some activity intended to redirect the action or thinking of the dreamer. It is sometimes combined with the surprise. It can also take the form of: a "knowing" character or event in the dream suggesting or directing or revealing new insight, awareness, or potential new direction; spoken or written words; or a moment of insight or discovery. It is typically in the form of a metaphor, thus rarely literal.

3. Reversal or acceptance—a point of change in the dream when the dreamer (or character the dreamer identifies with) accepts the guidance or reverses their thinking, actions, or direction. Drawing analogies to waking life reversals can be useful.

4. Emotional reinforcement—a positive reward often accompanied by pleasant color, light, and sometimes sounds. This typically occurs when the dream ego accepts or follows the guidance cues, thus reinforcing the learning (as in the example

that follows). It can also take the form of a warning (negative reinforcement) when the dream ego is engaged in something requiring correction.

The following example illustrates the appearance of these four activities in a dream. Bill was a corporate executive whose company was restructuring and eliminating top executives. He was holding out for the possibility that some position would open internally because he feared that if he looked elsewhere he would never find a good job at his age and would also lose his retirement package. The positions open to him internally, however, were uncertain and not well suited to his career, but he considered it too risky to look outside. He had the following dream: *"I am a passenger in a boat on a dark underground river trying to find a way out and a 'position' in the windows where I can see daylight. A tour guide appears behind me and points out an opening in the front of the boat that I had not seen before* [surprise] *and says, "You can walk out that door* [guidance]*." I didn't understand what he was saying at first and was reluctant since it didn't make sense, but finally at his constant urging I walked out the door* [reversal/acceptance] *and found myself out in front. At that point the boat emerged from the cave and into a bright beautiful sunlit setting of calm water* [emotional reinforcement]*."* In a follow-up, actual learning appears to have taking place. After the dream the executive decided to try looking outside and accepted what turned out to be a fantastic position in another company and he indeed "walked out the door."

Note that because these activities appear as metaphor, it is often difficult to understand fully what the dream is trying to do, even if some of them appear in the dream. The dream may also end badly or contain no closure or concluding direction. When faced with this situation, the dream can still be used as a platform to create a possible new metaphor for closure. We use a form of dream reentry and spontaneous visualization to complete the dream, similar to imagery rehearsal treatment (Krakow et al., 2001), which is often used in working with nightmare sufferers.

Whether the solution for moving forward comes from the insight within the dream or from the imagined new ending, it must first be tested. Dreamers need to think through whether it is healthy, practical, and appropriate, and won't leave them stuck in a new problem. If it is a healthy solution, then dreamers are encouraged to define the "next steps" or what they need to do to act on it.

## The Dream to Freedom Protocol

The following sections will take you through the full three-part, step-by-step protocol. Each step includes a suggested script, followed by a case example to illustrate it, as well as procedural notes that provide hints and tips for administering the step. A worksheet that can be used to administer the protocol can be downloaded at www.dreamscience.org (Energy Psychology button).

The illustrative case example that accompanies each step comes from a woman who woke terrified from a short and seemingly innocuous dream. In her waking life she was frozen with fear, unable to take the necessary action to move across country to take an exciting new job she had accepted. With 2 weeks to go she had not even put her house on the market. As we discovered from the dreamwork she had conflicts with her bosses and let go of two prior jobs. She was terrified that it would happen again if she took this job.

## Part 1: Dreamwork Discovery Phase (Problem Identification)

A session usually begins with some personal dialogue intended to bring dreamers to a comfortable and safe place as well as a discussion regarding their situation. If they did not offer a dream, you might ask if they had a recent one they would like to work with. An informed consent document is shared in this introduction as well. The EFT protocol formally begins with the dream. You might begin by asking the dreamer to give the dream a title as if it were a book or movie. It is useful as an identifier but also can create a revealing metaphor. Voice-recording the session is helpful for follow-up work; you will be surprised at the connections that pop out later.

**Step 1—Dream summary.** Script: "Reenter the dream (or if lengthy, the most emotionally charged segment) and describe it as if you are re-experiencing it, in the first person, present tense."

Case example: *"A friend of mine Jane is painting over my newly painted gray walls, red and blue. I try to wipe it off with a rag. I woke screaming!"*

Procedural note: Dream reentry is suggested even if the person has written the dream down. It provides a fresh view with richer metaphors than simply reading the narrative. If the dream had many segments or scenes it is likely testing multiple scenarios involving the same core issue, so mentally note the associations between each one. As you listen to the dream, try to write down or underline phrases that sounds like metaphors, figurative statements that might be describing something in the dreamer's life. Note any past dreams that the dreamer might spontaneously recall at that moment. There is likely a connection. Keeping in mind that the DTF protocol relies on working on just one or a few dream images, you will eventually want to concentrate on just the final few segments, or whichever one seems most important to the dreamer.

**Step 2—Waking life situation.** Script: "Describe any situations in your life around the time of the dream that were emotionally important or impacting, either negative or positive."

Case example: *"In waking life I am nervous about moving across the country to take a new job."*

Procedural note: The situation the dreamer brings up may or may not be the subject of the dream, but it is a start and it often links to the dream in some way. If the dream is an older one and they can't recall the situation at the time, don't worry; just ask them what generally was taking place at the time and what is happening in the present that is a bit stressful.

**Step 3—Dream-to-life analogy (metaphors/ associations/feelings).** Script: "Can you see any connections between the dream and your waking life situation? If so, describe the situation and how you felt at the time." If you noted any phrases that sound like they might be a metaphor, ask about it in some manner such as this: "Does this phrase _____ describe a feeling or something going on in your life at this time?"

Case example: There was nothing obvious other than a suspected metaphor in the phrase *painting over* the walls, so we asked: "Are you painting over something in your life at this moment?" The dreamer indicated that she was trying to avoid her concerns about taking her new job and moving.

Procedural note: It is helpful to point out and explore any possible metaphors you might see;

phrases in the telling of the dream that might also describe a situation or feeling in the dreamer's life. If there is a connection, an "aha" moment of recognition, encourage the dreamer to briefly discuss the situation and the feelings at the time. Take care not to impose any of your own personal projections at this point as an interpretation of the dream; the final "meaning" needs to come from the dreamer from whatever surfaces in the in-depth dreamwork yet to come.

**Step 4—Let the dream speak (scripted role-play).** Theoretically, almost everything in the dream is a visual representation of material being processed deeper within (perhaps an emotional conflict, memory, or situation with which the dream is dealing). At this point we want to explore the imagery that draws the dreamer's attention by virtue of the emotionally charged material it may represent. We do this by letting the dream imagery express itself, using a role-play technique derived from Gestalt therapy, guided by a standard script of six or seven questions.

**Step 4a—Chose a dream image to explore.** Script: "Again close your eyes and reenter the dream, perhaps at the most emotionally charged point, and look around the dream at all that is around you (all the characters and things you see in the dream). Notice if one of them draws your attention or is perhaps strangely curious to you— no matter if it is a lesser element or a dominant one."

Case example: *"The rag."*

Procedural note: We are trying to identify one salient issue to work on, which often comes from working with just one or two seemingly important dream elements. So the question becomes how to pick the best image(s) to work with. By asking dreamers to reenter the dream and pick something in the dream that draws their attention, we rely on the dreamer's unconscious for help. It is best to go with what dreamers are drawn to, but since they will eventually have to role-play and "become" that thing, some guidance is helpful. There are no hard-and-fast rules, but it is best that they pick something tangible rather than an action or feeling and pick one thing rather than a group. It is also well to avoid archetypal images, for example, geometric patterns or ill-defined masculine or feminine characters having no specific role. Fritz Perls considered things to sometimes have more important content than human characters. If dreamers pick a character from their waking life, it is likely borrowed to represent a personality characteristic. The character often represents a way the dreamer is acting in the waking situation, or alternatively a characteristic that the dreamer needs to adopt in order to better deal with the situation. On the other hand, if the character is an integral part of the waking situation the dream is dealing with, it may simply represent itself.

**Step 4b—Role-play.** Script: "Close your eyes again and bring that dream image (X) to your mind's eye. Lift your finger when you are there. Now take three deep breaths and on each breath bring X closer to you with the goal being that on the third breath you merge with X in the dream, and become it. Once there look out at the dream from its perspective and feel what it is feeling in the role it is playing in the dream. If you can't become that thing, then at least imagine how X might answer the questions that I will ask. I am now going to ask six questions and you are to answer as if you are that thing (X) in the dream, using first person, present-tense—'I am' or 'I feel'—responses. Don't think about the response, just say the first thing that comes to mind."

1. "What are you, name and **describe** yourself, perhaps how you feel in that role?" Case example: *I am a rag, in somebody's hands.*

2. "As X what is your **purpose or function**?" Case example: *"My purpose is to be handy and clean things up."*

3. "What do you **like** most about being X?" Case example: *"What I like about being a rag is being available, needed, and used."*

4. "What do you **dislike** about, or what is the downside of, being X? Case example: *"What I dislike about being a rag is getting thrown away after the job is done."*

5. "As X what do you **fear** the most, what is the worst thing that can happen to you?" Case example: *"What I fear as a rag is getting dirty and being thrown away."*

6. "As X what do you **desire** the most?" Case example: *"What I desire as a rag is staying clean and continuing to be used."*

7. Optional: "Now as X look out into the dream scene where you see the dreamer. What would you like to say to the dreamer?" (Suggested only when it fits the context of the dream story. It can be revealing when that thing in the dream is interacting with the dreamer or when it is in conflict with or impeding the progress of the dreamer in some way.) Case example: *"You will mess it up if you try to wipe it away."*

When they have completed the last question, tell the dreamer, "Now open your eyes and shake off the essence of that dream image, that thing in the dream, and come back to being yourself."

Note: If X is a known person, that is, one the dreamer knows, then an adjustment to the script is recommended. Question 1 is changed as follows in order to explore personality characteristics (in this case example, the image of her friend Jane):

1a) "Who are you? And describe your personality." Case example: *"I am Jane, I am a person who goes with the flow."*

2a) "How is your personality like that of the dreamer?" Case example: *"We are both ambitious and fun loving."*

3a) "How is your personality different from that of the dreamer?" Case example: *"I am more flexible and less hesitant when it comes to trying new things."*

Procedural note: For those who have difficulty, ask that they do their best to imagine how that thing in the dream might answer the questions you are going to ask it. When asking the question, record the answer as close as possible to the way the dreamers stated it. This is so that, when read back to them, dreamers can 'connect' with any phrases that sound like a feeling or something happening in their lives at the time. Try to limit the number of statements (usually one to three per question), unless you feel that some important discovery may take place by letting them continue. If you feel that the answers had little depth, then you might ask a qualifying question such as "What did you feel?" or "Why did you feel that way?" If you feel the need to add an additional question or two to fit the moment, it may be all right to go with your intuition; keep in mind, however, that the purpose at this point in the DTF protocol is not to initiate therapy but simply to identify a core emotional problem to work with. We warn against adding too many more questions or you may lead the dreamer into a lot of tangential issues. The six to seven questions usually provide more material than you will need.

**Step 4c—Waking life reflection.** Script: "I am going to read each response back to you.

Switch perspectives and listen to them *not* as if X is saying them, but as if it is *you* saying them about a way *you* have felt lately or a situation in *your* waking life. If any statement sounds like it describes a feeling or situation in your waking life, stop me and describe the situation and how the statement relates to the feelings involved." Procedural note: if any statements seem metaphor rich and fit together as pairs, try reading them back that way, for example: "Do these statements sound like a role you perceive yourself in? (read the 'I am…'" and "My purpose is…" statements). "Do these statements sound like conflicting emotions you are feeling about a situation in your life?" (read the 'I like…'" and "I dislike…" statements). "Do these statements sound like conflicting fears and desires that you are feeling?" (read the "I fear…" and "I desire…" statements).

Case example: In the case study, the dreamer felt every statement related directly to some aspect of the waking life situation. She stated: *"I do feel my career is in somebody else's hands. I do consider my purpose on the job is to be handy and clean things up. On my last two jobs, I was hired to do a job, but once that job was done, I was not kept on, I was told I was no longer needed and was let go—so, yes, I dislike being 'thrown out after the job is done.' I fear that on this next job I might mess up again and be thrown out—but will now have left my friends and family, sold my home, and be clear across country. I want to avoid conflict and continue to have my talents used."* The first two statements relate to the waking life role that the dreamer sees herself in; feeling like her future is in somebody else's hands and that her role is to be handy and clean things up. Her conflict is revealed in statements 3 and 4: liking to be needed and used, but disliking being let go after the job is done. The motivations (fears and desires) driving the conflict are revealed in statements 5 and 6: desires to have her talents used but fears messing up again and being "thrown out."

Procedural note: Make sure that when you read the statement back, you include the part of the question that preceded it so that it makes a complete expression in the context of the dreamer. For example, a role-play statement such as *"to clean things up"* or *"My purpose as the rag in the dream is to clean things up"* would be read back to the dreamer as *"My purpose is to clean things up."* If a statement fits or comes close to describing a waking life feeling or situation, then ask the dreamer

to let you know and then explore the situation a bit. If the dreamer makes no connection, even after reading them in the pairs as suggested, then have them go back into the dream and pick something else in the dream that attracts their attention.

**Step 5 (optional)—Exploring color.** Color can be an important part of a dream image because it combines with the other parts of that image to give it its full meaning and additional emotional component. Recent research exploring color content immediately upon subjects waking from sleep has demonstrated that almost all dreams contain color (Schredl, Fuchedzhiea, Hämig, & Schindele, 2008). The problem is recall. Color seems to diminish more rapidly than other content, but this can actually be an advantage in dreamwork since it is likely that we recall color images that captured our attention due to the higher emotional intensity they represent. Color is associated with emotion, in both the waking state and the dream state, and in much the same manner (Hoss & Hoffman, 2004). Research in the field of color psychology has shown that the human brain and autonomic nervous system respond to color subliminally (below our threshold of awareness). Color evokes a relatively common set of neural responses, different for different colors. Blue, for example, calms the parasympathetic branch, where as red excites the sympathetic branch, causing changes in heartbeat, respiration, and other autonomic functions (Lüscher, 1971).

Table 1 provides a tabulation of emotional phrases representative of the human subliminal response to color. It is derived from color psychology research and literature, including the Lüscher Color Test (Hoss, 2005). The focus is on subliminal response and, as such, it excludes cultural associations or popular meanings often assigned to colors. The table of colors and their associations does not describe the "meaning" of any color. It is simply an aid for triggering possible connections with the dreamer's own waking life situation or feelings. The statements provide a spectrum of emotions, from being filled with the emotion to needing more of that emotional stimulus. The table also references Jung's theories on darkness or black as related to the unconscious and light or white to the conscious. In his view, the appearance of both as a pattern signifies the forces of balance and integration at work in the dream (Jung, 1972, p. 5). This might be a useful observation when the dream is working out a conflict or integrating conscious and unconscious material.

**Table 1.** *Subliminal Emotion Associations with Color*

**Red**

1) I feel intense, vital or animated.

2) I feel transformed.

3) I feel assertive, forceful.

4) I feel creative.

5) I want to live life to its fullest.

6) I want to win, succeed, achieve.

7) I feel sexy or have strong sexual urges.

8) I have a driving desire.

9) I need something to make me feel alive again.

10) I need to be more assertive and forceful.

11) I need to get out and enjoy myself.

**Note:** Red can also appear in cases where the dream is focused on an injury or inflammation.

**Orange**

1) I want to expand my interests and develop new activities.

2) I want a wider sphere of influence.

3) I feel friendly and welcoming.

4) I want more contact with others.

5) I feel enthusiastic, outgoing, and adventurous.

6) I am driven by desires and hopes toward the new, undiscovered, and satisfying.

7) I feel driven but need to overcome my doubts or fear of failure.

8) I must avoid spreading myself too thin.

**Yellow**

1) I feel a sense of joy and optimism.

2) I feel alert.

3) I am seeking a solution that will open up new and better possibilities and allow my hopes to be fulfilled.

4) I feel the new direction I am taking will bring happiness in my future.

5) I am hopeful.

6) I need to find a way out of this circumstance or relationship.

7) I need a change.

8) I may be compensating for something.

9) I feel I may be acting compulsively.

**Green**

1) I need to establish myself, my self-esteem, my independence.

2) I want recognition.

3) I need to increase the certainty of my own value and status, through acknowledgment by others of my achievements.

4) Hard work and drive will gain me recognition and self-esteem.

5) My opinion must prevail.

6) I must hold on to this view in order to maintain my self-esteem.

*(continued)*

**Table 1.** (*Continued*)

7) I want what I am due.

8) I must maintain control of the events.

9) Things must not change.

10) Detail and logic are important.

11) I need to increase my sense of security.

12) I need more money to feel secure.

13) I want to withdraw or retreat into my own center.

14) I feel I am being healed or I need healing.

## Blue

1) I need rest, peace or a chance to recuperate.

2) I need a relationship free from contention in which I can trust and be trusted.

3) I need a peaceful state of harmony offering contentment and a sense of belonging.

4) I feel tranquil, peaceful and content.

5) I feel a sense of harmony.

6) I feel a sense of belonging.

7) I feel a meditative awareness or unity.

## Violet

1) I seek a magical state where wishes are fulfilled.

2) I yearn for a magical relationship of romance and tenderness.

3) I have a need to identify with something or someone.

4) I need more intimacy.

5) I often engage in fantasy perhaps because I feel a bit insecure about the situation.

6) I like to win others over with my charm.

7) I feel an identification or "mystic" union with something or someone.

8) I feel I am gaining a deep intuitive understanding of the situation.

9) I feel a sense of intimacy.

10) The feeling is erotic.

## Brown

1) I seek a secure state where I can be physically comfortable and relax or recover.

2) I am uneasy and insecure in the existing situation.

3) I need a more affectionate environment.

4) I need a situation imposing less physical strain.

5) I want to satisfy the physical senses (food, luxury, sex).

**Notes:** If the color is a natural or wood brown, try these Jungian associations: 1) I am concerned about matters of family, home, or my "roots;" 2) I am concerned with a son or daughter; 3) I am searching for my true self or natural state of being. A dirty brown color can sometimes accompany physical illness.

## Gray

1) I want to shield myself from those feelings.

2) I feel emotionally distant, only an observer.

3) It is as if I am standing aside, watching myself mechanically go through the motions.

4) I want to remain uncommitted, noninvolved, shielded, or separated from the situation.

(*continued*)

**Table 1.** (*Continued*)

5) I do not want to make a decision that will require my emotional involvement.

6) I have put up with too much and wish to avoid any further emotional stimulation.

7) I am trying to escape an anxious situation.

8) I may be compensating for something I don't like.

**Black**

1) I am anxious and don't know why.

2) I am fearful of or intimidated by the situation.

3) I have been dealt an unacceptable blow.

4) Nothing is as it should be.

5) I refuse to allow it or them to influence my point of view.

6) I can't accept the situation and don't wish to be convinced otherwise.

7) I feel the need for extreme action.

8) I am in revolt.

**Note:** To Jung, black and darkness represented the realm of the unconscious. The dreamer entering darkness might suggest exploring the unconscious self, a turning within, or a submission ("death of the ego") so that the new self can be "reborn." Something entering darkness might relate to suppression. Beautiful shiny black might be a positive view of the unconscious, from which a new self emerges.

**White**

1) This is a new experience.

2) I'm becoming aware of new feelings.

3) I'm experiencing a new beginning, a reawakening, a transformation.

4) I have a new outlook, a new awareness.

5) I feel pure and innocent.

6) I feel open and accepting.

7) I feel unprepared.

8) I feel alone, isolated.

9) It feels cold or sterile.

**Note:** grouping of colors with white might add a sense of newness (or emergence) to the emotions involved, and mixing with white (pastels) can add a calming or renewal tone.

**Pink**

1) I feel romantic or loving toward someone or something.

2) I am feeling very sensitive about something.

3) I feel nurturing or a need to nurture someone.

4) I am feeling compassionate.

5) I am avoiding aggression or want to calm my aggressive feelings.

6) I need romance.

7) I need nurturing.

8) I need something to calm me down.

9) Dealing with this feeling of assertiveness or driving energy is new to me.

**Note: Black and white patterns**
According to Jungian theory, this is an indication of positive integrating forces active within the psyche, a union of opposites, a bringing together of the conscious (light or white) and unconscious (darkness or black) so that they move together, thus bringing about balance and a state of wholeness within the psyche. This typically appears at a time of conflict resolution (opposing perceptions) or as internal change is taking place.

Script: "Were there any colors associated with the image X or in the remainder of the dream that stood out?" (Note: at this point refer to Table 1, and select the color that comes closest to the client's choice.) "I am going to read a number of statements to you. Close your eyes and listen to them. Raise your finger if you feel a 'connection' with any statement, if it comes close to describing a recent feeling or situation in your life." (Write down the results.) "I am now going to read these statements back to you" (read the ones they indicated from Table 1). "Describe the situation or feelings they remind you of." "Try rephrasing the statement(s) in a way that best describes your feeling." Procedural note: When there are two colors in an obvious pair, consider the possibility of them relating to two conflicting emotions. You might read the two and ask: "Do these two statements sound like a conflict you are experiencing?"

Case example: When the dreamer read the statements for the color gray (the color she used to paint the wall), she connected with *"I want to remain uncommitted, non-involved, shielded, or separated from the situation"* and *"I do not want to make a decision that will require my emotional involvement."* She related these to her emotional *"wall"* and desire to separate herself from making a decision to take the job and move. Her friend Jane (representing *"going with the flow"*) then introduces a conflict pictured as the color pair red and blue. For red she connected with *"I want to win, succeed, achieve"* and blue with *"I need a relationship free from contention in which I can trust and be trusted."* This she could relate to wanting to take the new job to *"succeed and achieve,"* which was in conflict with needing a relationship *"free from contention"* in which she *"can trust and be trusted,"* which she feared she might not have.

**Step 6—Pick the most emotionally charged statement or situation.** Script: "Let's review the role-play statements that you connected with in step 4 as well as any emotional statements related to color from step 5." (Read back the ones that the dreamer identified as significant.) "Pick the statement that feels the most emotionally charged or relates to the most stressful waking life situation. Summarize that situation and if necessary rephrase the statement to better relate to it."

Case example: *"I fear messing up and being thrown out."*

Procedural note: At this point the underlying emotional situation should be apparent; however, it is likely that more than one set of feelings or conflicts has surfaced. The objective is to identify the most emotionally charged situation that contributed to the problem so that the energy protocol can be applied to that stressful memory.

## Part 2: Energy Psychology Application and Stress Reduction

**Step 7—Recalling a specific stressful incident.** Script: "In order to work on the emotional barriers and stress underlying this situation, we need to go one level deeper. Think about the emotional statement or situation you picked, and the feelings involved. Then recall a specific incident when you felt that way and visualize the scene." "Let me know if at any point your stress level increases to a point where you are having difficulty and we will stop the exercise and let the feelings subside."

Case example: *"On my last job, I had a misunderstanding with my boss and I can picture the moment in my boss's office that she told me she no longer needed me!"*

Procedural note: At this point the dreamer should have been able to describe the situation that the dream has surfaced, and the feelings involved, at least in general terms. Although it is possible to tap on the general situation, it is best to go one level deeper, to a specific incident when the dreamer felt those feelings, a memory that the dreamer can visualize. We can then work on the stressful emotional response that was specifically encoded at that moment. A note of caution: Some memories, such as those of PTSD sufferers, can be so severe that recalling the incident can retraumatize the sufferer. So if there is strong resistance to recalling such a disturbing memory, then back off and tap on the more generalized feelings or problems (perhaps use the statement that the dreamer picked in Step 6). PTSD work should not be attempted by anyone but a trained professional.

**Step 8—Initial stress rating.** Script: "Become aware of your stress level right now as you picture the scene. Rate your level of stress from 0 to 10, with 10 being the most stressful."

Case example: *"It is an 8!"*

Procedural note: A stress measurement is used after each round so that you can judge progress (as the stress level decreases) and know when to stop or continue with tapping rounds until the stress level reduces to near or at 0. It is also useful in determining if the stress has increased due to new aspects (new associated memories) that may have arisen.

**Step 9—Affirmation.** Script: "I am now going to help you develop two phrases to be used to keep the emotional scene in mind and set your intention, while tapping: 1) an affirmation that pairs the negative problem or feelings with a positive intention or expectation, used to initiate or set up the procedure; and 2) a Reminder Phrase that is an abbreviation of the problem statement, used to keep the problem in mind while you tap on it."

**Step 9a—The affirmation.** "The affirmation pairs the negative statement of the problem with a positive intention in a phrase that sounds like this: 'Even though I have this problem or feel this way, I choose to, or I know I can (adding your positive intention).' First, let's define the problem or the feelings that arose when you visualized the specific scene in step 7. Check with the dreamwork statement in step 6 to see if that remains adequate to keep the problem in mind, or if not, redefine it." "Now that the problem is defined, let's add the second half—the positive intention. Check the 'I like' or 'I desire' statements from the role-play in step 4 to see if they provide an intention phrase that fits. In the end you should have a statement that reads, 'Even though I have this problem/feel this way (name the problem/feeling), I choose to or know that I can (name the positive intention).'"

Case example: *"Even though I feel thrown out, I know I can work well and stay clean."*

**Step 9b—Reminder Phrase.** We will use the full affirmation for an initial setup exercise, but we need a shorter version to keep the problem in mind while tapping on the various meridian points. So we pick a few words from the negative part of the longer Setup Statement that summarizes the problem or feelings."

Case example: *"Feel thrown out."*

Procedural note: Tapping works by changing the brain's stress response to an emotional memory. Neutralizing the response requires the stressful memory to be present in an atmosphere of calming sensations brought about by the tapping, such that its associated "meaning" is altered from threat to safety. The negative feeling or problem half of the affirmation is designed to hold the emotional memory in mind while tapping. The positive intention or expectation is added in order to accompany the calming sensations in altering the associations. In EFT literature (Church, 2012) it is called the "Setup Statement" and is structured as follows: "Even though I have (name of problem), I deeply and completely accept myself." In the DTF protocol, however, we try to use the unconsciously derived information from the dream as much as possible to help create the statement. Attempt to use the statements from Step 6 or 7 to create the negative problem half, and the "I desire" or the "I like" statements from the role-play (Step 4) for the positive intention. If the dreamer feels that the statement no longer fits, then work with the dreamer to define a statement that does.

**Step 10—Initial tapping round.** Procedural note: The DTF protocol is not specific to any particular energy psychology tapping protocol although we suggest the points and procedures described here as "standard" for the DTF protocol. Variations using more or fewer points or including or excluding the bridging technique are known to be effective as well; so if you are more comfortable with a slightly different set of points, feel free to use them. The tapping protocol begins with a setup exercise in which the dreamer stimulates the SI-3 (Small Intestine) meridian point (commonly called the Karate Chop point in EFT literature) by tapping on it, while stating the full affirmation and visualizing the scene. After this setup exercise, multiple tapping rounds are performed on the DTF standard set of acupressure points while keeping the problem in mind by saying the shorter Reminder Phrase. We typically tap on each point about 7 to 10 times, whatever feels comfortable. The stress level is reassessed after these two rounds. As a practitioner you would show the subject each set of points by tapping on yourself and asking the subject to follow you through them. Table 2 lists the location and description of the acupoints, adopted by permission from the *EFT Mini-Manual* (Church, 2012); note that the DTF tapping protocol varies slightly from the *Mini-Manual*.

**Step 10a—Preparation or setup exercise.** Script: "Now we will begin the energy work with a setup exercise, which prepares for the round of tapping by stimulating the SI-3 acupoint (see Table 2) as you state the full affirmation phrase while visualizing the scene. Follow me. The SI-3 acupoint (called the Karate Chop point in EFT literature) is on the side of the hand (either hand will do). It is located on the outside of the hand, the fleshy upper middle part below the base of the little finger (at the crease when making a fist).

**Table 2.** *Acupressure Tapping Points*

| Setup Tapping Point |
| --- |

**KC or Karate Chop point:** Located on the fleshy outer portion of the hand, in the upper middle about where the crease is when you make a fist, the part used in karate to deliver a blow (Small Intestine meridian, SI3). Tap the Karate Chop point with the tips of the four fingers of the opposite hand.

### Tapping Round Acupoints

**1. EB or eyebrow point:** at the start of the eyebrow where it joins the bridge of the nose (Urinary Bladder meridian, UB2)

**2. SE or side of eye:** on the outside edge of the eye socket (Gallbladder meridian, GB1)

**3. UE or under eye:** on the bony ridge of the eye socket under the pupil of the eye (Stomach meridian, ST2)

**4. UN or under nose:** under the center of the nose, one-third the distance between the nose and the upper lip (Governing Vessel, GV26)

**5. Chin:** between the lower lip and the chin, in the center (Central or Conception Vessel, CV24)

**6. CB or** collarbone points: located in a small depression under each collarbone on either side of the U-shaped groove at the top of the sternum (Kidney meridian, KD27)

**7. UA or underarm:** about four inches below the base of each armpit and about halfway between the front and back; for women, this is where a bra strap crosses, for men even with the nipple (Spleen meridian, SP21)

**8. KC or Karate Chop point**

**\*Gamut Point (for optional bridging procedure):** back of either hand a half inch toward the wrist from the point between the knuckles and the base of the ring finger and little finger (Triple Heater, TH3).

You tap on it with four fingertips of the other hand the entire time you are visualizing the scene and saying your affirmation phrase out loud, repeating it about three times: 'Even though I (have this problem/feel this way), I know that I can/I choose to (positive intention)'."

**Step 10b—Initial tapping sequence.** Script: "We will now tap on the problem, sending calming signals to your brain while keeping the problem in mind by saying your shorter Reminder Phrase."

1. **Initial round of tapping (Table 2):** "Follow me through the exercise tapping on each of the points (tap on yourself to show them) about 7 to 10 times with the balls of your fingertips or the balls of your index and middle fingers only, using either hand on either side of the body. Tap while repeating out loud your short Reminder Phrase."

2. **One more round of tapping:** "Let's do one more round of tapping." Note: whether you do the bridging sequence or not another round of tapping is recommended before reassessing the stress level; it is the same as the first round.

3. **Reassess the stress level:** "Now relax and picture the scene again; rate the level of distress you now feel from 0 to 10."

**Step 11—Subsequent rounds.** Procedural note: Assuming the stress level is not at 0, the tapping rounds are continued. The affirmation and Reminder Phrase are adjusted to include the word "still," to indicate that the stress still exists to some extent when the issue is brought to mind. Then repeat the tapping sequences of step 10, measuring the stress level after each round, until the level is near or at 0.

Script: "We will continue with another round of tapping to reduce the stress level further, but before we begin we will adjust the affirmation and Reminder Phrase to acknowledge that some stress remains by adding the word "still" to both of them. So modify your affirmation as follows: 'Even though I *still* (have this problem)' and the Reminder Phrase "*still* (have this problem)." Now let's use those statements as we repeat the tapping sequence." Repeat the setup exercise, step 10a, once with the new affirmation. Then repeat step 10b, the pair of 8-point tapping rounds, then stop and rerate the stress level. Continue the tapping rounds, 10b, until the stress reduces to near or at 0.

Case example: The affirmation was adjusted to state, *"Even though I still feel thrown out, I know I can work well and stay clean,"* and the Reminder Phrase to *"still feel thrown out."* The session in this example took three more tapping rounds to bring the SUD rating down to a 1.

**Step 12—If other aspects arise.** Procedural note: If after any round of tapping the level of stress did not diminish, or if it increased, then stop and explore the situation. Often other associated memories, perhaps more stressful situations, spontaneously surface. If the stress level is not diminishing or actually increasing due to an associated memory, it is generally ineffective to continue tapping on the original problem, as the person will be consumed with the new memory and the stress it brings about. To work on the new aspect or memory, go back to Step 7 and treat it as a new but associated incident. Ask dreamers to describe the new scene that came to mind and rate the stress level they are feeling as they picture it (Step 8). Create a new affirmation and Reminder Phrase for that new aspect or memory, just as you did in Step 9. At this point using a problem or intention statement from the dreamwork may no longer apply. Give it a look but don't force it; go with what the dreamer is now feeling and desiring based on the new memory. Once the new affirmation is defined then proceed with the tapping rounds as in steps 10 and 11. Once the stress level around this aspect is reduced to near or at 0, then ask the person to go back to the original problem and picture that scene again, and rate the stress. If it is now reduced to near or at 0, then go on to the closure protocol in Part 3. If it is still a bit elevated, then perhaps repeat with one or more rounds of tapping with that original memory and Setup Statement until a reduction occurs.

## Part 3: Closure Protocol

Once the stressful reaction to the memory is reduced, dreamers should be able to think more clearly about how they can now move beyond the problem. This is an ideal time to return to the dream for guidance. Dreams attempt to resolve internal conflict and as such may reveal the most creative natural approach to closure. Even if the dream did not reach a resolution, it may contain clues that can help formulate a more informed action plan.

**Step 13—Dream guidance.** Script: "Now that the stress related to the memory has been reduced and the emotional barriers decreased, we are ready to think about how best to find closure and move beyond the problem. Your dream was not only a reflection of the problem, but was also attempting to resolve it in creative and natural ways. So returning to the dream may provide valuable clues as to how best to move forward." "Close your eyes and reenter the dream, perhaps at the most emotionally charged point. Briefly review it until the end and restate how it ended."

Case example: the subject stated, *"I am trying to rub the paint off with a rag and wake screaming."*

**13a) Surprise:** "Did you experience a surprise at any point in the dream?"

Case example: *"Yes, I was surprised that it was Jane painting my walls."*

"If so, what was surprising about it and what was it that differed from your expectation?"

Case example: *"She is my friend and would never do that."*

**13b) Guidance:** "Did you experience any guiding actions, a new discovery or insight, perhaps a guiding character who gives you a suggestion or direction, written or verbal words, or a lesson from the dream story?" "In what ways was it trying to alter your actions or thinking in the dream?"

Case example: no obvious guidance

**13c) Reversal or acceptance:** "Was there a point where the guidance was accepted or a reversal in viewpoint or direction? If so, describe the change."

Case example: *"No, there was none."*

**13d) Positive ending:** "Did the dream end positively?" Alternatively, "Did it end with a demand or warning?" "If so, describe that ending and what specific sequence of events brought it about."

Case example: *"No, it ended with me waking up screaming. I felt terrified."*

**Life analogy:** "How might the answers in 13a, b, and c provide insight or guidance in relation to your waking life situation?"

Case example: *"Jane is a person who just goes with the flow; perhaps she is showing me to 'go with the flow.'"*

**Step 14—Finishing the dream.** Procedural note: When none of the activities in the previous step are apparent in the dream, or easily understood, or when the dream does not seem to conclude, it can still be used as a platform for determining how best to move forward. Through reentry and spontaneous imaging, the unconscious can be reengaged in creating a new ending that might produce a new metaphor or analogy to a waking life solution.

Script:

**Step 14a—Finish the dream.** "Close your eyes; take a deep breath and place yourself back at the end of the dream. Review what you were trying to do in the dream and specifically what happened that brought you to this point. Think about what you are feeling at this point. Now without thinking about it, just let the images flow; imagine continuing and finishing the dream from that point with a new ending that works out for you and those you are involved with in the dream. When finished, describe the new ending."

Case example: The dreamer reentered the dream and really immersed herself in it to the point that she surprised herself with the images that came forth, exclaiming: *"I let my friend finish painting the room red and blue...it looks great!"*

**Step 14b—Life analogy.** "How might the new ending provide insight or be analogous to a resolution for your waking life situation?"

Case example: *"Go with the flow, it might turn out just fine!"*

**Step 15—Closure.** Procedural note: Once the dreamer can relate the insight from Step 13 or 14 to their waking life situation, it is necessary to act on what is learned. To do so the insight, which the dream presents as metaphor, must be defined as a concrete solution. It must then be checked to make sure the metaphor was not interpreted in a manner that will leave the dreamer stuck again. Think through it to make sure it is healthy, practical, and appropriate. If it checks out, then the first step(s) toward putting it into action should be determined. Picking a solution-related image from the dream can also help as a reminder if the dreamer gets stuck in a similar situation in the future.

Script:

**Step 15a—Define the solution.** "Based on the insight from the exercises in steps 13 and/or 14, define what you learned in terms of a specific solution that will allow you to move ahead in your waking life situation."

Case example: *"Rather than fighting the situation, I accept and go with what is happening!"*

**Step 15b—Check it out.** "Is this a healthy, practical, and appropriate solution that allows you to progress, or might it leave you stuck again?"

Case example: *"Yes, it is a helpful solution that allows me to move forward."*

**Step 15c—Next steps.** "If the solution checks out positively, then what specific next step(s) can you take to bring it about? Imagine the next time you might be in that situation again and define specifically what you would now do."

Case example: *"I can put my house on the market and leave for my new job."*

**Step 15d—Token reminder image.** "It is often helpful to pick an image from the positive dream ending as a reminder of your solution, in the event you find yourself confronted with a similar situation in the future."

Case example: *"Jane (who goes with the flow)"*

Case example follow-up: After the session the dreamer put her house on the market, packed, and with the help of her friends (Jane included) moved to her new job.

## Conclusion

We hope that this protocol and the illustrative examples have provided you with an excellent tool to enable you to understand how dreamwork might be combined with whatever EFT or energy psychology tool you are using. If at times you need or want to work with a dream and the total protocol appears too lengthy for the specific circumstance, then the most important thing to remember is the following. The goal of the dreamwork is to discover the underlying emotional issues that the dreamer is dealing with so you can reduce the stress reaction triggered by those memories. This will rarely happen by cognitively working with metaphors or trying to project your own analysis on the dream. You will only tap into surface issues at best. If you really want to understand the dream and the dreamer, "give the dream a voice." As a bare minimum, have the dreamer "become" or imagine herself or himself as some important element in the dream and let it speak. Use the six-question script; it is fast, simple, often fun, and very revealing. Then use whatever energy tools you feel most comfortable with to diminish the stress around the emotional memory that has surfaced. Feel free to write to us at bob@dreamscience.org if you have further questions.

## References

Church, D. (2012). *The EFT mini-manual* (2nd ed.). Santa Rosa, CA: Energy Psychology Press.

Coutts, R. (2008). Dreams as modifiers and tests of mental schemas: An emotional selection hypothesis. *Psychological Reports, 102*(2), 561–574.

Feinstein, D. (2004). *Energy psychology interactive: Rapid interventions for lasting change.* Ashland, OR: Innersource.

Feinstein, D. & Eden, D. (2011). *Ethics handbook for energy healing practitioners.* Fulton, CA: Energy Psychology Press. See also: http://innersource.net/em/practitioners/ethics-code.html

Hartmann, E. (1996). Outline for a theory on the nature and functions of dreaming. *Dreaming, 6*(2). Retrieved from http://www.asdreams.org/journal/articles/6-2hartmann.htm

Hartmann, E. (2011). *The nature and functions of dreaming.* New York, NY: Oxford University Press

Hobson, J. A., Pace-Schott, E. F., & Stickbold, R. (2003). Dreaming and the brain: Toward a cognitive neuroscience of conscious states. In E. F. Pace-Schott, M. Solms, M. Blagrove, & S. Harnad (Eds.), *Sleep and dreaming* (pp. 1–50). New York, NY: Cambridge University Press.

Hoss, R. (2005). *Dream language: Self-understanding through imagery and color.* Ashland: Innersource.

Hoss, R. & Hoffman, C. (2004). *The significance of color in dreams.* Paper presented at the International Association for the Study of Dreams conference, Copenhagen, Denmark. Available at http://www.dreamscience.org/articles/significance_of_color.htm

Hoss, R. & Hoss. L. (2013). *Dream to Freedom: a handbook for integrating dreamwork and energy psychology.* Santa Rosa, CA: Energy Psychology Press.

Hover-Kramer, D. (2011). *Creating healing relationships: Professional standards for energy therapy practitioners.* Santa Rosa, CA: Energy Psychology Press.

Jung, C. G. (1964). *Man and his symbols.* New York, NY: Dell.

Jung, C. (1971). *The portable Jung* (Edited and with an introduction by J. Campbell). New York, NY: Viking Press.

Jung, C. (1972). *Mandala symbolism.* NJ: Princeton University Press.

Krakow, B., Hollifield, M., Johnston, L., Koss, M. Schrader, R., Warner, T. D., … Prince, H. (2001, August 1). Imagery rehearsal therapy for chronic nightmares in sexual assault survivors with posttraumatic stress disorder: A randomized controlled trial. *Journal of the American Medical Association, 286*(5), 537–545.

Lüscher, M. (1971). *The Lüscher Color Test* (Ian A. Scott, Trans.). New York, NY: Pocket Books.

Perls, F. (1969). *Gestalt therapy verbatim.* Moab, UT: Real People Press.

Perls, F. (1976) *The handbook of Gestalt therapy* (Edited by C. Hatcher and P. Himelstein). New York, NY: Jason Aronson.

Revonsuo, A. (2000). The reinterpretation of dreams: An evolutionary hypothesis of the function of dreaming. *Behavioral and Brain Sciences, 23*(6), 877–901.

Schredl, M., Fuchedzhiea, A., Hämig, H., & Schindele, V. (2008). Do we think dreams are in black and white due to memory problems? *Dreaming, 18*(3), 175–180.

Seligman, M., & Yellen, A. (1987). What is a dream? *Behaviour Research and Therapy, 25,* 1–24.

Stewart, D. & Koulack, D. (1993, December). The function of dreams in adaption to stress over time. *Dreaming: Journal of the Association for the Study of Dreams, 3*(4), 259–268.

Wakefield, C. (2012). *Negotiating the inner peace treaty.* Bloomington, IN: Balboa Press.

# Chapter 61
# The Power of Personal Choice in EFT: A Positive Option

*Patricia Carrington*

### Abstract

This chapter presents Dr. Patricia Carrington's EFT Choices Method, a unique way of introducing positive intention into the wording of the Setup Statements and Reminder Phrases used in EFT. The technique is outlined step by step, showing how to make it maximally effective by introducing words and phrases that increase the attraction of the user toward their desired goal. The use of Personal Resource States, a variation of the Choices Method that makes use of individuals' memory of times when they (or someone they have observed) have employed exceptionally effective coping skills to deal with a difficult situation, is also described. This approach transfers the requisite skills to the present situation though the use of EFT. The chapter presents case material to illustrate both the Choices Method and Personal Resource States so these approaches can be readily utilized.

**Keywords:** Choices Method, resource states, positive choices, meridian tapping

**Patricia Carrington, PhD**, EFT Master, is a clinical professor of psychiatry at the UMDNJ–Robert Wood Johnson Medical School in New Jersey. A pioneer in the field of EFT, she originated the widely used Choices Method and her books and audios are in the forefront of tapping therapy worldwide. Send correspondence to Patricia Carrington, 61 Kingsley Road, Kendall Park, NJ 08824, or pat@patcarrington.com. www.masteringeft.com.

## The EFT Choices Method

## The Choices Method: What It Is and Why

The Choices Method is a variation of meridian tapping that I developed before I ever heard of energy psychology or tapping. It was born from my disenchantment with the usual affirmations that people were recommending at the time. These positive self-statements were less than satisfactory for me for many reasons. They seemed to hold a special promise, but, though they made sense from a psychological point of view, I myself had not had much success with them, either for my clients or myself. This was despite the fact that some other people were apparently using them successfully.

When I investigated the reasons for my discomfort with the format of traditional affirmations, I discovered that a large number of people beside myself were reacting negatively to the essentially "contrary to fact" nature of these traditional affirmations. This was producing what psychologists call cognitive dissonance (an inner contradiction). When they were repeating affirmations such as "I have a wonderfully compatible and creative job that I enjoy," when in actuality they were working at a miserable job that they disliked intensely, a little voice in their head would say something like "Yeah, right!" or tell them, "That's not true and you know it!"

In the early 1980s, I found an unexpected answer to this dilemma. It was when I was teaching a self-development course known as DMA, created by Robert Fritz. The course used a form of affirmation I found to be immediately effective for just about everyone who encountered it. Fritz had inserted the words, "I choose" at the beginning of each affirmation and this turned it into a statement of intention rather than a contrary-to-fact declaration. This made all the difference. Using a "Choices" affirmation, I felt absolutely no inner contradiction what so ever and I began to get wonderful results doing this.

A positive spinoff of a Choices affirmation is that it puts those who make it into the "driver's seat" in their own lives. When they make a Choice (notice that I use a capital "C" for Choice because this is a special type of thinking), they are exercising their own will and deciding and committing upon a course of action. I soon found that this freely entered into commitment could have a powerful influence on the desired result. It made it far more likely to be obtained.

Actually, since I had not heard of energy psychology or EFT when I first encountered Choices, I was using Choices affirmations for years with my clients before EFT became the primary treatment modality that I adopted. It was in 1991 when I was already using EFT as a major component of my practice as a clinical psychologist that I thought of combining Choices affirmations with the EFT Setup and Reminder Phrases. At that moment the EFT Choices Method was born.

The reason I felt it so important to introduce this method into my regular practice of tapping was because I had been less than satisfied with the standard affirmation that appears in the last part of the Setup Statement—"I deeply and completely accept myself." It did not sit well with many of my clients, although it was obviously effective for others. This phrase is often difficult or impossible to use with people whose self-acceptance is extremely low to begin with; they experience it as artificial and it is extremely uncomfortable for them to repeat, and often they cannot do so. It also does not "fit" the situation for many newcomers. For example, if they are experiencing pain, it seems irrelevant and foolish to them to repeat the phrase "I deeply and completely accept myself" relative to the pain. I often found myself having to convince them to suspend their doubts and "say it anyway!" Though this sometimes worked, it did not address an even more fundamental problem I found with standard EFT as it was then taught.

Traditional EFT focuses on problems. Its tapping phrases start with statements like "Even though I have this headache..." or "Even though I can't meet my present bills..." and then completes that statement with the phrase "I deeply and completely accept myself." The treatment then proceeds by simply repeating the "problem" in each Reminder Phrase, saying at each tapping point such words as "this pain."

There's no doubt that with this form of EFT, you can definitely tap a problem away. But I wanted also to tap in a solution, and this is what I was able to do when I substituted a "Choices" phrase for the traditional EFT self-acceptance phrase. I did this by adding the words "I choose" to the last portion of the Setup Statement, and then using it in some of the Reminder Phrases, making it possible for a person to define a specific desired outcome by inserting a positive statement of intent after the words "I choose."

Using EFT with my own clients in psychotherapy, I soon discovered that I could get even better results if I allowed them to insert their own positive affirmations into the EFT statement in this manner. The Setup Statement could now become perfectly attuned to the problems they were addressing.

Here is how this would work. Say, for example, that a person's hand was throbbing. I would suggest an EFT Choices statement such as "Even though my hand is throbbing, I choose to have my hand be comfortable and pain-free." Contrary to the default self-acceptance phrase, "I deeply and completely accept myself," this kind of Choices statement immediately makes perfect sense to the injured person; it expresses precisely what that person wants to bring about—the cessation of pain and the healing of the hand.

I then refined the Choices Method by experimenting with my own clients. To use this method, individuals applying it are asked to identify the outcome they would truly like to have for their problem, and then they put this desired outcome into a phrase they use at the end of the Setup Statement (in place of "I deeply and completely accept myself"). This new phrase commences with the words "I choose…"

My method of injecting "Choices" into EFT soon developed into a systematic Choices protocol known as the "Choices Trio," which I have found to be extremely effective, not only for my own clients and workshop participants, but for many others as well. Soon after that I devised the formal Choices Method and began training other people in its use. This approach was almost immediately greeted with enthusiasm by the EFT community, and today many people worldwide are using EFT Choices statements. In particular, psychotherapists, counselors, and personal performance coaches make extensive use of it because it so precisely targets their clients' problems.

## How to Use the Choices Method

There are six rules for composing EFT Choices statements that I find particularly effective:

1. Be Specific.
2. Create *Pulling* Choices.
3. Go for the Best Possible Outcome.
4. State Your Choices in the *Positive*.
5. Make Choices That Apply to *You*.
6. Make Choices That Are Easy to Pronounce.

The fact is that really effective Choices use words that draw you in and make you feel involved. They are the opposite of dull, abstract statements. For example, suppose a person were trying to explain to another person (whose name happened to be Dorothy) their own point of view but felt that they were unheard by Dorothy, one way to formulate the Choices phrase in this person's tapping statement might be: "I choose to express myself in a way that gets my points across to Dorothy." This is a perfectly accurate statement of intent as far as it goes of course. But an even more appealing version might be: "I choose to find a *creative way* to get my points across to Dorothy." The word *creative* gives the statement excitement and suspense. You wonder what *would* be a creative way to get your points across. Curiosity is a powerful motivator!

*Surprise* is another word that can draw us in and get us emotionally involved in the outcome, so another effective Choices statement could be: "I choose to *surprise myself* by finding easy and enjoyable ways to get my points across to Dorothy." *Easy* and *enjoyable* are "pulling" words and they help to make this a compelling statement.

Or suppose someone felt sharp pain in one knee. Following these recommendations, you could add specific details about the pain, insert some interesting ideas about it, describe what the person would *rather have,* replace negative words (no, not, can't, won't, etc.) with positive words, and thereby create a personally rewarding Choices statement. Here are some examples:

> *Even though I have this sharp pain in my knee, I choose to enjoy a relaxed, pain-free game of golf tomorrow.*
>
> *Even though my knee has me crying out in pain, and I can't believe that this tapping is going to make any difference, I choose to give it a good try.*
>
> *"… I choose to enjoy doing these EFT exercises.*
>
> *"… I choose to have my knee feel completely normal.*

While tapping on the EFT acupoints, the Choices Trio also calls for having you try alternating between "problem" and "solution" Reminder Phrases.

For example, in the first round of tapping, you can use "problem" reminders:

> Top of Head: *stabbing pain*
> Inside Eyebrow: *so frustrating*
> Outside Eye: *terrible pain*
> Under Eye: *can't move without pain*
> And so on, through all the tapping points.

Or use the *same* complete "problem" phrase on all of the acupoints, such as:

> Top of Head: *I'm upset because my knee is so painful.*
> Inside Eyebrow: *I'm upset because my knee is so painful.*
> Outside Eye: *I'm upset because my knee is so painful.*
> And so on, through all the tapping points.

Then, in the second round of tapping, you could use only *positive* "solution" oriented phrases, such as:

> Top of Head: *better already*
> Inner Eyebrow: *pain-free*
> Outer Eye: *complete range of motion*
> Under Eye: *everything's easy*
> And so on, through all the tapping points.

Or you could use the same *complete* "solution" sentence on all of the acupoints, such as:

> Top of Head: *I choose to feel completely well in every way.*
> Inner Eyebrow: *I choose to feel completely well in every way.*
> Outer Eye: *I choose to feel completely well in every way.*
> And so on, through all the tapping points.

Using the Choices Trio in the third and final round of tapping you would then alternate between "problem" and "solution" phrases. Starting with the Inner Eyebrow you would say the negative phrase, then at the Outer Eye you would say the positive (Choices) phrase, then at the Under Eye spot you would say the negative again, and so on through all the tapping points, being sure to end on a "solution" phrase.

When doing this, it is usually easiest to alternate between the two complete sentences used previously:

> Inner Eyebrow: *I'm upset because my knee is so painful.*

> Outer Eye: *I choose to feel completely well in every way.*
> Under Eye: *I'm upset because my knee is so painful.*
> Under Nose: *I choose to feel completely well in every way.*
> And so on. Be sure your final phrase is positive (you should always finish on a positive note).

Many people find the Choices Method particularly effective because it helps them figure out not only what they *don't want,* but also what they *do want.* In addition, it installs positive intentions in a remarkably rapid and thorough manner and because of this it often brings about more profound and lasting results than standard EFT.

You can learn this method and practice it yourself by trying it out with many different issues using many different kinds of Choices, perhaps using my *Choices Manual* to attain mastery in this method. You will probably want to place this method in your collection of *truly useful* EFT approaches.

## Using Personal Resource States in the Choices Method

An important addition to the Choices Method has been my use of Personal Resource States, (a term borrowed from neuro-linguistic programming, or NLP), which denotes a key memory of a time in your life when you (or someone else) demonstrated an exceptional ability to cope with a difficulty. I have found that certain key memories that access Personal Resource States, when used with the Choices Method, can serve to remind us that we possess a great many powerful *coping abilities* of which we are unaware most of the time yet which can be invaluable.

If we know how to access them, these key memories can be called upon to help us with many problems that arise in our lives, even everyday problems. Unfortunately, most of us are largely unaware of this treasury of personal resources within us. The reason for this is twofold. We may have experienced a particular Resource State only *momentarily,* perhaps only once or a few times during our entire lifetime. We may therefore not consciously recall the incident and so have no clue that such a capability exists within us. Yet a memory of even *one moment* of outstanding competence (even if it took place within an insignificant context) can exert tremendous power for change. Consciously used and "tapped in," it can be extremely valuable in helping us handle challenges in a far more effective way.

Resource States are not limited to our own direct experience. We can also acquire magnificent coping skills second hand by observing others who display them. Human beings are great imitators; this comes naturally to us.

When I first found out that I could use Resource States to formulate effective Choices, I was extremely interested because, as a therapist, creating the best Choice for a given client is not necessarily an easy task. A key memory of powerful coping can be an enormous help in this process.

There are two main kinds of Resource States that people can use to create highly effective Choices:

1. A Resource State derived from one's own experience. This is a power memory that derives from your own *personal* experience; you have experienced it first hand.
2. A Resource State derived from observing another person or animal that you admire. This type of resource is created when we watch any living creature effectively cope with a difficult situation. It could be someone personally known, a relative, friend, mentor, etc., or it could be a fictional character, or a person or animal in a movie or novel. It is relatively unimportant *where* these lessons come from; to have a role model who demonstrates how to cope superbly with a difficult situation is extremely valuable wherever it comes from.

## Eliciting Resource States to Use as Choices

**1. Resource States derived from one's own experience.** In order to use a Resource State as a Choice, we must first do a little detective work. We have to discover the power memory that will work best for us, or for a client we may be treating. It is not unusual for us to be unaware of our own personal resources. There are two main reasons why this can happen.

It may be that we haven't used that resource in the *same area* as the problem being addressed. If we had, we would probably now be coping with that problem much more effectively. This resource may have been used in *other areas* of our lives,

perhaps very successfully in those areas, but simply never transferred to the particular area now causing difficulty for us.

For example, you might be wonderfully organized in the way you handle your personal appointments and social engagements but find yourself extremely deficient in the way you organize your physical surroundings. Clearly, you do have a capacity to organize or you wouldn't be able to handle your social engagements so well, but you have not transferred this ability so that you can use it when it comes to organizing your physical surroundings.

When using Choices, an appropriate way to work with such a lack of transfer would be to formulate a Setup Statement that incorporates the transfer as a Choice, such as: *"Even though I can't seem to organize my house (my papers, etc.), I choose to organize my house (papers, etc.) as effectively as my social engagements."*

If the issue still needs work after tapping on this statement, you could question yourself or a client you are working with by saying something like "Do you remember *any* time in your life when you have *ever* felt calm and confident as you went about organizing some event?"

You are directing that person's (or your own) attention to moments when you or they may have had the experience you now want to use as a Choice. By making a Choice based upon a remembered Resource State, you are learning how to make a transfer of your own capacities in one area into a new area where they are needed but have probably been underutilized.

Another example might be a woman who has difficulty understanding the motives of someone close to her and therefore is bewildered and hurt by that other person's actions. Let's say she is a person who habitually has a problem empathizing with others and understanding why they act as they do. If you are working with her, you might ask this question:

"Can you remember *any time in your life* when it suddenly dawned on you to wonder *why* somebody was doing something that puzzled you, and when you may have then said to yourself, 'Oh, of course! That's why they did it. I can see that now!'"

If the person locates such a memory, this will be extremely valuable. If not, you might pursue this question further by saying something like: "This doesn't have to be a major experience, just any moment at all when you had a feeling of, 'Oh yes, I know why they're doing that!'"

The fact is that most people have had such an experience at some time in their lives, even people who are not ordinarily sensitive to the motivations of others. Helping a person to locate that "fleeting moment" when they did experience such understanding can be the basis for an excellent Choices Setup Statement.

In this case, the Choice Setup might go: *"Even though I don't understand why* (so and so) *is acting the way they do, I choose to realize what they're about the way I did with* (insert the name of the original person in their past whom they understood, even if only for a moment)."

Here's an example of how this occurred in my own practice. David had consulted me for his fear of flying which, up until now, he had handled by avoiding plane trips whenever possible. His job had not required frequent traveling and, on the few occasions when he and his wife had traveled by plane, he had managed to quell a rising sense of panic by taking a few drinks and just "holding onto myself" as best he could until the flight was over. A week before consulting me, however, his company had told him that he was going to have to fly to a number of different cities and face some fairly extensive travel demands in the near future. He became immediately so anxious that he decided he should seek counseling to help him cope with this situation.

Although he had been afraid of flying for many years, an even more extreme fear of flying has been present in the last few years. He had not been fond of planes before, but the real fear started when he first experienced severe anxiety in an uneventful cross-continental flight. He still had no fear of takeoff or landing and, though he didn't like turbulence, that was not his problem either. What frightened him most he told me was when the plane seemed to be "not moving," when it felt as though it were suspended in the air. At such times he would get the feeling that he was "waiting for the bottom to fall out from under him." There were one or two other aspects to his fear of flying, but the one we tackled first was this fear of the plane seeming "motionless" and "hovering."

I helped him look for an appropriate Choice, one that could counter act his anxiety about hovering. The first part of his Setup Statement was easy to formulate: *"Even though I feel anxious when the plane seems to stand still..."* It was the last part of that sentence that eluded us.

I suggested as a default Choice, "I choose to feel calm and confident." Although he didn't reject this phrase entirely, I could see by the expression on his face that it didn't really hit home. Something more specific and compelling was needed.

In order to find a good Choice for him, I decided to look for one of his Resource States. Did he feel equally distressed when traveling under other circumstances and in other vehicles?

He told me that he had no trouble at all traveling in cars, buses, or trains, and that he loved driving in his own car, did so frequently, and was particularly comfortable when driving on long trips. This gave me a clue about where we might go in terms of a Resource State and I suggested to him that he might want to make a Choice that would go something like: *"I choose to feel at ease the way I would if I were driving my car."*

He immediately responded to this phrase with enthusiasm, and we started the tapping session. His initial distress rating (on a 0-to-10 scale) was between a 4 and a 5, but when he did the Choices Method using his Resource State he came down to a 0 in a single round. And when I purposely attempted to evoke anxiety about the feeling of a hovering plane by vividly describing the "hovering" (to test him), it no longer caused any reaction in him.

There was more work to do later on some of other aspects of his flying phobia, but we had made great strides by using this Resource State, and it actually proved to be transportable; that is, the exact same Choice was applicable to his other concerns about flying. *"Even though I'm anxious about an air disaster, I choose to feel at ease as if I was driving in my car"* was one of the Choices he now made. For each issue, choosing to feel at ease the way he was when driving his car did the trick. We had effectively shortened the treatment greatly by this strategy.

Another example might be a man who cannot imagine anyone coping with his financial state without alarm. A question designed to unearth a personal Resource State for him might be, "How do you cope with situations in your life that have nothing to do with finances? Do you have some situations that you think you handle pretty well?"

Most people will think of at least some areas of their lives that they handle pretty well or they wouldn't have survived outside of an institution where others would have cared for them. People generally respond by recalling some area in which they are at least reasonably capable.

At this point a further question might be: "Can you think of anything that's happened to you in the last 3 months that was troublesome—something having nothing to do with finances—which you coped with well?"

Most people will come up with some example of having coped pretty well with at least *one* situation that was difficult for them; it is almost impossible that this didn't happen. If they don't think of one right away, you can help them by asking something like "Can you think of *any* little thing that you handled to your satisfaction this whole year? For example, did the toaster oven go on the blink and you were able to fix it? Something like that?"

Few people are unable to think of even a small thing that they coped well with in the past year. Once you get an example from them, you have all you need. Now you can ask them how well they think they coped. Did the situation turn out okay? Is this ability to handle things satisfactorily something they would like to experience at other times in their life too?

If the man who is alarmed by a financial challenge in his life tells you he coped well with the flooding in his house when the main water pipe burst, you might help formulate a Choice along these lines: *"Even though I feel that I'm facing financial disaster, I choose to be as resourceful as I was when the water pipe burst."*

By using his Resource State as a Choice, you are using this man's own experience with the broken water pipe as a representation of the way in which, ideally, he could cope with his financial problems. It is a concrete example that symbolizes behaviors that would be useful for him to have more of in his life.

**2. Resource States derived from observing others.** The second type of Choice using a Resource State involves observing the effective coping behavior of another person or animal, and can be equally useful. A good plan, however, is to inquire first about a possible Resource State embedded in the person's own experience. Many

people do come up with an excellent Resource State that they have directly experienced, but if they can't recall one, moving on to the second type of Choices resource—the observed one—can be an effective next step.

To do this you might ask the individuals to think of someone who exemplifies for them the particular resource or coping ability that they need. Here are several examples of the use of such a vicarious Resource State for a Choice. They illustrate different ways in which this strategy can increase the effectiveness of the Choices method.

1. Roy had been injured in a water skiing accident, which was ironic because he was an avid water skier and had expert skill in this sport, as in all his other athletic endeavors. In his early life he had experienced himself as young, vibrant, and on top of the world. Then in a freak accident he cracked his back against the water, traveling at 90 miles per hour, and fractured several vertebrae. He could have been paralyzed for life. He was not able to recover easily and, although he worked with great deliberation at rehabilitation and could move about somewhat, in essence he was now a semi-cripple.

Moving from one job position to another and never really succeeding at any of them because he cared nothing for jobs that did not relate well to his image of himself, he became a discontent and a wanderer. In his mind he was still the "golden boy" with the supple body, except that at every moment of the day this image was smashed as he faced his obvious physical incapacities.

Roy entered counseling at the insistence of his current girlfriend who felt that he was taking out on her and the relationship his frustrations about no longer being physically capable. When he entered couples counseling, Roy's inner distress surfaced. He was clearly ready for help and consulted a social worker, one of my supervisees who works extensively with EFT. He suggested that Roy come to see him for one or two individual sessions as well as for couples counseling, but he was not at all sure that this suggestion would take.

Roy did come for the sessions, however, and because I was the supervisor of his therapist at the time, I was able to follow his case in detail. At first he and his counselor worked with his immense rage at fate, with Roy tapping vigorously and finally making a Choice, with guidance from his therapist, to "find a creative way of dealing with this (his disability)," despite his anger. The therapist was attempting to introduce some positive motivation into Roy's life and, in fact, Roy did begin to use his energy in a better way. He began to seek some solutions to his dilemma, something that had not occurred to him before as a possibility.

It was at this point that I suggested to the therapist that he might want to ease Roy into some EFT Choices that could steer him in the direction of a genuine acceptance of his disability and thereby free him to move on and create a life for himself.

Roy was unable to imagine how he could possibly accept his disability and so I suggested to his therapist that he share with Roy a description of a moving incident involving the world famous violinist, Yitzhak Perlman. I felt that if Roy were to read the description, he might become open to identifying with Perlman's somewhat similar dilemma and his remarkable way of handling it, and thereby open himself to healing. Here is the account that I gave his therapist to pass along to Roy:

"On Nov. 18, 1995, Yitzhak Perlman came on stage to give a violin concert at Avery Fisher Hall in New York City. There were standees for many rows; it was to be a major concert by one of the world's greatest artists. We awaited the performance with bated breath.

"Getting out onto the stage is for this man no small achievement for he was stricken with polio as a child. He wears braces on both legs and walks laboriously with the aid of crutches and to see him walk across the stage one step at a time, painfully and slowly, is awe inspiring. He walks painfully, yet majestically, until he reaches his chair. Then he sits down, slowly, places his crutches on the floor, undoes the clasps on his legs, tucks one foot back and extends the other foot forward. Then he bends down and picks up the violin, puts it under his chin, nods to the conductor, and begins to play.

"The audience knows him and is used to this ritual. They sit quietly while he makes his way across the stage to his chair. They remain reverently silent while he undoes the clasps on his legs. They wait expectantly and politely until he is ready to play.

"But this day, something went wrong. Just as he finished the first few bars of his piece, one of the strings on his violin broke. You could hear it snap—it went off like gunfire across the room.

"There was no mistaking what that sound meant and what he had to do. We who were there that night figured that he would have to get up, put on the clasps again, pick up the crutches, and limp his way offstage—to either find another violin or else find another string for this one.

"But he didn't do that. Instead, he waited a moment, closed his eyes, and then signaled the conductor to begin again. The orchestra began over again, and he played from where he had left off, and he played with such passion and such power and purity, as we had never heard before from him.

"Of course, anyone knows that it is impossible to play a symphonic work with just three strings. I know that, and you know that, but that night Yitzhak Perlman refused to know that. You could see him modulating, changing, and recomposing the piece in his head. At one point, it sounded as though he was de-tuning the strings to get new sounds from them that they had never made before.

"He played the entire piece this way, and when he finished, there was dead silence. There was a moment of silence and then the audience rose as one person, and began to cheer. They cheered and they shouted and they stomped and there came forth thunderous applause from every corner of the auditorium. We were all on our feet; we were all screaming ... we were doing everything we could to show how much we loved what he had done.

"He smiled, wiped the sweat from his brow, raised his bow to quiet us, and then he said, not boastfully, but in a quiet, pensive, reverent tone, "You know, sometimes it is the artist's task to find out how much music you can still make with what you have left."

"That final statement has remained with me ever since. It could be a prescription for life—not just for artists—for all of us. This man had prepared painstakingly for a lifetime to be able to create exquisite sounds on a violin of four strings, and then suddenly, in the midst of one of his greatest concerts, he had only three strings to work with—and he made music with the remaining strings, and the music he made that night with just three strings was more beautiful, more sacred, more memorable than any that he had ever made before when he had four strings to work with.

"Maybe it is our task in this fast-changing, bewildering world to make music at first with all that we have, and then, when that is no longer available, to still make our special music with what we have left. This may be the definition of quiet courage."

Though the story of Perlman's triumphant handling of his handicap had been inspiring to me and to his therapist, it was not initially accepted by Roy who became angry at the message conveyed in the anecdote. He became so angry, in fact, that the intensity of his reaction suggested to his therapist that on some level the anecdote had affected him deeply—else why the fury? He need only have shrugged his shoulders and said, "It doesn't mean much to me."

Because he was so strongly affected by it, his therapist persuaded him to look at his anger at Perlman's story and consider tapping on that. Roy agreed to do so.

*"Even though I hate stuff like this"* (referring to the Perlman anecdote) *"I choose to use it to my advantage"* (his therapist's suggested Choice).

He was able to repeat this with emphasis, although clearly the type of advantage he might get was not clear to him.

It took considerably more work to unearth the positive motivations in Roy, but interestingly, he kept coming back for individual sessions with his therapist, and no matter how much Roy protested, the therapist persisted in guiding him to reach toward a positive solution for himself.

When Roy admitted to his therapist, "If I could be like that guy (Perlman) I'd have it made," this paved the way for the following Choice, which again the therapist helped him formulate: *"Even though I hate stories like this, I choose to be a little bit like Perlman."* It was the beginning of a change, a first step. The therapist had helped Roy to make a modest, gradual step, to be "a little bit" like Perlman. A step however constitutes a bridge upon which client and therapist will now build, and with Roy's high energy and dogged persistence— the qualities that made him such a good athlete— he may eventually make an about-face and, like Perlman, play very well with "only three strings." It is a matter of when and how he will fully catch this vision. I assume that the Choice he made and the story's impression on him are now working beneath the surface. I think Roy will emerge much stronger.

## Peak Experience Used as a Resource State

A peak experience is an experience that is so vivid and compelling as to be often transcendent in nature. Such an experience can be used to bring about a life change that can at times border on the transformational, but it must be used with discretion and the person must be ready for it.

Not all people are open to recreating in other areas of their lives the impact of a peak experience. Psychologist Abraham Maslow, who was the first to write systematically about peak experiences, presented them as "aha" experiences, ones that open us to life and its profound beauty and meaning in a manner so remarkable that each is usually remembered as an outstanding moment of the experiencer's life. As such, a peak experience can have an extraordinary healing power when used as a Choice.

Here is one example. Dena had had a near-death experience following a car accident. She rarely spoke about it, but when she allowed herself to think of it, it represented a rare moment of truth for her. She had experienced herself away from this plane and in "an entirely different dimension," where there was a peace and love she could in no way describe—it had been all encompassing. Every problem she had ever had while on Earth was gone in those moments. When later she consulted me for a deep anxiety concerning her future (many years after this peak experience) and we were tapping on it using EFT, I asked her to help me formulate a Choice for her that would embody the state in which she would ideally like to be when facing this current crisis in her life.

She thought for a moment and then said, "The time after the accident happened, when I was in that state—there is nothing like it, it was unimaginable." As she talked, she was clearly reexperiencing the glow of that moment, its deep peace. She was then able to make this Choice: *"Even though I'm terrified of what will happen, I choose to remember the incredible safety of that moment."* Tapping on this Choice turned the situation around for her; it both quieted and stabilized her and enabled her to view her present circumstance in an entirely different perspective. She had drawn on this powerful resource within herself that resided in the memory she had half forgotten, and it served her in her time of need. This power memory was "installed" in her through the tapping, the words, and the ritual of EFT to achieve a superb result. If a peak experience exists in a person's life, it can be used to formulate a magnificent healing Choice.

In summary, key memories associated with Resource States are a fertile source of Choices phrases and are well worth the extra effort that may be involved in uncovering them because of their convincingness to the person using them. In fact, when used this way, these memories are indisputable and so are very powerful. Choices based on Resource States can move a person's personal growth light years ahead.

I hope you will make frequent use of the Choices Method as a powerful aid in your own personal growth and for your clients if you are a practitioner.

# Chapter 62
# Creative Languaging Patterns in EFT
*John Freedom*

**Abstract**

EFT (Emotional Freedom Techniques) is a therapeutic technique combining psychological exposure with acupoint tapping and cognitive reframing. As the most distinctive feature of EFT involves tapping acupoints, its cognitive components are often overlooked. Good clinical practice with EFT involves mastering what is known as the "art of delivery," one aspect of which is the verbal patter that accompanies tapping and gives it flow and continuity. The use of creative languaging has become somewhat controversial as a departure from the phrasings and formulations of the original EFT, while other practitioners continue to develop their own. This chapter discusses the cognitive aspects of EFT, explores the role of framing and reframing in treating psychological reversals and catalyzing therapeutic change, and presents examples of how to interweave creative language patterns with acupoint stimulation in the clinical practice of EFT.

**Keywords:** EFT, TFT, tapping, energy psychology, reframing, framing, psychological reversal, meridian therapy, creative EFT language

> *Words have a magical power. They can bring either the greatest happiness or deepest despair...Words are capable of arousing the strongest emotions and prompting all men's actions.*
>
> —Sigmund Freud

**John Freedom, CEHP,** is an educator, EFT practitioner and trainer. He is the author of *Heal Yourself with Emotional Freedom Technique,* and serves as chair of the research committee for the Association for Comprehensive Energy Psychology (ACEP). Send correspondence to John Freedom, PO Box 36532, Tucson AZ 85740, or research_committee@energypsych.org.

The question I hear most often following EFT Level 1 trainings is "How do I know what to say?" Proficiency in the art of EFT involves mastering what is known as the "art of delivery," the verbal patter that accompanies EFT and gives it flow and continuity. While many clinicians are skilled in both talking and tapping, it is not necessary to talk in order to tap. In developing Thought Field Therapy (TFT), Roger Callahan de-emphasized the use of languaging and eliminated use of the Setup Phrase. For clients who are kinesthetic, words can get in the way; some do better by simply accessing their somatic sensations and tapping nonverbally.

On the other hand, EFT lends itself well to cognitive interventions. Words are bridges, bridging the distance between another's experience and our own; by expressing our inner experience with words and emotions, they become real to others and ourselves. It is through languaging that we make sense of the world we see around us. In this chapter I will explore the use of creative languaging to build rapport, attune to felt experience, and enhance the therapeutic efficacy of meridian therapy interventions.

## Caveats

I wish to state upfront that some of the material in this chapter may be controversial. As in any field, there are purists and progressives, traditionalists and innovators. In his EFT Tutorial, Gary Craig (2012b) emphasizes what he calls "Official EFT": being very specific, working with aspects and roots, and using simple reminder and setup phrases. (Note, however, that Craig does sanction, after instruction in the Basic Recipe, the use of "extended setups" and combining the Setup and Reminder Phrases.)

The effectiveness of this approach is validated by research (see the introduction to this book) as well as the experience of thousands of practitioners. Basic EFT also has the advantages of being simpler and easier to learn, as well as being somewhat standardized. In addition, showing new clients a form of EFT with which they are already familiar builds rapport and credibility.

On the other hand, there is a great deal of innovation and experimentation going on in the field of meridian therapies. Just as Craig himself innovated by developing EFT from Roger Callahan's Thought Field Therapy, and created useful innovations such as the Tearless Trauma Technique and Borrowing Benefits, so now a second and third generation of new practitioners is doing the same. It is ultimately up to the practitioner to practice ethically and responsibly. To go back to basics: *primum non nocere,* first do no harm. Your most important goal and responsibility is your client's healing and well-being.

This chapter is intended for the mature EFT practitioner, not for beginners. As with any new skill it is important to *master the basics before attempting to innovate.* I recommend that students practice EFT's Basic Recipe for at least a year before attempting to experiment with the innovations presented here.

Further, complex wording does not work for everyone. For clients who are primarily kinesthetic, excess verbiage can be distracting, or even get in the way of accessing their felt experience (Gendlin, 1982). Rapport skills, reading body language, and behavioral flexibility are required to tailor your approach to different clients. As stated, it is not necessary to talk in order to tap.

Some of the approaches described in this chapter are suggestive, and are based on the practice of *pacing and leading.* This refers to a technique in hypnotherapy of first matching and mirroring the client's affect, behavior, body gestures, and language patterns and entering their "map of the world" *before* attempting to lead them somewhere else (Bandler, Grinder, & DeLozier, 1975). This involves building rapport, trust, and understanding of your clients and their situations. Please note that you must pace congruently before you can lead effectively.

Pacing and leading is implicit in the Setup Statement: *"Even though I'm feeling _____ (pacing), I deeply and completely accept myself (leading)."* The nuances of pacing, building rapport, matching and mirroring, and then leading are beyond the scope of this chapter. The simplest way to pace your client is to keep your reminder and setup phrases simple, and use their own words and phrases in your languaging of the client's issue. After first building rapport and pacing your client, it may then be appropriate to use one or more of the techniques described here.

## Languaging Intentions

Creative languaging begins with conscious intentions. We frame our intentions with our words and actions. Meridian therapies have a peculiar relationship to intention and expectation. On the one hand, as Roger Callahan first noted, they often work even when the client does not expect them to; when they do work, clients often attribute successful results to something else (the Apex Effect; Callahan & Callahan, 1996, p. 134). On the other hand, clinicians usually hold an implicit intention to alleviate suffering. This intention shows itself in little details we often take for granted, such as being punctual, keeping appointments, creating a safe space, listening empathically, and so on.

We can language our intentions by: saying a prayer, setting an intention for each session, eliciting the client's goals and outcomes, and/or writing a personal mission statement.

## The Art of Delivery

True finesse in applying EFT involves mastery of what Gary Craig (2012a) called "the art of delivery." How you deliver EFT goes far beyond reading a script or simple mechanical tapping. It involves understanding language patterns, reframing and creative use of Setups, uncovering and antidoting reversals, treating aspects and roots, and troubleshooting issues, as well as having a polished delivery.

The art of delivery begins before you meet your client, in your advertising and promotion, how you present yourself and create credibility, and how you answer the phone and answer questions. In starting your session, this includes the way you welcome your clients, thank them for coming in, and have them fill out intake forms. You may chat a little bit about their drive over, about the weather, or other topics for connecting and building rapport. After you sense that you both are feeling comfortable and are ready to dive in, you ask a question.

The questions you ask, and how you ask them, set the tone and frame for your work together. In linguistics the term *frame* refers to "a collection of facts that specify characteristic features, attributes, and functions of a phenomenon" (Fillmore, 1982). Frames are gestalts: their meaning is embedded in their relationship with the other elements of the frame. A simple word such as "ship" only has meaning in the context of the ocean, a captain and sailors, cargo and passengers. Thus any element of the frame (e.g., ship, sailors, or cargo) evokes the other elements of the frame.

We affect each other and ourselves by how we language our experiences, by how we frame them. No word is an island. Every word evokes a frame—a complex relationship with other elements that together give it meaning (Lakoff & Johnson, 2008). Stating that someone "has problems" will evoke a very different meaning and set of expectations than stating that one is "mentally ill," as compared to saying that the individual is "facing challenges" or is "working to achieve her goals." The meaning of a word is a function of its frame, its greater context.

We are continually framing the world we see, other people, and ourselves. These frames are often "tight," constricting and fear-based, and limit how we perceive, feel, and behave. They are also largely unconscious. Examples of limiting frames include the blame frame, the problem frame, the danger frame, the scarcity-and-competition frame, the disease/pathology frame, the right-wrong frame, and the black-and-white frame. Note that our dominant paradigms (frames), our fundamental maps of the world, were formed when we were small, vulnerable, relatively helpless, and (physically, cognitively, and emotionally) immature.

It has been estimated that our senses are taking in 12 million bits of information per second, of which we are consciously aware of perhaps 40 bits (Norretranders, 1998, pp. 143–144). This is like trying to figure out what a million-piece puzzle looks like, when you only have 40 pieces! In order to make sense of our complex, constantly changing, multidimensional reality we fill in the blanks with our own interpretations, with what Gary Craig calls "the writing on our walls." That is, we project our own paradigms (frames) onto the world we "see" around us. In the words of Anais Nin, "*We see things, not as they are, but as we are.*"

Questions themselves elicit frames and expectations. We create different expectations and elicit different answers, depending on the questions we ask. Asking "What seems to be the problem?" elicits the *problem frame:* Someone has a problem, it's problematic or difficult, the client cannot fix it by her/himself, and thus we need to fix it. Framing issues as problems evokes the experience of problems. Problems evoke a *blame frame;*

when there's a problem, there's usually someone (or something) to blame for it. Asking the question "How I can help you today?" may be said kindly and compassionately, but it implies that the person needs 'help' and is in a one-down position. Asking "What are you here to work on?" evokes the ideas that the client is here to work, that work is not fun, and that this work will require time and effort.

A very useful question to ask is *"What goals or outcomes are you planning to achieve?"* This focuses the client's attention on the goal rather than the problem. Another question I often ask is *"What would you like to shift or change today?"* Some people react with surprise to this question; they thought they were coming in to talk about their problems! This question is open-ended, and contains two implicit presuppositions (which I will allow you to discover for yourself).

A simple answer to the question "How do I know what to say?" is to listen carefully and jot down the client's own words. Then in your discussion of the issue, you can say something like "Let me see if I got that right: you're saying that…" and then feed their own words back to them. One of the biggest complaints people have about health professionals is "My doctor doesn't listen to me." When you listen carefully and then repeat their own words back to them, internally they relax because, finally, someone has heard them. Their own words are the keys to their internal "maps of the world" and evoke these maps cognitively, energetically, and physiologically.

After empathic listening and refining the issue, you create a Reminder Phrase and Setup Statement, using their own words. A Reminder Phrase is a succinct statement that keeps them focused on the issue. The mind can be like a drunken monkey, swinging from one thought association to the next. The Reminder Phrase keeps the issue front and center in the client's awareness, and emotionally and energetically engaged with it. Here are some examples:

Issue: Mary feels upset about a fight she had with her boyfriend, Bill.

Setup Statement: *Even though I feel upset about the fight with Bill, I deeply and completely accept myself.*

Reminder Phrase: *upset with Bill.*

Issue: Joe feels disappointed about losing a tennis tournament.

Setup Statement: *Even though I feel disappointed about losing the tournament, I deeply and completely accept myself.*

Reminder Phrase: *disappointed about losing the tournament.*

## Continuous Tapping

A simple way to combine verbal interaction with tapping is to do *continuous tapping*. Sometimes a client comes in, starts telling his story, and begins crying or emoting. Rather than interrupting him, asking for a subjective units of distress (SUD) rating, and so on, you just start tapping along with him as he talks (and taps). This is the basic practice of Simple Energy Techniques (SET), as taught by psychotherapist David Lake and psychologist Steve Wells from Australia (see Chapters 39 and 55). SET dispenses with both SUD and Setup, and encourages people to simply tap while telling their story (Wells & Lake, 2012a).

The advantage of this approach is that it is simpler and less structured than formal EFT. It is also somewhat more flexible, in that you simply allow clients to tap along with their own stream of consciousness. The disadvantage is that it sidesteps the issue of reversals (which may need to be addressed); it does not measure SUD, so it may be more difficult to assess progress; and it may not be as thorough as traditional EFT, which focuses on treating reversals and aspects as they arise.

Lake also teaches a variation called *Acceptance Tapping*. I'll let Dr. Lake describe it in his own words:

The basic principle is to pay attention to and work with what's there instead of changing it. If you try to change it, it often comes back. *The solution is in the symptom, so be present to it.* In essence you accept that the problem is there before anything else is changed. Then you simply add "continual tapping" to the problem pattern.

This simple technique works equally well in mental rehearsal of a positive behavior, where presumably unconscious blocking beliefs might be an issue.

I have found that the addition of tapping changes the routine behaviors of the problem significantly. It's a way of getting the client's attention in a new way, and of working creatively with the most intense part of the behavior while deciding on the best intervention, and the next part of the individual treatment. (Lake, 2012)

## Psychological Reversals

*We have met the enemy and he is us.*
 —Pogo/Walt Kelly

The "presumably unconscious blocking beliefs" that Lake refers to are *psychological reversals*. An understanding of psychological reversals and how to work with them are, in my opinion, one of the great contributions of energy psychology to clinical practice.

A psychological reversal (PR) is a block to healing associated with a belief or motivation that is opposed to your conscious intention. Reversals are one form of what is more commonly referred to as "resistance." This phenomenon can take many forms: "resistant" clients, "noncompliant patients," athletes who "go into a slump," salesmen who "hit a plateau," and addicts who are "self-sabotaging. Examples include:

> Possibility: *I can't get over this issue.*
> Willingness: *I'm not willing to get over this issue.*
> Worthiness: *I don't deserve to get over this issue.*
> Safety: *It's not safe for me to get over this issue.*
> Secondary gain: *I'm getting _____ from having this issue, and don't want to lose it.*
> Authority: *My doctor says I will always have this issue.*
> Identity: *This issue is part of who I am.*

Thinking about reversals has shifted over the years. Callahan originally defined PR as "a negativistic condition whereby one's motivation operates in a way that is directly opposed to the way it should work" (Callahan, 1991, p. 41). It was originally conceived of in energetic terms. "PR is best thought of in terms of electrical or electromagnetic poles…when the energy flow is in the 'wrong' direction…this reversal of energy flow accounts for the self-sabotaging behaviors, which are seen as epiphenomena of the electromagnetic substrate" (Gallo, 1999, p. 104). David Gruder pointed to their energetic nature when he reframed PR as "psycho-energetic reversals," but later emphasized their cognitive aspect by referring to them as "objections to success" (Gruder, 2001; ACEP, 2011).

Bruce Ecker and Laurel Hulley use different language to describe a similar phenomenon:

> [T]he coherence of the symptom—how it is necessary to have—is inevitably present in a very separately held, unconscious position of the client. We refer to this as the client's *pro-symptom position*—"pro" in the sense of being *for* having the symptom. The themes and purposes in this pro-symptom construction of reality comprise the deep sense and strongest emotional significance of the symptom in the client's world of meaning. To find the client's pro-symptom position is to find the emotional truth of the symptom. (Ecker & Hulley, 2000, p. 162)

Callahan discovered three ways to correct reversals: (1) tapping the Karate Chop point or other points or rubbing the Sore Spot (neurolymphatic reflex), (2) using an affirmation of self-acceptance (the Setup Statement), and (3) using the Bach Flower Rescue Remedy (flower essence formula available in health food stores). Callahan initially included the Setup Statement as part of the TFT algorithms but later dropped it in favor of stimulating the KC point or Sore Spot by themselves. Other points, such as the Under Nose and Index Finger points may be used with specific reversals as well (Gallo, 1999).

The Setup Statement in EFT is the correction for PR: *"Even though I have this _____, I deeply and completely accept myself."* This affirmation combined with stimulating the KC point or Sore Spot usually works well for (at least, temporarily) antidoting reversals. But sometimes, for reasons unknown, it may not. Then it can be useful to get more specific, and to uncover and address the reversal directly. (Note that Craig has dropped the use of PR, even though he has retained the use of the Setup Statement, the correction for PR; see Craig, 2012d.)

## Uncovering Reversals

Reversals may be seen as "objections to success" or as good reasons for doing the opposite of your conscious intention. They are often associated with specific beliefs, although the existence of a cause-effect relationship is not known. Many reversals are rooted in fear, in primal instincts to protect and survive. One way to uncover hidden reversals is simply to ask questions:

> *What fears do you have about getting or achieving this goal?*
> *What fears do you have about NOT getting or achieving this goal?*
> *What beliefs do you have about this _____?*

*What seems to stop you from _____?*

*What comes up when you start moving toward _____ ?*

Other useful questions include:

*If there was a good reason for having or keeping this issue/symptom, what would that be?*

*What are the advantages of having or keeping this _____?*

*What are the disadvantages of giving up this _____?*

## Ramping Up Self-acceptance

Self-acceptance is central to the Setup Statement. Some people balk at self-acceptance, saying that they can't or don't (or won't!) accept and love themselves as they are. Many of us hold the idea that we could and should be better, more talented, more successful. Others believe that they are unworthy and undeserving of love and acceptance. (Note that an unwillingness to accept oneself is a reversal, and is another aspect to be treated.)

Some hold on to self-judgment and self-criticism, believing that the whip is more powerful than the carrot. Yet, as Carl Rogers (1959) has noted, self-condemnation can keep us stuck, while paradoxically, *when we truly accept ourselves, as we are, we begin to change.* When we can we accept ourselves as we are, with all our faults and flaws, we begin to change and grow and heal.

We can also extend acceptance to the issue itself: *"Even though I have this _____, I deeply and completely accept myself, and I accept this _____."* What we resist, persists. Resisting what is causes resistance! When we're able to accept what is, even though we may not like it, it softens and shifts.

One way out of the quagmire of unworthiness and self-hatred is to build a semantic ramp up to self-acceptance (Freedom, 2007). We can ramp ourselves up to self-acceptance with statements such as:

*Even though I have _____, I am WILLING to accept myself.*

*Even though I have _____, I am WILLING TO LEARN to accept myself.*

*Even though I have _____, I am WILLING TO BEGIN TO LEARN to accept myself.*

*Even though I have _____, I am WILLING TO BEGIN TO CONSIDER THE POSSIBILITY that MAYBE SOMEDAY I MIGHT BE ABLE TO accept myself.*

We are often beset by fears and doubts, confusion and indecision. Although we may desire certainty and commitment, we are often lacking in both. Fortunately, complete certainty and commitment are not necessary. When we are willing to go somewhere, we begin moving in that direction. In the words of the poet Yevgeny Yevtushenko, "In the going, I am there…"

Other ways to express acceptance include:

*And that's okay.*
*I know I'm human.*
*And I'm willing to love myself anyway.*
*And I have a right to all my thoughts and feelings.*
*And I'm a really great kid.*

There are also ways to invoke acceptance without using the *A* word. EFT Therapist Karen Ledger writes:

After I say the usual *"I deeply and profoundly love and accept myself"* a couple of times, I then tell them, *"and now for the child part of you: Even though I'm feeling _____, I'm loveable and I'm okay."* Even the previously resistant to love and acceptance usually smile and visibly relax with this one.

A lot of men have issues with self-acceptance. One of my late-teen male clients uses the phrase *"Even though I feel _____, I'm the man!"* One of my veterans was a big burly guy who would not go anywhere near love or acceptance. We brainstormed Setup Statements, and came up with this: *"Even though I'm feeling _____, we're gonna go and git 'er done!"* (Ledger, 2012).

## Parts Work with Reversals

Another way of looking at reversals is that they represent inner conflicts. Part of us wants to heal, succeed, and get ahead in life, and another part of us has different agendas. Like an ostrich burying its head in the sand, a part of us seeks safety by hiding, ignoring, and avoiding. While this may be appropriate avian or infantile behavior, it's usually not the best strategy for solving our problems.

We have programs, which are subconscious patterns of feeling and behavior. These programs are sometimes called *parts,* semiautonomous personalities with their own beliefs, feelings, and behaviors. They often developed as strategies attempting to fulfill a need that made sense in the context of being a child but are no longer useful. Cutting or hurting oneself is not very loving but may make perfect sense to a child hurting herself to prevent others from doing so. All therapy involves parts work: recognizing, dialoging with, and reintegrating disconnected memories, behaviors, and aspects of self.

EFT Master Judy Byrne discusses how she works with parts in this way:

"I believe that all problems were once solutions. They are something that a part of us set up in response to a problem and was useful at the time but which the part keeps running and then becomes a problem in itself. Because these "solutions" are set up unconsciously, we cannot just make a rational decision to undo them. So I like to use tapping to *thank the part for its intention and ask it to find another way to achieve the same intended positive end.* This involves talking to both conscious and unconscious while tapping.

So a sequence might go something like:

Karate Chop: *Even though I have this critical voice that tells me I am not good enough and never will be, I accept myself.*

*Even though it stops me doing things, I accept all the parts of me, even the part that set up this voice and runs it.*

*Even though it causes me pain, I thank the part of me that runs this voice for its intention. I know it is trying to help me in some way. I accept and thank it for its positive intention and accept all the parts of me.*

Top of head: *Thanking this critical voice part of me for its intention.*
Eyebrow: *I know it is trying to help me in some way.*
Side of eye: *I understand its intention is positive.*
Under eye: *But I need it to know it is causing me pain.*
Under nose: *I want that part of me to know it really isn't helping.*
Chin: *I know it wants to help.*
Collarbone: *I appreciate that.*
Under arm: *And I really want its help.*
Top of head: *I would like to ask that part of me to be really creative.*
Eyebrow: *I want to ask it to find a different way to achieve the same helpful end as it intends.*

Side of eye: *I really want it to remain part of me.*
Under eye: *I want to ask it to be really creative and help me in a way that will not have negative side effects.*
Under nose: *"I am sure it can be creative in that way."*
Chin: *I want the part of me that runs this voice to know that what it is doing really is not helping.*
Collarbone: *I need it to know that.*
Under arm: *I want to ask it to find a different way.*

Problem parts are inevitably out-of-date. So it can be useful to add a further round like the following:

Karate Chop: *Even though I feel like a little girl, I know I'm a strong, mature adult, and I deeply and completely accept myself.*

*Even though I feel like a little girl, I know I'm a mature adult woman with children of my own, and I accept myself.*

Top of head: *I am ___ years old now.*
Eyebrow: *I have a responsible job.*
Side of eye: *I have children of my own.*
Under eye: *That problem (specify) I had when I was ___ is a yesterday thing.*
Under Nose: *I am ___ years old now.*
Chin: *I am married now.*
Collarbone: *I have children of my own.*
Under arm: *I am a responsible adult.*
Side of ribs: *Maybe I can do things differently now.* (Byrne, 2012)

## Customizing Setup Phrases

In my work I have found it to be more effective, creative, and fun to custom-design my own Setup phrases. Just as one of the keys to success with EFT is to get very specific, so also designing very specific Setups, tailored to the client's specific reversals, can greatly enhance the effectiveness of the whole treatment.

A simple yet elegantly powerful way to design your own Setups is to use the following template. I call this the Parts Setup, and it has three parts (Freedom, 2010).

*Even though A PART OF ME THINKS that _____, the REST OF ME KNOWS that _____, and I'm WILLING/CHOOSING to _____.*

After the first phrase, insert the reversal (usually a limiting belief or motivation). After the second, insert a *positive, truthful fact* that confronts and counteracts the limiting belief. After the third phrase, insert a *positive action* the individual is willing or choosing to take. Choosing a positive action is derived from Patricia Carrington's Choices Model (Carrington, 2006). "Willing" is more gentle, while "choosing" is more forceful.

I had a client who believed that she "could not do anything right." This was not true, of course, but that was her belief. So I had her custom-design her Setup phrases like this:

> *"Even though A PART OF ME THINKS that I can't do anything right,*
> *THE REST OF ME KNOWS that I do some things very well, and*
> *I'M WILLING to love and accept myself, whether I do things well or not."*
> *Even though A PART OF ME THINKS that I can't do anything right,*
> *THE REST OF ME KNOWS that I've held a responsible job for many years, and*
> *I'M CHOOSING to focus on what I do well, rather than on what I don't."*
> *"Even though A PART OF ME THINKS that I can't do anything right,*
> *THE REST OF ME KNOWS that I am intelligent, competent, and capable, and*
> *I'M CHOOSING to tap on myself, release these limiting beliefs, and get the results I want."*

I have my clients repeat the Setup three or four times, using the same PR/objection but with different antidotes and choices in the second and third phrases. After openly acknowledging, confronting, and correcting the specific PR, the presenting issue is then tapped away much more easily. It is also very useful in antidoting "mini PR," when the SUD (intensity) level goes down only 2–3 points and then plateaus there. The positive, truthful facts that we insert into the second part of the Parts Setup are called *reframes.*

## Reframing Our Parts

Reframing refers to the art of seeing things differently. Instead of thinking about it *that* way, think about it *this* way! One of the goals of therapy is to assist clients in shifting from narrow, limiting frames to larger, more flexible, more functional frames. Mental health involves flexibility, the ability and willingness to consider different points of view (Seligman, 2006; Siegel, 2010). Many people get attached to and stuck in their frames, in their limiting maps of the world. This can lead *to hardening of the categories,* or what David Gruder has called Paradigm Attachment Disorder (PAD).

Reframes go far beyond seeing the glass as half full or half empty. Meaning is a function of context: When you change the context, you change the meaning. A delicious meal served on paper plates in one's kitchen will have a different meaning than the same meal served in an elegant restaurant. For reframes to be effective, they need to be plausible and reality-based; that is, they need to be believable, larger, and more realistic than the limiting frame.

Reversals are limiting frames, which are opposed to our conscious intentions. These frames are often artifacts of the child ego-state; they may have been appropriate when we were small, vulnerable children, but no longer serve. Whenever a client says things like "I can't," "It's too dangerous," or "I feel afraid," the client is seeing through the limiting lenses of a little child.

A simple way to reframe is to change time frames. Sometimes the child part of an individual is stuck in a time warp (a time frame) and (subconsciously) believes he or she is still a powerless little child. EFT Master Jaqui Crooks (2012) switches temporal frames by having her clients say:

> *"Even though I felt terrified when my mother smacked me, IT HAPPENED, IT'S OVER, AND I SURVIVED; and I deeply and completely accept myself."* (You can also add, *"and I also accept my mother!"*)
> *"Even though I was terrified when my mother smacked me, THAT WAS THEN AND THIS IS NOW, and maybe it's finally safe for me to release those old feelings."*

Reframing sometimes involves giving the client/child-part new information, a larger, more expansive map of his or her world. Crooks (2012) sometimes tells her clients: *"Even though I've had this strategy for as long as I can remember and even though it probably wasn't even mine in the first place, I deeply and completely accept myself and those who created it."* She states, "It's wonderful to see the light dawn on their faces when they realize just where they picked it up from! It also makes it easy for them to let it go, when they know it's not really theirs."

Here are some other examples of giving the client (the child ego-state) new information:

*"Even though a (child) PART OF ME THINKS I can't,*
*the REST OF ME KNOWS that I'M A STRONG, MATURE RESOURCEFUL ADULT, and*
*I CAN DO MANY THINGS NOW THAT I COULD NOT DO BACK THEN."*

*"Even though a (child) PART OF ME THINKS that it's too dangerous,*
*the REST OF ME KNOWS that it was dangerous back then,*
*but I HAVE FRIENDS, SUPPORT AND RESOURCES NOW."*

*"Even though a (child) PART OF ME feels afraid,*
*the REST OF ME KNOWS that I CAN CONFRONT AND TAP THROUGH THESE FEARS AND FEELINGS NOW."*

Another way to suggest a plausible reframe is to offer your clients a choice. After a statement such as *"and maybe it's finally okay for me to release those old feelings,"* you can add *"and whether I do that now or later, either way I'm okay."*

Reframing, reprogramming, and reinterpreting are central to therapeutic process, and are inherent in such diverse therapies as Redecision Therapy, Re-evaluation Counseling (RC, or Co-Counseling), hypnotherapy, cognitive behavior therapy, Eye Movement Desensitization and Reprocessing (EMDR), and Coherence Therapy. Developing more functional, expansive perspectives is a hallmark of successful therapy. Like "little" Simba who sees the reflection of a mighty lion staring back at him in the pond, reframes can be catalysts for epiphanies, spontaneous perceptual transformations. These shifts in perception lie at the heart of therapeutic transformation (See Table 1.)

**Table 1.** *Frames and Reframes*

| Frame | Limiting Frame | Empowering, More Realistic Reframe |
|---|---|---|
| Temporal | The time is still back then. | This is now. |
| Location | The place is still back there. | Now I'm here (in a different place). |
| Part vs Whole | Part of me thinks that… Part of me feels stuck, wounded, powerless. | The rest of me knows that… Other parts of me are wise, adult, resourceful. I have other parts that are bigger, stronger, and wiser (besides this small wounded part). |
| Ego States: Child vs. Adult | I'm small, stuck, limited, powerless, vulnerable (Child ego state). | I'm adult, mature, capable, resourceful, expansive (Adult ego state). |
| Abandonment | I'm all alone, abandoned. | No man/woman is an island. I have friends, family, community. I am part of this larger human community. |
| Blame | It's all my fault. It's all their fault. | Everything happens. All phenomena have multiple "causes" and factors. Nothing is "caused" by any single individual. |
| Identity/stuck | I AM this… | I'm learning, growing, changing, evolving… |
| Survival | It's dangerous, I won't survive. | I have survived, and I'm okay now. |
| Overwhelm | It's too much: too hard, scary, dangerous. | I'm a strong, wise, resourceful adult. Whatever happens, I can and will handle it. |
| Permanence | I'm stuck, permanent. It's always been like this, it will always be this way. | All things (including me) are changing, growing, evolving. All things come and go, like clouds in the sky. The only constant in life is change. |
| Normalizing | I'm bad, sick, defective. I'm the ONLY ONE who's like this. | All human beings have faults, flaws, and issues. I'm human and imperfect, just like everyone else. |

Reframing can occur spontaneously: Francine Shapiro (1995) changed the acronym EMD to EMDR to acknowledge the role of reprocessing/reframing induced by bilateral hemispheric stimulation. Spontaneous reframing also occurs with meridian therapies, wherein clients experience sudden shifts in affect, perception, and cognition.

Note that reframes are not about getting your clients to see things the "right" way; they're about offering alternatives and possibilities. When presented with a plausible solution—a larger frame that fits the facts better—the mind seeking a solution will often accept it. Using permissive verbs and modifiers such as *can, could, maybe, possibly,* and *willing* are generally more effective than authoritarian statements.

Even though they may be "positive," reframes are not affirmations. In his EFT Tutorial Gary Craig (2012c) states: "Reframes offer another way to look at the issue, and thus add a healthy perspective that is generated from within the client. Positive language, on the other hand, tends to be artificially imposed from without and often dilutes the goal of truly eliminating negatives…When applied skillfully, reframes add a new dimension to the EFT process by presenting the problem from a different angle, or introducing a higher level of understanding to the situation."

## Paradoxical Approaches

Lake and Wells have developed an approach they call Provocative Energy Techniques (PET). This approach uses a humorous and paradoxical communicative style, developed by the psychotherapist Frank Farrelly (Farrelly & Brandsma, 1974). PET involves "humorously playing the devil's advocate with the client, siding with the negative half of their ambivalence towards themselves and towards change, revealing how they bind themselves in the situation, and doing all this in a way which promotes the client's self-knowledge and capacity for change" (Wells & Lake, 2012b).

PET utilizes deliberate provocation to get past the client's persona, to push his or her buttons, which brings emotional material to the surface for tapping. For example, a woman brought in her daughter who she was concerned was behaving poorly. Therapist (sensing Mum's fears): "So, you've given birth to a criminal!" This is a communicative style, with meta-messages that imply respect for the client simultaneously with implicit acknowledgment of the limiting belief system that holds him or her back.

Provocative therapy harnesses the power of paradox and exaggeration. Exaggeration in healing utilizes the *Principle of Amplification:* To change something, increase it rather than try to reduce it. If attention is already shrunken, shrink it more; amplify problematic emotional responses rather than try to decrease them (Wolinsky & Ryan, 1991). This approach is central to homeopathy ("like cures like") and may be found in psychotherapies such as psychodrama, Gestalt work and Ericksonian hypnotherapy.

You can inject humor and elicit underlying fears and issues by exaggerating clients' beliefs about themselves. Examples include:

A man who thinks he's not a good husband: *"Even though I'm the worst husband in the world, and any intelligent woman would leave me…"*

A woman who wants to quit smoking, but doesn't think she can: *"Even though I can't quit smoking, and even though I get more pleasure from smoking than from sex…"*

This exaggeration brings clients' worst fears and beliefs to the surface, where they can then be tapped and desensitized. Please note that, as with pacing and leading, it's best to build rapport before poking and provoking.

Another paradoxical technique involves using what EFT Master Carol Look calls *Argument Tapping.* She writes:

I love using this process in a group setting, because most people find it amusing and get something of value out of it. When you are tapping, voice both sides of an argument with another person. If your mother or father said, "You'll never amount to anything," you take both sides and argue the points while you tap, alternating the sides with each consecutive point.

For instance, start with the Karate Chop point, and say, *"Even though he said I was no good and wouldn't amount to anything, I choose to accept myself now anyway,"* and then tap the regular sequence as if you are arguing with another person:

Eyebrow: *You won't amount to anything…*
Side of Eye: *Yes, I will…*
Under Eye: *No you won't…*
Under Nose: *Yes I will…*

Chin: *Don't be ridiculous…*
Collarbone: *I'm smart enough…*
Under Arm: *Who are you kidding?*
Top of Head: *I know I can do it…*

Be sure to follow how the argument is "looping" in your memory, and vigorously argue both sides. This will help chop down a lot of "trees in your forest." This technique is wonderful for the brain, for the emotional release, and when the absurdity surfaces, it feels quite relieving.

Another variation of Argument Tapping is to argue with *yourself* while tapping. When you say something positive, for instance, *"I know I have what it takes to be successful,"* you might hear a tail-ender that says, *"No I don't!"* So it would sound like this:

Eyebrow: *I have what it takes to be successful…*
Side of Eye: *No I don't…*
Under Eye: *I am smart enough to figure this out…*
Under Nose: *No I'm not!*
Chin: *Yes I am!*
Collarbone: *No I'm not…*
Under Arm: *I accept my feelings…*
Top of Head: *I appreciate who I am.*
(Look, 2012)

A related technique I often use is *Polarity Tapping.* Reversals often show up as chronic stuckness. You can sometimes shift clients out of their stuckness by alternately tapping on both polarities of an issue:

As an example, a woman who feels unworthy of love:

Eyebrow: *I don't deserve to be loved.*
Side of Eye: *But I'm human, and all humans deserve love and kindness.*
Under Eye: *I don't deserve to be loved.*
Under Nose: *I have a few friends who love me.*
Chin: *I don't deserve to be loved.*
Collarbone: *I'm here, and I love me!*
Under Arm: *I want to feel like I deserve to be loved, but…*
Top of Head: *I'm willing to love me, whether I deserve it, or not.*

Another way to use Alternate Tapping is by *juxtaposing past and present* using the first two parts of the Parts Setup. For example:

Eyebrow: *PART OF ME USED TO THINK that I'll be stuck this way forever.*
Side of Eye: *But THE REST OF ME KNOWS that I'm not the same person I used to be.*
Under Eye: *A PART OF ME USED TO THINK that I'll be stuck this way forever.*
Under Nose: *But THE REST OF ME KNOWS that I'm still learning, growing, and changing.*
Chin: *PART OF ME USED TO THINK that I'll be stuck this way forever.*
Collarbone: *But THE REST OF ME KNOWS that all things change, like clouds in the sky.*
Under Arm: *PART OF ME USED TO THINK that I'll be stuck this way forever.*
Top of Head: *But THE REST OF ME KNOWS that other people have overcome this issue, and if they can, maybe I can, too.*

## Refusal Tapping

Another way of looking at PR is that *reversals are refusals.* They are good reasons why a part of the client refuses to achieve her or his goal. When clients experience particularly strong resistance, you can have them do what EFT Master Carol Look calls Refusal Tapping. She writes:

We have all been told what to do, controlled on a regular basis, influenced by others and manipulated all our lives, and when trying to change, it is very natural to experience an enormous amount of emotional resistance. Part of us believes the change is threatening to our survival. Try giving this part of you a voice for a change, and feel the relief of saying "No!" Don't be surprised when this act of refusing speeds up the change you were intending.

Your tapping sequence might proceed as follows:

Eyebrow: *I refuse to give this up…*
Side of Eye: *Don't even try to make me…*
Under Eye: *I am so happy I don't have to get rid of this…*
Under Nose: *I refuse to change…*
Chin: *You can't make me…*
Collarbone: *Ha ha, ha ha, I'm keeping this problem…*
Under the Arm: *You can't make me get over this…*

---

Top of the Head: *I REFUSE TO LET GO OF THIS ISSUE.* (Look, 2012)

## Probing Questions

Asking questions sensitively is a way of building rapport, gathering information, and getting to know the other person. It is as important to listen to *how* they say it as to *what* they say. Questioning is a way of going deeper and of uncovering tapping targets, aspects, and roots. Questions, like the question mark itself, are hooks; you toss them out into the great sea of the subconscious, and they will hook memories, traumas, feelings, and associations.

Do not attempt to ask your client (or yourself!) every single question here. Some of these are repetitive, and often just asking two to four questions is sufficient. You will know that you've hooked something significant when clients have an emotional reaction to the question; when they try to avoid the question (don't want to go there); or if they have an "aha" moment while answering the question.

*What do you notice in your body when you attune to this issue?*

*Where in your body do you feel this?*

*Where did this come from?*

*What do you think might be the cause, source, or origin of this _____?*

*What do you tell yourself when _____?*

*What are you telling yourself about _____?*

*What does this issue/symptom remind you of?*

*About how old do you feel when _____?*

*When did you experience this _____ before?*

*If there was an emotional contributor to this issue, what might it be?*

*If this issue/symptom were trying to communicate something to you, what would that be?*

*If this issue/symptom were trying to get you to do something, what might that be?*

*What image, symbol or metaphor comes to mind when _____?*

*What fears do you have, about either keeping or releasing this issue?*

*If there was a person or event in your life you'd rather have skipped, what would that be?*

*What seems to be stopping/preventing you from _____?*

*What are the advantages of holding onto this issue? (What are you getting out of holding onto this issue?)*

*What are the disadvantage(s) of giving up this issue? (What is holding on to this issue costing you?)*

*What was going on in your life in the 3 to 6 months before this symptom/condition first showed up?*

*What will you have to give up, in order to get _____?*

*What else comes to mind, when you think of this issue?*

When asking questions, notice how your client's body responds, with emotional shifts, shivers, yawns, or "AHAs." The body holds the truth of what happened, whether or not clients can recall a specific memory consciously. Even if they cannot recall a specific memory, they can always tap on the symptom itself, and on body sensations (which evoke body memories) as well. Listening to their inner "truth bell" will tell them (and you) when they've found their truth.

## Tapping in the Positive

When we're in a funk, we forget. It's hard to see the forest when we're trapped under a log. We forget and ignore the tremendous potentials we have within ourselves. Tapping not only removes inner blocks, it also removes outer blocks, the blocks to perceiving and feeling, so that we can begin to see and hear with new eyes and ears. When we do that, we literally see and experience a different world.

Human beings have tremendous untapped potential, in the form of internal states: courage, creativity, intuition, equanimity. These inner resources are always there; we simply need to invoke and attune to them. We can consciously connect with them by first tapping out the negative, and then tapping in the positive.

Caveat: Many clients (and clinicians!) want to focus on the positive and avoid the negative. This can be like building a beautiful penthouse on a rotting foundation. In EFT it's necessary to focus on and release the negative first, before attempting to tap in the positive.

1. Select a memory, issue, or belief you wish to change.

2. Attune to the experience in your body, and rate its intensity 0–10.

3. Plug your belief or experience into the Parts Setup, while tapping the KC point: *"Even though a PART OF ME THINKS THAT _____, the REST OF ME KNOWS THAT _____, and I'M CHOOSING TO _____.*

4. Tap one or more rounds as needed to defuse the emotional charge on the belief or experience.

5. Think of a positive belief or resource to replace the negative with. (Positive resources can include courage, creativity, balance, enthusiasm, love, etc.). Rate the positive belief or resource using the VOC (validity of cognition) scale, where 0 = not true, and 10 = absolutely true.

6. Do Alternate Tapping: starting on the Top of the Head point, tap while saying out loud:
Top of the Head: *PART OF ME USED TO THINK THAT _____,*
Eyebrows: *But NOW the REST OF ME KNOWS THAT _____.*
Sides of the Eyes: *A PART OF ME USED TO THINK THAT _____,*
Under the Eyes: *But NOW the REST OF ME KNOWS THAT _____.*
And so forth, for 2–3 rounds.

7. Do 1–3 final rounds of Alternate Tapping, focusing on the positive, as follows:
Top of the Head: *But NOW THE REST OF ME KNOWS THAT _____,*
Eyebrows: *And I'M CHOOSING TO _____."*
Sides of the Eyes: *NOW THE REST OF ME KNOWS THAT _____,*
Under the Eyes: *And I'M CHOOSING TO _____.*

And so forth through the sequence. After completing tapping, check in with yourself: What do the negative and positive beliefs feel like now? Then thank yourself for a job well done!

## Gratitude Tapping

A powerful method for opening the heart is Gratitude Tapping. Some people who study the Law of Attraction (LOA) believe that having an "attitude of gratitude" is the best way to raise your vibration and attract prosperity into your life. Many of us think we "should" be grateful, but it can be challenging to feel grateful consistently in a chaotic, fast-paced, at times unfair and uncaring world! Gratitude Tapping is a way of tuning into the power of gratitude, and integrating it in our minds and bodies.

There are several ways to do Gratitude Tapping. The deeper method involves first making an inventory and then clearing out the blocks to gratitude: angers, grudges, grievances, resentments, and disappointments. (For some of us, this will take some time!) The simpler, easier way is to make a Gratitude List, and just tap. See methods 1 and 2, as follows.

**Method 1.** Sit down and ask yourself, *"What seems to get in the way, of my feeling truly grateful for everyone and everything in my life, as it is right now?"* When you try to think of every aspect, some of which may be wonderful and some of which may not, you will likely think of several angers, grudges, or grievances, things that are "unfair" and "not right," about which you feel less than grateful. Jot those down on paper, give each one a SUD rating, and tap.

You can inject gratitude into your Setup Statement by finding something positive (you learned a lesson, you survived, people rallied around you) and inserting it like this:

> *"Even though A PART OF ME THINKS that this was a terrible misfortune, the REST OF ME KNOWS THAT everything is a learning opportunity, and I'M CHOOSING TO turn lemons into lemonade, and do the best I can."*
>
> *"Even though A PART OF ME THINKS THAT I was treated unfairly, the REST OF ME KNOWS THAT I could have checked out the details more closely, and I'M CHOOSING TO be more careful and vigilant in the future."*

This may take several hours—or days, if you're being thorough! Take your time with it. After clearing out disappointments and resentments, move on to method 2.

**Method 2.** Make a Gratitude List of at least 10 things you feel grateful for. Your list might include things like:

> *I feel grateful for my life.*
> *I feel grateful for my parents and family.*
> *I feel grateful for my wife/husband/partner.*
> *I feel grateful for my career.*
> *I feel grateful for my vacation last year.*

*I feel grateful for EFT.*
*I feel grateful to be here.*

You can either use a Setup Statement like the following, or simply tap (without the Setup):

*"Even though I don't always feel grateful and deserving,*
*I feel grateful for this opportunity to be grateful now, and I'm choosing to _____."*

Then tap on each item on your list, while focusing on feelings of gratitude and appreciation.

## Harnessing the Power of Forgiveness

Anger and guilt appear to be different emotions, but they are two sides of the same coin. Anger and guilt are the emotional results of judgment projected inward or outward. We feel angry when we blame another, and guilt/shame when we blame ourselves. Anger results from blame projected "out there" onto another; guilt and shame are the felt experience of anger projected inward at oneself.

All anger involves projection. When we see a personality characteristic in someone we don't like, it is a mirror or reflection of something we don't like within ourselves. There's a saying from the 12-step programs that's relevant here: "If you can spot it, you got it."

Forgiveness is a process of recognizing the reflection "out there," recovering the projection "in here," and then absolving oneself and the other of the guilt we seek to avoid by projecting onto her or him.

Forgiveness is the traditional antidote in both Judaism and Christianity for anger, guilt, and shame. In the words of *A Course in Miracles* (1975), "Forgiveness begins with the willingness to see things differently." Forgiveness involves a change of perception, a change of mind, and a change of heart. As Edward Bach (2005), developer of the Bach Flower remedies, noted, "There is no true healing unless there is a change in outlook, inner happiness, and peace of mind."

Many spiritual teachings sanction forgiveness, or teach that we should forgive. I find that people often want to forgive but are unable to. The reason why they can't forgive is because there is unresolved hurt or pain (i.e., trauma); even when they try to forgive, and consciously want to do so, the subconscious memory of the pain prevents them

from doing so. Another issue is fear, as revealed in the adage, "Forgive, but don't forget." So long as there is fear or anticipation that "it could happen again," there is no true forgiveness.

The inability to forgive is another form of reversal. Psychologist Philip Friedman (2009) states unequivocally that "underneath all other emotional and psychological problems there is one core problem—unforgiveness—and one core solution, which is forgiveness." He recommends using this phrasing while tapping:

*"I release this _____, and all of its roots and causes, and all of its effects on me and everyone else in my life, and I choose to feel calm, relaxed, at peace, and confident."*

He then has his clients repeat the following three times while rubbing the Sore Spot:

*"I love and forgive myself unconditionally, despite my problems, limitations, and challenges;"* and then three times, *"I am entitled to miracles."*

Psychotherapist Meryl Beck (2012) uses this languaging:

*"I totally and completely forgive myself, and I intend to forgive everyone else involved;*

*I totally and completely forgive myself, and I ask for the wisdom to see that everyone involved was acting from a place of unmet needs."*

When people have difficulty forgiving, it can be helpful to name the specific judgment they're holding against the other or themselves, and then including the willingness to forgive in the Setup Statement. For example:

*"Even though A PART OF ME BLAMES MY MOTHER for everything that's wrong in my life,*

*the REST OF ME KNOWS THAT she was acting out of her own pain and programming, and I'M WILLING TO LEARN TO love, accept, and forgive her and myself as we are."*

*"Even though A PART OF ME JUDGES MYSELF as being lazy,*

*the REST OF ME KNOWS THAT I often work many hours a day, and I'M WILLING TO LEARN TO love, accept, and forgive myself, whether seemingly lazy or not."*

*"Even though A PART OF ME JUDGES Sam for being dishonest,*

*the REST OF ME KNOWS THAT I am not always 100% honest myself, and I'M CHOOSING TO look at the mirror, find the projection, and learn to love, accept, and forgive Sam and myself as we are."*

## Harnessing the Power of Spirituality

Clients' spiritual beliefs can be a rich source of resources. However, your languaging must be congruent with your client's belief system. Preaching Jesus to a Jew, or Buddhism to an atheist is not the best way to build rapport! When taking a thorough case history, I ask clients about their religious backgrounds and spiritual beliefs (if any). Then I language my interventions in terms of their "maps of the world." As stated previously, you must pace congruently before you can lead effectively.

The standard setup is rooted in self-acceptance. Some people believe that they are sinners, that they deserve to be punished, or that they are unloveable. If they are religious and believe in a loving God, they will usually be open to the idea that God loves them.

Psychotherapist Daniel Benor (2008) recommends adding this phrase to the traditional setup: *"…and God/The Divine/The Infinite Source loves and accepts me wholly, completely, and unconditionally."*

Alternative setups can be phrased as follows:

*"Even though I have _____, I'm WILLING to remember that God/Higher Power loves and accepts me as I am."*

*"Even though I have _____, I'm WILLING to remember that God/Infinite Source has a far greater perspective than my little ego perspective."*

*"Even though I have _____, I'm WILLING to OPEN UP to the possibility of a loving Creator loving and accepting me as I am."*

Beck (2012) uses this phrasing: *"I bring in Higher Power (Spirit/God/Light) into all the branches to the deepest roots around this issue/craving and ask for healing for the highest good,"* while tapping the Top of the Head, followed by *"I release all this _____ in all the branches to the deepest roots around this issue/craving"* on other points in the sequence. Psychotherapist Phillip Mountrose (2012) uses what he calls the "miracle reframe": "Even though I have this _____, anything is possible, and miracles are happening now. (http://www.gettingthru.org/miracles.htm)

Another useful reframe is: *"Even though I have this _____, I welcome this invitation from my Soul to heal, and I'm choosing to _____."*

## Research on Languaging and Therapeutic Process

Eugene Gendlin and colleagues at the University of Chicago spent 15 years researching the factors involved in therapeutic outcomes. He discovered that therapeutic success resulted more from what clients were doing internally, rather than the skill of the therapists or the method they used. Gendlin found that the successful subjects were intuitively focusing on their internal bodily awareness, what Gendlin later termed the "felt sense." He found that this skill was teachable, and developed the method he called *focusing* (Gendlin, 1982). In EFT, the process of tuning, rating, and repeating a Reminder Phrase that "resonates" parallels the steps of focusing.

Affirmations are popular in the business, coaching, and self-help communities. Ever since the publication of books such as *The Power of Positive Thinking* (Peale, 1952) and *Think and Grow Rich* (Hill, 1966), the idea that thinking positively can increase one's health, wealth, and success has taken root in the American psyche. The evidence for the efficacy of affirmations is mixed. In one study, Wood, Perunovic, and Lee (2009) divided subjects into two groups. Those with high self-esteem who repeated a positive self-statement (e.g., "I'm a loveable person") felt mildly better. Subjects with low self-esteem felt worse than those who did not repeat the statement. The authors speculated: "Messages that fall outside one's 'latitude of acceptance' are thought to meet resistance, and even to have the potential to backfire, leading one to hold one's original position even more strongly." In a related study, Leippe and Eisenstadt (1994) asked participants to identify a trait they would like to possess but believed they lacked. When they were later told that they actually did possess that ideal trait, participants felt worse, rather than better. Evidence indicated that positive feedback led subjects to consider counter-examples that contradicted that feedback.

There are several studies documenting the efficacy of *affect labeling* (i.e., putting feelings into words). Pennebaker and Beall (1986) found that having undergraduates write about "earlier traumatic experience was associated with both short-term increases in physiological arousal and long-term decreases in health problems." Matthew Lieberman and colleagues (2007) at UCLA found that "affect labeling...diminished the response of the amygdala...to negative emotional images. Additionally, affect labeling produced increased activity in a single brain region, right ventrolateral prefrontal cortex (RVLPFC).... these results suggest that putting feelings into words may activate RVLPFC, which in turn may dampen the response of the amygdala, thus helping to alleviate emotional distress...." Affect labeling is central to the first part of the setup phrase, and to the Reminder Phrase as well.

More recently, Ecker, Ticic, and Hulley (2012) point to the role of *juxtaposition* in therapeutic change. Animal researchers discovered that there is a short window during which memories are labile and can be changed, prior to reconsolidation. Experiential juxtaposition occurs when pairing an expectedly emotional stimulus with an acupoint-induced relaxation response, and also in the pairing of a stressful experience with self-acceptance in the Setup phrase.

## Other Phrasings

Many clinicians have their own favorite phrases and wordings. Psychologist John Diepold (2013) uses this version:

*"I deeply love and accept myself even though I have this problem, its cause, and all that it means and does to me."*

Psychologist Holly Timberlake (2013) sometimes uses this phrase, *"Even though I have woven this belief into my personality and experience, perhaps I can begin to let go of it."*

Here in the Southwest, I often end Setup Statements with: *"And que sera, sera!"*

This chapter has presented examples of creative languaging. Part of mastery of the art of delivery involves developing your own repertoire of phrasings, finding those words that flow easily for you and that 'resonate' and connect for your client. When you're attuned and have rapport, however, your intuition opens and the "right" words just arise. It's not a matter of thinking, having a plan, or trying to figure it out. When you watch master practitioners working with clients, you'll notice how easy and effortless the dance between talking and tapping is. I find that as I continue tapping on myself every day, my fears, blocks, and inhibitions soften and release, and I am naturally open, attuned, and in the flow.

## Conclusion

Recent review articles have suggested that the rapid desensitization observed in TFT and EFT is the result of psychological exposure combined with acupoint stimulation (Feinstein, 2012; Lane, 2009). Roger Callahan emphasized the importance of tapping meridian points to "collapse perturbations in the thought field," and de-emphasized the role of cognitive interactions in TFT. Gary Craig innovated the use of reframing and creative languaging in his development of EFT. Following his example, a new generation of practitioners has developed cognitive interventions that complement tapping. Although mechanism studies to determine the "active ingredients" in TFT and EFT have been proposed, clinical experience shows the energetic and cognitive aspects of EFT to be quite complementary, and possibly even synergistic. It is recommended that clinicians remain sensitive to clients' needs by attending to their affect and body language, finding those words and phrases that connect and resonate, and tailoring cognitive interweaves to their clients through sensitive pacing and leading.

## References

ACEP. (2011). *Essential skills in comprehensive energy psychology: Level one workshop.* Ardmore, PA: Association for Comprehensive Energy Psychology (ACEP).

Bach, Edward. (2005). *The essential writings of Dr Edward Bach.* London, UK: Ebury.

Bandler, R., Grinder, J., & DeLozier, J. (1975). *Patterns of the hypnotic techniques of Milton H. Erickson, M.D.* Cupertino, CA: Meta Publications.

Beck, M. H. (2012). *Stop eating your heart out: The 21-day program to free yourself from emotional eating.* San Francisco, CA: Conari Press.

Benor, D. (2008). *Seven minutes to natural pain release: Pain is a choice and suffering is optional—WHEE for tapping your pain away.* Bellmawr, NJ: Wholistic Healing Publications.

Byrne, J. (2012). Personal communication to the author.

Callahan, R. (1991). *Why do I eat when I'm not hungry?* New York, NY: Doubleday.

Callahan, R. & Callahan, J. (1996). *Thought Field Therapy and trauma: Treatment and theory.* Indian Wells, CA: Thought Field Therapy Training Center.

Callahan, R. & Trubo, R. (2002). *Tapping the healer within.* New York, NY: McGraw Hill.

Carrington, P. (2006). *The magic of personal choice in EFT: An introduction to the EFT choices method.* E-book retrieved from http://masteringeft.com/masteringblog/eft-choices-manual

*A course in miracles.* (1975). New York, NY: Penguin.

Craig, G. (2012a). Retrieved from http://www.emofree.com/eft/about-videos.html

Craig, G. (2012b). Retrieved from http://www.emofree.com/eft/phrases.html

Craig, G. (2012c). Retrieved from http://www.emofree.com/eft/reframing.html

Craig, G. (2012d). Retrieved from http://www.emofree.com/index.php?option=com_content&view=article&id=40:how-to-eft&catid=25:tutorial-contents&Itemid=192

Crooks, J. (2012). Personal communication to the author.

Diepold, J. (2013). Personal communication to the author.

Ecker, B. & Hulley, L. (2000). Depth oriented brief therapy: Accelerated accessing of the coherent unconscious. In J. Carlson & L. Sperry (Eds.), *Brief therapy with individuals and couples* (pp. 161–190). Phoenix, AZ: Zieg, Tucker & Theisen.

Ecker, B., Ticic, R., & Hulley, L. (2012). *Unlocking the emotional brain: Eliminating symptoms at their roots using memory reconsolidation.* New York, NY: Routledge.

Farrelly, F. & Brandsma, J. (1974). *Provocative therapy.* San Leandro, CA: Shields Publishing.

Feinstein, D. (2012). Acupoint stimulation in treating psychological disorders: Evidence of efficacy. *Review of General Psychology, 16,* 364–380. doi:10.1037/a0028602

Fillmore, Charles J. (1982). Frame semantics. In Linguistic Society of Korea (Eds.), *Linguistics in the Morning Calm* (pp. 111–137). Seoul: Hanshin.

Freedom, J. (2007). When self-acceptance becomes a problem. Available at: http://www.danachivers-eft.com/emofree/Articles2/ramping-up.htm

Freedom, J. (2010). Refinements to EFT. Available at: http://eftuniverse.com/index.php?option=com_content&view=article&id=4404:creating-your-own-custom-designed-setup-phrases&catid=47:refinements-to-eft&Itemid=3212

Freedom, J. (2011, August 13). Energy psychology: The future of therapy? *Noetic News.* Retrieved from http://www.noetic.org/noetic/issue-thirteen-august/energy-psychology/

Freedom, J. (2013). *Heal yourself with Emotional Freedom Technique.* London, UK: Hodder & Stoughton.

Friedman, P. (2009). *The forgiveness solution: The whole-body rx for finding true happiness, abundant love, and inner peace.* San Francisco, CA: Red Wheel/Weiser.

Gallo, F. (1999). *Energy psychology: Explorations at the interface of energy, cognition, behavior, and health.* Boca Raton, FL: CRC Press.

Gendlin, E. T. (1982). *Focusing.* New York, NY: Bantam.

Gruder, D. (2001). *Energy psychology desktop companion.* San Diego, CA: Willingness Works.

Hill, N. (1966). *Think and grow rich.* New York, NY: Hawthorn Books.

Lake, D. (2012). Acceptance Tapping: A powerful EFT treatment variation for severe compulsive disorders and bulimia. Retrieved from http://www.danachivers-eft.com/emofree/addictions/compulsive-disorders-bulimia.htm

Lakoff, G. & Johnson, M. (2008). *Metaphors we live by.* Chicago, IL: University of Chicago Press.

Lane, J. (2009). The neurochemistry of counterconditioning: Acupressure desensitization in psychotherapy. *Energy Psychology: Theory, Research, & Treatment, 1*(1), 31–44.

Ledger, K. (2012). Private communication to author.

Leippe, M. R. & Eisenstadt, D. (1994). Generalization of dissonance reduction: Decreasing prejudice through induced compliance. *Journal of Personality and Social Psychology, 67,* 395–413.

Lieberman, M. D. Eisenberger, N. I, Crockett, M. J., Tom, S. M., Pfeifer, J. H., & Way, B. M. (2007, May). Putting feelings into words: Affect labeling disrupts amygdala activity in response to affective stimuli. *Psychological Science, 18*(5): 421–428.

Look, C. (2012). Top 10 tapping tips. Retrieved from http://www.attractingabundance.com/eft/top-10-tapping-tips

Norretranders, T. (1998). *The user illusion: Cutting consciousness down to size.* New York, NY: Viking.

Peale, N. V. (1952). *The power of positive thinking.* New York, NY: Prentice-Hall.

Pennebaker, J. & Beall, S. (1986). Confronting a traumatic event: Toward an understanding of inhibition and disease. *Journal of Abnormal Psychology, 95,* 274–281.

Rogers, C. R. (1959). A theory of therapy, personality and interpersonal relationships, as developed in the client-centered framework. In S. Koch (ed.), *Psychology: A study of science* (pp. 184–256). New York, NY: McGraw Hill.

Seligman, M. (2006). *Learned Optimism: How to change your mind and your life.* New York, NY: Vintage Books.

Shapiro, F. (1995). *Eye Movement Desensitization and Reprocessing: Basic principles, protocols, and procedures.* New York, NY: Guilford Press.

Siegel, D. J. (2010). *The mindful therapist: A clinician's guide to mindsight and neural integration.* New York, NY: W. W. Norton.

Timberlake, H. (2013) Personal communication to the author.

Wells, S. & Lake, D. (2012a). Simple Energy Techniques (SET). Retrieved from http://www.eftdownunder.com/SET.html

Wells, S. & Lake, D. (2012b). What is Provocative Energy Techniques (PET)? Retrieved from http://www.eftdownunder.com/eftpet.html#WhatisPET?

Wolinsky, S. & Ryan, M. (1991). *Trances people live: Healing approaches in quantum psychology.* North Bergen, NJ: Bramble.

Wood, J. V. Perunovic, W. Q., & Lee, J. W. (2009, July). Positive self-statements: Power for some, peril for others. *Psychological Science, 20*(7), 860–866. doi:10.1111/j.1467-9280.2009.02370.x

# Chapter 63
# Tapping Deep Intimacy: EFT for Relationships
*Dawson Church*

**Abstract**

Relationships often carry elevated emotional charge. Close relationships such as marriage and family relationships can be nurturing and rewarding from the point of view of the individuals involved. More often they are the source of conflict and emotional distress. Relationship behaviors are often strongly conditioned, originating in childhood attachment experiences, leading to repetitive dysfunctional patterns of behavior within and across a range of adult relationships. Clues to the origin of these persistent behaviors are now emerging from disparate fields, such as evolutionary biology, epigenetics, psychoneuroimmunology, endocrinology, and neural plasticity. Biological forces predisposing relationship behavior include neural plasticity, stress hormones such as cortisol and adrenaline, gene expression, inherited gene silencing, autonomic nervous system dysregulation, excitatory neurotransmitters, and limbic system activation. An examination of these biological underpinnings of relational behavior reveals leverage points through which conditioned behaviors may be changed. Evidence and case histories are presented here to demonstrate that EFT is able to quickly countercondition even strongly conditioned behaviors that impair relationship quality and, in so doing, clear internal obstacles to deep intimacy.

**Keywords:** EFT, intimacy, relationships, stress, conditioning

**Dawson Church** is a health writer and researcher in the field of energy medicine. He is the author of the award-winning best-seller *The Genie in Your Genes*, editor of the peer-reviewed professional journal *Energy Psychology*, executive director of the National Institute for Integrative Healthcare (niih.org), and CEO of Energy Psychology Group (EFTUniverse.com). Send correspondence to Dawson Church, 334 Fulton Road, #442, Fulton, CA 95439, or dawsonchurch@gmail.com. The author receives income from books and speaking engagements on the approach described in this chapter.

laudette, a woman in her mid 20s, was asked, as part of an exercise at an EFT workshop I taught, to find a minor annoyance to tap on. She said that her annoyance was that her partner, Jim, "doesn't pull his weight around the housework."

When asked to tune in to what she felt in her body when thinking about Jim and housework, she said she felt pressure in her head. I asked her about the earliest time she had ever felt such pressure, and she described times when, as a little girl, she had watched her father and uncles lounging around the house while her mother did all the housework and waited on them. She pictured several specific occasions when this occurred. "I was so angry," she said. "They sat around, drinking and talking, watching my mother work." Using EFT's Basic Recipe, Claudette tapped on her emotional intensity till each of these scenes was at a 0 on a SUD (subjective units of distress) scale from 0 to 10, with 10 representing maximum intensity.

"Tell me again about Jim and housework," I asked. Claudette spoke slowly and thoughtfully, in contrast to her earlier torrent of complaints. "He actually does quite a lot," she said. "The real problem is me. I'm too demanding, always ragging on him, pointing out every deficiency."

Claudette's chances of having a successful relationship had just increased substantially. Jim hadn't changed one iota. By going to the childhood origins of her pain and tapping on those events, Claudette had defused one of the detonators that threatened to blow up their relationship.

Claudette's reaction had little to do with the present situation, even though she believed that Jim was causing her emotional response. In reality, early childhood memories buried deep in her memory were producing her current response. Due to her strong emotional reaction during those early experiences, Claudette's brain recorded those events with the type of heightened importance it assigns to threats to physical survival. Her brain did the smartest thing possible in evolutionary terms: It attached a "red tag" indicating danger to certain situations. The brain then compares current situations to past threats, and if it finds a match, it initiates a stress response. This vital protective mechanism allows Claudette's brain to identify new situations that might hold similar threats, and react accordingly.

A brain that does this well is a valuable asset to those living in a primal environment. For our distant ancestors a million years ago, the ability to respond quickly to threats meant the difference between life and death. The brain evolved accordingly, generation by generation. In each generation, those with the fastest stress response were the best equipped to notice and react to dangers such as predators and enemies. They were more likely to live, and pass on their genes. Their more amiable companions were more likely to fall victim to those predators, and thus fail to produce offspring. With each generation, the stress response became more finely honed. Modern humans are the product of hundreds of generations of refining the most exquisitely sensitive stress response. That's why, like Claudette, we react so quickly to problems.

## How Your Brain and Body Sabotage Good Intentions

An analogy for your brain's threat-response system is a platoon of soldiers. Imagine a group of miniature warriors in the middle of your brain, your personal Imperial Guard. If they are highly alert and give the alarm quickly when an enemy attacks, the whole organism, like a whole country, survives. If their response time is slow, the whole organism dies.

Although this ability was essential to the survival of our Paleolithic ancestors, it is less helpful when trying to navigate the world we find ourselves in today. There are few predators in our environment. The only place we're likely to see lions or tigers is in a movie or in a zoo. Yet the brain's Imperial Guard is always on high alert, hardwired through thousands of generations to identify and respond to danger immediately. The guard has little ability to differentiate between a real enemy and an imaginary one. If our spouse or partner says or does something that triggers us, our Imperial Guard sounds the signal for attack. It overrules our logical mind. That mind, located in the prefrontal cortex of the brain, just behind the forehead, is responsible for executive functions such as decision-making and discernment. It can think coolly and rationally when faced with a problem. Our logical mind could be viewed as the Wisdom Council of the kingdom. It can weigh alternatives, examine different aspects of a problem, sort fact from fiction, and consider the future consequences of an action.

When the Imperial Guard kicks down the door, however, yelling, "We're under attack!" the whole kingdom springs into action. The Imperial Guard overrules the Wisdom Council and takes control.

It doesn't have the ability to weigh long-term consequences, only immediate safety. It acts fast; the genes that code for the neurochemicals our bodies produce under stress reach peak expression in about 3 seconds (Rossi, 2000). For that reason, they're called "immediate early genes." Fast action is essential to survival, and it occurs much faster than the conscious deliberative processes in the prefrontal cortex. Noted brain researcher Joseph LeDoux calls this "the hostile takeover of consciousness by emotion" (LeDoux, 2002).

Minutes or hours after you've responded to a stress cue, and perhaps said something angry to your lover in the heat of the moment, your prefrontal cortex collects itself and thinks of many smarter things you might have said. In the moment of stress, however, under the influence of those fast-acting immediate early genes, your brain prompts you to blurt out a hurtful statement that would have been better left unsaid.

## The Brain's Threat-Assessment Machinery

The responsibility for responding to threats is located in our midbrain and hindbrain (Krasnegor, Lyon, & Goldman-Rakic, 1997). Our hindbrain, or brain stem, controls basic survival functions such as respiration and circulation. In evolutionary terms, this brain is ancient, and common to many species that predate mammals on the geological scale. The brains of dinosaurs were essentially the same as our hindbrain. Reptiles have hindbrains, as do birds and sharks.

Our midbrain or limbic system, located above the hindbrain, is a more recent evolutionary innovation. Among other functions, the midbrain processes emotion (Phelps & LeDoux, 2005). Mammals have midbrains, which distinguishes them from reptiles. The limbic system contains several distinct clusters of neurons that act together to interpret information from the environment. Two parts of the limbic system hold particular importance in activating the stress response: the amygdala and the hippocampus. The amygdala is like a smoke alarm. Once it sounds, it signals the hindbrain to enter survival mode. The hippocampus is like a military historian. It maintains a file of possible threats, situations that have been "red tagged" as threats to survival. It evaluates new situations against the file. If one fits the profile of a possible threat, it signals the amygdala to sound the alarm.

When the alarm is sounded, the hindbrain activates the full catalogue of biological responses to threats, the fight-flight-freeze response, or FFF. FFF was strongly adaptive for our human ancestors, even though the part of the brain that activates it is as old as the dinosaurs. When archaic humans encountered an enemy or predator, those who fought, ran away, or froze were more likely to survive. Those who fought might successfully beat off an invader. Those who fled might be able to hide till the invader was gone. Those who froze might have been taken into captivity as slaves, but that was still better than death. Each of the three FFF behaviors is preferable to the alternative, so they have been built into the fundamentals of our body's biology (Lane, 2009).

The limbic system is also the emotional brain, which further aids our survival. Fear is the emotion that allows the hippocampus to assign a "red tag" to a memory. If, for example, you've had a frightening experience with a big dog, your hippocampus attaches a red tag to the image of a dog, and when you see another dog, even though it might not be threatening, you respond with fear. In this way, emotion is another layer boosting our survival capabilities.

## The Autonomic Stress and Relaxation Responses

The part of the nervous system that regulates basic biological functions such as respiration, circulation, digestion, and reproduction is called the autonomic nervous system. It runs inside the spinal column down from the hindbrain, sending signals throughout the body from the brain. When first named and identified, it was believed to act autonomously, that is, outside the control of the conscious, directive parts of the brain. More recent research has demonstrated, however, that many supposedly automatic physiological functions such as heart rhythm may be influenced by conscious decisions as well as emotions (Rein, Atkinson, & McCraty, 1995).

The autonomic nervous system has two divisions, the sympathetic and parasympathetic branches. The sympathetic branch is responsible for the stress response, while the parasympathetic governs the relaxation response. Individuals under stress show heightened sympathetic arousal, whereas in relaxed states, the parasympathetic system dominates.

Large nerves from both the sympathetic and parasympathetic branches emanate through the vertebrae. These neural bundles connect to every important system in the body: the musculoskeletal system, digestive system, reproductive system, respiratory system, endocrine system, immune system, and circulatory system. When we're stressed, our sympathetic nervous branch produces a large-scale redeployment of biological resources toward systems required to get us out of danger, such as the musculoskeletal system, and away from nonessential functions such as reproduction, immunity, and digestion. In the previous analogy, the sympathetic system is under the command of the Imperial Guard, whereas the parasympathetic system is guided by the Wisdom Council.

## Fight or Flight in Relationships

FFF is a lens through which we can view relationship behaviors. Each of the three Fs corresponds to typical patterns in which you or your loved one might act. Here's an abbreviated version of a typical male-female spat. Jack has a habit of leaving his dirty clothes lying around the house, and Jill is growing tired of picking up after him.

Jack: Where are my work boots?
Jill: I think I saw them in a pile in the corner of the dining room.
Jack: What are they doing there? (Fight)
Jill: I wish you'd pick up after yourself. (Fight)
Jack: I have so much going on at work. I don't need this. (Flight)
Jill: You only think about your own needs. What about me trying to take care of the kids after a full day at work? (Fight)
Jack: There's no point in talking to you. You're so irrational. (Flight)
Jill starts sobbing. (Freeze)
Jack: I don't need this. (Flight)
Jack goes into his den and watches TV. (Flight)

On the surface, this looks like a disagreement about picking up the clothes. Yet it's actually a reenactment of behavioral patterns that are as ancient as the dinosaurs. Jack and Jill feel emotion, which activates their limbic systems. Their reptile-like hindbrains are then activated, using the autonomic nervous system to send danger signals through the entire body.

The way our brains have evolved, though perfectly adapted to the archaic world in which they developed, wreaks havoc in our love relationships. We may respond out of all proportion to an imagined offense. These responses are strongly encoded in our neural networks and are difficult to change. As a thought experiment, you might begin analyzing your problems with your relationship partners by tagging which of the associated behaviors reflect fight, which look like flight, and which resemble freeze. You'll likely be surprised to notice that virtually all your emotionally charged interactions fall into one of those three categories.

The FFF response doesn't just involve our brains. Survival was so important to our ancestors that multiple redundant backup systems evolved to ensure it. In particular, the endocrine system, which produces hormones, plays a key role in the stress response. The two primary stress hormones are adrenaline (norepinephrine) and cortisol. When you feel emotionally triggered, your endocrine system floods your body with an increased dose of these two hormones. They are "messenger molecules," triggering cascades of molecular changes in all the other systems of your body (Lutgendorf et al., 2000). Adrenaline acts fastest, within a couple of seconds, while cortisol takes a few seconds longer. The signals they produce affect your biology in profound ways. Your circulatory system recalibrates. Your heart pounds, and the vessels carrying blood to your muscles enlarge. Your breathing speeds up, as your respiratory system goes into high gear, forcing more oxygen into your bloodstream. Your liver dumps glucose into your bloodstream, giving you a quick energy boost of sugar. The pupils of your eyes dilate to take in more light.

Nonessential body systems are shut down. You don't need functions such as digestion, reproduction, or immunity when a tiger is chasing you. You need the ability to get out of harm's way: FFF. Cortisol triggers changes such as constriction of the vessels carrying blood to your digestive system and reproductive system, forcing that blood into the muscles. Your immune system and all the biological mechanisms of cell repair and regeneration are downregulated. The balance of other messenger molecules called neurotransmitters is altered; the levels of stress-related or "excitatory" neurotransmitters such as dopamine rise, while the levels of relaxation-related or "inhibitory" neurotransmitters such as serotonin fall and heart rate variability becomes less coherent (Stadler,

Evans, Hucklebridge, & Clow, 2010). When you're under stress, much of the blood in your forebrain is shunted to your peripheral muscles (Takamatsu et al., 2003). The evolutionary utility of this is obvious: You don't need the ability to compose a symphony or perform calculus when a lion bursts out of the grass.

Because of that blood flow out of your forebrain, you're not very smart when you're stressed. When you're upset, anxious, fearful, or angry with your relationship partner, your Imperial Guard is running your body's show, and your Wisdom Council is offline.

If you've gone to couples counseling, you've probably discovered that the agreements you make in the therapist's office rarely survive the first fight after you get home. You made vows when you got married, and your Wisdom Council forebrain, the thinking part of your brain, really believed them. Yet when you get stressed, the Imperial Guard in your midbrain takes over, and you violate your vows. You might have set intentions or said prayers with a minister or spiritual counselor, and promptly failed to implement them when real life called upon you to do so. You might have felt very bad about what you did to your spouse, but you couldn't help yourself, driven by these very strong primitive urges. That's because, in the therapist or priest's office, you were in a safe environment without the stress of real life. Your Wisdom Council was in charge, and you could talk about your marriage rationally and calmly. Back home, when triggered by your spouse, the Wisdom Council is overthrown, and the Imperial Guard controls you. You say and do things you would never say or do in the therapist's office, or in front of the priest. Your best intentions go out the window, and you're back in caveman behavior.

You act from your reptile hindbrain and your fearful limbic system, forgetting all the fine cognitive tools you learned in couples therapy. When you're flooded with fear hormones, you don't have the ability to empathize, or relate to your partner other than as a fear object. You act out your old dysfunctional scripts, despite your best intentions.

## Your Negative Emotions Rewire Your Brain

These dysfunctional behaviors are reinforced by neural plasticity. When you perform a behavior many times, it becomes stronger, just the way your golf swing improves with practice. When you practice any behavior over and over, you increase the number of neural connections that govern that action. Research by Nobel prize–winning physician Eric Kandel, MD, showed that within an hour of repeat stimulation, the number of neural connections can double. (Kandel, 1998). Just as practicing your golf swing hour after hour increases the neural connections related to that skill, practicing anger, resentment, or other negative emotions toward your spouse builds increased capacity in those neural pathways. You literally increase the size of the anger circuits in your brain.

Your hormonal system reinforces this change. The number of cortisol receptors on the surface of your cells can increase as stress hormones bombard them. As you flood your body with stress biochemicals repeatedly, you reinforce the ability of your cells to respond to them. Angry people tend to become more angry and faster at getting angry as they practice the behavior over time. You've had early life experiences of the FFF response and, unless you find some way to change, you may wind up increasing the strength of your stress response as you get older. Negative relationship behaviors that were a small problem when you were younger can later become a big problem.

## Multigenerational Relationship Dysfunction and Gene Expression

A series of animal and human studies by McGill professor Moshe Szyf highlighted the role of nurturing in the development of the stress response (Szyf, 2009). Szyf examined the differences between litters of rat pups who were raised by nurturing females, and those raised by non-nurturing females. Nurturing female rats lick and groom their pups, which non-nurturing mothers do not. Szyf found that, in the group that was not nurtured, the genes that dampen the stress response were silenced. As adults, these rats were less able to manage their response to a stressful environment. They had all the same genes as the rats who had been raised by nurturing mothers, but the genes were silenced. Szyf calls such silenced genes "frozen assets."

Szyf then extended his work to humans by examining the brains of people who had died in accidents, and comparing these to the brains of schizophrenics who had committed suicide (Poulter et al., 2008; McGowan, et al., 2008). He found massive gene silencing of the stress-management genes in the brains of the suicides. Again, they had the genes required to dampen stress, but epigenetic cues had "switched off" these genes.

Other studies likewise demonstrate gene expression differences between the brains of humans who have been nurtured and those who have not (Binder et al., 2008; Haeffel et al., 2008). One of the founders of the field of marriage and family therapy, Virginia Satir, drew an analogy from biology to illustrate her observation that dysfunctional behaviors are often passed from generation to generation. She defined "marriage" as the attempt by two sets of dysfunctional family patterns to propagate themselves into the next generation (Satir, 1983).

New evidence from epigenetics shows that behaviors may be associated with the silencing of groups of genes across generations. Once silenced in one generation, they may be silenced in the next generation, and the generation after that. Though the genes are still present in the cells of the offspring, they are silenced at some point after conception. (Akitake, Macurak, Halpern, & Goll, 2011). Previously, it was believed that a newborn had its full range of genetic potential available, and that the process of gene silencing as the result of adverse experiences began after birth or after conception. The new evidence, however, shows that epigenetic influences may begin before birth, so that genetic configurations are passed from generation to generation, just as genes themselves are inherited.

## Hopelessness

The biological factors predisposing us to repeat strongly conditioned behavior thus include neural plasticity, stress hormones such as cortisol and adrenaline, immediate-early gene (IEG) expression, inherited gene silencing, autonomic nervous system dysregulation, excitatory neurotransmitters, and limbic system activation.

When our conscious forebrain attempts to change our behavior through volition, decision, intention, or willpower, it may succeed during periods of relaxation. But when we're stressed, the weight of our biological heritage overwhelms those conscious directives.

This is deeply distressing for many people. They may try very hard to improve their relationships using the executive functions of their forebrains. Yet they fail repeatedly. Over a period of years or decades of failure to change dysfunctional

behaviors, individuals can become discouraged. Their difficulties may persist through several marriages, or many different love relationships. In my social circle, I observe many men and women in their forties, fifties, and sixties who feel hopeless about their relationship future. They've tried a variety of interventions. They've been through counseling, read many relationship books, taken workshops, and set intentions. The Wisdom Council in their brains has attempted, over and over again, to improve their relationships. Yet their Imperial Guard has sabotaged every one and, after many such experiences, they give up on themselves, and on the prospect of lasting love. Even if they stay in a marriage for decades, they're haunted by a sense of lost potential, that their sense of satisfaction might have been much greater, or that life has passed them by.

## The Possibility of Change

Since our nervous systems and bodies are hardwired to act this way, how then can we change? The biological odds appear stacked against us. Helping professionals, such as therapists, counselors, priests, social workers, and life coaches are familiar with the phenomenon of clients who try to change yet have been unable to do so despite the best efforts of both practitioner and client. The path to growth and transformation is often lined with frustration and failure.

In my experience, EFT is one of the very few tools capable of changing these behaviors. It accomplishes this in several ways.

First, it breaks the spell of strongly encoded memories. Claudette's memories had been encoded early in her life, with "red tags" attached to experiences similar to the problem in her current relationship. If she had not broken the influence of those strongly encoded childhood memories, she might have left Jim, and gone on to the next partner—only to repeat the same pattern. She might never have identified the true source of her feelings of frustration. When EFT counterconditioned her childhood memories, she had a radical shift in her perception of the current relationship problem. Her conscious mind reframed the problem in such a way as to give her the leverage to solve it. The following is another case history of a client whose perception of the problem changed entirely when the underlying childhood issues were addressed with EFT.

## Hiding Your Pain

At an EFT workshop, one of the participants, "Nancy," a college professor, said she resented her husband. "I go to his professional conferences, but he doesn't go to mine," she said. "There was one I really wanted him to go to, but he refused. I hid my pain."

One of my favorite sayings is: "The problem is never the problem." A current problem is almost always an echo of an earlier problem. The current problem has upset us only because it has an "emotional signature" similar to that of an earlier problem. Once the emotional signature is evoked, we attach meaning to the current situation as the cause of our distress. But focusing on the current situation simply distracts us from the real problem, amplifying our old patterns. It displaces our attention from a place where emotional resolution is possible (the early problem) and onto a location where full emotional resolution is unlikely (the current problem). A productive way in which a practitioner can reframe a current problem for a client is to suggest that it may simply be a new manifestation of an old pattern that requires healing. This by itself can remove some emotional charge from the current situation by facilitating the client's perceiving it as a healing opportunity rather than as a hindrance.

I asked Nancy where in her body she felt the resentment toward her husband, and she said it was in her throat. The intensity level was a 5 on the SUD scale. I asked what was the earliest time she could recall having a similar physical feeling.

"When my mother pushed me," she said. "I was 5 years old. She pushed me down the steps. A neighbor saw her do it, and rushed over and asked if I was alright. My mother said, 'She's a stupid girl, she wasn't moving fast enough.' So I hid my pain and said I was fine."

There were several layers of trauma in this experience. Young Nancy experienced physical pain. The pain was the result of unexpected behavior by her mother. She was then blamed for the situation, after which she disguised her suffering. Nancy's SUD level was a 9 on the pushing incident before we began tapping, but it quickly dropped to a 2.

I said, "Nancy, I bet you were an expert at hiding your pain by the age of 5. You'd had lots of practice. Tell me about an earlier incident when you hid your pain."

Unhesitatingly, she replied, "I was at preschool, on the playground. I was all alone, sitting on one end of a seesaw (teeter-totter). A teacher realized I might be lonely, so she picked up another little girl and put her on the other end. Her end of the seesaw went down and mine went up. I'm seeing the eyes of that girl right now. She didn't want to be with me. So she jumped off. I fell down hard, and jarred my spine. But I hid my pain."

Nancy started to cry. I began to say something, but she cut me off and said, "I *really want* to feel this right now. I'm used to stuffing it away. Don't make me try and feel better!" When a client is in touch with their feelings, the practitioner doesn't always require a SUD rating. The fact that Nancy was *not* hiding her pain represented a shift.

Nancy tapped until the seesaw incident went down to a 2. I asked, "How do you feel about your husband not going to conferences with you?" She replied with a laugh, "I can take care of myself, and actually I have more fun when he's not there!"

This cognitive shift is typical of people who've resolved an emotional distress. My guess is that Nancy could have tapped on the adult disappointment around her husband and experienced an improvement. But she would not have resolved the core issue, "I hide my pain." That could only happen when she dealt with the problem behind the problem: the childhood hurt that still lived in her emotions, encoded in her hippocampus, and which was awakened when her husband didn't want to attend one of her professional conferences. If Nancy had continued to project the source of her emotional distress onto her husband, and invest her time and energy into changing him, the likely outcome would have been further frustration and feelings of invalidation. Only when she focused on the source of the negative emotions did she provide herself with the opportunity for healing.

## Stress Biochemistry and Emotional Health

The previous cases present ways in which EFT can disrupt conditioned behavior by counterconditioning strongly encoded memories. The second way EFT disrupts conditioned behavior is by signaling your brain that the negative interaction you're having with your significant other is not a threat to your survival. You start to have the argument, your Imperial Guard comes to attention, but then you tap. The act of tapping is soothing, and signals the guard, "Don't worry, we're safe," so it stands down and relaxes. The guard gets one signal from your environment: the nascent argument. It then gets a second, conflicting signal: the soothing sensation of tapping. The second signal cancels out the possibility of threat generated by the first signal. By tapping you break the association encoded in your neural circuits between a disagreement with your partner and the stress response.

The third way EFT interferes with the stress response is by reducing cortisol levels.

Along with colleagues Garret Yount, PhD, of the California Pacific Medical Center, and Audrey Brooks, PhD, of the University of Arizona, I performed a randomized controlled trial of EFT for cortisol (Church, Yount, & Brooks, 2012). Because cortisol is a "master" hormone, regulating a cascade of genetic and molecular changes in response to stress, we reasoned that if EFT reduces emotional triggering, the results might be evident in an individual's stress biochemistry.

Participants were recruited, ostensibly for a "free cortisol test" in order to keep them blind to the true target of the study. We divided the 83 subjects into three groups. One group received a one-hour EFT session from a life coach. The second received a talk therapy session from a psychologist or family therapist. The third group simply relaxed in the office. The study, performed at five integrative medicine clinics in California, recruited participants with relatively normal levels of cortisol.

We measured the cortisol levels of participants before and after their session. We also tested their levels of anxiety, depression, and other mental health conditions. We found that talk therapy improved their mental health symptoms about as much as resting, whereas EFT improved them more than three times as much. We also found significantly greater drops in cortisol levels in the EFT group. The study revealed a significant correlation between the drop in mental health symptoms in the EFT group and the drop in cortisol. In other words, as the participants felt better emotionally, they produced fewer stress hormones. This study, published in a prestigious peer-reviewed psychiatry journal, the oldest in the United States, called the *Journal of Nervous and Mental Disease,* was a groundbreaking demonstration of the link between emotional and physical health.

There are many studies showing the link between the emotional quality of a marriage and health. Studies find that high-quality relationships confer increased immunity and a variety of health benefits (Repetti, Robles, & Reynolds, 2011). In one study, researchers measured the levels of healing proteins called cytokines circulating in the bloodstreams of couples (Kiecolt-Glaser et al., 2005). They then had the couples remember a past disagreement and spend half an hour discussing it, after which the researchers measured their cytokines a second time. They found that their cytokine levels dropped. Couples who had the most negative interactions fared worst on measures of their health. These couples, when asked to remember an old disagreement, quickly escalated the discussion into a new argument. The cytokine levels of these angry couples dropped by as much as 40%.

As cortisol levels go up, the levels of the hormones and neurotransmitters responsible for immunity and cell repair go down. As relationship partners practice EFT whenever they're stressed, they're likely to be lowering their cortisol levels regularly. Those receptor sites on their cells that were previously being sensitizing by elevated cortisol levels are no longer being activated. Over time, the body becomes habituated to a lower stress level. With biological resources no longer being recruited by stress, more are available for protective functions such as cell repair and immunity. Whereas previously, stress drove blood away from digestion and reproduction, now relaxation promotes their optimal function. Instead of the FFF response, individuals cultivate a relaxation response, which improves overall health. By lowering cortisol, EFT has a positive effect on all the body's systems.

There are a number of studies of EFT used for physical problems, including tension headaches, psoriasis, pain, and fibromyalgia. A study I conducted involving 216 health care professionals (doctors, nurses, chiropractors, psychotherapists, and alternative medicine practitioners) found significant changes after a one-day EFT workshop (Church & Brooks, 2010). The study, published in the professional journal *Integrative Medicine,* found that symptoms of mental health conditions such as anxiety and depression decreased by an average of 45% ($p < .0001$) and physical pain dropped by 68% ($p < .0001$). I had the participants measure their pain before and after an EFT exercise that lasted about 20 minutes. A two-thirds reduction in pain in that short a time frame, using only a safe behavioral intervention, represents a highly promising result. A randomized controlled trial with veterans with PTSD also found that their pain reduced significantly after EFT (Church, 2013).

One study examined the symptoms of women with fibromyalgia who took an online EFT course (Brattberg, 2008). As their psychological health improved, their pain and fibromyalgia symptoms dropped significantly. Another study of people with psoriasis, a skin disease, also found large drops in symptoms as mental health improved after EFT (Hodge & Jurgen, 2011). The common thread to these studies is that, as we tap on psychological and emotional triggers, the natural healing responses of our bodies reassert themselves. I have witnessed this phenomenon frequently with clients, as in the following example drawn from an EFT workshop.

## 20 Years of Rheumatoid Arthritis Pain Disappears After EFT

"Jennifer," presented with arthritis on the first day of an EFT Level 1 class I was teaching, and volunteered for a demonstration in front of the 60 participants present. She was 22 years old and reported that her first symptoms had appeared at the age of 2, and that the years between 2 and 16 were a "health crisis" for her. She had been treated in various ways, including hydrocortisone injections into her knees starting at the age of 2. The symptoms had abated at the age of about 18, and then returned in full force 2 years later.

When asked for the current location of the pain, she reported pain in three locations: her right ankle, her left knee, and her left elbow. Asked to rate the intensity of the pain using a scale from 0 to 10, with 0 representing no pain, and 10 representing the greatest pain possible, she rated the pain in her elbow as 3, her knee 8, and her ankle 5.

When I asked Jennifer to associate her physical symptoms with an emotional event, she was unable to find one. I asked what happened around the age of 2, when the symptoms began and, despite several probing questions, she was still unable to identify a specific event. I asked her about her relationships with her father and mother, and she said that they often fought. She began to cry. I asked her to remember a particular fight, and she could not identify one, so we tapped on "Mom and Dad fighting." Although EFT is designed to work on specific emotional events, it is recommended that in cases of excessive emotional intensity, practitioners tap on generalities to reduce the

level of client distress that might be evoked by specifics. Once the client's degree of intensity has subsided enough for the client to be able to think about specific events, you might then explore further to identify some of those events.

In this case, after we'd tapped on the generality and taken the edge off, Jennifer was still so upset she could hardly speak, so I just made up likely phrases, such as "the big fight" and "all the fights Mom and Dad had" and "their raised voices" and "it's scary when parents fight" and "I don't feel safe when they're fighting," and so on. These are all obvious elements of parental conflict and a child's reaction to it, so we could make progress with EFT despite the lack of specific events to target, or the ability of the client to articulate her experiences.

During this session, Jennifer spoke in a very low, hesitant voice. She had large brown eyes and an open, childlike face. Her suffering was so evident that many people in the room were moved to tears. Before the session, I had asked for permission to tap on her during the session, should the need arise, and she had assented. She was in such distress that I would normally have begun tapping on her, as her hands were shaking, she was crying so hard she could not speak, and she was so engrossed in her story that she was barely able to focus on the tapping points. I did not tap on her as planned, however. Not only was her emotion excessive, but mine was too. I simply had to keep tapping on myself to be able to handle my own emotional reaction to her suffering.

After the demonstration, which lasted about 25 minutes, she reported a reduction in pain to 1 in her elbow, 5 in her knee, and 3 in her ankle. I asked her to note any other changes in her symptoms in the course of the training. On the second day, she reported she had no pain in her elbow and ankle, but there was still some pain in her knee. She said she felt it was "not safe to let go of all the pain yet." I encouraged her to let it go at her own pace, and not force the process. This is important because when an EFT client has had an ego identity linked to a physical symptom for a long time, that identity can feel lost and disoriented without the symptom. It is prudent to allow time for a new self-concept to take root before the old one is extinguished. That second day, Jennifer's appearance had also changed noticeably. She smiled and participated lightheartedly, in contrast to the heavy sense of oppression she'd exhibited the day before.

In Jennifer's case, we used only the simplest form of EFT's Basic Recipe, as that was as far in the curriculum as the class had progressed, and I wanted to model basic rather than advanced skills. In a normal private session, I might have used many other interventions, including "empty chair" work from Gestalt therapy, calming acupoints taught in other energy psychology schools, meridian reflow adjustment methods taught in Eden Energy Medicine, and visualizations from transpersonal psychology. I also stressed to the class participants that, though many advanced EFT techniques are available and EFT is also often combined with other methods in the therapeutic toolbox, even the simplest form of EFT's Basic Recipe is effective in most situations, even those involving excessive emotion and when working with severe emotional and physical pain.

Although there are not yet studies of how biological measures like cytokines or cortisol change in relationship partners who use EFT, it is reasonable to suppose, given the improvement in subjective physical symptoms such as pain, that improved relationship quality after EFT might translate into improved physical health.

## Mental Health Symptoms and Relationships

As illustrated throughout this chapter, conditioned behavior creates problems in relationships. The case examples demonstrate that EFT can interrupt conditioned behavior by: (1) breaking the hold of strongly encoded memories, (2) signaling the brain that adverse relationship interactions are not threats to physical survival, and (3) reducing cortisol levels. The fourth way that EFT improves our ability to function in a relationship is by reducing the anxiety, depression, and other mental health conditions that compromise relationships. An individual who is anxious, depressed, phobic, or suffering from the symptoms of posttraumatic stress disorder is impaired in his or her ability to function successfully as a relationship partner. Much research demonstrates that EFT substantially reduces the symptoms of mental health problems, and that subjects maintain their gains over time.

Lastly, EFT changes habitual behavior patterns. Once you've signaled your Imperial Guard that Jack not picking up his clothes is not a threat to your survival, you don't have to transmit the same message every time. Transmitting it once

or twice is usually sufficient. Once you break the association between the stimulus (messy clothes) and the response (FFF) with one use of EFT, your Imperial Guard no longer springs to alert at the sight of messy clothes.

Before EFT, the brain's ability to rewire itself leads to an increase in the capacity of the neural pathways associated with stress. After EFT, neural plasticity becomes an advantage. Eric Kandel's later work showed that if a neural circuit is unused, it starts to decay within 2 weeks. If Jill doesn't react to Jack's clothes a few times, the neural circuits she had built to handle the phenomenon start to disappear. Free from those habitual responses, Jill starts to think creatively about the problems in the relationship and comes up with a range of creative choices, from ignoring the problem to piling all Jack's scattered belongings in the garage once a week and letting him sort it out from there.

## Conclusion

Not only is EFT effective in itself, it also allows us to get more out of whatever other tool we're using to improve our lives and love relationships, whether that tool is meditation, psychotherapy, couples counseling, prayer, a support group, a workshop, or an online course. The way it amplifies the utility of other approaches is that reduced stress leads to improved learning and retention. An effective tool means that, when we are stressed, we remember what we learned in couples counseling, instead of having our conscious intentions swept away by emotion. After EFT, we better remember learned tools such as active listening or Nonviolent Communication.

Another way in which EFT fosters intimacy is that it enhances safety. If a partner lives in fear of the other's emotions such as fear and anger, that partner will typically adopt a defensive posture. The FFF response is typified by the predator-prey relationship found in the wild. A predator stalks and attacks prey, with both exhibiting elevated stress levels. If one partner is potential predator and the other potential prey, there is little stress-free neutral ground in which the relationship can flourish. When partners are safe from their own and the other's emotions, having found in EFT a tool to reduce emotional triggering before it enters the shared space of the relationship, a fertile field for intimacy has been created.

The final way in which EFT reinforces connection in relationships is enhanced *presence*. Free of their own reactivity, partners are much better able to pay attention to each other. They listen better. They are more sensitive to cues like the other's tone of voice and body language. The whole of their attention is no longer consumed by their own emotional experience, opening up space for attention to the other partner. When you're in the FFF state, your primary relationship is with your own fear. EFT allows you to escape the FFF state, to enter instead into a relationship with your partner. In these ways, EFT opens up a space in the relationship for growth and deep intimacy.

In the course of working with many couples, I have been gratified to witness profound changes in their attitudes toward self and other. Some have never had a safe space in a relationship before, and find one after EFT. Others are afraid of their own unpredictable emotions, and learn to master them with EFT. Most have a sense that relationships can be much more satisfying than they currently experience. Some have started their first session ready to get divorced, after years of dysfunctional behavior, and decide to recommit to their marriage after experiencing the breakthroughs possible with EFT. Others tap away barriers to intimacy, and discover the power of attentive listening and emotional presence. EFT is able to create the conditions for connection and emotional health in which relationships can thrive.

# References

Akitake, C. M., Macurak, M., Halpern, M. E., & Goll, M. G. (2011). Transgenerational analysis of transcriptional silencing in zebrafish. *Developmental Biology, 352*(2), 191–201.

Binder, E. B., Bradley, R. G., Liu, W., Epstein, M. P., Deveau, T. C., Mercer, K. B., ... & Ressler, K. J. (2008). Association of FKBP5 polymorphisms and childhood abuse with risk of posttraumatic stress disorder symptoms in adults. *JAMA: The Journal of the American Medical Association, 299*(11), 1291–1305

Church, D. (2013). Reductions in Pain, Depression, and Anxiety Symptoms after PTSD Remediation in Veterans. *Explore: The Journal of Science and Healing*. In press.

Church, D. & Brooks, A. J. (2010). The effect of a brief EFT (Emotional Freedom Techniques) self-intervention on anxiety, depression, pain and cravings in healthcare workers. *Integrative Medicine: A Clinician's Journal, 9*(4), 40–44.

Church, D., Yount, G., & Brooks, A. J. (2012). The effect of Emotional Freedom Techniques (EFT) on stress biochemistry: A randomized controlled trial. *Journal of Nervous and Mental Disease, 200*, 891–896. doi:10.1097/NMD.0b013e31826b9fc1

Haeffel, G. J., Getchell, M., Koposov, R. A., Yrigollen, C. M., De Young, C. G., af Klinteberg, B., ... & Grigorenko, E. L. (2008). Association between polymorphisms in the dopamine transporter gene and depression : Evidence for a gene-environment interaction in a sample of juvenile detainees. *Psychological Science, 19*(1), 62–69.

Kandel, E. R. (1998). A new intellectual framework for psychiatry. *American Journal of Psychiatry, 155*(4), 457–469.

Kiecolt-Glaser, J. K., Loving, T. J., Stowell, J. R., Malarkey, W. B., Lemeshow, S., Dickinson, S. L., & Glaser, R. (2005). Hostile marital interactions, proinflammatory cytokine production, and wound healing. *Archives of General Psychiatry, 62*(12), 1377.

Krasnegor, N. A., Lyon, G. R., & Goldman-Rakic, P. S. (Eds.). (1997). *Development of the prefrontal cortex: Evolution, neurobiology, and behavior.* New York, NY : Brookes.

Lane, J. (2009). The neurochemistry of counterconditioning: Acupressure desensitization in psychotherapy. *Energy Psychology: Theory, Research, and Treatment, 1*(1), 31–44.

LeDoux, J. (2002). *Synaptic self: How our brains become who we are.* New York: Penguin.

Lutgendorf, S., Logan, H., Kirchner, H. L., Rothrock, N., Svengalis, S., Iverson, D., & Lubaroff, D. (2000). Effects of relaxation and stress on the capsaicin-induced local inflammatory response. *Psychosomatic Medicine, 62*, 524–534.

McGowan, P. O., Sasaki, A., Huang, T. C., Unterberger, A., Suderman, M., Ernst, C., ... & Szyf, M. (2008). Promoter-wide hypermethylation of the ribosomal RNA gene promoter in the suicide brain. *PLoS One, 3*(5), e2085.

Phelps, E. A. & LeDoux, J. E. (2005). Contributions of the amygdala to emotion processing: From animal models to human behavior. *Neuron, 48*, 175–187.

Poulter, M. O., Du, L., Weaver, I. C., Palkovits, M., Faludi, G., Merali, Z., ... & Anisman, H. (2008). GABA-A-receptor promoter hypermethylation in suicide brain: Implications for the involvement of epigenetic processes. *Biological Psychiatry, 64*(8), 645–652.

Rossi, E. (2000). *The psychobiology of gene expression.* New York: Norton.

Rein, G., Atkinson, M., & McCraty, R. The physiological and psychological effects of compassion and anger. *Journal of Advancement in Medicine.* 1995; 8(2):87–105.

Repetti, R. L., Robles, T. F., & Reynolds, B. (2011). Allostatic processes in the family. *Development and Psychopathology, 23*(3), 921–938.

Satir, V. (1983). *Conjoint family therapy.* Palo Alto, CA: Science and Behavior Books.

Stalder, T., Evans, P., Hucklebridge, F., & Clow, A. (2010) Associations between the cortisol awakening response and heart rate variability. *Psychoneuroendocrinology 36*, 454–462.

Szyf, M. (2009). The early life environment and the epigenome. *Biochimica et Biophysica Acta, 1790*(9), 878–885.

Takamatsu, H., Noda, A., Kurumaji, A., Murakami, Y., Tatsumi, M., Ichise, R., & Nishimura, S. (2003). A PET study following treatment with a pharmacological stressor, FG7142, in conscious rhesus monkeys. *Brain Research, 980*(2), 275–280.